Praise for the new edition

This second edition of *Researching Business and Management* is the inspiring book that our students need to engage in solid research. Not only does this book provide a rigorous approach to research, but it takes the students' point of view and accompanies them through every stage of their project, answering and discussing key questions and suggesting additional resources. This book is an ideal guide to strong research in business and management!

> Monique Aubry, Professor of Project Management, School of Business and Management, Université du Québec à Montreal, Canada

Academic textbooks about research usually struggle with the balance between being thorough and being accessible. This textbook, however, provides both. The '4-D' structure provides a clear and simple framework for students and academics to structure their research projects. The content of the different chapters provide sufficient depth to enable students to design, perform and report these projects successfully. In other words, Harvey Maylor, Kate Blackmon and Martina Huemann succeeded in providing an up-to-date, complete and easy-to-read textbook on research. A new core-textbook for every business or management program!

> Gilbert Silvius, Professor of Project and Programme Management, LOI University of Applied Sciences, the Netherlands

As research became an increasingly important part of undergraduate and postgraduate taught education, there was a definite gap in textbooks explaining how to do business research for such students, until the first edition of this book came along. This second edition brings the content up-to-date but also includes important material on areas such as reflection and ethics to give a more rounded book. The book manages to be process-based (which students need) without becoming prescriptive or giving a recipe for research. And there are plenty of resources online to accompany the book. This is an essential book for the academic bringing on new researchers at any level.

> Terry Williams, Professor of Project Management, Hull University Business School, UK

First I would like to congratulate the authors for writing such a wonderful book on researching business and management. The best part of the book is that the authors have clearly understood the need and learning styles of the students and placed their intellectual capability in such a way that students are able to foster an understanding of the concepts. This book is well written, has a logical flow, addresses relevant content and forms good connections with real life business problems. I personally would like to use this book as a main book for my undergraduate students and reference book for my postgraduate students.

> Aftab Haider Rizvi, Associate Professor of Advanced Business Research Methods, School of Business, Manipal University, Dubai

Finally, a book that coaches and directs business and management students through all the relevant phases to develop and finalize their research projects successfully.

> Yvonne Schoper, Professor of Project Management, HTW – University of Applied Sciences Berlin, Germany

Maylor, Blackmon and Huemann's writing and style is really accessible. They pick up on and explain a number of issues that the students typically struggle to understand. The level of explanation is very accessible and overall *Researching Business and Management* is somewhat different from other texts – less bulky and more concise with lots of good points and explanations.

Maria Adamson, Senior Lecturer in Organisational Behaviour and Human Resource Management, Middlesex University Business School, UK

From the outset this book is written in a 'user-friendly' way based upon anecdotes, vignettes, case studies, metaphors and dialogue that encourages the researcher to develop their research interests through reflection and question-generating. I like the key questions posed at the beginning of each chapter as they are an example of good practice. At the same time, the work does not shy away from making the reader realise that research links business and management practice and theory with a disciplinary foundation. Conceptually the chapters are strong and the writing style is exemplary. This would be a sound text for 2nd or 3rd year undergrads and I would have no qualms recommending this for masters students.

Dave Needham, Senior Lecturer in Business Research Methods, Nottingham Trent University, UK

Praise for the first edition

The authors provide detailed sections in a friendly but challenging manner. Students undertaking research methods will find the material easy to read, grasp and understand. If you want to write a good project, befriend this book.

Denis Hyams-Ssekasi, Lecturer in Business Research Methods, University of Bolton, UK

This book makes the process of preparing for, and undertaking, a research project much clearer. The structure of the book covers all key points required to work toward a successful research project.

Rachelle Andrews, Programme Leader for MSc Business and Organisational Strategy, University of Hertfordshire Business School, UK

2nd edition

Researching Business and Management

Harvey Maylor
Associate Fellow, Saïd Business School, Oxford, UK

Kate Blackmon
Associate Professor in Operations Management,
Saïd Business School, Oxford, UK

Martina Huemann
Professor and Academic Director in the Department
Strategy and Innovation, University of Vienna, Austria

 macmillan education palgrave

First edition 2005
This edition 2017

Published by
PALGRAVE

Palgrave in the UK is an imprint of Macmillan Publishers Limited, registered in England, company number 785998, of 4 Crinan Street, London, N1 9XW.

Palgrave® and Macmillan® are registered trademarks in the United States, the United Kingdom, Europe and other countries.

ISBN 978–0–230–22212–0 paperback

This book is printed on paper suitable for recycling and made from fully managed and sustained forest sources. Logging, pulping and manufacturing processes are expected to conform to the environmental regulations of the country of origin.

A catalogue record for this book is available from the British Library.

A catalog record for this book is available from the Library of Congress.

In memory of my mum, Jean Maylor (HM)

To my parents (KB)

To my students (MH)

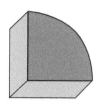

Short Contents

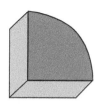

Long Contents

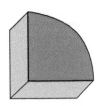

List of Figures

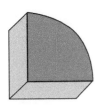

List of Tables

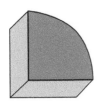

Preface to Lecturers

This book started life in 2000 as a handout we prepared for our own undergraduate and master's students called 'How to fail your project (without really trying)'. It was born out of the frustration that both of us experienced in working with many students in their general quest for knowledge, or simply to finish courses and dissertations. Our frustration came from knowing that the students were not making the most of the learning opportunity that their projects presented to them, often for the same reasons, year after year. Not only were they having problems conceptualising and designing their research, they also had problems with providing any critique of the literature that they were using, despite having access to the research methods texts that were available at the time.

Believing we could do better, we set out to write a book that would help our students do good or even excellent research, that would deal with a large percentage of their questions, and that would simultaneously allay our frustrations at the learning opportunity frequently wasted by our students. We were convinced that our book would be welcomed by lecturers and students alike because:

- Our starting point was not that knowledge of research and research methods is useful in itself, but that it needs to be applied for a student to produce excellent work
- We described research methodologies in an unbiased, easily accessible way, recognising the difficulties many students have in understanding the terminology and often abstract ideas
- We encouraged reflection on the business and management literature and had taken a broad and inclusive view of research approaches
- We had used illustrative examples from real-life student research projects, as well as professional research, to illustrate the points being discussed wherever possible and to keep students grounded in reality
- We recognised that good research combines good process with creativity, intuition, self-reflection and just a little serendipity, and these elements can be stifled if the process is made overly complex

That led us to the first edition, published in 2005. It largely met its objectives, and the feedback was almost universally positive on the approach we had taken. Since 2005, whilst many of the fundamentals remain unchanged, there have been shifts in the way that student research is carried out. Firstly, the proliferation of web-based tools for research has fundamentally changed the way that students access the knowledge base in their subject areas. Secondly, the explicit ethical requirements for research have taken a large step forward. There are many other changes too in the methods that we saw students and colleagues experimenting with. But then one of our friends and colleagues persuaded us to develop a second edition. Enter Professor Huemann. Her penance for this was that she had to join the writing team.

This new edition takes a number of steps forward, whilst retaining the above five features. Apart from the obvious updates, we finally arrived at a demarcation in research terminology that we were happy with and could use consistently (we hope). The separation of research into quantitative and qualitative is not perfect and we realise won't please everyone, but is in our view, the best pedagogical solution to the problem of describing research approaches.

We continue to take a student-centred and process-based approach to research projects, following the typical life cycle of a project from concept through to submission of the final report, using our four-stage model. In doing so:

- We have covered the issues that students find the most challenging – not least finding a topic, managing their projects and communicating the results – and have avoided the intimidating terms and language that many students encounter when academics start to talk about research methods
- We have recognised the prevailing modes of research that students use and provided particular guidance on these – particularly the use of case studies
- We have included chapters on interpreting findings, and reflecting on the project, critical to producing good work and making the most of the learning opportunity, yet not covered in most other research methods textbooks.
- We have added a new chapter on ethics and plagiarism

And finally…

- We have put the role of the internet into perspective as a useful but not exclusive medium for research
- We demonstrate how a good project could be made excellent
- And, in all this, we have tried to retain a sense of humour and not lose the excitement (and fear) that comes with doing a research project – particularly when one is trying to do this for the first time.

There is a companion website to accompany the teaching of this book which includes problem-based learning questions with answers, PowerPoint slides and notes, weblinks, and tools to help students when designing and writing up their projects. The companion website can be accessed at www.palgravehighered.com/maylor-RBM-2e. Please tell us if you think there are other resources needed, or if you have any comments that you wish to make on this book. We would be delighted to hear from you.

HARVEY, KATE AND MARTINA

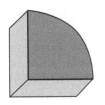

Preface to Students

Welcome to our book.

The first edition of this book (2005) originated out of discussions between two of the authors concerning student research projects. Both of us were supervising undergraduate, master's and doctoral research students, as well as teaching research methods courses, Harvey to undergraduate and MBA students, and Kate to postgraduate research students.

We found ourselves frustrated by not being able to find the 'perfect' book to recommend to our students. Although many excellent books have been written about business and management research projects, and we mention many of them in this book, few books seemed to combine the process of research with the content of research. As a student you need to know what to do, how to do it and why you are doing it. This book was our attempt to bring these three aspects of research together.

Martina Huemann joined the writing team for this edition as we have sought to improve on the original book and make sure it is sufficiently up-to-date to be of most use to you. Business and management programmes continue to evolve, alongside the regulations governing and the tools available to our students. However, there are many constants since the world of the first edition. For instance, research projects are still used to develop skills that are difficult to practise in a single academic module, and many still progress as team projects.

There is of course a health warning. No research methods book can be comprehensive, especially if it is to be of reasonable size. Therefore, we aim to cover only the issues that are most relevant from an academic or a practical perspective. In order that you can explore particular issues in more depth, we highlight additional resources in every chapter to which you might refer.

We have also aimed to predict and answer the queries and concerns students very often voice during research methods courses and in writing their dissertations. We have avoided intimidating or over-complicated terms and language to make all the important aspects of research more easily accessible and relevant to you. Additionally:

- Our starting point is not that knowledge of research and research methods is useful in itself, but that it needs to be applied for a student to produce excellent work
- We have described research methodologies in an unbiased, easily accessible way, recognising the difficulties many students have in understanding the terminology and often abstract ideas
- We recognise that good research combines good process with creativity, intuition, self-reflection and just a little serendipity, and these elements can be stifled if the process is made overly complex
- As a result, in this book, we take a student-centred and process-based approach to research projects, following the typical life cycle of a project from concept through to submission of the final report, using a four-stage model

This is reflected in the content of this edition.

- We have dealt with some of the issues that students find the most challenging – not least finding a topic, managing their projects and communicating the results
- We have included chapters on interpreting findings, and reflecting on the project, critical to producing good work and making the most of the learning opportunity
- We have written a new chapter on ethics and plagiarism

And finally…

- We demonstrate how a good project could be made excellent
- And, in all this, we have tried to retain a sense of humour and not lose the excitement (and fear) that comes with doing a research project – particularly when one is trying to do this for the first time.

There is a companion website to accompany this book which includes tools to help students when designing and writing up their projects. The companion website can be accessed at www.palgravehighered.com/maylor-RBM-2e.

We wish you every success with your studies.

HARVEY, KATE AND MARTINA

Acknowledgements

The authors would like to heartily thank the many colleagues, students and reviewers who provided feedback on the first edition and on our ideas to 'improve' it. We hope we have done justice to your insights.

We are also very grateful to the many people who allowed us to reproduce their work here, not least Professor Saleem Gul for his contribution on computer aided analysis.

Lastly, we are grateful to one reviewer who noted that our quotation from Napoleon ('always have two plans, leave something to chance') may not have been so wise; his planning clearly wasn't so great as he lost most of his army on the retreat from Moscow.

Introduction

There are open-topped bus tours in each of the cities where we live, Bath, Oxford and Vienna. These are a most pleasant way to see the city and each tour provides a view in a relatively short time of what each city has to offer. A tour will not make you an expert in The Pump Rooms, the Bodleian Library or the Schönbrunn Palace but it will provide a view of the landscape of that city. Once complete, there may be somewhere you identify that you wish to explore further.

We have designed our book like this – an open-topped bus tour of the world of research. There are stopping-off points at the end of each chapter, with signposts to other sources so you can explore a particular matter further. We cannot make you experts in research, but we hope you will emerge with a view of the landscape and where you might begin your own journey in research.

This book is especially intended for you if you are an undergraduate or postgraduate or advanced student in business and management, or are working in business and management and need to conduct some research. Specifically, we aim for this to help you with a research methods course, coursework generally or work leading up to a dissertation or thesis. This may be as the sole researcher, or if you are working as part of a team.

Research

Academics are by nature curious about the world. That is why, after we probably should have taken 'proper jobs', we love to explore why organisations perform as they do and to understand what are inevitably highly complex social systems, in all their bizarre and colourful ways. Why, for instance, when a particular approach to management has been proven, do organisations fail to adopt it, and instead carry on with practices that causing them great harm, especially when they have recognised them as harmful? Why, when they are trying to trim budgets, do organisations economise a small amount of spend one year in return for a much larger spend in the following year? Why is human resource diversity still an issue? What is stopping organisations from becoming properly sustainable? So many issues, and even more questions, for which current knowledge does not furnish us with acceptable answers. Research can provide some answers to these big questions, but also help make decisions on much more specific matters – where to locate a facility, what people think about a product, what the impacts are of a particular government policy on business.

So whether your interest is in the general or the specific, you will need to understand what to do, how to do it and, most importantly, why you are doing it. We have found that books that clearly explain the 'why' of research are usually aimed at experienced researchers or postgraduate research students, and rarely link back to the 'how' of doing research. Most books aimed at the new researcher take what we will describe as the 'cookbook' approach to research, which suggests that doing research is mainly a matter of picking out the right 'recipe' and following the instructions. You can learn a lot from a cookbook, but rarely do you end up with a clear understanding of the overall logic that guides what you are doing so that you can apply it for yourself. The purpose of this book is to explain what, how and why, so that you can learn not only to follow a 'recipe', but also to develop your own judgement and style.

To continue with the 'tour' metaphor, once you have stepped off the bus, each research project becomes a personal journey. We do recognise that once off the bus, even in the best-planned research projects, rarely do we end up exactly where we set out to go. The book will help you to overcome some of the obstacles along the way that might keep you from doing good research. This will in no sense reduce the challenge of the journey, but it will remove some of its uncertainty by making your research more systematic.

Research takes inputs such as previous business and management research and data and transforms them into knowledge that is supported by evidence and theory. Compared with a repetitive process such as manufacturing a television or an automobile, the research process is disorderly and sometimes even chaotic. However, we can progress systematically because we can place a structure on it and in doing so make the best of your time and efforts.

The structure we use for research and of this book is based on the 4 Ds.

- D1 – Defining your research
- D2 – Designing your research
- D3 – Doing your research
- D4 – Describing your research

This 4-D model (**Figure I.1**) illustrates how your activities will progress from defining what you will study to reporting what you found out. Throughout this book, we will use this model to identify the key activities and ideas that are the most critical during each stage. These activities, and the process itself, are well established. Your challenge is to adopt them for – and if necessary adapt them to – your own research project.

Although this model might suggest that you will go through each stage in turn, in reality you may find yourself revisiting previous stages. Research is also cyclical, not a linear process. For example, as you are designing your project you may discover some information that affects how you have defined it, requiring you to briefly return to the project definition stage to revise your definition. Iterating, revisiting previous work to make sure that you are heading in the right direction or to check your course, will help you strengthen your research project.

 ## Part 1 – Defining your research

The three chapters in Part 1 focus on defining your research project, initially by gaining an understanding of what research is and isn't (**Chapter 1**). We then lead you through the opportunities presented in choosing and clarifying your topic (**Chapter 2**). To ensure this is building on work already carried out, rather than starting all research with a blank sheet of paper, is a key reason for seeking more information via a literature review (**Chapter 3**).

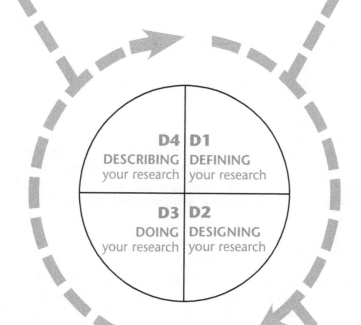

Relevant chapters
13 How do I write up my report?
14 What do I do now?

Key challenges
● Making sense of your findings
● Presenting your research to others
● Reflecting and learning from your research

4

Relevant chapters
1 What is research?
2 What should I study?
3 How do I find information?

Key challenges
● Understanding what academic research is
● Generating and clarifying ideas
● Using sources of information

1

D4
DESCRIBING
your research

D1
DEFINING
your research

D3
DOING
your research

D2
DESIGNING
your research

Relevant chapters
9 How do I do field research?
10 What do my quantitative data mean(1)?
11 What do my quantitative data mean(2)?
12 What do my qualitative data mean?

Key challenges
● Practical considerations in doing research
● Describing data using simple statistics
● Carrying out statistical tests
● Interpreting words and actions

3

Relevant chapters
4 What is my research approach?
5 How do I do quantitative research?
6 How do I do qualitative research?
7 How do I do case study research?
8 How do I make sure my research is ethical?

Key challenges
● Choosing a research approach
● Choosing a research design
● Collecting data using quantitative methods
● Collecting data using qualitative methods
● Integrating quantitative and qualitative methods

2

Figure I.1 The 4-D research model

Part 2 – Designing your research

The five chapters in Part 2 will explain how to transform your project definition into a research design. There are many different ways to carry out business and management research, and so we start by identifying two generic research strategies (quantitative and qualitative) that underlie particular research designs, and explain what the choice of a particular strategy signifies for your research project (**Chapter 4**). **Chapter 5** identifies the most popular research designs for quantitative research, while **Chapter 6** does likewise for qualitative research. **Chapter 7** addresses issues related to one of the most popular approaches used in student research – the case study. **Chapter 8** is new for this second edition and sets out the ethical issues that may arise during your research, whether it be a piece of desk research or work that involves direct contact with organisations or the public.

 Part 3 – Doing your research

The four chapters in Part 3 focus on using the research design you developed in Part 2 to collect and analyse your data, and to interpret the results, and to do so in a way that meets the requirements of 'ethical research'. **Chapter 9** considers the highly practical issues associated with field research. **Chapters 10 and 11** identify basic and advanced techniques for analysing quantitative data. **Chapter 12** describes structured and unstructured approaches to analysing qualitative data.

 Part 4 – Describing your research

Your research is only partially complete until you have told other people what you have found out, including any academic and business advisors who you need to report to. The two chapters in Part 4 help you complete your research project by communicating the results of your research and reflecting and improving on what you have learnt. **Chapter 13** explains what to do with the information you find; that is, how to interpret the results of your data and analysis to see if you have answered your research questions, and to present your results in a written project report and/ or oral presentation. **Chapter 14** looks at how to learn from what you have done.

How to use this book

If you are consulting this book for guidance on specific issues, you can read the chapters in this book out of sequence, but we have tried to structure the book so that we deal with issues in much the same order that you will if you are conducting a major research project, or are taking a course in business and management research. You may want to skim through this book quickly to get an idea of what we will be covering and when.

Throughout this book, you will find different kinds of research examples used to illustrate our discussion. '**Student research in action**' boxes present examples from our own students' projects. These examples illustrate both good and bad practice, sometimes both in the same project. We will also occasionally describe some interesting projects that other researchers have published in the 'Research in action' boxes, to show how more experienced researchers have faced similar issues to those you will face. We also discuss some of our own research, again with examples of both good and bad practice. Finally, we will use some classic research projects, which we describe in more detail in **Chapter 1**, as a continuing theme or motif in the discussion, including classic management studies such as Frederick Taylor's scientific management, the Hawthorne experiments, and classic psychological studies such as Stanley Milgram's laboratory experiment on obedience to authority.

We love the research process. We hope you will, too.

Enjoy the tour!

Harvey, Kate and Martina

About the authors

Dr Harvey Maylor is an Associate Fellow at the Saïd Business School, University of Oxford, and a Visiting Fellow at Cranfield University. He was previously Director of the International Centre for Programme Management at Cranfield, successfully delivering a $US4m programme of research with Hewlett Packard Enterprise, and before that, founding and running Cranfield's MSc in Programme and Project Management. He is the author of the bestselling text *Project Management* (5th edn, Prentice Hall 2017). He has taught postgraduate programmes in project management and research methods at University of Bath, Warwick Business School, Cranfield and Copenhagen Business Schools, at NIMBAS in Holland and Germany, and at Kasetsart University, Bangkok, Thailand. He is also a consultant and trainer, and has received funding for his research from the Project Management Institute, the UK government, the EU and industry.

Dr Kate Blackmon is an Associate Professor of Operations Management at the Saïd Business School and a Tutor and Fellow in Management Studies at Merton College, both at the University of Oxford. Her teaching includes research methods on the MSc in Major Programme Management, and she takes a part in research ethics oversight at departmental, divisional and university levels. She has also held academic positions at the University of Bath, London Business School, and IMD (Lausanne). During 2014–15 she was the Senior Proctor of the University of Oxford.

Dr Martina Huemann is a Professor at the WU Vienna University of Economics and Business. She heads the Project Management Group in the Department of Strategy and Innovation and is the Academic Director of the Professional MBA Program: Project Management. She has supervised over 150 master's theses of graduate and postgraduate students. In her research she believes in co-creation processes with other researchers and practitioners and she pursues strong industry collaborations. In 2015, she was honoured with the IPMA Research Award. She has strong international links in the research and practice communities. Outside of academia, she is a trainer and consultant and has co-founded enable2change – a network of independent experts who enable organisations and people to achieve their goals.

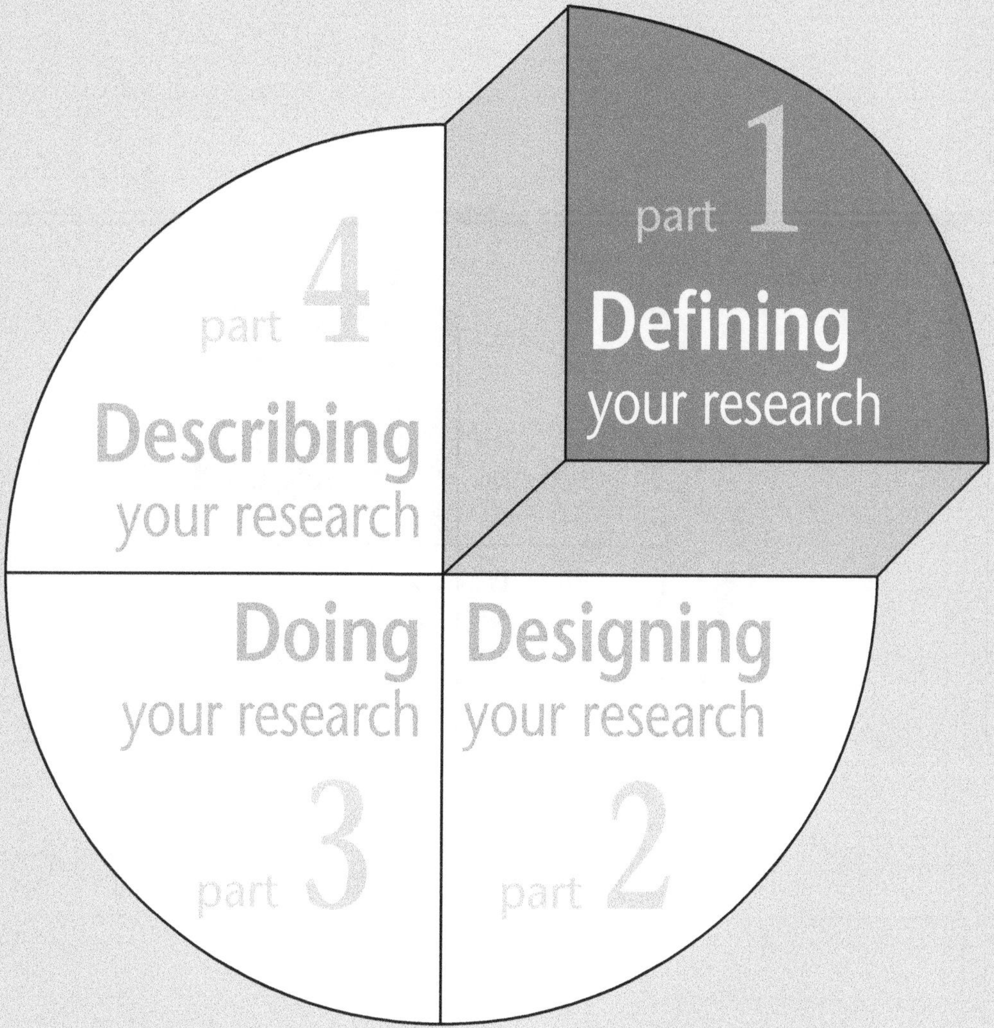

part 1

Defining
your research

part 4

Describing
your research

Doing
your research

part 3

Designing
your research

part 2

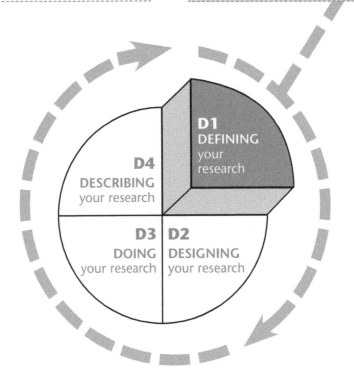

Relevant chapters
13 How do I write up my report?
14 What do I do now?

Key challenges
● Making sense of your findings
● Presenting your research to others
● Reflecting and learning from your research

4

Relevant chapters
1 **What is research?**
2 What should I study?
3 How do I find information?

Key challenges
● **Understanding what academic research is**
● Generating and clarifying ideas
● Using sources of information

1

D1
DEFINING
your
research

D4
DESCRIBING
your research

D3
DOING
your research

D2
DESIGNING
your research

Relevant chapters
9 How do I do field research?
10 What do my quantitative data mean(1)?
11 What do my quantitative data mean(2)?
12 What do my qualitative data mean?

Key challenges
● Practical considerations in doing research
● Describing data using simple statistics
● Carrying out statistical tests
● Interpreting words and actions

3

Relevant chapters
4 What is my research approach?
5 How do I do quantitative research?
6 How do I do qualitative research?
7 How do I do case study research?
8 How do I make sure my research is ethical?

Key challenges
● Choosing a research approach
● Choosing a research design
● Collecting data using quantitative methods
● Collecting data using qualitative methods
● Integrating quantitative and qualitative methods

2

1 chapter

What is business and management research?
Introducing the research process

 Key questions

- What is business and management research?
- Why do we do business and management research?
- What are the benefits of taking a systematic approach to a research project?
- What critical issues should you consider as you get started?
- Who are the key project stakeholders?
- What is the 'real' project life cycle and how do I manage it?

 Learning outcomes

At the end of this chapter, you should be able to:

- Explain what business and management research is, and why we do it
- Describe a systematic research process for doing research
- Identify the issues you should address before starting your project

Contents

Introduction

Mini-Case

HOW HARD CAN IT BE?

Dave was a senior manager in a large multinational firm. His team provided human resource support (recruitment, training, development, promotion) for thousands of managers globally. Following one reorganisation, he was asked to provide a report on the learning and development needs of these managers. Whilst there were a number of options open to him, he didn't feel he had the right information to decide between them. He was able to decide that – as he was asked about so many – a survey would be appropriate. So far, so good.

How was he to go about this, though? What were the steps he needed to take? How would he ask questions and of whom? What kind of questions might people both understand and respond to? Were there any ethical issues with carrying out such a survey, and how would he both analyse the results and be able to work out what they meant? It was all a bit more complicated than it originally looked.

He therefore decided to approach a team of researchers for whom this kind of work was not unusual. They advised on the mix and type of questions, on the scales to use, on how to work this up from a pilot (test) into a full study, on confidentiality (which was critical) and on the sample size and limitations with analysis, and they made some suggestions for the type of analysis he could conduct.

Research is a familiar part of our everyday lives. Its dictionary definition is *to investigate systematically* (www.oed.com). You are investigating something when you collect and use information to solve a practical problem, such as searching for the latest specification of a new bicycle, using social media to find out what friends are up to, or asking people their opinions on a topical matter. You may be investigating things using the library, internet, newspapers and other sources of information to find out more about organisations, people or events. Most of us do this without having to consciously think about it and without explicitly thinking about it as research.

Managers and organisations constantly conduct research to meet particular needs, as shown in the opening example of this chapter. Sometimes this research is obvious to the outsider – someone approaches you in the street or contacts you via telephone or email asking you to answer a market survey on behalf of a company. Less obviously, they collect information on you as a customer using 'cookies' and other software when you visit a website or through customer loyalty cards when you visit a shop. As a result of this research, when you next visit, you are 'remembered' and promotions tailored to your previous enquiries are given prominence.

New information about business and management gained from research also constantly bombards us. Newspapers report stories about organisations and people, management consultants present their analyses of clients' problems and make recommendations to solve them and organisations themselves churn out a steady flow of information for shareholders, analysts, regulators and the general public.

If you are already doing research, why should you study or learn more about research methods by reading this book? The second word in the dictionary definition – *systematically* – suggests that there is much to be gained. For instance, if you were interested in a question such as '*How much should executives be paid?*' there are many possible ways you could answer this. You could simply argue based on your own bias or intuition, or you could take two other positions:

1. As much as they are worth to their employers, as determined by the current market rates and their performance.
2. Only a specified multiple of the salary of the lowest-paid employees of the firm (as is the case in some Scandinavian firms).

If what you know now is not sufficient, how would you find an answer based on more than this? You could require a more systematic appraisal – for instance through looking at published statistics on the salaries of executives in different countries around the world, at how their remuneration is made up (salary, shares, allowances etc.) and at the many studies of executive pay that have been published. This would give you a stronger basis to answer the question, of course adding in your own interpretation of the findings.

This systematic approach to investigation is at the root of successful business and management research. You can apply the skills you develop through studying a research problem in depth, as well as the learning and self-reflection that come from the process, in your studies and career. Competently doing research is a key skill in studying (as part of a course) and in managing (solving an organisational problem – such as that described at the start of this chapter). Whichever applies, you can benefit from a better understanding of the research process. Furthermore, research can help you to become a more critical consumer of what you hear and read in the course of your studies.

This chapter provides a general introduction to business and management research. **Section 1.1** provides an overview of the nature of business and management research. **Section 1.2** explains the wider context of business and management research. **Section 1.3** discusses some critical issues that you should think about as you begin learning about research.

To get you started on thinking about research as a systematic process, this chapter will:

- Describe business and management research
- Show how research fits in the context of business and management
- Introduce some practical considerations for your research.

1.1 What is business and management research?

Our goal in writing this book is not only to present you with the information needed so that you can pass a research methods course or carry out a particular research project, but also to help you develop skills and understanding that let you manage **research** through taking a **systematic approach**. This systematic approach is based on the 4-D model of the **research process** we outlined in the **Introduction**. Positioning your research project within this more general framework lets you identify the choices you will make as a researcher about what to research and how to research it, and the logic that guides these choices. Even if some aspects of research are always uncertain and unpredictable, a systematic approach to research will help you manage this uncertainty.

You might think of research as a process that consists of a specific set and sequence of activities, with tangible and intangible inputs and outputs, such as information, time, resources and knowledge. *Something* (such as knowledge about the world and actions that are taken based on that knowledge) is transformed as a result of the research process. With this understanding, you can manage research rather than being managed by it or simply hoping that it will all happen for you.

1.1.1 What research *is*

Even before you started reading this book, you probably had some ideas about what business and management research might be. *Researcher* may conjure up an image of a white-coated scientist beavering away in a laboratory, but business and management research generally doesn't involve 'ivory tower' research in a laboratory; *investigator*, on the other hand, may suggest a hard-boiled private eye snooping around to try to uncover some piece of evidence and thereby solve a crime, but your research is unlikely to involve undercover investigation (though we will see some good examples of each of these in the professional research field).

For the purposes of this book, the scale of business and management research we are considering is projects that involve considerable time and effort, much more than a basic internet search. 'There are a lot of things that we don't know and that we could find out', according to Phillips and Pugh (2005), and 'what' questions are very important.

Although gathering information is an integral research skill, research – as opposed to simply intelligence gathering – also requires that you use this information to do something; that is, to solve a problem that is relevant to business and management. Research involves identifying a problem, understanding what information is relevant to addressing that problem, getting the information and interpreting that information and its context. This problem can be a practical one faced by a real individual or organisation, or a theoretical one posed by a gap in management knowledge.

To reflect this larger role and our focus on the *process* of research (through our **4-D model**), we define research as:

A systematic process that includes defining, designing, doing and describing an investigation into a particular problem.

What business and management researchers study

It is much harder to draw neat boundaries around business and management research than in, for example, inorganic chemistry or nuclear physics, because it covers diverse areas of business and management activity, including accounting, finance and economics; human resources and organisational behaviour; strategy and international business; marketing; operations, management science and information systems, as shown in **Figure 1.1**.

Moreover, these investigations may be approached from any one of the business and management disciplines. They also may investigate a particular problem associated with a particular social unit. From this, you can see the huge range of possible subjects facing the business and management researcher. Whilst this seemingly endless set of possibilities is undoubtedly a great feature of the business and management area, it can leave you rather spoilt for choice!

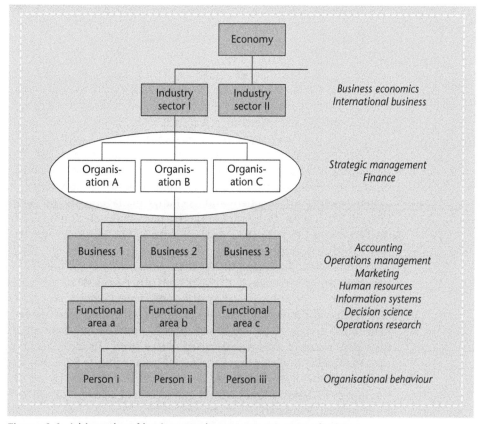

Figure 1.1 A hierarchy of business and management research objects

What other areas of knowledge business and managers draw from

Business and management research often draws on underlying academic areas or disciplines, such as mathematics, statistics, economics, psychology, computing, sociology, anthropology and law. If you wanted to study the causes or effects of the current financial crisis, for example, you would undoubtedly need some knowledge in both economics and mathematics, because finance draws heavily on these two areas. Mathematical theories of complexity have provided management strategists with an interesting stream of research – modelling the behaviours of organisations as complex systems (e.g. Stacey 2001). Similarly, the application of behavioural theories to the science of economics gave some of the most lauded insights in research in modern times (Kahneman and Tversky 1979).

Drawing on an academic discipline to approach a problem can be referred to as taking a 'theoretical lens' on that problem; for example, using psychology could be called taking a '*psychology lens*'. Because of the many disciplines and problems that are available to the researcher, business and management research is incredibly varied. However, your choices are not limited to the lens and the problem. Where more than one discipline is used (*multi-disciplinary* research) the objective of the research is to combine the insights or views that each lens provides. This approach is typically taken by research teams, where each lens is taken by one or more individuals, rather than individuals, who rarely have expertise in more than one area.

Even within a specific management area, there are multiple options for your lens. For instance, within operations management, you could investigate a specific problem from a product (concerned with hard attributes such as dimensions or durability) or a service (concerned with customer feelings towards the service they have received) perspective, or a combination of the two. Within marketing, you could use a business to business (B2B) or a business to consumer (B2C) view, or within business economics you could use a classical or behavioural economics perspective. It is also not unusual in business and management research to combine different management areas or disciplines in an investigation. For instance, in 2011 work carried out at Cranfield University took a *multi-disciplinary* view on the case of a major change programme carried out by Desso as it became a sustainable 'cradle-to-cradle' producer of carpet tiles (see www.desso.com). The group studied Desso's supply chain, its marketing, its human resource management and its change management, and developed a teaching case study (www.thecasecentre.org). The researchers each approached the case using their own lens but with the overall objective of combining these lenses to provide a richer picture of the change.

If business and management research spans nearly every type of human activity, is there anything that makes it different from other areas such as economics, psychology or sociology that study many of the same issues? Many academics and managers believe that the ultimate goal of business and management research should be to help individuals, groups, organisations and networks improve a particular aspect of their performance. This performance ranges from efficiency to profit maximisation to sustainability and corporate and social responsibility. So, a major focus of business and management research is on the practices that are associated with desirable performance of whatever kind, with the objective of achieving *impact* – the opportunity for beneficial change to be achieved.

Research can focus on many different 'social units'

Business and management researchers study a diverse set of 'social units' or groupings of people, ranging from individuals to nations and even regions of the world:

- **individuals**, such as employees, managers or executives in organisations, and other individuals such as customers and suppliers who interact with them. These shareholders, directors, managers, workers, customers, clients and external activists, for instance, are 'organisational actors'.
- **groups** of individuals, such as teams, who act together to achieve common aims, or who interact, such as frontline employees and customers.
- **organisations**, formal or informal groupings of people, including firms and other businesses, and not-for-profit entities such as charities, government agencies or non-government organisations (NGOs).
- **broader context** – in which the other levels have to operate, including society, environment and networks of organisations, such as a supply chain (the flow of goods and services through multiple organisations to an end user), a number of organisations within an industry sector, nation, or region of the world.

Within each of these four levels, a researcher can focus on the actions of *social units* (individuals, groups, organisations, networks), or the *interaction between social units*. For instance, corporate research at Amazon (and most other retail sites) tracks the

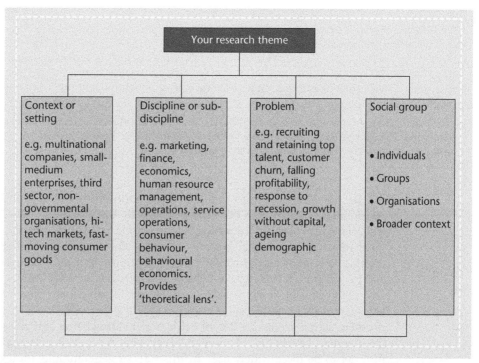

Your research theme			
Context or setting e.g. multinational companies, small-medium enterprises, third sector, non-governmental organisations, hi-tech markets, fast-moving consumer goods	**Discipline or sub-discipline** e.g. marketing, finance, economics, human resource management, operations, service operations, consumer behaviour, behavioural economics. Provides 'theoretical lens'.	**Problem** e.g. recruiting and retaining top talent, customer churn, falling profitability, response to recession, growth without capital, ageing demographic	**Social group** • Individuals • Groups • Organisations • Broader context

Figure 1.2 Four dimensions of your research theme in business and management research

buying preferences of individuals, groups (e.g. Kindle users), organisations (through corporate accounts), and geographic regions (e.g. EU), and how each interacts with their offerings and those of its competitors in a market. Considering the interaction between social units is often a fertile approach to research. For instance, the issue of organisations and their relationship with their broader context (the governments in whose countries they operate) is a perennial issue, particularly when it comes to the topic of taxation or social justice issues such as 'the living wage'.

These options are shown in **Figure 1.2** as the four dimensions of topic choice for business and management researchers.

1.1.2 What research is not!

Even if business and management research is diverse, it is not so broad that any problem you could investigate qualifies as research, as shown in **Research in action 1.1** below.

Research in action 1.1
CHECK THE ASSUMPTIONS

One company continually worked hard to reduce new product lead times – that is, how long from start to finish it took it to develop new products. Reducing lead times became a real obsession in the firm, but whenever anyone was asked why it was so important, they usually answered: 'Oh, you know that study ...'. However, not one person could identify the original source of 'that study'.

From detailed questioning of the managers, it became clear to the researcher that this study was actually a one-line statement quoted in *Fortune* magazine based on some simplistic calculations carried out by a consultancy. Perhaps not coincidentally, the consultancy trained companies to reduce new product lead times. If the managers had approached the study from a more critical perspective, they might have raised questions such as: How reliable is this study? Do these recommendations apply to us?

The point is that we must be able to evaluate the foundations on which we are basing our work or decisions. The *Fortune* study referred to was not research – it was a piece of what we know as 'bad science' – but qualified as a suitable source in journalism.

It can sometimes be hard to tell research, **journalism** and **consulting** apart. There are significant differences between a systematic investigation – the journey you are embarking on – and activities such as journalism or consulting. Business and management research is more than simply collecting and reporting information; it involves creating new knowledge by analysing, interpreting and reporting that information, and by integrating this new knowledge with what we already know.

A major goal of business and management research is to create knowledge that will help other people to solve a similar practical problem or understand a **research problem** better. Academics describe this as generating better and more widely applicable theories (we will discuss more precisely what we mean by 'theory' in **Chapter 2**). In order to be more widely used in this way, or generalisable, professional business and management research must be rigorously checked by other academic researchers (peer review, which we discuss in **Chapter 3**), at least if it is to be accepted as true and get published in management journals. It is constantly revised or even replaced over time.

Research is not journalism

Many students find it difficult to distinguish between journalism and academic research. A common purpose of both journalism and research is to gather information and present it in an appropriate format. (We will discuss the credibility of sources in **Chapter 3**.) Journalists report information about business and management organisations, people and trends in newspapers such as the *Financial Times* and the *Wall Street Journal* and magazines such as *The Economist* and *Fortune*. Information that is published in newspapers, magazines, books or websites may be interesting and useful for your research. However, a journalist's job is to report the news – what is new or novel – to sell newspapers or magazines or attract television or radio viewers. '*Man bites dog*' makes the news headlines because it is new or unusual, not because it adds to our knowledge, or helps us to understand deeper truths about the world or solve particular problems.

An important difference between journalism and research is that checking and challenging is an essential element of the systematic investigation process presented in this book. Other researchers must verify research findings before they are published. Newspapers and magazines, however, seldom carry out independent factual checking of the information they report, and so fall well short of the standards of peer review. Information provided by journalists is not always reliable, therefore, even if it is eye-catching and timely. Student reports often refer to websites, which, on viewing, have little or no basis in fact. Just because someone has written something doesn't make it right or useful, and websites are almost entirely unregulated in what they can say.

Of course, journalism and academic research are not always mutually exclusive. Journalists report on noteworthy research findings and the presentations and ideas of leading academic researchers. Some investigative journalism even comes close to or surpasses academic research; however, it is unlikely to have been peer reviewed.

Similarly, many academic researchers cross over into journalism, appearing on news programmes and chat shows; writing blogs; providing 'sound bites' on the topic of the day; writing books, magazine articles and newspaper columns for popular audiences; and even presenting television and radio programmes. However, even if someone has immense credibility as a researcher, if what they are saying has not been arrived at through a systematic research process and been checked and challenged by other academics, it is still opinion and/or journalism and not research. Whilst their opinion may offer a useful perspective, as researchers we would challenge whether this was authoritative and could therefore be relied on. As one of our colleagues so eloquently put it, *'You don't abdicate your professional standards just because you are writing for a newspaper or someone had shoved a camera in your face.'*

Research is not consulting

Journalism and academic research are typically done by different people and reported in different places, but **consulting** and academic research, on the other hand, are often done by the same people and reported in the same places (for example *Harvard Business Review*). Professional consultants publicise their ideas and promote their services in books and in-house journals modelled on academic publications (e.g. *McKinsey Quarterly*). Some academics wear both hats, carrying out consulting projects and reporting their work as research findings: Michael Porter and Gary Hamel run consulting companies, teach business and management, and publish in academic and non-academic forums.

To understand the difference between consulting and research, then, we need to take a closer look at what consultants do. A consultant is typically engaged by an organisation to solve an organisational problem and must gather, analyse and interpret information to generate a set of recommendations based on this information, describing how the company should solve the problem. For example, a consultant hired by an organisation to provide advice on how to restructure the organisation will need to gather information about the organisation, including finding out the organisation's current structure and defining its objectives. Her report would describe how to restructure the company and address any potential problems in how it might be implemented.

In deciding whether a project is consulting or research, you should consider both the means and the ends: whether it qualifies as research depends on what the consultant then does with that information. Most consulting engagements begin and end with the specific organisational problem, although a consultant will build up a stock of expertise over time and consulting companies often specialise in particular areas of expertise. Consultants value the information they gain in a consultancy engagement primarily as an input to future consulting engagements and may want to keep that knowledge proprietary. When consultants do report their work, it is typically to advertise this expertise in order to attract clients rather than increase the sum of business and management knowledge. As a result, consultants rarely have to justify how and what they investigate except to their client and employer, because the quality of their work is judged by how well it lets the organisation solve a particular problem, not whether it would help other organisations solve similar problems.

Professional researchers, on the other hand, have a primary responsibility to create and share knowledge. This means that they must link their research to previous research on the subject, and show that they are adding something new to that knowledge as a result of their investigation. Research by its nature is meant to be shared, not hidden.

ACTIVITY

The site www.ted.com illustrates the convergence of academic research, journalism and consultancy. Some Ted Talks are based on academic research that is then conveyed through compelling stories (good journalism) resulting in prescriptions for organisations (therefore consulting). Others start with the ideas of one individual or group, which may draw on existing research in the development of their stories, but may just rely on the emotive 'sell' and popular appeal of their narrative. We suggest you watch one and decide – is it academic research, journalism, a shameless attempt to sell you the individual's consulting services, or some combination of these?

 ## 1.2 What are the characteristics of business and management research?

As well as defining business and management research as being neither journalism nor consulting, we can also define it by what it is, a form of social science research and of research in general. Three characteristics of research projects – originality, relevance and immediacy – make them unique and create challenges for researchers.

1.2.1 Research is original

The goal of academic research is to make an original contribution to knowledge. A professional business and management research project therefore needs some degree of originality – it is not a copycat of someone else's research. On the other hand, a student research project will typically aim to apply existing business and management knowledge in a new context or add a small bit of new knowledge to what we already know. Student research therefore doesn't necessarily have to make a 'great discovery' or suggest a 'grand new theory'. Originality may come through building on existing knowledge but providing:

- new or improved insights or evidence
- new or improved methods for doing research
- new or improved analysis of data
- new or improved concepts, or applications of existing concepts or theories
- new or improved questions for further research.

For instance, a student research project to look at the suitability of managers for particular roles examined their competence and response to particular challenges or complexities in major projects. The work contributed to the knowledge of the research team of which his supervisor was a part by providing some good insights – how managers are chosen for their roles was not by their competence – and highlighted questions for further research, including whether current competence measures were appropriate for their context.

1.2.2 Research is relevant

Business and management research focuses on asking questions to solve a problem of incomplete knowledge, which may be practical or theoretical. Thus, as we will see in **Chapter 2**, the first step in the research process is to identify a research problem that you want to find out more about. A research problem can come from a **practical problem** (real-life situation) based on an issue that you have observed in a real-life setting, for example receiving poor service in a store might lead you to study how stores handle customer complaints. A practical problem could also come from issues that have been identified in your courses, or problems that face your organisation or other setting you are interested in investigating. Good business and management research may well start with a problem that could be identified through consulting or journalism – this ensures the relevance part of what we do.

More rarely in student projects, you may start with a **theoretical problem** (general principles or observations) posed by a business or management topic about which you would like to know more but for which there is incomplete information, for example the best way to consistently achieve organisational change. Such problems often emerge as you think about how to apply the theories and models learnt in your coursework to real-life settings, or try to understand which of several competing theories best explains how people or organisations actually behave. For example which is better for understanding corporate strategy, Porter's five forces or the resource-based view of the firm? It is not always possible to answer either type of problem completely by what you find out in a single research project.

A good research problem leads you to ask one or more questions about your research problem in order to understand more about it. Vice versa, you may start with questions that lead you to research problems that you can turn into research projects. **Chapter 2** will show you a systematic process for identifying research problems and questions, and how these problems and questions can be used to structure your research project. For example, if you were interested in urban renewal, you might research whether hosting a major sporting event (Olympics, Commonwealth Games, football World Cup) really does have any lasting legacy effect. You could investigate:

- the practical problem presented by turning venues designed for a single and relatively short event into permanent operational amenities;
- the health and economic benefits to local communities;
- the impact on urban renewal schemes in other areas which may be seen to suffer as a result of the focus on the area where the event is being held (e.g. Rio vs. other regions of Brazil for the 2016 Olympics).

Professional researchers are primarily concerned with increasing knowledge. This knowledge may be applied to improving individual and organisational performance

Table 1.1   Three types of research activity

Stage in research	Role of this type of research
Basic research	Research that is conducted to increase knowledge, with little consideration of future applications. Many social science researchers consider their work to be of this type. For instance, research on the behaviour of people under certain conditions may be undertaken (as in Milgram's experiment at the end of this chapter).
Development	This involves taking an original idea, possibly a basic research project, and looking for applications. This may include combining it with other ideas, or changing the original intention. For instance knowing that people behave in a certain way, considering how this might be applied in practice, for example as part of a training package for in-company use.
Commercial	This involves taking an idea from the possibility of application through to commercial usage. This is a particular skill set of consultants. For instance, they may take the behavioural work developed above and sell it as part of a training package. There could be further research to evaluate its usefulness in practice.

(relevant) but must be conducted in a systematic and supportable manner (rigorous). This requirement for rigour and relevance is termed 'the double hurdle' (e.g. Pettigrew 1997).

1.2.3   Research has immediacy

Research projects that start with a practical problem often need to be answered right now; that is, they have high immediacy, whilst those that start with a theoretical problem can wait; they have low immediacy. In academic and industrial research, different levels of immediacy lead to the description of three general types of project as basic research, development and commercial projects. These three types are described in **Table 1.1**.

A series of research projects that starts with basic research and carries the same kind of investigation through to development, or vice versa, is known as a stream of research. An individual research project may fit into more than one classification. You might start by investigating a practical problem and then use your findings to add to the knowledge about a theoretical problem, or you might investigate a theoretical problem in a specific practical context and then identify how to solve similar problems in other practical contexts.

1.3   What are some practical considerations when starting business and management research?

Always have two plans; leave something to chance.
(often attributed to Napolean)

We will look at three considerations in this section – how you usually like to work, the real stages of a research project, and setting some appropriate objectives.

How do you do? Type 1 or Type 2?

Type 1. As soon as the topics for the assignment are issued, Type 1 people rush away to start work. They plan out the tasks and, working steadily through them, finish with several weeks to spare. This time can be spent polishing their work, and occasionally gloating over Type 2 students. (Smug bastards.)

Type 2. As soon as the topics are issued, Type 2 students head to the bar. No use rushing the project, of course. It is only in the last few weeks before the deadline that they can ignore it no longer. Panic ensues; caffeine keeps them going during the long nights. As all the Type 2 students are queuing for the printer, the project report has a high chance of being submitted late.

If you are a Type 2, this approach may have worked for you in the past, but you are leaving your project's success to chance – and this time is different. Your research project is likely to be one of the biggest and most complex pieces of work you will have attempted. You can gain many benefits if you adopt at least some Type 1 practices in managing yourself. Like the research itself, it requires a systematic approach. If you define your research project, develop a credible research design and follow through in executing your project, the systematic approach should maximise your chances of project success.

We cannot say too strongly that *time is key* – particularly when you are working on a research project that involves many different people. We have observed that people who carry out projects successfully have consistently made good use of their time by planning. To make the best use of time, you must plan your project carefully. Over and over, students ignore all the good advice to manage the research process systematically, and hope that 'it'll work out in the end'. However, the old saying 'if you fail to plan, you plan to fail' is well illustrated by many research projects that went on to fail. Planning is not the enemy of creativity – as evidenced by just about every major product innovation company today. Committing effort to plans frees up time and head-space to explore relevant and interesting areas creatively. However, whatever way you choose to proceed, you will encounter 'the real project life cycle', the topic of our next section.

The real project life cycle

Rather than talk about idealised life cycles, the reality is that like most researchers, you may encounter these emotions at one time or another (although not always in this order, and not necessarily separately), as shown in **Figure 1.3**:

- **Enthusiasm** – You have just started the project and you are excited about it.
- **Despondency** – You realise how much you have to do and how much time it will take.
- **Running down blind alleys** – You are wasting time on interesting information or activities that will not contribute to your finished research project.
- **Panic** – You realise that you have too much work to get it all finished in the remaining time.
- **Elation** – You have completed a significant activity or the entire project.
- **Deflation** – You cannot figure out what to do next.

After the original rush of enthusiasm wears off, even experienced researchers can become despondent and lose their momentum, because the task can appear to be

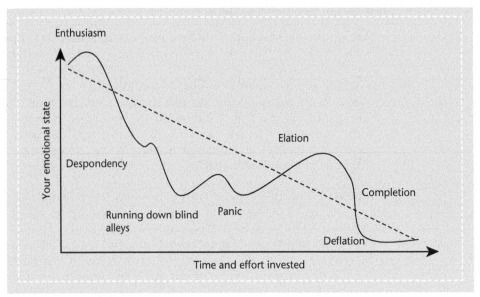

Figure 1.3 The real project life cycle

overwhelming. The result usually is a kind of mental paralysis which needs to last as short a time as possible. You can minimise the despondency phase by breaking down your project into manageable chunks of work – then just working systematically through them. Keeping the tasks a manageable size is crucial. For instance, the task of 'do literature review' is just too big. Working out your process and questions for the literature review is more manageable.

Most researchers can tell you how much time they have wasted investigating *blind alleys*. These are project directions that initially masquerade as interesting and relevant but ultimately will not help you to solve your research problem or answer your **research questions** and so represent wasted effort. If you aren't sure whether a certain area is relevant to your research project, check with your project advisor. When you are faced with a new line of enquiry, you should ask yourself the 'so what' question – how will pursuing this help you to answer one or more of your research questions? As a 'reality check' for a potential blind alley, you should ask:

- What aspects of my research problem (practical or theoretical) does this tell me more about?
- What new information does this add to what I already know about this research problem?
- How would I explain to my academic supervisor or project sponsor what this adds to my research project?
- If it is interesting, but outside the scope of this research project, can I come back to it later as an 'area for further investigation'?

There may come a time when you realise that the work you have left to do will take longer – sometimes far longer – than the time you have available for doing it. This results in another project inevitability – panic! Breaking down the remaining work and setting the scope of that work carefully (reducing the scope to fit the time available) is the Type 1 response.

Elation is good, but is usually followed by deflation. Having notes of what to do next collected as you go is a good source of where you might go next. However, this is early in your project and we will cover strategies for this last phase in the final chapter of this book. For now, the most important part of what has to be done is in structuring the activities that will follow. For this we use the SMART approach, described below.

1.3.1 Thinking about research in general

> I keep six honest serving-men, they taught me all I knew. Their names are what and why and when, and how and where and who.
>
> (Kipling [1902] 1998: 69)

Some of the most successful research projects we have supervised began with students visualising the final project report and then deciding how they would make it happen. We call this beginning with the end in mind, and we think that it is one of the keys to successful research (see Covey 2005). We can use Kipling's six question words to start thinking about research in general (by way of summary of the chapter so far) or to amend the questions for a particular project:

1. **What is research?** A systematic process that includes defining designing, doing and describing an investigation into a research problem.
2. **Why do research?** To find out things about business and management; to improve practices or performance.
3. **When is research carried out?** When we need to solve a problem of theoretical knowledge or practical importance.
4. **How does research change anything?** It provides the basis for improved theory or informed action.
5. **Where is the information that I need?** In the current literature on the area of interest and in the research field.
6. **Who else has a stake in research?** Anyone who is involved in the research process (people you study, research supervisors, managers) or the outcome (people reading your study or affected by the decisions based on the results).

You can apply these six questions to your own research project, as illustrated below.

What is my research?

What is the problem that I want to explore – how is it manifested and what are the effects of the problem? We explore this further in **Chapter 2**, with your objective being to develop a research question. What is the process that I need to follow to demonstrate that I have systematically investigated my area of interest?

Why am I doing research?

There are many reasons that you might be carrying out a research project, but these are the two we most commonly find – extrinsic and intrinsic. *Extrinsic* reasons for doing research might be to pass a course or carry out a work assignment, and a consideration of how this will be assessed (e.g., formal assessment criteria or utility of recommendations as perceived by key people). *Intrinsic* reasons to do research might be to be a more critical consumer of the results of research, to be able to demonstrate your research skills, to develop your understanding of the area you are researching.

When is my research to be carried out?

The first aspect of this question concerns the practicalities of the process you are involved in – when does it start, when does it have to be finished, and what are the key dates in between that I need to meet? The second aspect concerns the nature of the data that you will be considering. Is it historic (based on past records), real-time (happening now) or in the future (e.g. technology forecasting)?

How will I have changed anything?

The two general aspects are of contribution to theory or contribution to practice. It is worth thinking of how your work will be viewed in the future.

Where is the information that I need?

Which libraries, databases, people, organisation archives or other sources will you be consulting?

Who else is involved in my research?

You should also think about the different people who will be involved in your project and the impact your work might actually make on the world. Who will be carrying out this research project? What will I be doing or be responsible for? How should I work with my supervisor? How should I work with any external **stakeholders** for my work? What are the requirements of any assessment body? At this stage, one of the key stakeholders in your work is your supervisor. This is the subject of the next section.

1.3.2 Your relationship with your supervisor

Your main advisor is an important **project stakeholder** (person or group with an interest in the process of your work or its outcome). This will be typically your academic supervisor, but sometimes your project sponsor if you have one. The role your main advisor plays may vary according to the kind of project; for example, project supervisor implies much more 'hands-on' involvement than project coordinator. In coursework projects or job-related research projects, your supervisor will set the project assignment, and may even be the person who marks or assesses it.

Finding out what other students think about a potential supervisor can help you to decide whether he or she might be a good match for your project. If you have a chance to choose your own supervisor or project coordinator, you should try to find out:

● What do other students that he or she has supervised think about him or her for this specific type of project?

- Is he or she interested in the research you will be doing?
- Does his or her personality complement or conflict with your personality?
- How quickly can he or she provide feedback on your work?
- What are his or her plans for the period of research?

Project supervisors who can provide quick, accurate feedback on your research are worth their weight in gold. A good sign is whether your proposed supervisor takes an interest in this kind of project, especially if he or she is interested in the topic and/ or research approach you will be taking. However, interest alone is no guarantee of success: every student–supervisor relationship is unique. Personal habits, administrative and other teaching duties, and the number of students he or she supervises can detract from your academic supervisor's time and attention. Furthermore, whether your supervisor is available to provide feedback and other guidance can be affected by sabbaticals, leave of absence, taking a job at another university, retirement or plans to spend the summer sailing around the coast of France.

Whether or not you are able to choose your supervisor, you should think carefully about the relationship you are about to embark on. Students sometimes make unrealistic assumptions about their advisors, which can only lead to disappointment. You can use the issues listed in **Figure 1.4** to manage your expectations of what your supervisor will and will not do. In particular, you should understand the extent to which you are expected to work independently, a valuable skill in itself.

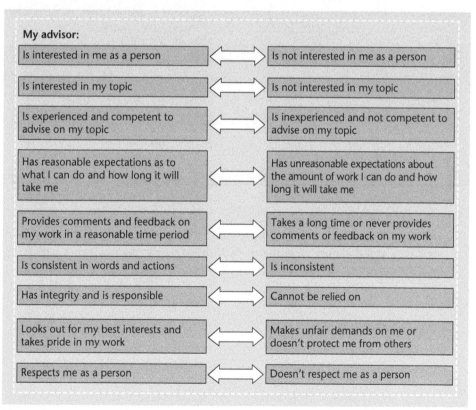

Figure 1.4 **Issues to consider in working with a project supervisor**
Source: Based on Davis and Parker (1997: 44)

Table 1.2   Example guidelines

The student's responsibilities	The supervisor's responsibilities
The student will be expected to: ● Submit a research proposal to the format and timetable as set down in the guidelines ● Draw up a timetable of activities ● Submit an outline of the project report showing what each chapter will cover ● Submit an agreed chapter to generate supervisor feedback ● Keep his/her supervisor informed of any holidays or trips that may affect his/her performance ● Keep the project coordinator and supervisor informed of any circumstances that may affect the submission of his/her project ● Work with an allocated supervisor who may not be his/her first choice ● Be aware of the supervisor's availability during the period of the project (July, August and September are problematic in Europe because of conferences and holidays).	The supervisor will provide general guidance in the conduct of a research programme and will act as a 'sounding board' to test various ideas and help in deciding appropriate courses of action (this can include referral to appropriate specialists within the school). This is to help to ensure that the progress made throughout the project and the writing up of these activities will fulfil the academic requirements of the school. It is expected that a supervisor will: ● Discuss and assist in the development of the submitted proposal ● Agree a timetable of activities ● Discuss the structure of the written report; that is, chapter coverage and purposes ● Comment on one chapter to advise on how well it matches the set purpose for that chapter and the style of writing ● Advise on issues relating to the theory and/or methodology used in the project ● Examine and mark the completed project. A supervisor will not: ● Keep track of a student's progress and chase him/her when deadlines are not adhered to ● Read an entire draft copy of the finished report ● Arrange access to organisations used as part of any field work ● Visit any organisations as part of any field work ● Necessarily be an expert in the theoretical or methodological area of a project he/she is supervising.

Because this relationship can have such a large impact on a research project's process and outcomes, many institutions now explicitly state what each person is responsible for. The guidelines given in **Table 1.2** are just one example, but you can see how they set out the ground rules right from the start of the project.

Other people who play a role

You may be working on the project not only with other project team members, but all the project's stakeholders. These include those people who have the information you need and those to whom you will report your findings or make your recommendations. A key research skill is managing everyone involved in the research project: you will also need to manage other project stakeholders besides yourself and your supervisor. They may or may not be the same people. You should identify these people and start to work proactively with them from the start of your project, since they can help but can also hinder your work. How well you manage them can affect how smoothly the process goes and how successful your project is.

1.3.3 Being 'SMART'

Your objectives should include both what you want to achieve from your research project and any personal objectives. Your research objectives should include satisfying your project requirements (coursework, degree, work assignment). Your **personal aims** should include anything else that you want to achieve, such as supporting your career development, personal interests or job prospects.

We suggest that you try to make each of your objectives **SMART**, which stands for:

- **Specific** – Where is this research journey taking you? What do you hope to achieve from it? Write it down and use this as a basis for future decision making
- **Measurable** – How will you determine whether your objective has been achieved (particularly more intangible objectives such as quality)? What steps are on the way to this?
- **Achievable** – Is the target you have set yourself physically possible?
- **Realistic** – Given all that you will be doing at the same time as this, will you really have the time and energy to give this project what it needs?
- **Time-framed** – How long do you have to accomplish each objective?

Aims help to guide your decisions before and during the project. These set the course for your journey. **Student research in action 1.1** shows how simple this process can be.

 Student research in action 1.1
IDENTIFYING SMART OBJECTIVES – KATYA

Katya was undertaking an MBA and wanted to do a research project in the logistics industry. She identified the following aims and objectives:

- To complete the MBA by submitting a project by the submission deadline – the project to score in excess of 65%;
- To gain a working knowledge of leading-edge practices in the logistics industry;
- To determine, by the end of the in-company research period, whether this was likely to be an area where she would work in the future;
- To make 30 contacts during the period of the project that would be useful in her future career.

Each of these met the requirements of the SMART objectives – they are specific, measurable, achievable and time-framed by the project period, and she prioritised her life so that she could make them realistic by giving the project the time necessary to achieve in excess of 65%.

Summary

In this chapter, we have addressed three main issues about business and management research. First, we have given you an overview of business and management research, and tried to draw a boundary between what research is and is not. Second, we have explained the benefits of understanding business and management research, doing a business and management research project and why you should approach it as a systematic and structured process.

Third, we argued that doing research helps you to understand and critically assess research carried out by other researchers, including the research presented in text-books, academic journals and the popular press. Without this ability to critically assess other people's arguments, as Carl Sagan commented: 'We become a nation of suckers, up for grabs by every charlatan that comes along' (Sagan 1997: 42). (More of this in **Chapter 3**.) Finally, we have explained some issues that you need to consider as you are getting started on your research project, including why you are doing it, what you want to get out of it and who else will be involved in it.

Answers to key questions

What is business and management research?

- It is a process that starts with the determination of a research problem or question, based on an issue of interest.
- Research is not journalism or consulting, although there are parallels in the processes with both these activities.
- Business and management research considers the roles of organisations, organisational actors and their actions and interactions.

Why do we do business and management research?

- Research is conducted for a wide range of intrinsic and extrinsic reasons, including the possibility of discovering new things about something of interest, testing ideas and making sense of complex situations.
- Basic research is carried out to establish ideas or principles.
- Developmental research is carried out to take these ideas or principles on and bring them one step closer to commercialisation.

What are the benefits of taking a systematic approach to a research project?

- A systematic approach allows you to identify the choices you will make as a researcher and the logic that guides these choices.
- A systematic approach will remove some of the uncertainty from the process, and allow you to manage the remainder.
- The research life cycle is defined by the 4-Ds, from definition to designing to doing the research and then describing your work.
- The process is not linear, but iterative.

What critical issues should you consider as you get started?

- Begin with the end in mind.
- Look for previous work in this or similar areas, key themes and hot topics, consider methods and look at your timescales and available resources.

Who are the key project stakeholders?

- Yourself.
- Other members of the project team (if applicable).
- Supervisors.
- Participants (e.g. respondents to your survey, case study informants).
- Examiners/university.
- Project sponsors (if applicable).

What is the 'real' project life cycle and how do I manage it?

- The real life cycle is something of a rollercoaster emotionally, as we begin usually with great enthusiasm, followed by various periods of despair when progress is not in line with our expectations.
- Recognising that this is a normal part of the process helps. Working closely with your supervisors and others can help minimise how much time you spend in the less pleasant parts of the life cycle.

References

Covey, Stephen R. 2005. *The Seven Habits of Highly Effective People*, revised edn. London: Simon & Schuster.

Davis, Gordon B. and Parker, Clyde A. 1997. *Writing the Doctoral Dissertation: A Systematic Approach*, 2nd edn. Hauppage, NY: Barron's Educational Series.

Kahneman, D. and Tversky, A. 1979. Prospect theory: An analysis of decision under risk, *Econometrica: Journal of the Econometric Society*, 17(2): 263–91.

Kipling, Rudyard [1902] 1998. The elephant's child. In *Just So Stories*. London: Puffin.

Milgram, S. 1974. *Obedience to Authority*. New York: Taylor & Francis.

Pettigrew, Andrew M. 1997. What is a processual analysis? *Scandinavian Journal of Management*, 13(4): 337–48.

Phillips, Estelle M. and Pugh, Derek S. 2005. *How to Get a PhD*, 4th edn. Maidenhead: Open University Press.

Roethlisberger, F.J. and Dickson, W.J. 1939. *Management and the Worker*. Cambridge, MA: Harvard University Press.

Sagan, Carl 1997. *The Demon-Haunted World: Science as a Candle in the Dark*. New York: Ballantine Books.

Stacey, R.D. 2001. *Complex Responsive Processes in Organizations: Learning and Knowledge Creation*. London: Routledge.

Taylor, F.W. [1911] 1998. *The Principles of Scientific Management*. London: Dover Publications.

Whyte, William F. 1955. *Street Corner Society*. Chicago: University of Chicago Press.

Additional resources

Collis, Jill and Hussey, Roger 2013. *Business Research*, 4th edn. Basingstoke: Palgrave Macmillan.

Easterby-Smith, Mark, Thorpe, Richard and Lowe, Andy 2012. *Management Research: An Introduction*, 4th edn. London: Sage.

Gill, John and Johnson, Phil 2010. *Research Methods for Managers*, 4th edn. London: Sage.

Goldacre, Ben 2009. *Bad Science*. London: Fourth Estate.

Jankowicz, A.D. 2000. *Business Research Projects*, 3rd edn. London: Cengage Learning EMEA

Partington, David 2002. *Essential Skills for Management Research*. London: Sage.

Pigliucci, Massimo 2010. *Nonsense on Stilts: How to Tell Science From Bunk*. Chicago: University of Chicago Press.

Robson, Colin 2002. *Real World Research*, 2nd edn. Oxford: Blackwell.

Saunders, Mark, Lewis, Phillip and Thornhill, Adrian 2012. *Research Methods for Business Students*. 6th edn. Harlow: Financial Times/Prentice Hall.

Sekaran, U. 2000. *Research Methods for Business*, 3rd edn. Chichester: Wiley.

Zikmund, W.G. 2000. *Business Research Methods*, 6th edn. Orlando, FL: Dryden Press/Harcourt College.

Key terms

consulting, 10, 11
journalism, 10
personal aims, 21
practical problem, 13
project stakeholder, 18
research, 5
research problem, 10

research process, 5
research questions, 16
SMART, 21
stakeholders, 18
systematic approach, 5
theoretical problem, 13

Discussion questions

1. Identify five ways in which organisations gather information about you for business and management purposes.

2. Can a single research project satisfy the needs of both academic research and consulting? Academic research and journalism?

3. Why do we argue that research reports published in newspapers or business magazines are less credible than those published in journals where they must be reviewed by other researchers before they are published?

4. Review **Table 1.1**. What are examples of research from each category?

5. What do business and management researchers study? Identify at least one study from your classes or textbooks for each level of the hierarchy presented in **Figure 1.1**.

6. What research projects have you carried out so far in your course of study? Why did you do them? What did you find out?

7. Which of the projects would we classify as academic research projects, and which as practical research projects, and what are the differences between the two?

8. Which is more important in business and management research – solving practical problems or increasing knowledge?

9. What are the four stages of business and management research?

10. How can project stakeholders influence the definition, design, doing and description of a research project?

11. Identify the stakeholders in a recent research project or other project you have carried out. What were the needs of each stakeholder and how were they expressed, if at all? If you have carried out projects previously, what have you learnt about the management of stakeholders from this experience?

Workshop

Read the six mini-cases below, each describing a particular research project carried out by either students or professional researchers, and then answer the questions at the end.

1: The good student project

A student was asked by a regional development agency (RDA) to investigate how effective the RDA was in promoting good business practice in the region. Early on, the student identified two key customers for this report, the university and the RDA, so she worked with both to make sure that she understood their requirements. The university's requirements were laid out in the project guidelines, which she clarified with her academic supervisor. Her main contact at the RDA put his requirements in writing at an early stage, giving her a definable end objective.

Based on these two sets of requirements, the student decided that the best way to approach the project was from an economic perspective, in which she identified and narrowed down the relevant research done by other people in similar areas, and organised these findings into a framework for evaluating the RDA's practices based on work done elsewhere. The findings reported by other researchers also provided a point of comparison when she evaluated what the agency was doing. Her further investigation of the roles that other agencies were reported to be playing allowed some small-scale benchmarking of the RDA's activities against other agencies.

The project was a phenomenal success. The university awarded it a prize and the agency came away with a much better understanding of how it was supporting businesses in order to innovate. This success reflected an understanding of the needs of both the university and the sponsoring organisation – not always an easy task – and the fact that these needs could be converted into products.

2: The bad student project

The project started with the student demonstrating to the supervisor a piece of software he had been involved in writing. 'This is what managers today need to help them to manage', he confidently stated. 'I want to use my project to validate that this is the case.' Despite objections from his supervisor, he proceeded with his work and tried to construct tests to prove this. As he saw this as 'a practical project', he dismissed any prior academic research as irrelevant to his work. He also rejected using established methods for collecting and analysing data in his testing, preferring to invent these methods himself.

The project failed. It lacked key facets that must be present in all academic projects. These include a basis in prior research – this shows that you have covered what is known already before you start reinventing anything. Furthermore, the use of any method is not self-validating. Justifying your methods is vital to demonstrate that you are able to conceptualise, design, carry out, analyse and report research. This is valued in most academic qualifications.

3: A professional laboratory study: Milgram's experiment

Stanley Milgram (1974) conducted one of the most well-known experiments in the study of human behaviour. His objective was to study obedience to authority. He constructed a laboratory-style experiment using human subjects – in this case male adults residing in New Haven aged 20–50, and selected from a wide variety of occupations. He carried out the experiment twice, using 40 new participants for each experiment.

Each test was carried out on a pair of test subjects. The initial briefing given to the subjects told them that the test was designed to test memory and learning. Unknown to one of the pair was the fact that the other was actually a confederate of the researcher. Each was paid and told that their performance in no way affected their pay.

Following a short introduction to memory and learning, a rigged draw took place in which the (naive) subject was assigned the role of teacher, and the confederate the role of learner. A white-coated experimenter stayed in the room with the 'teacher'. The 'learner' was taken to an adjacent room and strapped into an electric chair. The experimenter told the subject that he had to teach the learner a list of paired words. Subsequently he was to test the learner on his recall of the list and to administer an increasing level of electric shocks to punish him for each mistake in the test. The 'teacher' was instructed to increase the intensity of shock by one level for each mistake. The dial was marked with 30 shock levels (15–450 volts), labelled from 'slight shock' to 'danger: severe shock'. The learner, according to the plan, provided many wrong answers, so that before long the subject would have to administer the strongest level of shock. Increases in shock level were met by increasingly insistent demands from the learner that the experiment be stopped. However, the experimenter kept instructing the teacher to continue. (The confederate was not really being shocked, but behaved as though he was increasingly being shocked, up to the level of no response, implying that he was unconscious or even dead.)

Milgram recorded that only 14 out of 40 people withdrew from the test before they thought they had administered the maximum shock. All participants administered at least slight shocks. The remaining majority, despite stating that they would rather not hurt the presumed victim, felt obligated to follow the orders of the experimenter. Although admitting that they had ultimate control over the switch, the experimenter exerted sufficient pressure by simply urging that the experiment must continue to create behaviour antithetical to personal and social ideals. (All the subjects were carefully debriefed following the experiment and reconciled with their 'victim'.)

4: The professional ethnographic study: Street Corner Society

Whyte (1955) studied groups of young men who socialised together in a thinly disguised Boston in the 1940s. Whyte lived and socialised with these 'disadvantaged' youths, even going bowling and generally living as they did for the period of the study. This gave him a unique insight into the complex social dynamics of the groups – he was able to get 'inside their heads' to understand their thinking processes, in a way that an external observer would never be able to. In this study he 'went native' – completely immersing himself in the environment for the purposes of the research.

5: The professional in-company study: F.W. Taylor's studies of work

F.W. Taylor has been credited with inventing the whole science of 'time-and-motion studies'. In these, a work task is analysed in scientific terms to determine the optimal way for it to be carried out. The time that it takes and the way that it is carried out are the subject of analysis. Taylor developed his techniques in the early years of the last century in a foundry. He studied many manual tasks that were carried out, including the shovelling of ore and ashes into and from furnaces. He would analyse the elements of each task – in the case of ore shovelling, pushing shovel into ore stack, turning and throwing ore in a particular direction at a particular height. By carrying out extensive experimentation and measurement (watching and recording the times and movements on hundreds of occasions), he was able to conclude that the optimum load for a shovel was 21 pounds for the people that he was studying. This meant that they would need different-sized shovels – for instance one for ore (small) and a different one for ash (much larger). Redesigning the shovels also increased the productivity of the people doing the shovelling. Other aspects of the job, including the placement of piles of work, were likewise optimised. He also paid the workers a bonus for this increased productivity in return for using his scientifically derived methods (see Taylor [1911] 1998).

6: The professional in-company study: Roethlisberger and Dickson's Hawthorne studies

The study started as an experiment with a small group of workers in 1927 to determine the conditions that led to fatigue in workers. By doing so, the researchers hoped to be able to determine the optimum conditions under which people could work to increase their productivity. The researchers were very confident about their method and that they would be able to isolate the key variables that would enhance productivity. As is so often the case in research, what they found was not what they expected.

One small part of the study concerned the impact of lighting levels on the productivity of a group of workers. By isolating the group from the rest of the factory, other factors could be eliminated, providing near-laboratory conditions.

Initially the lighting level was raised and it was noted that the productivity increased. At the end of the experiment, the levels were lowered again, and the productivity increased again. This was not expected. The researchers changed their approach to try to uncover why this was happening. They discovered that what was underlying these changes in output were not any of the influences of management (for example through incentives). They found that it was the social processes in the group and their accepted norms (particularly relating to output) that determined their productivity (see Roethlisberger and Dickson 1939).

Discussion questions

1. What question or problem do you think the researcher was addressing in each case?
2. How did each researcher go about his/her task? Briefly summarise the method for his/her research.
3. What were the resource requirements in each case in terms of time, level of expertise, and so on, for the researchers and how applicable would each approach be for a student project?
4. What were the key findings of each project?
5. How generalisable are the findings in each case; that is, could the finding apply to environments other than the one in which they were carried out?

Relevant chapters
13 How do I write up my report?
14 What do I do now?

Key challenges
- Making sense of your findings
- Presenting your research to others
- Reflecting and learning from your research

4

Relevant chapters
1 What is research?
2 **What should I study?**
3 How do I find information?

Key challenges
- Understanding what academic research is
- **Generating and clarifying ideas**
- Using sources of information

1

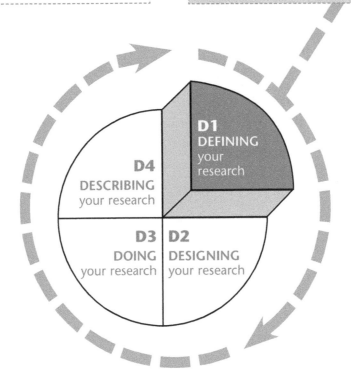

Relevant chapters
9 How do I do field research?
10 What do my quantitative data mean(1)?
11 What do my quantitative data mean(2)?
12 What do my qualitative data mean?

Key challenges
- Practical considerations in doing research
- Describing data using simple statistics
- Carrying out statistical tests
- Interpreting words and actions

3

Relevant chapters
4 What is my research approach?
5 How do I do quantitative research?
6 How do I do qualitative research?
7 How do I do case study research?
8 How do I make sure my research is ethical?

Key challenges
- Choosing a research approach
- Choosing a research design
- Collecting data using quantitative methods
- Collecting data using qualitative methods
- Integrating quantitative and qualitative methods

2

2 What should I study?
chapter
Generating and clarifying ideas for a research project

 Key questions

- Where do ideas for research topics come from?
- How can I choose between several potential research topics?
- What characterises a good research topic?
- Why should I use research questions to focus my research?
- How can I use a project proposal to define my project scope?

 Learning outcomes

At the end of this chapter, you should be able to:
- Find ideas for your research project
- Select the best idea to develop further into a research problem and questions
- Develop that idea into a research proposal

Contents

Introduction

According to Craig Lundberg (1999), you should use a systematic process for generating, selecting and refining your ideas. The systematic process we present in this chapter will help you identify your research topic and develop it into a research problem and research questions, giving you a sound basis for your research design. This is the first step on the way to a successful research project.

Your first stage is identifying ideas that may lead to a research topic. This may be challenging, either because you don't know what you want to do or how to come up with ideas, or because you have too many ideas and don't know how to choose the best one. **Section 2.1** explains how to generate ideas for business and management research using the academic literature, real-world problems and your own personal interests and experiences, through methods such as brainstorming and mind mapping.

You will need to narrow down your ideas into a researchable topic. **Section 2.2** describes how to take potential research topics and select the best one (and a backup). You should choose your research topic carefully, because you will have to live with your topic, often for a long time. Finding a suitable topic will depend on the project requirements, the characteristics of a good research project, and your own interests. Not all research topics will satisfy your project guidelines and assessment criteria, so read them carefully when you are defining your project and keep filtering your ideas against them. Even if you have been assigned a research problem, you can bring some creativity to generating and selecting ideas about what to research and how to research it.

A good research topic is not only interesting and worth doing, but also manageable in scope – you can get it done in the time and with the skills and other resources you have. **Section 2.3** describes how to define the scope of your project, once you have selected a promising idea, and how to prepare a project proposal. Your project proposal tells your project stakeholders what you are going to do and, just as importantly, what you are not going to do in your project. This makes it easier for them to provide support and feedback, and for you to know when you are done.

After you have finished this chapter, you should be much clearer about what you are going to research. You may have to revise your initial project proposal once you have done further reading about your topic, which we will cover in **Chapter 3**; otherwise, you may be trying to solve a problem that has already been solved, or one that no one can solve. Such revisiting is not unusual in research projects, but if you use a systematic approach you should waste much less time and effort in this stage of your research if you need to revise your original research topic.

2.1 How can I find an idea for my research project?

Deciding what your project will be about and where and with whom it will be conducted is an important part of your research project (Blaikie 2009), so taking a systematic approach to generating, selecting and refining ideas is key to project success (Gill and Johnson 2010). We strongly recommend that you don't decide what you will research just because you want to try out a particular way of gathering data (such as a survey), or a particular way of analysing data (such as building a *structural equation model* as described in **Chapter 11**), unless your project requires this. While you should definitely take research methods into account, 'if the only tool you have is a hammer, everything starts to look like a nail'. Start with the broader picture.

2.1.1 How do I generate ideas?

Good research often starts with an issue that 'catches your attention'– something that presents a puzzle or is interesting, according to Karl Weick (1992). Good ideas for research projects come from many places: the business and management world, the subjects you have studied in your course and your own personal interests. Booth et al. (2008: 36) suggest that you think of a **research idea** as an interest or a general area of enquiry that you want to pursue. Lundberg (1999) lists potential types of research ideas as:

- a phenomenon
- an issue
- a problem
- a question to study
- a general theme
- an area of behaviour
- a body of theory.

Although you may find ideas to explore anywhere, projects most often start with something that interests you in real-world business and management settings (*practical problems*) or from business and management research (*theoretical problems*). You may also find ideas in your own personal interests and experiences, the subjects you have already studied and projects that other students have already carried out, or even from brainstorming. Early on, your ideas may be as broad as 'service management', 'research and development', 'the film industry', or 'humour in organisations'. These ideas are too general to research, but we describe how you can focus them into research topics and then into research problems and research questions. The rest of this section will describe some different areas where you might find research ideas.

As you generate ideas, try to identify a potential **research topic**, a general area of business and management that the idea might link to. A good research topic will lead to either a practical or a theoretical problem that you can address in your research. Booth et al. (2008) identify two kinds of research problems: **theoretical problems**, 'What do we not know that we ought to know?' and **practical problems**, 'What can we not do that we ought to be able to do?' A research problem starting with a gap in theory might be *'what are the structural factors that create a gender gap in business leadership?'* while a research problem starting from evidence about the gender gap in business leadership might be, *'why are there not more women CEOs?'*

2.1.2 Finding ideas

Write your ideas down as you go along, no matter how silly they might seem, so that you don't lose them. The quality of your ideas at this point is less important than their quantity: you should aim to generate plenty of good ideas so that you can choose the most promising idea (the one you will try to develop into a research proposal) and a backup (an alternative in case the first one doesn't work out as planned).

Through further reading and some library research, you can nurture your best topic into research problems and research questions. As well as a research topic and research problem, you will eventually need to identify a research setting where you will conduct your work, and a sample of people, groups, organisations or the broader context (as described in **Chapter 1**) where you will collect your data.

Finding ideas in your studies

Starting with a project based on your studies, such as a class material or an assignment, may make it easier for you to identify the main topics and further reading about those topics. Classes that you have enjoyed or where you have performed your best usually reflect your natural interests and abilities. This may indicate what you will be successful at: it is difficult to do a good project if you don't have the interest, knowledge and skills to carry it out. One of Harvey's students initially refused to consider a finance project because he didn't intend to pursue a career in that area, even though his best marks were in finance. When he subsequently considered his personal goals for the project and his course, he decided to do a project in financial management and carried it off with distinction.

Have you already completed a short assignment that you could expand or follow up, to investigate a topic more deeply given more time? This will be important when you get started on your literature search, as we will see in **Chapter 3**. This may also make it easier to identify an academic supervisor who can support your research project, if you still need to choose. Your academic supervisor or lecturers may have some suggestions for you to investigate.

Finding ideas in business and management research

You can also use business and management research that has already been done as a source of research ideas. You may have read about a particular idea or topic and want to know more about it, or disagree with it and want to challenge it. Good places to look include:

- Academic journals such as the *Academy of Management Journal* or the *European Management Journal*;
- Managerial or academic books such as Womack et al.'s *The Machine that Changed the World* or Latour and Woolgar's *Laboratory Life*;
- Textbooks such as Kotler et al.'s *Principles of Marketing* or Grant's *Contemporary Strategy Analysis*;
- Newspapers and magazines such as the *Financial Times* or *The Economist*.

If you haven't got any clues about what ideas or topics you might pursue, flipping through the tables of contents of some current management journals may give you some ideas about what is currently 'hot or not' on the research agenda. **Student research in action 2.1** illustrates how Kate combined a general research idea – why does technological change make existing firms fail? – with the (then) new 'hot topic' of absorptive capacity in her doctoral research. (A doctoral thesis is usually a much more substantial piece of research than an undergraduate or master's level project, but the issues and challenges are similar in nature, even if larger in scope.)

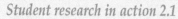

Student research in action 2.1

TRYING OUT AN EXISTING MODEL IN A NEW REAL-WORLD CONTEXT

Intrigued by research on technology cycles by Tushman and Anderson (1986), Kate decided to investigate how radical changes in product technology affected company survival in high-tech industries. Her supervisor brought an article on a new theoretical concept, absorptive capacity (Cohen and Levinthal 1989; Cohen 1990), to her attention as a factor that might affect company survival in turbulent environments. To study whether companies with higher absorptive capacity were more likely to survive, Kate needed to find at least one industry or sector where she could gather data. She investigated a number of industries, and narrowed them down to reduced instruction set computing microprocessors, high-definition television (HDTV) and supercomputers. Even though all three industries were interesting, a chance conversation with a venture capitalist during a transatlantic air flight on the way to a conference on HDTV convinced her to study supercomputers for her thesis.

You could also start by thinking around an existing topic such as organisational citizenship behaviour (OCB), the positive and negative behaviours associated with people in organisations. Potential questions might be:

- What behaviours should we include in OCB? (concepts)
- Are there differences in OCB between full-time and part-time workers? (context)
- Do Western models of OCB apply in China? (context)
- Does OCB affect customer loyalty? (outcomes)
- Does deviant workplace behaviour affect business unit performance? (outcomes)

Here, your main goal is to extend knowledge or fill in any 'gaps' in what we know about it. Very broad ideas such as the relationship between organisations and the governments of the countries in which they operate, discussed in **Chapter 1**, are a particularly promising sources of potential research ideas. For example, are practices such as ISO 14000 (international standard for environmental management systems used by most large organisations) developed in the context of large, multinational companies applicable in other contexts such as small and medium-sized enterprises (SMEs) or public services? Look at the existing research in this area to see whether you can confirm, disprove or extend the research that has already been done. You can identify what ideas researchers have already investigated, and also where there are gaps where your own research might fit. We describe this as starting with a *theoretical problem*, because you are trying to address a gap in knowledge (or theory, which we will describe in **Section 2.3**), rather than starting by trying to solve a real-world problem.

Another strategy is to test an existing piece of research by extending it to a different real-world **research setting** such as a different country, industry, type of organisation or social group, to see if what you find out is similar or different. What happens if you can apply a model of employee motivation developed for manufacturing employees to lawyers, or lean production in a hospital context? If you find out that the model does apply, this makes it more universal or more 'robust'. If you use this strategy, your research should strive to increase knowledge by extending or filling at least a small gap in what we know about the research topic in real-world applications. This often ensures that your research has relevance to practical problems faced by organisations and managers. Projects that start with established knowledge claims often benefit from a degree of serendipity in finding a real-world context, because you are finding out 'what if' you try to apply a theory or model in a new context besides the one in which it was developed, as illustrated in **Student research in action 2.1** and **Student research in action 2.2**.

Student research in action 2.2 gives an example of how a student took an idea from one context and examined its application in another.

Student research in action 2.2
APPLYING IDEAS IN NEW CONTEXTS

As a committed vegetarian and ethical consumer, Catherine was interested in farmers' markets, farm shops, and other places that people could buy organic fruit and vegetables besides the major supermarket chains. In her MSc dissertation, Catherine had surveyed customer attitudes towards online grocery shopping. For her next research project she decided to combine her ethical interests with her interest in e-business and find out more about what kinds of customers bought organic fruit and vegetables online, and how small organic producers tried to market their products to customers. As she worked on her idea, she realised that it would be interesting to test whether the models of service quality that she had applied in studying online supermarkets could actually extended to small producers.

At the time of writing some 'hot' topics include whether banks and other financial institutions are too heavily or too lightly regulated; the role of social media such as Twitter and Facebook in marketing; whether there should be quotas for women on executive boards; and whether regions are better as part of bigger countries or as independent economic entities. If you find an interesting article in the table of contents of a journal, you can look at the 'areas for further research' at the end of the article, where the authors describe the next logical step (or steps) following on from their research. These provide 'hooks' on which you can hang your work.

Finding ideas with real-world managers and organisations

Many interesting ideas come from practical problems that the business and management organisations need to solve in the real world. If you are sponsored by an organisation or are working in an organisation while you are doing your research, you will probably be expected to focus on a practical problem identified by either you or the organisation. An idea may also be the result of personal experience at work, as in **Student research in action 2.3**.

Student research in action 2.3
FINDING IDEAS IN WORK EXPERIENCE

Before he started as a postgraduate research student, Elmar was an IT consultant. He was appalled by the number of large IT projects that failed despite the millions of euros spent on them. When he started his studies, he found that many newspaper and academic articles investigated the failure of IT projects, but no one had any justifiable answers to the problems that stood up to testing. Indeed, the literature was littered with prescriptions that did not appear to provide any benefit to managers in managing their projects successfully. Clearly, there was an opportunity for him to do some interesting research. The research project that followed had clear practical implications for managers and organisations in how they treated risks.

If an organisation or professional association is sponsoring your research, it probably has a specific practical problem in mind rather than 'blue sky' research on an academic problem. Your organisation or sponsor may need to answer questions such as:

- Implementing a particular practice: How can we reduce our purchasing costs? Should we develop a supply strategy that reduces our numbers of suppliers to allow them to focus and we get the benefits of greater volumes, or do we diversify and try to benefit from greater competition in our supply base?
- Solving a particular organisational problem: How can we retain customers who are defecting? Should we improve our customer service?
- Improving the organisation's performance: How can we get more undergraduate students to apply for our credit card?

Journals such as the *Harvard Business Review* or the *European Management Journal*, magazines such as *Fortune* or *Management Today*, and newspapers such as the *Financial Times* or *The Wall Street Journal* are good sources of practical problems that currently face many organisations. You might focus on a practical problem of interest to:

- **An industry**: Should fast-food companies be allowed to advertise before the 9pm TV 'watershed'?
- **A type of organisation**: Should charities substitute for government activities (the volunteer society)?
- **An organisation**: How should Starbucks respond to binges and boycotts by opposing groups of consumers?
- **An organisational problem**: Should companies adopt flexible working policies so that men can take on equal parenting responsibilities?
- **A group of employees**: Do women managers still face a 'glass ceiling' in investment banks?
- **A group of consumers**: How do children exercise 'pester power' to get their parents to buy them products advertised on television?

Finding ideas in your personal interests

Many students overlook an obvious source of ideas: their own interests. After all, you have to live with the project – sometimes for up to a year – so it may as well be something that inspires you! Even if you are working on an assigned project or as part of a research team, you need to 'own' some part of the project, even if it is just part of the process, such as finding out how to design a questionnaire, using a particular statistical technique that you are interested in, or taking responsibility for editing or doing the graphic design of the finished report. Whilst this is not always necessary or even possible, you may be able to develop one or more of your hobbies, sports and other interests into a topic that reflects your own personality and character.

Some examples of projects that students have developed from their own interests are given below. Each student developed a research project that allowed him or her to explore a personal interest, and also led to a research problem with both practical and theoretical aspects:

- A football fan combined his love of Manchester United with his interest in marketing to develop a study of the impact of sports sponsorship on the sponsoring organisation.

- A student with a serious interest in 'retail therapy' carried out a study of the e-marketing potential of luxury goods.
- A highly entrepreneurial student studied the practices and associated success (or otherwise) of local entrepreneurs.
- A student who did a lot of work with local charities conducted a human resources study of the work performance differences between the voluntary and the private sectors.
- A student who had served in the military conducted research into commercial project management, and used the project to establish an interest, which subsequently led to a job.

Finding ideas in past projects

You may be able to find lists of previous student research projects in the projects office or library. A look at projects that other students have completed might spark off some ideas. You may even be able to look at some past projects, to get a feel for what yours might look like.

The following are some examples of recent projects that conducted investigations into:

- Knowledge management in the use of rehearsal for natural disaster planning
- The impact of ISO 14000 on company performance
- The role of regional development agencies in improving business performance
- Whether a mobile phone company should offer an existing customer a cheaper deal if they threaten to leave
- The use of storytelling in management
- How the stadiums built for the football World Cup in South Africa are being used now, and how this compares with the original legacy plans for them and other global event venues
- How Nike uses social media platforms to engage with disadvantaged youth groups

Other sources of ideas

What if you have considered these sources and still don't have any ideas? If you are stuck for ideas and haven't been able to identify any practical or theoretical problems that really 'grab you', you might want to be a bit more creative. Why not brainstorm? **Brainstorming** is a technique for generating and selecting ideas. You should try to come up with as many ideas as you can, without censoring them or subjecting them to critical review. Brainstorming is probably more practical for a group than an individual, but try sitting down somewhere quiet with a blank sheet of paper and free-associating. Include a variety of potential sources of ideas for brainstorming such as your personal interests, your studies or other students' projects. If your idea doesn't interest you, you probably won't be committed enough to do a good project.

If you get this far and you still haven't come up with any ideas that seem appealing, you might consider:

1. **Reflecting on your own personal experiences related to business and management.** Frustration is often a great seed for management research ideas. If you have had a bad experience of service quality in a shop, you may want to find out just how widespread bad service is or the causes of such encounters.

2. **Thinking back to lecturers and other speakers you have heard.** Has anyone presented you with an idea that was particularly well thought out or that you could relate to and wanted to find out more about?
3. **Talking to other people to see what they are interested in.** What are the pertinent issues at the moment? For example, you might find out that someone you know has bought or sold something interesting on eBay. This might lead to a question such as 'Can we start to make all our purchases through eBay or other auction sites?'
4. **Reading general articles, journals, books and newspapers.** Good sources for current topics include the *Financial Times*, *The Economist*, *Harvard Business Review*, and trade publications such as *Computer Weekly* and *The Grocer*. These can help you to identify 'hot topics' that may present good opportunities for both interest and career, and add some relatively unique element to the work.
5. **Surfing the internet.** Do a random search such as Google's 'I feel lucky' just to see where it takes you.

2.1.3 How many ideas should I generate and when should I stop?

While some projects may not allow you any leeway in defining your topic, nearly every project has enough flexibility that you can – or are even required to – be creative about what you are going to study and how you are going to study it. As you can see in **Figure 2.1**, some people start with no ideas, and others with many ideas. Most people

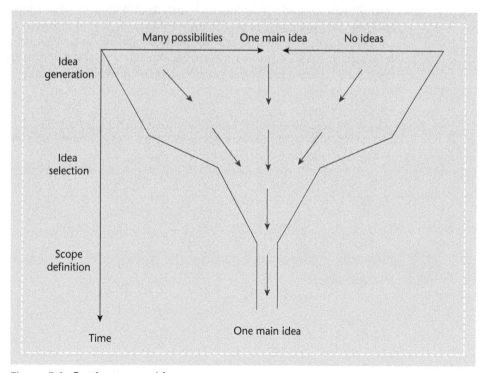

Figure 2.1 **Getting to one idea**

start somewhere between the two extremes with a few ideas. If you start with no ideas, you should aim to generate several ideas that you can choose from. If you start with many ideas, you should aim to converge on a few possibilities, and then select one main idea. If you are one of the few people who start with one main idea, you should revisit that idea to see whether it will actually lead to the best project that you can do.

Even if you already know what you want to, or must, do, don't stop generating ideas too early. Identify as many good ideas as you can, rather than only one 'perfect' idea. If you generate enough ideas, you can choose the best one; otherwise, you ignore the chance to learn or you may feel overwhelmed. You can often incorporate features of the ideas you reject into your research project. Creativity, according to some (see Stacey 2001), lies on the border between order and chaos. Your best idea is one that suits you and satisfies your project stakeholders, including your supervisor and business sponsors. You will learn how to rank and select the best one in **Section 2.2**.

Although this representation may make the process seem simple – generate some ideas and pick the best one – many students find this stressful. Some have absolutely no idea of what they would like to research or how to come up with ideas. You cannot truly own your project unless you want to find out more about something that academics or managers care about. We have suggested how to overcome this in **Section 2.1.1**.

Other students come unstuck the first time they are asked to come up with their own ideas and told they can do anything within the entire subject area of business and management – resulting in an overload of possibilities and uncertainty about where to get started. The combination of uncertainty and the pressing need to get on with the project leads to **project paralysis**. If this describes you, don't worry, there are many ways out of it and we will be describing them in **Section 2.2**.

As supervisors, we find that the most difficult students to work with are those who start off with a single fixed idea, an unshakeable view of what they are going to do and how they are going to do it. This is more risky than no ideas or too many. If you choose your topic without exploring other possibilities and rush into making a choice too early, you are likely to run into significant problems later on in your research project. You have probably not considered the possibilities adequately, have missed what you might learn from the early exploration of alternatives, and might have to change your topic significantly anyway, as illustrated in **Student research in action 2.12**. Explore your research topic and come up with possibilities to investigate further. Once you start to explore potential ideas, you will find that your certainties are replaced by questions, rather than vice versa.

A good research project starts off with one question and finishes with ten. This isn't just a job creation scheme for academics, but a recognition that *'the more you know, the more you realise you don't know.'*

How do I select the best idea to develop into a research proposal?

Once you have developed a list of potential research topics that might be developed into a research project, the next step is to decide which idea to actually go forward with. For an individual project, this may be the idea that interests you the most, but if you are not sure which one you should pick, or if you are working in a project team, you might need a simple means to decide.

At this stage, you do not have to be highly detailed on the research topic; we are setting you on a path rather than committing you definitely and irrevocably to a specific research project (Blaikie 2009). We suggest that you spend a few minutes now to make sure that you could transform any of your ideas into a good research topic. Before you select a research topic to develop further into your research proposal, make sure that it is not a 'dead end' in practical or theoretical terms. An idea is only worth exploring if you can develop it into a contribution to academic and practical knowledge; just being interesting does not mean that it is worth studying. This means showing your contribution to solving (in a small way) either a practical problem or theoretical problem or both. If you can restate your research topic as a problem at this stage, you are ahead of the game.

In **Section 2.2.1**, we describe some of the characteristics of a 'good' research topic, whilst in **Section 2.2.2** we describe how to actually narrow down the contenders into one or two ideas that you can take forward. We suggest that you ask the following questions about each of your ideas:

1. Does it meet the project requirements?
2. Is the scope of my research project manageable?
3. Can I do it with the time and resources available to me?
4. Will my project be successful no matter what I find out?
5. Will my findings and recommendations satisfy all of my project's stakeholders?
6. Will I be able to get good marks on the project?

You should also consider whether your project is worth studying in the larger sense – will it make a contribution to the world, or is it an 'academic exercise'?

7. Will my project contribute to business and management knowledge?
8. Is it relevant to at least one practical problem faced by business and management?
9. Is it relevant to at least one theoretical problem faced by business and management researchers?
10. Can I identify a research setting and research sample in which I could gather data, and can I get access to it?
11. Am I interested in doing it?

We suggest that you score each of your ideas using the following system: 0 = No, 1 = Yes, 2 = Outstanding. You should drop any projects that score one or more 0s from further consideration. We will explain in **Section 2.2.2** how to choose the best idea out of those that are feasible. Use your project requirements to think about what your project needs to do and the criteria it needs to meet.

If you forget to apply the second and third criteria above to potential research topics, this can create significant difficulties later in your research process.

2.2.1 Will this research project satisfy my stakeholders?

A key concept for your study is to identify just who the stakeholders for your project are and what they want from it. **Figure 2.2** shows some of the stakeholders.

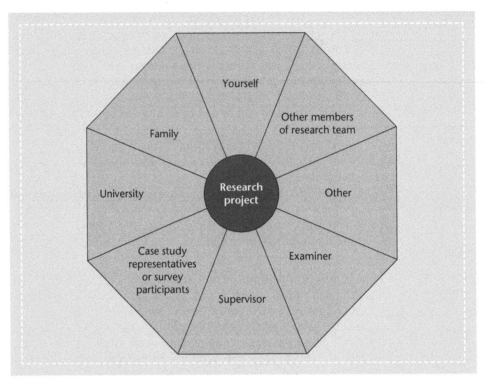

Figure 2.2 **Some stakeholders in your research project**

The most basic requirement is to make sure that your report enables you to pass the course you are taking. The next question then is what we term *a qualifier* – without being able to answer 'yes', no matter how much effort it takes or how clever it is, it won't do you any good.

Does my project satisfy the project guidelines?

At a minimum, your project must satisfy your project requirements as set by your project supervisor and your examiners. This is so important we will discuss it below in **Section 2.2.2** and again in **Chapter 14**. Your project requirements may list specific skills and knowledge you need to demonstrate in your project, such as:

1. Demonstrating your knowledge of the work covered during the course.
2. Identifying and constructively critiquing the work already carried out in the area.
3. Relating theory/best practice to actual practice in organisations.
4. Designing appropriate research questions and selecting appropriate methods to carry them out.
5. Analysing and reporting your findings.
6. Drawing conclusions from the work.

To see how to meet these criteria, you may find it helpful to look at some project reports submitted by former students, as we suggested in **Section 2.1.2**, to see how much work you will need to do and what standard of work you need to achieve. You might also want to talk to your supervisor and/or sponsor to see what effort they expect. For a dissertation, you may well be expected to put in as much effort as you would for a full-time job. This would obviously affect your ability to take paid work during this period. For other projects, you might be expected to put in the equivalent of one day per week during the project period.

A sponsored or placement project must also satisfy your manager and the organisation's expectations as agreed in the project brief or sponsorship agreement. Balancing the needs and expectations of your academic and project sponsor can be tricky, as we discuss in **Section 9.2**, because they can often come into conflict.

Is the scope of my research project manageable?

Many students aim to 'change the world', or at least significantly 'fix it'. Whilst we applaud this sentiment, you will rarely be able to achieve this – nor is it really appropriate – in a student project. A good research problem has a well-defined and realistic purpose, and an identifiable beginning, end and boundaries. It doesn't try to change the world. Your idea must be focused enough for you to do a thorough job, but not so small that it is trivial. Realistic goals might be to understand a particular area better or to apply something you have learnt in your course to solve a particular problem. Finding out something revolutionary is a bonus, not an objective.

Can I do it with the time and resources available to me?

A research project is not worth considering unless you can investigate it in the time and with the other resources and skills that you have available. Although this sounds obvious, students often propose ideas for research projects that require more time than they have to spend, access to resources beyond their means, or skills they do not possess.

Nearly all student projects have to be completed in a set time. As a rough guide, you should rule out any project that will take more than 80% of the time you have available to work on it.

What other resources besides time you will need to investigate this topic? If you plan to investigate the marketing strategies of blue-chip companies by interviewing the CEOs or Marketing Directors of Fortune 500 or FTSE 50 companies, unless you already have personal contacts in those firms who already have agreed to take part in such a study, it is unlikely that you will be able to contact even one manager based on 'cold calling' (see **Chapter 9**). As you will have to rely on publicly available information, which rarely gives any particular insight into the actual strategies being pursued or why and results in unsatisfactory projects, you should reconsider.

Will my project be successful no matter what I find out?

Your proposed research should have **symmetrical outcomes**; that is, no matter what you find out, your findings are both interesting and relevant, and your recommendations are valid and relevant. Even if you will not be formally assessed on your research project's outcomes, you will have put in a lot of time and effort, so you should make sure that whatever the outcome of your early work you will still have a project to work on and your findings will not be irrelevant or trivial. This is especially important if your research is done in sequential stages: one part of your project depends on what you find out in an earlier part. If you are investigating a 'yes or no' question, and the answer is only interesting if you find one of these, not having symmetrical outcomes will be fatal to your research. This is often true of exploratory or qualitative projects. The importance of symmetry is illustrated in **Student research in action 2.4**.

Student research in action 2.4

MAKING SURE THAT YOUR RESEARCH WILL HAVE AN OUTCOME

Bruce was asked to investigate a major supermarket's supply chain for fresh fruit. The project brief stated that he should investigate the supply chain and identify where in Northern France suppliers were consolidating their products. The question was put as: how might the supermarket influence the supply chain by providing additional facilities, warehousing, and so on?

In the first phase of his study, Bruce found that suppliers mainly consolidated and stored fruit in the UK. This meant that the second part of Bruce's project, which had originally been intended to be the main part of the investigation, was now irrelevant because the supermarket already had enough warehouse facilities in the UK. Thus, he could only complete half of the project, which left him without enough material to flesh out a full research project. If Bruce had only known about the concept of symmetric outcomes, he could have framed his research questions so that the second half of his project would be worth doing no matter what he found out.

If you find that your proposed research will not have symmetrical outcomes, think about how you might reframe your research questions to achieve this. The research question 'Why do lower income households tend to die younger?' assumes that – 'People from lower income households (however you define this) die younger.' If you can show that people from lower income households do die younger, for example using national statistical records, you can investigate the question, 'Why might this be true?', but if you find out instead that people from lower income households don't actually die younger, the answer to your question is, 'Well, they don't', and your project would not be wildly successful. It might be better to restate your question as 'How does household income affect health and mortality rates?'

Will my findings and recommendations satisfy all of my project's stakeholders?

Students often find that academic and business sponsors have different ideas about what they should do in their project. If you have different project stakeholders who each have conflicting needs and expectations, you may find it difficult to satisfy all of them. You need to think about these competing project stakeholders from the start and make sure that you build in the necessary work to meet the needs of each into your project plan. We cover more of the issues of managing in-company research projects in **Chapter 9**.

Your examiners will probably focus on how your research can help them to understand a theoretical problem – aspects of your topic that they want to know more about. Your academic institution requires an academically sound piece of work that demonstrates knowledge of the subject area and an ability to design and carry out research, and present, analyse and draw conclusions from the results.

On the other hand, your business sponsor or collaborator will probably focus on how your research can help them to understand a practical problem – aspects of business and management practice that they need help with. They will worry less about how this was arrived at than whether your recommendations can be implemented and whether they will help to solve that particular problem. Sometimes, and this can be very difficult for students to resolve, you may be expected to produce recommendations that support what the manager has already decided, not what the best solution is for the organisation, as illustrated by **Student research in action 2.5**.

Student research in action 2.5

SORRY, THAT'S NOT THE ANSWER WE WANTED

A team of students spent a year studying the excellent community outreach work being done by a faith-based organisation. One of the major findings was that very few of the underprivileged young people being helped by the organisation were actually aware of its strong religious beliefs, and those who did know did not want to be associated with that particular religion. Although this was an interesting finding, with significant implications for their sponsor, the students were told in no uncertain terms that they should not mention this finding in their project report. This meant that they could not use their most interesting finding in the report for the organisation, because this was not acceptable to one of their stakeholders. They were able to highlight it in their academic report.

You may even need to write a different report for each important stakeholder. Few managers will wade through a 20,000-word report to reach your recommendations in your last chapter, even if your report is beautifully bound and laid out! One managing director commented to Harvey, 'If the blurb on the front doesn't grab me, I don't bother reading it.'

You may need to go through several rounds of identifying a practical problem and attempting to link it to an area of business and management knowledge, or identifying a theoretical problem and seeing if you can possibly link it to a research setting. No matter whether you start with a practical or a theoretical problem, you must bring both of them together when you define your research problem. So, if you start with a practical problem, you can use theoretical knowledge from your business and management studies to solve that practical problem. If you start with a theoretical problem, you can add to our understanding of that problem by investigating a practical situation. You can see this in **Figure 2.3**.

Will I be able to get good marks on the project?

In keeping with our mantra of 'beginning with the end in mind', we strongly suggest that you should stop now and consider whether your project ideas are not only interesting and worthwhile, but also that you will get maximum return on your effort when it comes to the marking process. In order to do this, you should think about the people and processes by which the final examination of your project will take place. If you want to do well, it is worth spending some time understanding how your research project will be assessed even before you choose your research topic, as we suggested in **Chapter 1**, so that you can target your work accordingly.

Three key questions you should consider at this point are:

- *Who* will be marking your project?
- *What* are the marking criteria they will use?
- *How* will they assess your project?

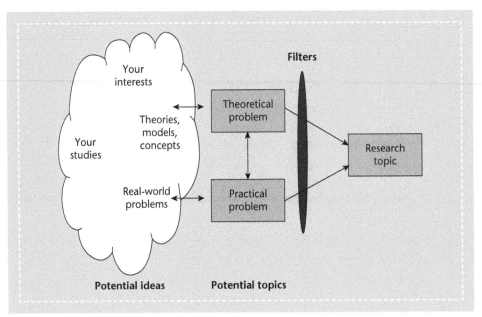

Figure 2.3 Research definition

Students often assume, based on experience with the marks they receive versus the marks that they think they ought to have received, that marking is entirely arbitrary. They imagine that examiners use the *stairs method* for marking, in which the examiner drops the pile of reports from the top of a flight of stairs. Any paper that lands on the top step receives 40%, the next step 50%, and so on, down to the paper that travels the farthest receiving the highest mark. Although this would certainly save lots of time, in reality marking is a strictly regulated process. *Project marking*, as we shall see below, is more of a craft than an exact science, but we can draw some lessons from our professional experience that may help you to put the finishing touches to your current work.

Who will be marking your project?   Students (and even professional researchers) sometimes get so wrapped up in their research that they forget that they are doing it for someone else, not themselves, the rest of the group, or other students. Research is only complete when you have presented it to your project stakeholders. The first stakeholder is whoever will be marking your research project. Use your project guidelines to identify everyone who has input into your project mark.

Your programme specifications and/or project guidelines should spell out in detail the number of examiners who will mark your project report and the categories from which they will be drawn. These may include:

● Your project supervisor
● Internal examiners, other academics from your programme who are not supervising you
● An external examiner, an academic who is not a member of your university
● Your business sponsor
● Other group members

Internal examiners are academics from your university who will mark your research project, usually people who teach on your degree programme but not always. Typical academic marking practices in the British higher education include *double marking*, where two examiners mark independently of each other, and then agree the final mark, and *moderation*, where one marks the project, and the second examiner checks to make sure the first examiner's mark is correct. Whilst internal examiners may include your project supervisor, this is becoming less common because the gold standard for marking is *double-blind* marking of *anonymised work*, where the student does not know the identity of the people marking the report, and the people marking the report do not know the identity of the student. This is obviously difficult if the project supervisor is doing the marking, or if a mark is being given for an oral presentation! Double-blind marking minimises positive or negative bias.

Your project supervisor will be able to give you advice on these aspects of the marking process at your institution. Even if your supervisor will not be marking your report, your supervisor will certainly be reading it through the eyes of a prospective examiner (see **Student research in action 2.6**). If your project supervisor will be one of your internal examiners, pay special attention to any *cues* that he or she gives you about likes and dislikes. How does your supervisor feel about reports written in the first person? Little winds up a supervisor more than seeing that a student has wasted his or her time by asking for advice or feedback and has then ignored it. Kate prefers that students avoid the use of footnotes or endnotes, because they detract from the flow of the paper, so seeing them in a project report really, really annoys her, not least because the student has clearly not listened to her explicit instructions. Furthermore, even if your project supervisor is not marking your project, he or she may be asked to provide some guidance to the examiners on your performance in the research project.

 Student research in action 2.6

FOLLOW THE INSTRUCTIONS AND PAY ATTENTION TO FEEDBACK

Mansoor failed his first submission of his research project because he completely ignored most of the detailed project guidelines that he had been given, including leaving out several required sections entirely. One of the examiners gave him extensive feedback on why he failed and what he should do to pass on his second (and final) submission. This feedback emphasised the importance of following the guidelines and including all of the required elements, not just some of them. When Mansoor submitted his revised project, he had completely ignored this advice. Needless to say, the project was failed – again.

In many countries, an *external examiner*, an academic from another university who is appointed to monitor and benchmark your programme impartially, also plays an important role. The external examiner's main job is to audit the examination process and the overall distribution of marks, but in some universities he or she may also check the marks on every paper, or on a sample such as representative papers, first-class or distinctions and fails, and borderline papers.

If you know who will be marking your work, you may want to take this into consideration as you prepare your project report for submission (but see *caveats* below) and please note that approaching any other examiner, for example emailing your external examiner, will be considered unethical. We are not suggesting that you 'pander' to them, but they are human and the marking process is somewhat subjective. You may want to make sure you consider how your research links to their interests and expertise.

If your examiner is an expert in a particular topic or method, this will probably be what they focus on most critically in your report. If your examiner:

- Specialises in the academic topic or research context that you have researched, make sure that everything that is related to that area is as complete and perfect as you can make it. For example, if she specialises in corporate finance you should double-check any financial data you present.
- Has done relevant research in this area, make sure to read it and to mention it in your literature review, even if critically. This said, don't mention irrelevant research by 'Professor X' just to 'soft-soap' him or her. A successful examiner will have seen his or her name in print many times before.
- Has written a book on your particular research method, you should make sure that you have described and executed it perfectly. If your examiner has written 'the book' or 'the article' on case study research, for example, and you have used a case study approach, make sure that you have taken their advice on board.

Beware of over-targeting your work to a particular examiner, though. Most institutions have a dual-marking system where more than one person assesses each major piece of work. Furthermore, there may be a last-minute change or substitution, and someone else entirely might end up marking your work.

In some sponsored or placement projects, your *project sponsor* may provide feedback that describes the value of your research to the company, and also whether you behaved ethically, to the examiners, who will usually take this feedback seriously. It is worth checking what level of input they have.

Although it is unusual, your *project group* may be asked to rate the performance by each group member during the research process. This may be used to adjust the group grade for each individual member, or it may be used to select particular group members for oral examinations, or vivas.

What are the marking criteria?   Examiners are typically given a detailed list of *guidelines* including *assessment criteria* that they must following in marking research projects. A sample marking scheme is shown in **Table 2.1**. Marking criteria minimise guesswork and judgement calls because they guide examiners in determining what mark an individual project report should be given. This ensures that the whole marking process is traceable and reproducible. This is good, because examiners cannot impose additional requirements on your project that have not been stated earlier, but also bad, because they must assess you on those guidelines, even if what you have done something that is excellent but outside the guidelines. There is rarely much leeway for examiners to interpret – or reinterpret – how you will be assessed.

2.2.2 Will my project contribute to business and management knowledge?

You should select a research topic that you can link to at least one area of business and management research (or research in supporting disciplines such as economics or

Table 2.1   Marking criteria

	Distinction level:	Addresses all aspects of the assessment criteria. Presents a well-structured and coherent research design for investigating a significant problem. Draws on the breadth and depth of the relevant literature. Takes a critical perspective on debates and unknowns. Writes fluently and correctly.
80–100	Superb work	Meets all of the criteria above for a 'distinction'.
75–79	Excellent work	Meets most of the criteria above.
70–74	Fine work	Meets some of the criteria above.
	Pass level:	Addresses all aspects of the assessment criteria. Presents a reasonable research design for investigating a research problem. Draws on the relevant literature. Identifies the key debates and unknowns. Writes to a reasonable standard with a minimum of errors.
65–69	Strong pass	Meets all of the criteria above for a 'pass'.
55–64	Good pass	Meets most of the criteria above.
50–54	Pass	Meets some of the criteria above.
	Fail:	Fails to fulfil the assignment criteria. Draws on an insufficient range of the relevant literature, misses relevant research, or draws on the wrong literature. Does not apply a critical perspective. Writes poorly or incorrectly.
45–49	Marginal fail	Meets at least some criteria for a pass but fails on a significant number of criteria.
0–44	Outright fail	Meets few criteria for a pass and destroys knowledge as we know it.

psychology) so that you can develop the theoretical underpinnings of your research. As we will see in **Chapter 3**, you will need to use previous studies when you define your research problem and questions, and when you select your research methods. You will need to develop a literature review (**Chapter 3**) and discuss key findings (**Chapter 13**).

This can be a problem if you are looking at leading-edge technologies or other new areas. For example, when the web was first becoming popular in the 1990s, students researching e-commerce found it difficult to find enough articles to do a good literature review, because the area was so new.

What you find out in your research should contribute to our knowledge of a practical or theoretical problem, that is, it has *at least one original aspect*. You *do not* have to provide a new grand theory or make a substantial addition to our existing knowledge, but you should enable us to understand one small aspect of what you have covered a little better than when you started, unlike the example in **Student research in action 2.7**.

Student research in action 2.7
TALENTED!

His interest in talent management meant that Dirk was drawn to look at the impact of particular personality types on the career paths of managers. Specifically, he was interested in a group of project managers and which of the personality types had had the most successful careers. So far so good. There was a good literature on personality profiling and much research to base his work on. The gap he identified was that previously nobody appeared to have done this in the project environment. The problem was not the topic or the gap, but what he wanted to do with it. He reasoned that a particular personality type would be the most successful and wanted to prove it. This was where the problems started. His plan – ask a group of project managers their profile and then what level they were at in their organisations. His group of A-team profiles would, he reasoned, have risen higher than the rest. What could possibly go wrong with that?

Is my topic relevant to managers?

In business and management research, your findings and/or recommendations should be relevant to managers (or other stakeholders). This usually requires that your research outcomes are beyond the particular company or sample that you have studied; that is, someone else could take your findings and apply them to other companies or people, or use your project as a starting point for further research or application. Results that are only relevant to an underpinning discipline such as mathematics may be of little interest to managers.

Balancing theoretical and practical problems

All business and management research has both a practical and a theoretical side, but the balance between the two may vary. Business and management research is more than information gathering (journalism) or applied problem solving (consulting) as we argued in **Chapter 1**: research adds to our knowledge about business and management.

So should you start with a theoretical problem or a practical problem? If you start with a theoretical problem, you will usually emphasise your contribution to knowledge, the findings about the particular theory, model or concept that you have investigated in your particular research setting. Your findings should contribute to knowledge about that theory or model. This does not always mean that you have to come up with a new theory or a new model. Your project might simply add to our understanding of which theories and models do or do not apply in this type of organisation (or other context) and find out something new that can be used to improve the model or theory, or even, in some cases, discredit it.

If you start with a practical problem, you will usually emphasise your contribution to organisations. This will often determine the **research setting** where you will do your research: the organisation you are sponsored by, are working in or are interested in. You might study a part of the organisation, the entire organisation, its supply network or its industry. On the other hand, you may want to study another research setting to find out information that will be useful to your focal organisation. For instance, when looking at the level of evidence used in managerial decision making, researchers have compared the setting with that faced by medical practitioners. You do hope that your doctor makes their decisions based on evidence, don't you? (See Rousseau 2012, and Söderlund and Maylor 2013 for further discussion.)

Research on charities may involve investigating for-profit firms. The challenge with working across contexts is to be able to identify the similarities and differences, and for instance determine how transferable this makes any practices.

You may need to start with a practical problem if you are working with an organisation; they will expect you to deliver some useful output, usually in the form of an analysis, recommendations and an implementation plan. Research that starts with a practical problem often focuses on developing recommendations for solving the particular practical problem in that particular context. If you are working on a sponsored project, you need to keep in mind that the organisation's main focus is on resolving the practical problem it faces.

Remember the discussion in **Chapter 1**, though, so that you can keep your project from being strictly a consulting project (unless that is your remit): you will need to link your research back to larger issues of business and management knowledge. You need to be clear on how your project will contribute to business and management knowledge if your research project is being assessed against that.

Increasingly, research funders such as the government – through research councils and research assessment exercises to decide how much funding universities receive – emphasise the need for research, including business and management research, to solve practical problems as well as or instead of theoretical problems. A focus on theoretical problems has been termed **mode I research**, whilst a focus on practical problems has been called **mode II research**. We have already discussed the differences between research that is to increase knowledge without any immediate application or that is immediately relevant to solving industry's problems as the differences between basic research, development and commercial research in **Chapter 1**.

There are a few words of wisdom that we can offer at this stage about theoretical problems and practical problems. Many research projects fail when a student falls in love with a computer model or other abstract solution and tries to force fit it to a business or management problem, or propose it as the solution to a problem that doesn't actually exist. This happens because the student has not identified a real-world or academic problem for which the research project is a solution. If you just want to gather information, you might ask yourself whether it is really research. A theoretical problem needs to have some link to a practical problem.

Moreover, not every interesting or even worthwhile real-world problem is relevant to academic knowledge. Many research projects fail when the solution is already well known, and there is nothing new about applying it, but the student hasn't done enough reading to see that this has been discussed already. Remember the hammer analogy, or to put it less kindly, *a fool with a tool is still a fool*. Addressing some aspect of a theoretical problem is critically important if your guidelines require you to apply or test academic theory or models.

A structure for integrating theoretical and practical aspects

We have found that a good starting point for refining ideas for your research project is Toulmin's *structure of argument*. This was developed by the philosopher Stephen Toulmin in his book *The Uses of Argument* (1958), and later simplified by Booth et al. (2008) into the model we present here. The main elements are shown in **Figure 2.4**.

The central elements of Toulmin's model are the knowledge claim and evidence. A **knowledge claim** is a testable statement that you believe is true, that can be generated and investigated through doing research, and that you will try to persuade other

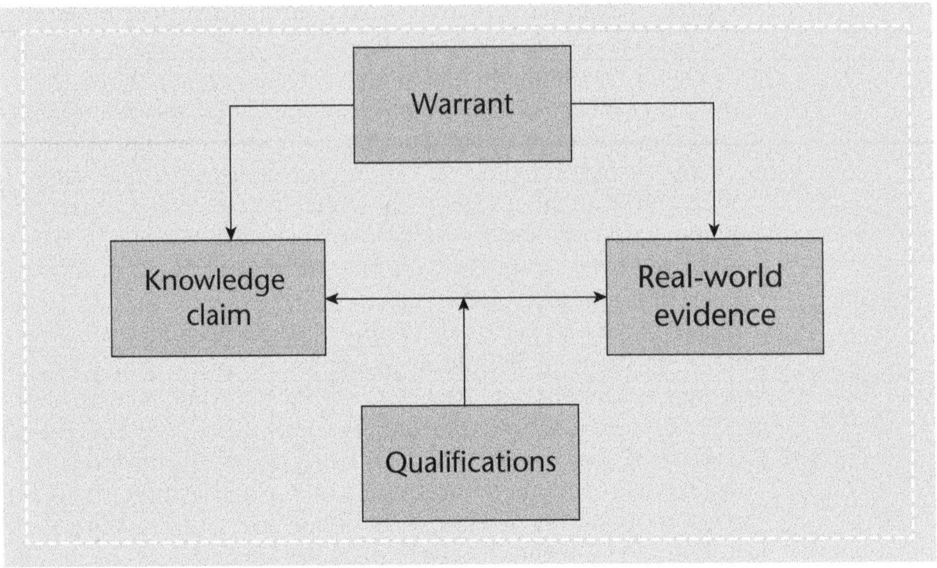

Figure 2.4 **Toulmin's structure of argument**

people is true. A knowledge claim can assert that a relationship exists: 'Adopting agile production techniques will improve manufacturing performance' or that a relationship does not exist: 'Increasing CEO pay will not improve a business's financial performance.' We make knowledge claims about the world, whether we are deciding to accept what someone else wants us to believe, or trying to convince someone else of something we want them to believe.

Simply asserting that their performance is – or should be – better is not research but speculation. Evidence for the knowledge claims above might include identifying companies who have adopted agile production techniques and comparing their manufacturing performance before and after their adoption, or comparing their performance with comparable organisations who haven't adopted the techniques. Research uses data rather than speculation or anecdotes to build or test our knowledge claims, so we need to use **evidence** to generate a knowledge claim or to test it. Without evidence, a knowledge claim is merely personal opinion or speculation.

There are two main strategies for linking knowledge claims and evidence:

● Develop your knowledge claims before gathering and analysing data (*a priori*) to test those knowledge claims, or
● Develop your knowledge claims from evidence after gathering and analysing your data (*post hoc*).

So far, this is pretty general – every time you write an essay or get in an argument in the pub about whether a team or individual can win a particular event, you are working with knowledge claims and evidence. However, for the purposes of carrying out research, Booth and his colleagues (2008) argued that two more important elements of Toulmin's structure of argumentation must be included.

The first of these, the **warrant**, links the knowledge claim and the evidence. Is the evidence actually relevant to the argument, and vice versa? The weaker this link, the

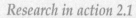

less believable your research is. This is why behavioural experiments carried out in laboratory conditions or computer simulations often fail in the real world: they apply to one context, but not necessarily the other. **Research in action 2.1** illustrates the importance of the warrant in research.

Research in action 2.1

THE STRENGTH OF A WARRANT

An article in the UK newspaper *The Guardian* reported on research linking bottle-feeding infants and their health in later life. Because babies who were bottle-fed had to do less work for their milk, it was said, they were likely to overeat, become obese, and develop heart disease in later life. The research was based on two studies where newborns were given either standard baby formula or enriched baby formula. The lead scientist concluded that 'it supports the case in the general population for breastfeeding – as it is harder to overfeed a breastfed baby'.

Source: www.theguardian.com/lifeandstyle/2010/sep/30/bottle-feeding-babies-adult-obesity

---

Do you think that the lead scientist was justified in making a knowledge claim for breastfeeding based on his evidence? Try to state the warrant in your own words. If he had also drawn on a study that included breastfed babies, would this have made his claim about the link between breastfeeding and obesity stronger?

The second of these is **qualifications**, which explain the circumstances under which the link between our knowledge claim and evidence is true. If our evidence applies to large multinational corporations, will it also be true for small owner-managed ones? If it is true today, will it be true tomorrow? Researchers often want to make much grander claims for their research than their knowledge claim and evidence actually can support.

We suggest that you take a reading linked to your strongest idea and use Toulmin's model to identify at least one knowledge claim, the evidence linked to it, the warrant, and the qualifications. You can then think about how you might use your own research project to build on that research, for example:

- Strategy 1: Test the knowledge claim with different evidence
- Strategy 2: Use the evidence to develop a different knowledge claim
- Strategy 3: Test the warrant, the relationship between knowledge claim and evidence
- Strategy 4: Test the qualifications, the limits to applying knowledge claim and evidence

You may find two main types of readings particularly useful in identifying prospective research:

- General overviews of your topic, for example textbooks or review articles
- Model studies – the type of study you would like to carry out, which yours can add to, provide points of discussion or generally be based around in some way, as shown in **Student research in action 2.8**.

Student research in action 2.8

BUILDING A RESEARCH PROJECT AROUND A KEY READING

Barclay and Benson (1990) reported that fewer than 8% of the managers they studied were aware of any recent published studies on the areas in which they were working. Doug decided to investigate their claim that the management literature did not actually affect managers' behaviour by investigating whether his study would find similar low levels of awareness, and then try to find reasons for the low level of awareness. This research would both replicate Barclay and Benson's findings and try to extend them.

2.2.3 Evaluating potential research topics

You can use the characteristics of a good research topic that we list below as the baseline for identifying suitable topics and ideas. You should discard any project ideas that will not meet your project requirements, but there are other characteristics of a good research topic that you should use to filter research topics as they emerge and revise others. They will also help you decide among different projects you might pursue.

Which idea should I pursue?

So, how do you identify the best project? We suggest that you follow the process described in **Student research in action 2.9**. You can construct a similar table by listing your ideas and rating them against the assessment criteria and any other criteria you decide are important. You can make the ranking process more complex by using numerical ratings and/or weighting the factors by their importance. Whether you use a simple or more complex table to rank potential projects, this structured approach

Student research in action 2.9

DECISION MAKING: I PREDICT A RIOT

As part of a course at the University of Bath, a group of students must run an event or carry out a particular task to demonstrate their ability to plan, execute and review a group project. They are assessed on the originality of their idea, the quality of the planning process and the content of the report reflecting their experiences during the project.

One group had a meeting and came up with a number of ideas. The group wanted to choose the best project out of the following:

- Producing a yearbook for their class group
- Developing a short video to promote the course they are studying
- Organising a formal ball for the entire department
- Organising a treasure hunt one Sunday
- Organising an 'accident awareness' day for schoolchildren.

The group's next activity was to decide what criteria to judge the proposal against. They first identified three criteria based on how the project would be assessed:

- whether the idea was original
- whether the idea would demonstrate project management skills
- whether it would enable them to produce a good report.

The group then added four more characteristics of their own that they wanted their project to have. These were:

- it should sufficiently stretch the group
- it should not depend too heavily on other people for its success
- it must not require them to undertake any large financial risk
- it must be fun for the group to do.

They then put the projects into a table, and agreed a set of ratings, as shown in **Table 2.2.**

Table 2.2   **The group's rating table**

	Originality	Demonstrates skills	Produces a good report	Stretching	Independent of others	Avoids financial risk	Fun
Yearbook	✗	✓	✓	–	–	✗	✗
Video	✓	✓	✓	✓	✓	✗	✓
Ball	–	✓	✓	✓	✗	✗✗✗	✓
Treasure hunt	✗	–	✗	–	–	✓	–
Accident awareness day	✓	✓	–	✗	✗	✓	–

allows you or your project team to make a reasonable choice based on your own criteria, and can greatly assist the group in uniting behind a particular decision.

Given these ratings, there was one clear choice – the video – as it had the most ticks. They also saw that they needed to manage the project's financial risk (cost of hiring editing facilities and production of the finished product) carefully.

Even if one idea is clearly ranked higher than others when you have gone through the ranking process, we recommend that you identify a second project as a backup in case the first one doesn't work out. Having an alternative or 'safety' project available is especially important when your first project is risky, for example if you need to arrange access to an organisation or data set, as such access often falls through.

2.3 How do I develop my idea into a research proposal?

Once you have identified your research problem and research questions, you need to communicate what you want to do to both yourself and other people. You might try writing down what you want to do as:

- A 'working title' – doesn't have to be snappy, just a few words that say what it is you are doing.
- A 'sound bite' or 'elevator pitch' – imagine a friend asking you what you are doing for your project. You have precisely 15 seconds to tell them, before their eyes glaze over and they rush off. What will you tell them about your work?

- An **abstract** – 100–150 words that summarise what you are thinking of doing.
- A visual representation – some people find it most helpful at this stage to draw a mind map, or represent their project with a picture, photograph, collage or drawing.
- A research proposal – a formal document that describes what you plan to do in your project.

2.3.1 How do I refine my research topic?

Once you are down to a single research topic that you have identified or been assigned, what next? For most students, this is narrowing down the research topic to a manageable *scope*. It is not unusual for us to see topics so broad it would take a thousand students working for a thousand years to finish the project, so scoping the project is a crucial step.

Use research questions

Your research topic describes the general area you will investigate. Your **research questions** focus on specific areas of your research topic you will investigate. For example, you might develop a research topic of 'service quality' from service management, or 'dual-career ladders' from 'research and development'. These topics could then generate research questions. The research questions define the project, because they identify the scope of the work and guide what you do in the project. Further, they will determine the existing research that you use to support your project, the data you collect and how you report your research.

Zina O'Leary (2013) suggests that your research questions should:

- Define your research topic – the business or management phenomenon that you will focus on
- Define the nature of your research – whether your main goal is to describe, explore or explain this phenomenon
- Define the issues you will explore – what aspects of the phenomenon you will find out about
- Provide the basis for investigating relationships between the concepts you are exploring – develop any propositions or hypotheses.

Any good research problem should lead to research questions that are interesting to both managers and academic researchers. **Student research in action 2.10** describes how one student developed some potential research questions from an area of personal interest.

⊕ *Student research in action 2.10*
DEVELOPING RESEARCH QUESTIONS AROUND A RESEARCH TOPIC

Alex needed to come up with an idea for her summer (MSc) research project. She was a passionate fan of the Arsenal football team, which she had followed since she was a child. Putting together the idea of doing research on one or more football teams with the topics she had studied in service management, Alex came up with some potential research questions, including:

▶

- Were football stadiums trying to become friendlier to female fans?
- Were football clubs focusing more on retailing merchandise or entertaining fans?
- What physical aspects of football stadiums encouraged or discouraged female fans from attending?

Alex also made sure that there was enough support in the academic literature to support her project at a level appropriate for an MSc. She identified previous studies of female sports fans by Coddington (1997) and Crawford and Gosling (2004) that she could use for her academic framework.

Most students find that they need to cycle between their research topic, research problem, and research questions several times to end up with a suitably focused research topic and a feasible set of research questions. Students doing a PhD may spend a year clarifying their research questions, even if they have started with a well-defined research topic, but most undergraduate or master's students don't have the luxury of spending so much time! As you develop your research questions, keep the following points in mind.

Avoid asking questions that have already been answered

Avoid asking research questions that have already been answered, as although what is termed replication has its place you run the risk of doing trivial research. On the other hand, if we only think we know an answer, because it is 'common sense', the question might well be worth asking. **Research in action 2.2** demonstrates where a researcher believed that the 'everyone knows' answers to a particular question were inadequate, and went on to make a major contribution to business and management research as a result.

 Research in action 2.2
QUESTIONING 'WHAT EVERYONE KNOWS'

At the time Henry Mintzberg started his doctoral thesis, researchers and managers accepted descriptions of what managers do, such as Henri Fayol's 'plan, organise, control and coordinate' as being representative of how managers made decisions. For his doctoral research, Henry Mintzberg watched five managers for a week each, and recorded what each one did during that week. He analysed their incoming and outgoing post, and listened to their conversations. Mintzberg concluded that Fayol's and other formal models of managerial decision making did not describe adequately what managers actually did. After analysing his data, he identified 10 different managerial roles (Mintzberg 1971). As well as being a significant triumph of 'fact over folklore', Mintzberg's research led to significant new research in managerial decision making.

Avoid biased or self-answering questions

Avoid research questions where you have already determined by how you frame the question what the answer will be before you start your research. Even if you expect to find a certain answer, based on your experience, the theory or model you are using or what your academic supervisor or project sponsor expects, you should frame your research questions so that you remain open to contradictory evidence or unexpected findings. Also remember the concept of symmetrical outcomes above! If you don't, you may miss out on the opportunity to discuss what you have found. In **Student research in action 2.11**, the student was open to findings that were not expected and as a result produced a most interesting piece of work.

 Student research in action 2.11

LEAVE ROOM FOR UNEXPECTED FINDINGS

Anjali was studying how small and medium-sized companies recruited and selected their employees. She expected to find that they used selected structured methods, as these were widely discussed by both academics and practitioners. However, in the firms who had agreed to give her access to their recruitment methods, it became clear that they selected employees based on interviews only, and that supposedly 'objective' methods (for example personality profiling) were not used. This presented great opportunities for discussion, and then gave rise to further questions, including 'Why didn't these firms use structured techniques for recruitment?'

Unexpected findings have led to some of the biggest breakthroughs in business and management research. In the Hawthorne experiments (**Chapter 1**), researchers failed to find any link between lighting and worker output, but this led them to question what factors actually influenced output in the relay assembly group. Was it the style of supervision? Was it the chance to make more money? Was it the attention from the supervisor? Elton Mayo's explanation that strong social ties created higher performance, even if his interpretation of the data has been challenged by later researchers (see Gillespie 1993), was significantly more interesting for management research than the original question about electric lighting, since it opened up many possibilities for research into the human and social side of managing employees.

Avoid unanswerable questions

Beware of research questions that you cannot answer by gathering and analysing data. Some research questions are simply unanswerable, for example metaphysical questions about good and evil, or right or wrong. This is not the same as the study of business ethics or topics such as corporate social responsibility, though!

The work that you do now exploring the area is vital, and will initially expand the possibilities for your studies. You may find this easier to do if you use a mind map, a hierarchy of concepts or a Venn diagram, which we describe below.

If you can't find at least one business and management area that your topic fits into, then you will find it difficult to develop and support the theoretical side of your research. Although this sounds obvious, we have seen students take such a narrow view of a research topic that they conclude that no one else has ever identified it, as shown in **Student research in action 2.12**.

 Student research in action 2.12

MAKE SURE THE 'GAP' IN KNOWLEDGE IS REALLY A GAP

Roy walked into his potential supervisor's office and claimed that the issue of staff pay and rewards in lean manufacturing systems had not been properly studied, but 'the rest of the management world had been too dull to notice'. When the potential supervisor asked him to support this claim,

▶

Roy said that he could find little of any relevance on this topic in the operations management literature, and his research project would therefore break new ground.

Roy's proposed research topic was clearly important, relevant and of interest to business. It was also probably true that there was little research in operations management on pay and rewards. So what might be wrong with this picture?

Management has been formally studied for over 100 years, and the chances that everyone had ignored such a major research problem are small – not zero, but small, as most topics have been covered in some way, in some form. Relatively little is completely new in management. Roy's potential project supervisor, therefore, found it hard to believe that no research had been done on the topic and, in fact, he knew that a major study of pay and rewards in lean manufacturing had been published by Delbridge and Lowe (1997) and subsequent studies.

Roy had ignored the fact that pay and reward is a major concern of human resource management (HRM). Not surprisingly, a brief review of the HRM literature revealed that his proposed topic had been extensively studied. Even so, there was scope for him to investigate this topic by building on the existing research on pay and rewards in HRM and lean manufacturing in operations management (OM). If Roy had identified the two different concepts he wanted to study as 'pay and reward' and 'lean production' and realised that they belonged to two different areas, he would have realised that he should be looking at his topic not only as 'how pay and reward affect lean production' but also 'lean production affects pay and reward', which would have led him to both the HRM and the OM literature.

Then, rather than trying to invent a new area of study, with the risk that his project findings would merely replicate previous research such as Delbridge and Lowe's study, he could have used this research to focus or frame his study more clearly. For instance, he could have tested the findings of Delbridge and Lowe's study in his own sample of manufacturing firms that had adopted lean production. This would have added to both the HRM and OM literature, since his findings could be used to validate Delbridge and Lowe. Furthermore, he could potentially have used Delbridge and Lowe's research methods to help to design his own research study, which would have saved a lot of time and effort.

As this example suggests, someone, somewhere has covered almost any business and management topic you could think of. (Kate has actually experienced students claiming in her research methods class that 'no research has been done' on a topic that she has researched.) Don't try to reinvent the wheel unnecessarily. Most research projects that are worth doing build on one or more existing areas of knowledge, and in **Chapter 3** we will discuss some ways you can identify those areas. This also presents a challenge if you can draw on more than one area: you will need not only to select your topic carefully, but also to consider what subject or perspective you will approach that topic from. This will make a big difference in how you define and execute your research topic, and help you to avoid some problems that commonly plague students.

Use a mind map

Figure 2.5 shows a mind map (aka a spider diagram) that Omozo, an MBA student, used to help structure his thoughts on his project on graduate recruitment practices in UK retail banking. He put the main topic in the centre of the map and the main issues related to this around it. The sub-issues are then clustered around each of the main issues.

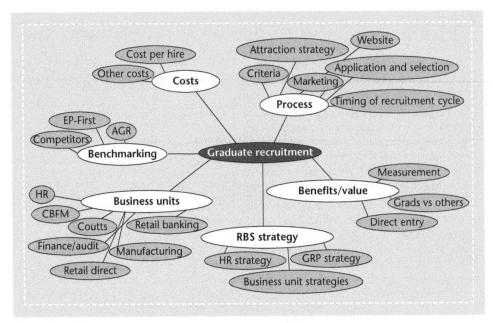

Figure 2.5 Mind map of graduate recruitment project
Source: Courtesy of Omozo Ehigie

Use a hierarchy of concepts

Drawing a **hierarchy of concepts** will help you get specific with your practical and/or theoretical problem. Some students start off with a really broad focus, such as: 'Why do organisations fail?' This is a perfectly good starting point, but it would be impossible to investigate in a single research project. Often, students need to go through several iterations on each concept in their research questions to narrow them down into a manageable topic and questions.

For example, if your particular interest is marketing, this can be broken down into business-to-business marketing (B2B) and business-to-consumer marketing (B2C). You decide that your interest is in the B2C area. How might this area be broken down? The potential hierarchy of concepts for this project is shown in **Figure 2.6**.

Many concepts easily fall into hierarchies. Thinking about how your research might fit into a conceptual hierarchy can be useful at many points in your project. If you go up a level in the hierarchy, you have a more abstract, and therefore broader, concept to deal with; if you go down a level, you have a less abstract, and therefore narrower, concept to deal with.

Use a Venn diagram to identify overlapping knowledge domains

Some research topics are studied only within one field, for example the ethics of marketing to children is mainly of interest in marketing. Many research topics, however, fit into several areas. For example, inter-organisational relations (IOR) is a substantial topic in both operations management and marketing. Some research topics are even studied within business and management's base disciplines, such as economics, sociology or psychology.

If your proposed research project fits into more than one area, you may want to use a mapping technique such as the **Venn diagram** to show where your topic fits and

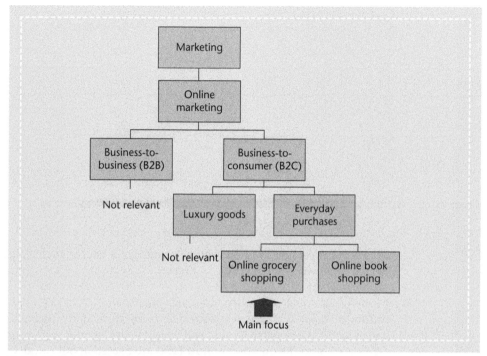

Figure 2.6 **A hierarchy of concepts**

where people have already done research (see **Chapter 3**). Interesting work often takes place at the intersection between different areas of study, because you can then draw on relevant aspects of each, but also combine multiple views of your topic. As shown in **Student research in action 2.13**, by looking at the overlap(s) you can narrow down the scope of your topic considerably and search for previous research. In this case, although each of the areas was well known, originality came from integrating the three.

Student research in action 2.13

TALK TO ME

Amit was interested in call centres. He started by trying to identify previous research on the specific topic of 'call centre management', but not much had been published under that specific topic heading. After talking to his supervisor, he realised that call centre management was studied in three areas: HRM (well understood), OM (well understood) and service management (also well understood). Amit could not possibly investigate HRM, OM and services in a single project. The project therefore existed at the intersection of the three areas, as shown in **Figure 2.7**.

His next step was therefore to choose one as his main perspective on the topic. For instance, Amit could choose to take an operations-based approach, if he were mainly interested in the process (what people do), a service-based approach to study the way in which the employees interact with the customers, or an HRM-based approach to look at the human interactions with the system.

Represent your ideas as a diagram

We suggest that you use your research questions to develop a diagram containing the key ideas you want to work with, and the relationships between them. This is sometimes

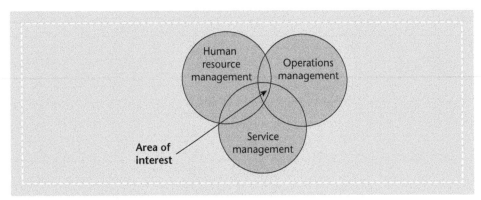

Figure 2.7 **A Venn diagram for investigating call centres**

called *a conceptual framework* and can help guide your background reading around your research topic and then later on your research design. If you are interested in conceptual frameworks, you might find Bacharach (1989) interesting to read. For examples of how professional researchers use conceptual frameworks to guide their work, the *Academy of Management Review* is known for being particularly useful. Refining the conceptual model is a key activity that will continue throughout your research.

This leads onto the question of how ideas are related in our research. Students who have been exposed to natural sciences research often wonder whether they should develop formal hypotheses which propose a link between two or more ideas before they develop their research design. As you will see in **Chapter 4**, the answer is, 'it depends'. In some research projects, you may be expected to further refine your research questions into more specific hypotheses about what you expect to find in your research project at this point. In other research projects, you may start collecting data without any formal hypotheses, and let the data guide you towards identifying some **propositions**. You may need to read **Chapter 4** and then come back to this section to see whether this is the case for your own research project. Even researchers who are doing relatively open-ended research usually start with some sort of conceptual framework. Mintzberg, who was interested in what managers actually did, did not set out trying to study everything about managers.

2.3.2 Writing a research proposal

Once you've narrowed down your topic area and identified your research problem and research questions, you can now formally state them in a **research proposal** to your academic advisor and/or business sponsor as part of your project. Whether or not you are required to present a formal project proposal, we recommend this as part of your research process. There are many reasons that you should do this, including to:

- Clarify your own ideas
- Document your ideas so that you can discuss your project with other people, including potential supervisors, partners and collaborators
- Provide a formal starting point for the project and a point of reference that you can come back to during the study should things not progress as you plan.

Table 2.3   **An example of an initial research proposal**

Project objectives	What do you hope to achieve by carrying out this research? What are your personal aims? What do you hope to find? (Make objectives SMART.)
Research theme	Title – not a major concern at this time, just a few words that summarise your ideas Research questions – what would you like to be able to answer?
The problem	What issues are the people/teams/organisations working with this problem facing? What is the evidence and how do you know this?
Context/setting	What is the context for the project? Why is it important? How did this idea come about – was it your idea? If not, how did it emerge?
Discipline/ sub-discipline	What are the subject areas you are interested in working with (Venn diagram)? What are the main articles or works you will be drawing on? Is there a particular 'hook' article?
Social unit	What industry/sector/organisation/group of individuals are you interested in studying?
Some practicalities	Who have you discussed your ideas with? Anything you wish to specifically include or exclude at this stage? What are your milestones? What resources will you need to do this project? What risks does the project pose? Have you read the requirements and regulations?

If you have been given a proposal format to follow by your organisation, you should follow it. If you haven't, use the format of **Table 2.3** to provide a structure for your thinking. It is worth putting some effort into completing the proposal at this point. If you can fill in all the boxes, you have at least considered the major issues up to this point in the process and covered at a high level the four dimensions of your research theme from **Chapter 1**. We will return to each of these in the next two chapters.

 Summary

In this chapter, we have described how to generate ideas for your research project. Some research will start with a practical problem. You may be interested in this practical problem, or you may be assigned a project brief by a business sponsor. Other research starts with a theoretical problem, a problem of incomplete knowledge that you may discover or are assigned by an academic supervisor or lecturer. Either way, business and management research usually involves finding both a practical and a theoretical aspect to your research topic.

This chapter has also provided some guidance on generating research ideas and filtering them to find the best idea. If you start with too few ideas, you may not have enough to select a high-quality idea. On the other hand, if you start with too many ideas, you may not be able to narrow them down. We have discussed a ranking mechanism for selecting the best idea for your research project.

Once you have selected a topic, you should be able to develop a project proposal – a document for communicating to others what you plan to do. You can use a project proposal to gain academic approval and practical support for your project.

Answers to key questions

Where do ideas for research topics come from?

- By creating some initial chaos, reading, discussing a wide range of potential issues, creating a number of possible topics, then focusing your work onto one issue that you will develop.
- The process of developing ideas includes reflection on experience, teaching and looking at previous projects, as well as considering why you are doing the project, then choosing the subject perspective you will use to approach the topic.

How can I choose between several potential research topics?

- You should choose between topics by defining the criteria your project will be evaluated on and selecting the one that most closely matches the criteria. If there are areas that do not match the criteria, the project should be specified to make sure that key criteria are met.

What characterises a good research topic?

- These can be summarised in seven general points – a well-defined purpose, wider implications than the project context, it is feasible, there is a basis in the literature but there is something novel about the study, it is practical, the outcomes are symmetrical and the project satisfies the stakeholders.
- It must interest you.
- It must fit with the requirements of your institution.

Why should I use research questions to focus my research?

- A main overall question will provide a focus for your work.
- Breaking the main question down into smaller research questions should provide a comprehensible breakdown of the activities you will need to carry out.
- Research questions are a readily understandable means for you to explain 'what my research project is about'.

How can I use a project proposal to define my project scope?

- The proposal will allow you to demonstrate the background and importance of your work, the research questions, hypotheses and propositions, state the intended methods for carrying it out and the basis for it in the literature.
- The proposal requires you to start being specific about your ideas – to define what you are going to investigate and, just as importantly, what you are not going to investigate.

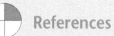

References

Bacharach, Samuel B. 1989. Organizational theories: Some criteria for evaluation, *Academy of Management Review*, 14(4): 496–515.

Barclay, I. and Benson, M.H. 1990. The Effective Management of New Product Development, *Leadership and Organisation Development Journal* Special Issue, 11(6): 1–37.

Blaikie, Norman 2009. *Designing Social Research*, 2nd edn. Cambridge: Polity Press.

Booth, Wayne C., Colomb, Gregory G. and Williams, Joseph M. 2008. *The Craft of Research*, 3rd edn. Chicago, IL: University of Chicago Press.

Coddington, A. 1997. *One of the Lads: Women who Follow Football*. London: HarperCollins.

Cohen, Wesley M. and Levinthal, Daniel A. 1989. Innovation and learning: The two faces of R&D, *Economic Journal*, 99(397): 569–96.

Cohen, Wesley M. 1990. Absorptive capacity: A new perspective on learning and innovation, *Administrative Science Quarterly*, 35(1): 128–52.

Crawford, Garry and Gosling, Victoria K. 2004. The myth of the 'Puck Bunny': Female fans and men's ice hockey, *Sociology*, 38(3): 477–93.

Delbridge, R. and Lowe, J. 1997. Manufacturing control: supervisory systems on the 'new' shopfloor, *Sociology*, 31(3): 409–26.

Gill, John and Johnson, Phil 2010. *Research Methods for Managers*, 4th edn. London: Sage.

Gillespie, Richard 1993. *Manufacturing Knowledge: A History of the Hawthorne Experiments*. Cambridge: Cambridge University Press.

Grant, R.M. 2004. *Contemporary Strategy Analysis*. Oxford: Blackwell Publishing.

Hebb, D.O. 1963. The semiautonomous process: Its nature and nurture, *American Psychologist*, 18(1): 16.

Kotler, P., Saunders, J. and Armstrong, G. 2004. *Principles of Marketing: European Edition*. Harlow: FT/Prentice Hall.

Latour, Bruno and Woolgar, Steve 1979. *Laboratory Life*. Beverly Hills: Sage Publications.

Lundberg, Craig 1999. Finding research agendas: Getting started Weick-like, *The Industrial-Organizational Psychologist* 37(2): 32–9.

Mintzberg, Henry 1971. Managerial work: analysis from observation, *Management Science*, 18(2): 97–110.

O'Leary, Zina 2013. *The Essential Guide to Doing Research*, 2nd edn. London: Sage.

Rousseau, D. 2012 (Ed.). *The Oxford Handbook of Evidence-Based Management*. Oxford, UK: Oxford University Press.

Söderlund, J. and Maylor, H. 2012. Project management scholarship: Relevance, impact and five integrative challenges for business and management schools, *International Journal of Project Management*, 30(6), 686–696.

Stacey, R.D. 2001. *Complex Responsive Processes in Organizations: Learning and Knowledge Creation*. London: Routledge.

Toulmin, Stephen 1958. *The Uses of Argument*. Cambridge: Cambridge University Press.

Tushman, Michael L. and Anderson, Philip 1986. Technological discontinuities and organisational environments, *Administrative Science Quarterly*, 31(3): 439–65.

Weick, Karl E. 1992. Agenda setting in organizational behaviour: A theory-focused approach, *Journal of Management Inquiry*, 1(3): 171–82.

Womack, J.P., Jones, D.T. and Roos, D. 1995. *The Machine That Changed the World: The Massachusetts Institute of Technology 5-million-dollar, 5-year Report on the Future of the Automobile Industry*. New York: Rawson Associates.

Additional resources

Alvesson, Mats and Sandberg, Jorgen 2003. *Constructing Research Questions: Doing Interesting Research*. London: Sage.

Andrew, Richard 2003. *Research Questions*. London: Continuum Research Methods.

Campbell, John P., Daft, Richard L. and Hulin, Charles L. 1982. *What to Study: Generating and Developing Research Questions*. Beverly Hills, CA: Sage.

Collis, Jill and Hussey, Roger 2013. *Business Research*, 4th edn. Basingstoke: Palgrave Macmillan.

Daft, Richard L. 1984. Antecedents of significant and not-so-significant organizational research. In T.S. Bateman and G.R. Ferris (eds), *Method and Analysis in Organizational Research*. Reston, VA: Reston Publishing.

Davis, Murray S. 1971. That's interesting: Toward a phenomenology of sociology and a sociology of phenomenology, *Philosophy of Social Science*, 1: 309–44.

Easterby-Smith, Mark, Thorpe, Richard and Lowe, Andy 2012. *Management Research: An Introduction*, 4th edn. London: Sage.

Jankowicz, A.D. 2000. *Business Research Projects*, 3rd edn. London: Business Press/ Thomson Learning.

Kaplan, Abraham 1964. *The Conduct of Inquiry: Methodology for Behavioural Science*. San Francisco: Chandler.

Lawrence, Paul R. 1992. The challenge of problem-oriented research, *Journal of Management Inquiry*, 1(2): 139–42.

Lundberg, Craig C. 1976. Hypothesis generation in organizational behavior research, *Academy of Management Review*, 3(1/2): 5–12.

Maslow, A.H. 1970. *Motivation and Personality*, 2nd edn. New York: Harper & Row.

Partington, David 2002. *Essential Skills for Management Research*. London: Sage.

Robson, Colin 2002. *Real World Research*, 2nd edn. Oxford: Blackwell.

Saunders, Mark, Lewis, Phillip and Thornhill, Adrian 2003. *Research Methods for Business Students*, 3rd edn. Harlow: Financial Times/Prentice Hall.

Sekaran, U. 2000. *Research Methods for Business*, 3rd edn. Chichester: Wiley.

Taylor, Frederick W. 1947. *Scientific Management*. New York: Harper & Row.

Söderlund, J. and Maylor, H. 2012. Project management scholarship: Relevance, impact and five integrative challenges for business and management schools, *International Journal of Project Management*, 30(6): 686–96.

Weick, Karl E. 1983. Management thought in the context of action. In S. Srivastva (ed.), *The Executive Mind*. San Francisco: Jossey-Bass.

Weick, Karl E. 1989. Theory construction as disciplined imagination, *Academy of Management Review*, 14(4): 516–31.

Wren, Daniel A. and Greenwood, Ronald G. 1998. *Management Innovators: The People and Ideas that Have Shaped Modern Business*. Oxford: Oxford University Press.

Zikmund, W.G. 2000. *Business Research Methods*, 6th edn. Orlando, FL: Dryden Press/ Harcourt College Publishers.

Key terms

Frequently asked questions

Q. Does the project have to be leading edge in management terms: does it have to address a hot topic from the current management literature?

A. No – the project does not have to be fashionable to be good. Many topics have disappeared from the management agenda for no reason other than that the field appears to have moved on to the next big idea. For instance, during the 1990s, many firms adopted particular approaches to quality management and then abandoned them when other ideas came along. Quality management is still a good topic for investigation – as there is plenty written on it and practitioners are still interested in to how to gain benefit from good quality management.

Q. How do I know the precise objectives of the project and the balance that is required between theoretical and practical issues?

A. The precise objectives of the project should be set out in course documentation and are always worth referring to – not least because they can clarify the requirements of the project and the balance point between theoretical and practical issues. The discussion of the role of theory/best practice and other practices is in **Chapter 4**.

Q. Why do I need to include this theory when what I am looking at is profoundly practical?

A. This is easy to understand, but where does this theory generally come from? It comes from people studying the practical, and theorising from it. As Hebb (1963) famously commented, 'There's nothing so useful as a good theory.' In addition, you will usually need to show that you have covered the existing knowledge on a topic – it is usually a central purpose of the project work. Moreover, the existing knowledge base should help you to make sense of, or at least structure, the issues in the area that you are considering.

Q. Do I really have to prepare a written scope and proposal?

A. Whilst some institutions require you to present a written proposal, others will accept a discussion of your proposals. We suggest that the few minutes that it takes to prepare the proposal are worthwhile, as it provides a point of reference for the project as it progresses and will help to keep you on track, if you refer back to it regularly.

Discussion questions

1. If you have access to a set of project requirements for your academic work or business project, use them to answer this question. What are the requirements of projects that you will be carrying out? Investigate the documentation provided by your institution and compare them with the characteristics of a 'good project' included in this chapter.

2. 'Previous work is so yesterday. Why not just start it again? After all, it was about time there was some fresh thinking in management.' What do you think of this statement?

3. What are the sources of ideas that you could usefully use for your project either to start you off or expand on the ideas that you have?

4. Does every research project have to be linked to a particular business and management area of study? Why or why not?

5. What are the ethical implications of using previous student projects as a source for your own project ideas?

6. How would you express your ideas at different stages in the development of those ideas? How would a mind map be used here?

7. How can filling out a research proposal improve the quality of the research process?

8. How can defining your project scope at this stage of the research process improve the quality of the research project?

Workshop

This workshop comprises two short group exercises, intended to illustrate the different processes that people go through in trying to reach a decision when there are a large number of possibilities for that decision.

10-minute exercise (1)

Your group has been awarded a (fictitious) potential business start-up grant of £100,000. What are you going to do with this? You have 10 minutes to agree on an idea and present it in order to 'win' this money.

Debrief discussion questions (1)

1. What are your ideas (summarise to one idea per group)?

2. How did you choose which of your ideas to run with?

3. What happened in the 10-minute session – was there any structure to the activity? Did all people contribute or was it dominated by one person? How was the information collected?

4. How effective was this process at getting to 'the best idea'?

5. Plot the process that the group went through onto **Figure 2.1**. How did each of you respond to such a wide brief?

10-minute exercise (2)

We now introduce some 'rules' for the process:

1. At the start of the next exercise, the first three minutes are to be conducted in silence to allow everyone to develop their ideas first.

2. Appoint someone as facilitator (not the most dominant person from the first exercise). The role of the facilitator is to clarify ideas and help to ensure that everyone is assisted in making their contribution.

▶

3. No ideas are rejected and nobody is criticised for ideas (some of the wackiest ideas when combined with others can produce superb concepts).

4. Combine but don't eliminate ideas.

5. Use Post-its (or index cards) to write your ideas down (one idea per Post-it or index card) and then compile a mind map of the issues as in **Figure 2.5**.

Task

You have been assigned to a project team to carry out a research project. The general area that you have come up with is the evaluation of critical success factors for small businesses. Your initial evaluation of the area shows it to be large and you will need to focus the topic onto a more limited question that you want to ask.

1. For three minutes, working individually, write down your ideas.

2. For two minutes review each other's ideas, without discussion.

3. For five minutes, arrange the topics into a mind map (as **Figure 2.5**).

Which is the most interesting of these that the group would pursue?

Debrief discussion questions (2)

1. What were your main ideas?

2. How did the group work this time round (better or worse)?

3. How did you make decisions?

4. What would you do differently in group situations in future – both to avoid the potential for failure from the issues you have identified, and in terms of the process for making decisions in project groups?

Task

Use the basic idea you have identified to complete a project proposal similar to the one provided in **Table 2.3**.

1

Relevant chapters

1 What is research?
2 What should I study?
3 How do I find information?

Key challenges

- Understanding what academic research is
- Generating and clarifying ideas
- **Using sources of information**

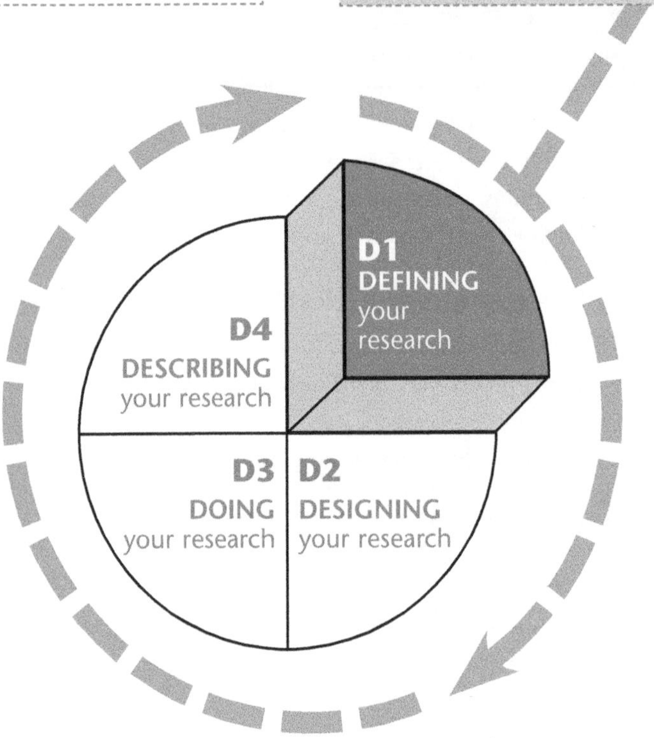

2

Relevant chapters

4 What is my research approach?
5 How do I do quantitative research?
6 How do I do qualitative research?
7 How do I do case study research?
8 How do I make sure my research is ethical?

Key challenges

- Choosing a research approach
- Choosing a research design
- Collecting data using quantitative methods
- Collecting data using qualitative methods
- Integrating quantitative and qualitative methods

3

Relevant chapters

9 How do I do field research?
10 What do my quantitative data mean(1)?
11 What do my quantitative data mean(2)?
12 What do my qualitative data mean?

Key challenges

- Practical considerations in doing research
- Describing data using simple statistics
- Carrying out statistical tests
- Interpreting words and actions

4

Relevant chapters

13 How do I write up my report?
14 What do I do now?

Key challenges

- Making sense of your findings
- Presenting your research to others
- Reflecting and learning from your research

3

chapter

How do I find what is already known about this topic?

Using knowledge resources

 Key questions

- Where and how do I find information to develop my research project?
- What methods for collecting and analysing data have other researchers used?
- How do I find more information about my research setting and sample?
- How do I assess the relevance and quality of business and management research?
- How do I use this information?
- What is a literature review and how do I write one?

 Learning outcomes

At the end of this chapter, you should be able to:

- Plan your search for information
- Use the internet and library to find information
- Organise information so that you can readily retrieve it for use
- Critically analyse research on your topic in a literature review

---

Contents

Introduction

Harvey gained a key insight in a conversation with a management consultant. When he asked how the consultant gained the information he required to provide guidance to his clients, the consultant's reply was 'research'. This sounded very promising until Harvey asked him to clarify this. '*Simple,*' he replied. '*Research is using Google. Deep research is using Google and Wikipedia.*'

Clearly, there are many different perspectives about what 'research' means. **Chapter 2** guided you through a systematic process for identifying your potential research topic and questions, a key step towards *defining* your research project. This chapter will help you identify what information to use in your research project, where and how to find this information, and how to use it effectively.

Using your readings effectively is critical to good research, according to O'Leary (2013). Your reading in the business and management **literature** will help you to:

- narrow down what you will study,
- provide a foundation for your work and
- identify suitable frameworks for investigating your research problem and questions.

Building on the work of others will enable you to create new knowledge in your own project. Sir Isaac Newton is often quoted having said: 'If I have been able to see farther than others, it was because I stood on the shoulders of giants.' You will use the business and management literature to support your theoretical underpinnings, your research design, and your data collection and analysis. As you find out how other people have investigated similar problems, your readings will also help you think about how you will find evidence to answer your research questions. **Part 2** of this book will then help you turn this into a research design to collect and analyse data to answer those questions.

Section 3.1 should help you answer the following questions about your research project:

- Where can I find research that other people have done that will help me develop and refine my research questions?
- Where can I find information about research methods that I might use to answer my research questions?
- Where can I find information about the people or organisations I want to study?

You will use your time and other resources more effectively if you plan *before* you start searching for information. **Section 3.2** shows you how to formulate a clear **search** strategy that will help you make best use of your knowledge, skills and time. As with other aspects of your research project, a systematic search is more likely to turn up the right and, more importantly, a manageable amount of, information. A search that is too broad will turn up an overwhelming amount of information; a search that is too narrow or in the wrong place will turn up too little, or perhaps even none. This section also highlights different online and print information sources that you may find useful and briefly explains how you can assess the quality of different sources of information so that you know what to use and what not to use.

Section 3.3 presents some additional practical skills for finding and using information effectively and also describes how to make best use of these resources. Keeping careful records as you work with information sources is essential and there are tools that can help. This is important because giving appropriate credit to other people for their words and ideas avoids plagiarism and other intellectual property issues such as **copyright**, which we consider in detail in **Chapter 8**. We also provide a brief discussion of some software that you may use to keep track of your information sources, which will be useful not only in this stage but also when you are writing up and presenting your research (covered in **Part 4**).

You may find your initial enthusiasm for your research project slipping into despondency, or even despair, at this point (part of the 'real' project life cycle presented in **Chapter 1**). Do not fear! Searching systematically for information will help you to develop a research project that is both interesting and sufficiently original.

3.1 What do I need to search for and why?

Chapter 2 focused on defining your research problem and questions, and this chapter shows you how to refine them through your readings. How much time and energy you now spend gathering information depends in part on your overall *research approach*, which we cover in **Chapter 4**. As a brief preview, if you are using what we will call a *quantitative research design*, you will carry out a comprehensive **literature search** before you start gathering data. Quantitative research designs include web or postal questionnaires or experiments, in which the researcher develops hypotheses from existing theory before data collection starts, and collects and analyses data to test these hypotheses. If you are using this approach, you may write a draft of your literature review, conceptual framework, and research methods chapters, and design your data analysis, before you start collecting any data. This means you will rely heavily on using your search skills early on in your project life cycle.

On the other hand, if you are using what we will call a *qualitative research design*, you will carry out only a brief literature search and review, but postpone your main search and review until you have started collecting your data or analysing it. If you are using a qualitative approach, you may only conduct a quick information search to sketch out the broad detail of what you want to study and then do further reading in parallel with your field research as different themes emerge from your observations and propositions from the data itself.

No matter which approach you choose, it would be unusual – and we suggest highly unwise – for a student researcher to start collecting data without *any* background investigation at all. In our experience as supervisors, students who spend too little time on this often encounter problems that might have been prevented if identified early, or remedied easily, but that become difficult or impossible to correct later. Students have missed major areas of interest because the literature review was incomplete, thereby missing the opportunity for comparison with work that has already been done in the area. **Research in action 3.1** illustrates one such case from our experience.

We have made the case that it is necessary at this stage to look at previous research to establish what has already been done. However, there are some time-traps that need to be avoided where considerable time may be spent investigating the literature without yielding any high-quality outcomes. A good literature search will help you narrow down your research topic and develop your research problem and questions. It will also help you identify the variables that you will measure and the relationships between them (which **Chapter 2** further developed into the idea of a *conceptual framework*), either to guide your data collection and analysis or to make sense of what you have found out. Achieving that balance between breadth, depth and relevance of the work is best achieved in short iterations, and is a crucial time to be drawing on your supervisor's experience.

Looking for relevant readings

The four areas that you should investigate are what other researchers studying your proposed (or related) areas have found out about your:

1. **Research problem and questions** – What other researchers have found out about the area you propose to study;
2. **Conceptual framework** – What concepts and relationships they have studied in their research;
3. **Research methods** – How they have collected and analysed data;
4. **Research setting or context** – Details of the people, organisations, or other settings where you will collect data.

We will look at specific search strategies in **Section 3.2**. As part of your finished research project, you will also need to support your research and possibly to critically analyse previous research in a literature review (sometimes called theoretical background) as part of your research project (see Gill and Johnson 2010), which we turn to in **Section 3.3**. A **literature review** is a systematic *critique* of previous research done on your theoretical or practical problem.

3.1.1 What readings are relevant to my theoretical problem?

What is my topic and what have researchers found out about it?

Your priority here is to find information that will let you identify 5–10 key readings related to your research problem and the key theoretical perspectives that other researchers have applied in studying it. If you have chosen a topic that you have already studied, we suggest that you start with your reading list or textbooks to identify at least one or two key articles or authors who work on your research topic. If you get stuck getting started, ask your project supervisor for some helpful suggestions. Even if you don't end up keeping all those suggested by your supervisor or from the reading lists in this core set, this is definitely easier than starting with a random search of books, academic journals and the web.

Don't narrow down your search too much. Some research topics fit neatly within a single field, while others cut across fields or even into other disciplines. One way to keep track of this is to use techniques such as mind mapping, the hierarchy of concepts or the Venn diagram presented in **Chapter 2** to help you to identify all the relevant perspectives on your research topic. **Figure 3.1** shows an example of a mind map used by a student, which demonstrates the complexity of the area she was studying.

What are the key 'building blocks' of this topic?

As you are reading, you should be noting what concepts, variables and measures other researchers have used in investigating your topic. These are the building blocks from which they have built the *conceptual model* for their studies, and which you might use in building your own conceptual model (see **Chapter 2**). There is no 'standard' conceptual model for any given research topic: different researchers will include different concepts based on what theoretical lens they are applying, and what particular research questions they are asking. They may also propose different relationships between those concepts. You should keep track of these, so that you can justify your own conceptual model (whether you develop it before your data collection starts or afterwards). **Research in action 3.2** shows how one conceptual model was constructed from the same building blocks as previous studies, but with a slightly different twist.

Research in action 3.2(a)
DEVELOPING YOUR CONCEPTUAL FRAMEWORK: VIRAL MARKETING EXAMPLE

Viral marketing, where an advertising campaign uses social media and word-of-mouth communications to increase customer awareness of a product or service instead of the usual advertising media, is a relatively new phenomenon. The research on it has just appeared in the last decade. For emergent topics such as this, a key issue will be finding relevant research. This is unlike traditional advertising using television and print media, for instance, where the main issue would be narrowing down the literature to a manageable amount.

As an example, a well-established belief in marketing is that increased advertising spend results in increased product awareness which results in increased sales. Viral marketing may challenge this relationship between advertising spend and sales; it may not be so straightforward.

In researching this, you would look for information on the key concepts advertising spend, product/brand awareness and sales, and the relationships between these. The arrows, well defined in

76

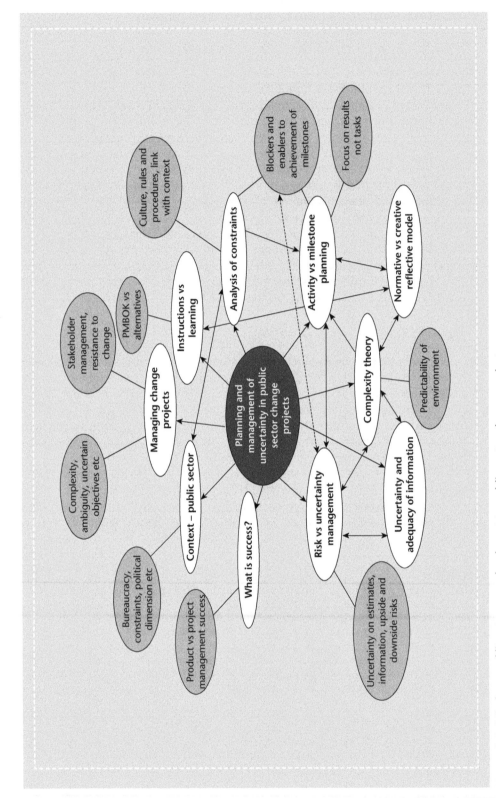

Figure 3.1 Mind map of literature search relevant to public sector change projects

Source: Courtesy of Liz Heywood

traditional marketing, become questions in the viral marketing model and show the kind of studies that could usefully be conducted to explore the nature of the relationships involved. A starting point in building the conceptual model for a study on viral marketing might therefore be to take a traditional marketing model and then consider whether it needs to be 'rearranged', for example to analyse how the effectiveness of viral marketing could be evaluated in contrast to traditional marketing. **Figure 3.2** presents two conceptual models, one for traditional marketing and one for viral marketing.

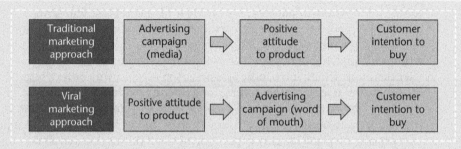

Figure 3.2 Simple conceptual frameworks for viral marketing study

What evidence have researchers used to answer their research questions?

As you investigate past research on your topic, you should also start to notice what research designs and – in particular – what research methods researchers have used to investigate your research topic. Academic researchers describe these in detail when they write up their research, and often provide helpful **references** to the research methods literature that guides their data collection and analysis.

You also need to understand whether there seems to be a consensus around a specific research method (e.g. questionnaires in market research, archival or secondary data studies in economics, simulations in operations research, observation in organisational studies), or there is a variety of approaches. Even if there is a consensus, this should inform, but not dictate, how you approach your research. This does not prevent you from recognising the limitations of one approach and taking another that complements it, although you will need to justify it. We will discuss research approach further in **Chapter 4**, and research designs and methods in **Part 2**.

Research in action 3.2(b)
VIRAL MARKETING (CONTINUED)

Continuing with our example, research into the relationship between advertising spend and product sales can be based on information produced by advertising agencies based on point-of-sale data. This is, as you'll see in **Chapter 5**, a form of secondary data analysis. The same approach could be taken for our viral marketing example – the spend to produce a viral marketing video could be quantified, and put against any uplift in sales. But is this the best way to study such an emergent approach (viral marketing)? If we look at the conceptual model in **Figure 3.2**, you will see that there is an intervening concept between the marketing activity and the increased spend – the product/brand awareness. What, for instance, is the nature of this product or brand awareness? How does the change in awareness from viral marketing differ from that achieved by a traditional advertising campaign? How have such differences been researched in marketing?

3.1.2 What is known about my research context?

You will also need use your readings to consider the potential real-world context or setting in which you will conduct your own research project. You can apply the same principles that we have applied to searching for information about conceptual models and research methods to finding out about the real-world contexts or *research settings* where researchers have collected data.

Your **research setting** defines the specific real-world context in or about which you collect information to address this problem of incomplete knowledge. We suggest that you keep note of the research settings in which your topic has been researched. The newspaper, brewing, and automobile industries have all been used as research settings for studying organisational evolution, for example.

Furthermore, when you choose – or are given – your own context/setting, you will need to justify it as a suitable setting for gathering **evidence** to answer your research questions. You might choose to use one of these in your own study, or to show how your choice has similar characteristics to these industries that make it appropriate. This will also help you identify gaps in the research (if this research about professional services applies to medical doctors, does it also apply to accountants?). **Research in action 3.3** gives an example.

Research in action 3.3

USING READINGS FOR 'VIRTUAL' EVIDENCE GATHERING

Researchers were working with a group from the UK police service recently. It became clear that this group believed that their context was (1) unique and (2) demonstrated practices significantly behind those of industry in project execution. A brief review of the literature on project execution in different sectors was carried out and compared with the practices being used by the police. This demonstrated that there were more similarities than differences in the challenges faced, and that the police practices were not so different from those used elsewhere. This was important, as it allowed the researchers to build on key literature as points of reference in subsequent studies.

Exploring your research setting through your reading can improve the quality of your research relatively easily. For instance, if you are studying an organisation in a particular industry or the industry as a whole, you might try to identify who the key players are in that context, what is the size of the industry, its geographic distribution, its history and trajectory, financials and so on. A study of airport management might entail finding out who the major firms are, what airports they manage, what their business models are and how they make money (which has nothing to do with landing planes, by the way). As we will see in **Chapters 5** and **6**, you may even be gathering your data to answer your research questions indirectly rather than through direct contact with people or organisations.

Use your reading to identify a research gap or original contribution

You can combine what you have learnt in your reading about your research topic, research design, and research setting to identify the unique contribution that your research will make. (Remember from **Chapter 2** that this only needs to be an element of novelty, not a 'change the world' discovery.) Searching the literature will help you

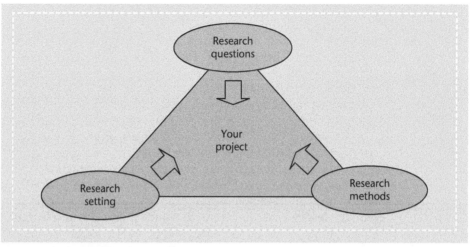

Figure 3.3 Positioning your research project

identify different combinations of research topics and questions, research settings and research methods before you make your final decision, as **Figure 3.3** suggests. This can be fundamental, as shown in **Student research in action 3.1**.

Student research in action 3.1

USE YOUR READING TO WIDEN YOUR RESEARCH HORIZONS

As we saw in **Student research in action 2.2**, Catherine's research project started with her interest in organic food retailing over the internet as a new phenomenon. Catherine had already done a research project investigating customers' perceptions of the service quality of online supermarkets, and, for her next research project, she decided to extend this to the context of online small organic food retailers. As she read the literature on web service quality, she realised that customers might not be simply substituting online purchasing for grocery shopping: they might actually have different motives for buying organic food over the internet.

This led Catherine to look at the consumer marketing literature, which she hadn't looked at before. She realised that she needed to take into account the fact that people purchase goods not only for their utility, but also for satisfying emotional needs, displaying an affiliation with certain groups, marking a significant life passage or expressing personal and social aspirations. She identified Thorstein Veblen's theory of trickle-down consumption as a possible explanation of consumer behaviour. Since nearly all the research on website quality had been written from a technical perspective focusing on the design and efficiency of transactions, she identified the potential to do research that would fill in a knowledge gap.

3.1.3 What am I *actually* investigating?

One of the key benefits of doing thorough but focused reading at this stage is that it will help you move from a broad, unfocused topic to a narrower set of research questions and a **conceptual framework**. Although this part of your research is simple in theory – identify a problem, develop a search strategy, make sense of the information you find – it is often challenging in practice. As **Figure 3.3** showed, focusing your research project requires identifying a specific research topic and specific research setting. We suggest that you separate your research problem into your theoretical problem of incomplete knowledge that you want to find out more about, your practical problem and your research setting where you will gather the information to answer your research questions.

Understanding what you are actually studying turns out, surprisingly, to be one of the most difficult parts of the 'defining' stage of a research project. Even experienced researchers sometimes get confused between the theoretical problem they are investigating – research topic, problem, questions, and conceptual framework of concepts and relationships – and the research setting in which they are doing their data collection. Moreover, searching only for past research that covers both your research problem and setting simultaneously can lead to a false conclusion that 'no one has ever done research on this before', as shown in **Student research in action 3.2**.

 Student research in action 3.2

AVOID FOCUSING YOUR SEARCH TOO NARROWLY

Yuraporn decided when she started her research that she would study 'the implementation of human resource management (HRM) information systems in Thai subsidiaries of multinational corporations (MNCs)', because she had worked in this area before starting her studies. She was adamant that there was no relevant academic research that she could use to write a literature review, because *no one* had done any research in this area, as she couldn't find even a single article on the topic. However, she had limited her search to HR, information systems, Thailand and MNCs simultaneously. She consequently missed out on relevant research on 'HRM information systems', on implementing information systems in multinational corporations, and on implementing HR systems in overseas subsidiaries of MNCs, all of which could have been used to define the research topic and research questions.

Searching for everything that has been published on HRM, and everything that has been published on multinational companies, and everything that has been published on companies in Thailand would create a different set of problems, including how to read millions of pages in the time you have available. If you understand the difference between your theoretical problem and your research context/setting, then you will be able to deal with the complexity of the literature search better. Talking it through with other people, including your project supervisor, your reference librarian, and other knowledgeable parties is often helpful.

3.2 How can I search for information?

Once you have a general idea of why you are searching for information and what you should be searching for, your next questions become 'Where should I be looking for this information?' and 'How should I be looking for it?'

Since we wrote the first edition of this book, how researchers search for information has changed dramatically. Whilst the overall goal of searching is the same, the 'where' and 'how' has become dramatically different. In 2005, the library was still the 'go-to' place for information, with the electronic library and internet being supplementary resources. The vast majority of information search and retrieval now takes place online. Search engines have replaced library catalogues (and the older physical card catalogues). As we write this second edition, you may be used to using only the electronic library and internet for getting both academic and company information.

General internet searches (such as Google or Wikipedia) are useful for quickly identifying the density of information and popular themes, suitable for establishing a topic. Published information – whether in printed or electronic form – is expanding so fast that any library can only hold a small sample of it. You can search the web for text, images, sounds and videos using various search engines. The web has billions of pages: to search through them efficiently, knowing how to use search engines such as Google is important.

However, this does not replace a well thought-out strategy for your research project and producing your literature review. **Section 3.2.2** will explain the principles of how to search, and then focus on how to make the best use of more specific electronic databases. Because you may need to search for historical and/or other non-electronic sources of information, we also briefly review the essentials of using the library and print resources. For instance, you don't want to miss that significant article from 1981, because your database only includes articles published from 1982 onwards. This is surprisingly common!

3.2.1 Where can I find what I'm looking for?

Googling for information is now often the first thing most people think of when looking up information, but we suggest that you should search for academic resources through your library resources (electronic or physical) first, and then use the web to follow up any useful references you find. Google or Wikipedia may give you an answer that is good enough for pub quizzes or Trivial Pursuit, but as of the time we are writing this is less useful for academic research. Since the library has 'gatekeepers', who determine what publications and databases to provide access to, it still has the edge on reliable information since anyone can publish anything on the web. (The Pacific Tree Octopus (http://zapatopi.net/treeoctopus/) is a favourite demonstration of this.) Knowing whether what you have found is accurate and useful may be difficult. So, how do you know what sources are 'good enough' for doing your research project?

Quality and published material

Students often end up getting in a muddle because of the variety of types of information and their many different sources. This confusion isn't helped by the specialised shorthand that experienced researchers use: 'the literature', 'literature search', and 'literature review'. What researchers mean by 'the academic literature' is sometimes a bit fuzzy. Is it any information related to the research project? Just articles in academic journals? As we noted earlier, research papers generally contain information about both the theoretical background of the research and the research setting (industry, company, social group, etc.) in which a particular piece of research was carried out. The 'academic literature' refers specifically to information that has been published in academic journals and books by professional researchers for other researchers.

But what about textbooks? Business magazines, such as *Fortune* and *Business Week*? Practitioner journals such as *Harvard Business Review* and *McKinsey Quarterly*?

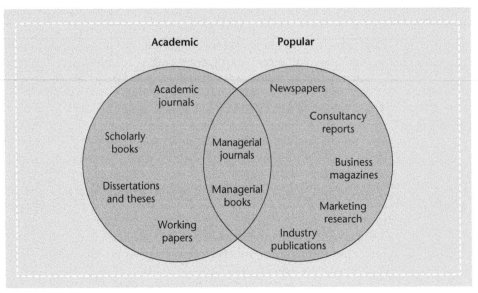

Figure 3.4 Major sources of information and their audiences

Wikipedia? Company sites? Random web pages? **Figure 3.4** suggests a rough classification, although, as it suggests, there is overlap between the 'academic' and 'popular' literatures, which can lead to even more confusion.

The most helpful source for identifying and refining the theoretical problem (and therefore the research topic, research questions, conceptual model and theoretical background) for your research project will be articles in periodicals (especially academic journals), followed by scholarly books from academic presses. The other sources are often useful for helping identify problems that would be worth investigating further.

Periodicals

We have listed the different types of **periodicals** you might need to consult in your research below. (In **Section 3.2** we will focus on *how* to find them.) These include:

- **Scholarly publications** – **Academic journals**, scholarly books and other resources;
- **Conference proceedings** – Papers presented at annual meetings of academic or other professional societies, such as the Academy of Management;
- **Managerial publications** – Non-academic periodicals, popular books, company reports and other resources
- **General periodicals** – publications that appear regularly – daily, weekly, monthly or yearly – or irregularly.

Table 3.1 gives examples of one type of periodical – the journal – that you are likely to encounter in your search for relevant readings, and their intended audiences.

Papers published in *general management journals* are aimed at academics with a good level of general knowledge of the discussions being undertaken in the papers, compared with those in *discipline-specific journals*, where a detailed knowledge of the

Table 3.1   Examples of journals by audience

Type	Examples	Remit
General management	• *Academy of Management Journal* • *British Journal of Management* • *European Management Journal*	Cover a wide range of management topics written by academics for an academic audience
Specific management area	• *International Journal of Operations and Production Management* • *Journal of Finance* • *International Journal of Project Management* • *Journal of International Business Studies* • *Journal of Business Venturing* • *Human Resource Management* • *MIS Quarterly* • *Marketing Science*	Cover a range of management topics within a specific subject area
Management-oriented	• *Harvard Business Review* • *MIT Sloan Management Review* • *California Management Review* • *Business Horizons*	Cover a wider range of management topics written by academics for a managerial audience

discipline is almost always required. These are sometimes published in more accessible form in **managerial journals** targeted at general managers such as *Harvard Business Review* or *California Management Review* or more specific publications aimed at specific managers. Whilst they tend to skip over the heavy academic content, they may still be worth looking at because they tend to have shorter lead times than academic journals (typically six months to a year) and therefore more current information. Telling the difference between the two types can be difficult – the *Journal of Supply Chain Management* is aimed primarily at academics, whilst *Supply Chain Management: An International Journal* is aimed at academics and managers.

Other useful periodicals include **magazines** of general interest (e.g. *The Economist, Fortune* or *Management Today*) or special interest (*The Grocer*), and **newspapers** which are daily or weekly publications of general interest (e.g. *The Times*) or special interest (the *Financial Times*). These write about people, organisations, industries, countries and economies, and are published frequently, but remember that their main goal is to sell articles, not report on academic research.

A number of journal lists have been published that purport to identify the quality of different journals, including the list published periodically by the Association of Business Schools, and the list published by the *Financial Times*.[1] We take these lists with a large pinch of salt, as they are based on opinion rather than data, although this is educated opinion (at least). There is no single order of merit for journals. For instance, there are also lists based on journal 'impact factor', but these have different problems with being 'true' indicators of a journal's quality. Plus, the quality and impact of articles in a single journal can vary widely, and some very influential articles have been published in obscure journals.

Although lists can be generally helpful, we argue that the two best indicators of the quality of a journal are (1) the quality of the editor and editorial team and (2) the process that they use to decide whether to publish an article. Similar indicators apply to books – where the quality of the press is a good, but not perfect, indicator. A high-quality journal generally has a leading academic as the editor, and other leading academics on the editorial team and as reviewers. **Peer review** describes the process that academics use to check the quality of books, articles and conference proceedings before publication. It is called 'peer' because other academics working in the same academic area review a proposed publication and decide whether it meets accepted quality standards. Peer review is designed to minimise personal bias in deciding what papers will be published. The highest standard of review is **double-blind review**, where the reviewer does not know whose work they are reviewing, and the author does not know who is reviewing their work, so that neither reviewers nor authors know who the other is. However, just because a supposedly great paper is published in a supposedly great journal, doesn't automatically mean it will be useful for your study.

Books (not dead yet!)

Books can be useful especially for broad surveys of an area or in-depth explorations of particular issues. Scholarly books include **monographs**, academic books on a single subject by one or more authors; **edited volumes**, academic books on a single subject by one or more authors under the direction of one or more editors; and **dissertations** and **theses**, book-length reports on research projects submitted by undergraduate or postgraduate students. These are appropriate sources for your literature review. You should judge books by the same sorts of criteria as we mentioned above for periodicals.

You may also want to consult **reference books** such as dictionaries, encyclopaedias, yearbooks, writing guides, thesauruses and statistical abstracts, and **textbooks**, and *mass-market books* written for a general business audience, such as *In Search of Excellence* (Peters and Waterman 2004), *The One Minute Manager* (Blanchard and Johnson 1982), *Who Moved My Cheese?* (Johnson 2003), or *From Good to Great* (Collins 2003). Although textbooks are useful for finding basic information about a field and as a starting point for identifying where to go for further information, they are unlikely to be authoritative, comprehensive or up-to-date, so you should not stop there, especially if you are doing an extended or narrowly focused research project. Popular business books may be written by academic authors and published by reputable presses such as the Harvard Business School Press or commercial publishing houses such as the Free Press, but they typically do not undergo the peer review or sometimes even professional editing – so 'let the buyer beware'.

Books are increasingly available in non-print form, including PDFs, electronic books on Kindle and iTunes, and digitised manuscripts on Google Scholar. Your electronic library may subscribe to Books 24/7 or other collections of e-books. The Gutenberg Foundation's (www.gutenberg.org) has a collection of thousands of out-of-copyright books.

The criteria against which you should judge books include:

- Do the book's authors and/or editors have scholarly expertise in the topic, do they have managerial expertise, or are they journalists/consultants? Scholarly expertise is likely to be signalled by the authors holding a faculty position at a major research university or their list of publications.

- Has the book been published by an academic or a commercial press? Many universities have their own presses (e.g., Oxford University Press, the University of Chicago Press), but there are also commercial publishers who specialise in academic books (e.g. Palgrave Macmillan, McGraw-Hill, Routledge and Sage Publications). These are likely to have academic input on what books are published and their content. Other books published by generalist presses, self-published by their authors or published by 'vanity' presses (where the author pays for publication rather than being paid) are unlikely to have undergone any kind of quality review. There is a growing trend for self-publication of books (e.g. Lulu) which may not have had any review at all.
- What audience is the book targeted to? Is it written for academics, students, managers or the general public, or to grab attention in airport bookstores?
- Has a book had a major impact? *Good to Great* has definitely been impactful, and there are many cogent arguments presented between the covers and many glowing testimonials. This is a useful criteria but against research the content and how the ideas have been tested needs careful evaluation.

Databases

Databases are collected resources of economic and other statistical data that contain structured information. These can be in printed format (e.g. OECD publications), or electronic formats (e.g. magnetic media, CD-ROM, or networked). Popular business and management databases are now available to multiple users on networked CD-ROMs, including corporate finance databases such as AMADEUS (Analyse MAjor Databases from European Sources) and FAME (Financial Analysis Made Easy), Bloomberg, Capital IQ, Datastream, Thomson Deals, Computstat, and market reports such as Forrester and Mintel – a UK database of market reports in key areas of retail, leisure and finance. We will describe these in more detail in **Chapter 5** when we discuss the analysis of secondary data. Company publications include news releases, brochures, financial reports, product specifications and so on.

3.2.2 How can I find what I'm looking for?

The growth in electronic library resources and the internet has undoubtedly made finding information easier, but finding the *right* information for a research project more difficult. Googling 'My topic' or 'My research setting' is likely to result in an overwhelming number of hits, most of which will be of dubious quality. This is where searching through your library can be helpful, as the material has already been 'curated' or pre-selected for you.

Electronic library resources

University libraries currently spend significantly more on electronic publications, whether in the form of electronic versions of printed books, articles or other publications, or publications that only ever existed in electronic form, than on printed resources. Make sure you understand how to use the resources in your electronic library to your best advantage. There are usually self-help guides online that will give you a general overview of the electronic library, and others that explain how to use specific resources. Most libraries offer an induction session, and some offer tutorials and frequently asked question lists. If all else fails, ask a librarian to help you, but don't wait too long to ask; we have collectively found our librarians to be both knowledgeable and helpful, whilst usually asking some great questions.

The internet

Although search engines let you search the entire internet in milliseconds, we have found that students don't always take advantage of the internet's possibilities or recognise its limitations. You should check before you use a search engine:

- How to construct a search
- How to use limiters
- How to search for specific types of resource, e.g. PDFs
- How to search safely

As always, we have to mention that searching safely is important. Make sure to keep anti-virus and anti-spyware programmes up to date, and be wary of clicking on web pages. If you are searching for images or videos, you may also want to use your 'family filter' setting to cut down on 'adult content' results in your search. (Kate was rather surprised to find many non-safe-for-work images when she was preparing to teach a Harvard Business School case study on industrial glue and Googled images of Superglue.)

Finally, beware using unverified web pages for academic information. Pages can disappear as quickly as they appeared, so you may not be able to count on continued access to information. If you are in any doubt about the veracity of websites, please see the sad fate of the endangered Pacific Tree Octopus.[2]

The physical library

Although libraries nowadays may function more as computer labs and group/individual study spaces than as places to look up books and bound copies of journals, the library has traditionally been and is still your most important resource for finding academic and real-world knowledge. Your library may employ a **subject librarian** who specialises in business and management studies, or a generalist in social sciences who takes responsibility for business and management studies. Different libraries (typically national, university, divisional, departmental and specialist) vary in the range and volume of resources; some offer much more access to business and management studies resources than others. For instance, a **copyright depository library** such as the British Library gets a copy of every book published in the country while some libraries are little more than a room with teaching resources. If you identify a resource that looks interesting but isn't held in your electronic or physical library, it might be worth checking with your library and/or subject librarian whether it is possible to borrow the resource or have a copy made through the interlibrary lending system. In the UK, it is possible to borrow many books from the British Library through such loans. If you are on a placement in or sponsored by an organisation, you may also have access to a corporate or organisational library.

The library and the internet are your most important knowledge resources. Although the resources on the internet have increased and improved dramatically, the best place to start your search for information is still your library, not only for books and journals, but also as a gateway to all kinds of printed and electronic information. The internet holds much more information than any library, as well as powerful search engines that will help you find it. However, you should rely on it mainly as a source of data rather than a definitive academic reference.

3.2.3   How do I find just the right amount of the right information?

As noted in **Section 3.1**, you will need to find information about your area of interest (what you will study), and to begin designing it (how you will study it). If you spend a little time developing a *search strategy*, you will spend less time searching and be more likely to find what you are looking for.

We will describe two search strategies that you can use to search the library and web. An ideal search starts broadly and quickly narrows down to a focused search for just the right amount of information. Even starting with what seems to be a focused research problem, you turn up many more leads than you could investigate. It's easy to waste hours or even days in the library or on the internet and come up with a lot of interesting information that doesn't help you to make progress in your research. As usual, you may need to consult more specialised resources to help you design and execute your search – see the **Additional resources** at the end of this chapter for some helpful guides.

If you can find the name of at least one key author in your topic area in a textbook or assigned reading, you can use a **snowball** or **egocentric** search. First, identify one or more key works – usually books or articles – by that author on the topic. By looking at the reference section, you can see what previous research that author has used – a sort of intellectual genealogy or 'family tree'.

Next, see what sources these authors refer to – the 'grandparents' of this work. Specialised citation databases such as the International Social Science Citation Index keep track of references and citations, and Google Scholar (www.scholar.google.com) does this too. For instance, if you look at the work on *Images of Projects* by Winter

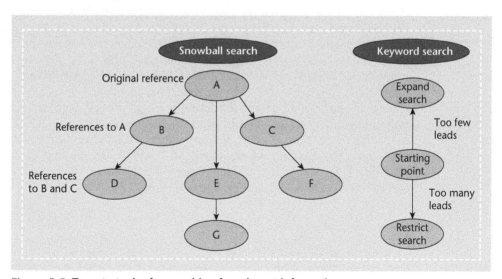

Figure 3.5 Two strategies for searching for relevant information

and Sczepanek, the 'grandparents' they cite include Burrell and Morgan (*Images of Organizations*), Edgar Schein, and Peter Checkland (*Soft Systems Methodology*). Keep this search strategy going until you have run out of likely looking authors to pursue. You can also see what authors have been influenced by your original author – the work's 'children' and 'grandchildren' so to speak. One problem with this strategy, though, is knowing when to stop. This requires some pragmatism in determining whether the sources identified provide something you are interested in pursuing.

You can also create a systematic search strategy around identifying a key concept, theoretical perspective, or other key idea that gives you focused **keywords** which you can use to search, such as 'organisational citizenship', 'behavioural finance theory' or 'ISO 14000'. You can use a **keyword search** of your library's **catalogue** and/or databases such as Business Source Premier to identify a starting set of authors and articles. We discuss keywords below in the context of searching more efficiently.

Searching more efficiently

Your results when you search your library's catalogue, electronic databases or the web will only be good as your search strategy, including the sources you are searching, the means you use to search them and the terms you use to define your search. If you don't know what you're looking for, or you don't use the right search terms, you will only get mediocre results – too many, too few, or not very useful results. You should put some effort into identifying the best keywords to describe the key concepts you are investigating, your keywords should be neither too broad (too many results) nor too narrow (too few results). Business Source Premier, an electronic publications database, includes a thesaurus that lets you see what terms you can use to search effectively. Be aware of variants, important synonyms or close alternatives for your keywords. For example, if you wanted to find out more about total quality management, relevant results might be listed under 'total quality management', 'total quality', or 'TQM'.

You will have a better search if you understand the particular **syntax** used by a database for entering your search terms and combining these search terms to increase the relevance of your results. Most search engines also give you the power to search by either one criterion at a time or two or more criteria using Boolean logic, in which the basic operators are 'true', 'false', 'not', 'and', and 'or'. You can increase the number of results by searching for, for example, 'Frederick W. Taylor' OR 'Scientific Management', which will show everything including either search phrase, or decrease the number of results by searching for 'Frederick W. Taylor' AND 'Scientific Management', which will return only those including both phrases. You can also use fields to narrow down or widen the search, for example restricting results about the psychological contract to only those books or articles with 'psychological contract' in the title: TI psychological contract. Don't forget that American and British spellings often differ, so that you may want to search for both 'organisational' and 'organizational' to identify works from both sides of the Atlantic. Some search engines allow wild cards such as '*' or '#', so 'organi#ational' would capture both spellings.

When is enough?

So when should you stop looking and move on? Is there some magic number of references that you need for your research project? (If there were, this book's authors would have a lot more hair left.) The right answer is: 'Enough to get the job done.'

At this point, you need to have done a robust enough search to enable you to finish defining your project and get ready to move on to designing it.

Ultimately, project examiners pay more attention to the quality of the sources that you use, and not the quantity. Try to identify a few high-quality academic articles closely related to your research topic, rather than everything that someone has written about your research topic. Inevitably, some of your literature finds will prove impenetrable, written using obscure phraseology and words designed to show the erudition of the author rather than achieving any sort of communication. You may find the books by Girden and Kabacoff (2011) and Locke et al. (2009) useful in understanding how to read academic research.

You will not have the time to read more than a few articles or books thoroughly, anyway, or skim read more than a few dozen. We will return to this theme later, but have in mind your core set of 5–10 articles that will provide your foundations.

3.3 What should I do with what I find?

No matter how many articles and books you accumulate, they won't help your research project unless you actually read them and get something out of them. How well you take notes will affect not only how useful the information you get out of your sources will be to your research project, but also whether you can give credit to these sources and avoid plagiarism. By beginning with your final project report in mind, you will save yourself valuable time at the end (when you don't want to be looking for that study that you vaguely remember …!).

3.3.1 How can I keep track of the contents of my readings?

Locke and his colleagues (2009) suggest that you are less likely to be overwhelmed by your reading if you take a systematic approach to recording the details of your reading and organising your records. They suggest that for each article you read, you should record the following information on a single sheet of paper:

1. **Citation** – the complete details of the study (authors, title, source details)
2. **The purpose of the study** – why did the authors do it and why did they think it was important?
3. **Theoretical background** – how does the study fit with the literature?
4. **Sample** – who did the authors study?
5. **Research setting** – where did the study take place?
6. **Method** – how were the data gathered?
7. **Data** – what data were gathered?
8. **Analysis** – how were the data analysed?
9. **Results** – what were the primary results of the analysis?
10. **Conclusions** – what did the authors say about the results?
11. **Limitations** – how should we interpret the study?
12. **Significance** – what did you learn from this study?

Keeping track of what you have found is critical to doing a good research project. Managing the sheer amount of paper or number of PDFs that accumulate in the course of a research project is a task in itself. If you file your materials in an organised way as you go along, it will be much easier to lay your hands on that critical paper in that three-foot high stack of paper at the last minute when you need inevitably need it, or find that PDF instead of having to search frantically in all of your folders for it.

Whatever your source material, you should:

- **record your sources**, not only for your **reference list** but also so that you can easily find them again.
- **record the information in your sources**, and make sure that you distinguish clearly between quoted (or narrowly paraphrased) material and summarised material.

You should carefully record information about web pages and other internet sources that you consult, especially those you find using a search engine, **metasearch engine** or portal, since there is no guarantee that a page you consult today will still be around tomorrow, even if you have bookmarked it. If you are making notes directly on tablets or computers, you can set up a database in Word or Excel that you can search or sort, and you can cut and paste your references directly into your paper. If you are doing a large research project, you may even want to use the reference manager built into your word processor (recent versions of Word give you the ability to manage citations and bibliographies directly), find an add-on to the word processor, or use a commercial reference management software such as EndNote (www.endnote.com), ReferenceManager (www.refman.com), or open-source software such as Zotero (www.zotero.org) for Mozilla Firefox, or Mendeley (www.mendeley.com).

Back in the day (!), researchers made handwritten notes on index cards. These days notetaking may use specialised software as noted above, or even a simple Excel spreadsheet. Whatever you use, it is this process of 'coding' – extracting relevant information for your study – that is the core skill. That you do it is much less important than how you do it.

3.3.2 What is a literature review and how do I prepare one?

In most research projects, you will need to write a literature review that summarises the past research on your topic, identifies any gaps and unknowns, and gives the foundation for your own research. A good literature review will:

- Demonstrate that you clearly understand the research topic
- Identify major studies related to the topic
- Identify the different points of view on the research topic
- Draw clear and appropriate conclusions from prior research
- Clearly state a research problem
- Propose a way to investigate the research problem
- Demonstrate the relevance and importance of the research problem (Hart 1998: 198).

As we noted at the beginning of this chapter, if you are taking a quantitative approach, you may be expected to do this at the beginning of your project; if you are doing a qualitative approach, most of this will be delayed until you are analysing your data. We will return to writing up the literature review in more detail in **Chapter 13** and **Chapter 14**.

Depending on your level of study and the size/importance of your project, you may also be expected to *critically* analyse the academic research on your topic in your **literature review**. 'Critically' means that you are analysing the strengths and weaknesses of this research, in particular any gaps or opportunities for contribution. This aspect constitutes one of the differences between research and journalism or consulting that we identified in **Chapter 1**: a good literature review does more than summarise other people's research.

If you are expected to write a formal literature review as part of your project report, you may find it worth consulting more detailed guides to searching the literature and writing a literature review. Chris Hart has written two excellent full-length books for the social sciences, *Doing a Literature Review* (1998) and *Doing a Literature Search* (2001). Other books are listed at the end of this chapter in **Additional resources**. Hart (1998) identifies three structures for writing up the literature review as *summative* – here is everything that we know about the research problem; *analytical* – here is the basis for investigating the research problem; and *formative* – here are the various points of view on the research problem.

Another way of organising your literature review is *conceptually*, structuring one section around each of your key concepts, as suggested by Creswell (2013). For example, if you are examining the relationship between customer satisfaction and the steps that organisations take to recover from service failures, you might write a section on the literature on customer satisfaction, one on service failure and another on service recovery. You would then need a final section that explains the relationship between failure/recovery and customer satisfaction, which acts as a 'hook' to set up your own research project.

Or you can organise your literature review *thematically*, around the themes that emerge across various researchers who have studied your issue, or subsets of those researchers, as you read the literature. What common ideas or categories emerge? For example, Golhar and Stamm (1991) identify three key themes in the just-in-time (JIT) literature as JIT's role in global productivity, differences between JIT and other systems such as manufacturing resource planning (MRP) and optimised production technology (OPT), and the practices associated with JIT, and classify the articles they read into one of these three key themes.

Lastly, you may organise your literature review *temporally*. We have found this helpful when wanting to demonstrate the development of a particular subject area. For instance, if you were interested in leadership, it could useful to consider how the *traits* view of the early 20th century gave way to the *situational* approaches of the 1970s, and to the notion of *the incomplete leader* in the early 2000s.

You may find it helpful to look at some literature reviews, especially if you can find one or more that have been published in your topic area. Blackwell's *International Journal of Management Reviews* specialises in management reviews; the well-established *Journal of Economic Literature* does the same for economics. There are also some useful disciplinary reviews, such as *Research in Organizational Behavior*. You should also search your electronic publications database for literature reviews that have been published as stand-alone articles. For example, Kate found a number of literature reviews on 'work-life balance' when she was working on that area recently.

If the literature review is either the core of your research project (with minimal empirical work) or if you find a particularly large literature exists on your topic, then the approach of **systematic literature review** may be appropriate. Should this be worth exploring, the example of Geraldi and his colleagues (Geraldi et al. 2011) is included in the reference list at the end of this chapter.

When you write your literature review, you need to know how to use correctly the material you have found. Giving appropriate credit when you use someone else's words or ideas is a crucial research skill. You need to learn the principles of **citation** and referencing, so that you can refer to other people's research when you are writing. This will help you to avoid **plagiarism**, which is intellectual property theft and taken seriously in academic institutions. You should also avoid violating copyright law by understanding the limits to the fair use of other people's published and unpublished information, including web resources. We will provide guidance on how to use these words and data in future chapters, particularly **Chapter 8** on research ethics and **Chapter 13**, on writing up your research report.

Summary

Being able to identify, find and make use of information from the library, internet and other knowledge resources in your research is a key skill and one that will affect the quality of your research project. Understanding how to define and set up searches is a useful skill.

The internet gives you global access to information, but the quantity and variable quality of information can create problems. Global search engines and other search engines, along with subject-specific portals, can help you to deal with the size and complexity of the web.

Your physical library contains books, periodicals and multimedia resources that will help you investigate the academic research on your research problem and the available knowledge about your research setting. **Virtual library** resources provide electronic access to even more resources, including financial and economic databases and periodicals. Your librarian can also be a valuable resource in helping you to refine your search and telling you about extended library services such as interlibrary loans and access to other academic and **specialist libraries**.

Once you have found relevant information, you need to manage and use it. A literature review covers the theories, frameworks, concepts and research methods employed by other researchers investigating the same or relevant research problems. You also need information about your research setting.

Answers to key questions

Where and how do I find information to develop my research project?

- Your physical and virtual library should give you access to books and periodicals that tell you what previous research has been done on your research problem.
- Textbooks, monographs, edited books, conference proceedings, reference books and periodicals (especially academic journals and annuals) which report previous research are your main sources.

- You can use the internet to search for additional information, such as working papers and reports.

What methods for collecting and analysing data have other researchers used?

- You can collect information on how researchers have collected and analysed data in previous research on your research problem.
- See if there are any different methods being applied in related research problems.
- You can consult the research methods literature itself – specialist books, journals and articles on research methods, including general research guides and specific technical guides.

How do I find more information about my research setting and sample?

- Business and trade publications, including newspapers and magazines.
- Books and reports on specific areas, including marketing reports from organisations such as Mintel, and financial databases such as AMADEUS and FAME.
- The web may be especially useful in searching for information about your research setting, since many businesses, organisations and so on have web pages.

How do I assess the relevance and quality of business and management research?

- Primary research – information you collect yourself from people and/or organisations.
- Secondary research – information you collect from already published sources.
- The internet can be used to identify and acquire information about your research project and research setting.

How do I use this information?

- Good notes will help you to make sense of the information.
- Giving other researchers appropriate credit for their words and ideas is a key skill here.

What is a literature review and how do I write one?

- Writing a literature review will help you make sense of what previous researchers have done and found, help you to develop a research design and give you a head start on writing your project report.

 ## References

Blanchard, K. and Johnson, S. 1982. *The One Minute Manager*. New York: Morrow Books.

Collins, James C. 2003. *From Good to Great: Why Some Companies Make the Leap and Others Don't*. London: William Collins.

Creswell, John W. 2013. *Research Design: Qualitative, Quantitative, and Mixed Methods Approaches*, 4th edn. Thousand Oaks, CA: Sage.

Geraldi, J., Maylor, H. and Williams, T. 2011. Now let's make it really complex (complicated): A systematic review of the complexities of projects, *International Journal of Operations and Production Management*, 31(9): 966–90.

Gill, John and Johnson, Phil 2010. *Research Methods for Managers*, 4th edn. London: Sage.

Girden, Ellen R. and Kabacoff, Robert 2011. *Evaluating Research Articles from Start to Finish*, 3rd edn. Thousand Oaks, CA: Sage.

Golhar, Damodar Y. and Stamm, Carol Lee 1991. The just-in-time philosophy: A literature review, *International Journal of Production Research*, 29(4): 657–76.

Hart, Chris 1998. *Doing a Literature Review: Releasing the Social Science Research Imagination*. London: Sage.

Hart, Chris 2001. *Doing a Literature Search: A Comprehensive Guide for the Social Sciences*. London: Sage.

Johnson, S. 2003. *Who Moved My Cheese?* New York: Andrews McMeel.

Locke, Lawrence F., Silverman, Stephen J. and Spirduso, Waneen W. 2009. *Reading and Understanding Research*, 2nd edn. Thousand Oaks, CA: Sage.

O'Leary, Z. 2013. *The Essential Guide to Doing Research*, 2nd edn. London: Sage.

Peters, T. and Waterman, R.H. 2004. *In Search of Excellence: Lessons From America's Best-run Companies*. New York: Profile Business.

Additional resources

Baker, Michael J. 2000. Writing a literature review, *Marketing Review*, 1(2): 219–47.

Booth, Wayne C., Colomb, Gregory G., and Williams, Joseph M. 2008. *The Craft of Research*, 3rd edn. Chicago, IL: University of Chicago Press.

Collis, Jill and Hussey, Roger 2013. *Business Research*, 4th edn. Basingstoke: Palgrave Macmillan.

Davis, Murray S. 1971. That's interesting! Towards a phenomenology of sociology and a sociology of phenomenology, *Philosophy of Social Science*, 1: 309–44.

Delamont, Sara, Atkinson, Paul and Parry, Odette. 2004. *Supervising the Doctorate*. Maidenhead: Open University Press.

Dunleavy, Patrick 2003. *Authoring a PhD: How to Plan, Draft, Write and Finish a Doctoral Thesis or Dissertation*. Basingstoke: Palgrave Macmillan.

Easterby-Smith, Mark, Thorpe, Richard and Lowe, Andy 2012. *Management Research: An Introduction*, 4th edn. London: Sage.

Fisher, D. and Hanstock, T. 1998. *Citing References*. Oxford: Blackwell.

O'Dochartaigh, N. 2001. *The Internet Research Handbook*. London: Sage.

Oxford University Press 2013. *The Oxford Style Manual*. Oxford: Oxford University Press.

Ridley, Diana 2012. *The Literature Review: A Step-by-Step Guide for Students (SAGE Study Skills Series)*, 2nd edn. SAGE Publications Ltd.

Rugg, Gordon and Petre, Marian 2010. *The Unwritten Rules of PhD Research*, 2nd edn. Maidenhead: Open University Press.

Saunders, Mark, Lewis, Phillip and Thornhill, Adrian 2012. *Research Methods for Business Students*, 6th edn. Harlow: Financial Times/Prentice Hall.

Turabian, Kate L. 1996. *A Manual for Writers of Term Papers, Theses and Dissertations*, 6th edn. Chicago: University of Chicago Press.

University of Chicago 2003. *The Chicago Manual of Style: For Authors, Editors and Copywriters*, 15th edn. Chicago: University of Chicago Press.

Resources on copyright and plagiarism

Lyons, P. (ed.) 1998. *JISC/TLTP Copyright Guidelines*. JISC and TLTP.

Oppenheim, C., Phillips, C. and Wall, R.A. *The Aslib Guide to Copyright*. London: Aslib

Web documents

The Copyright Licensing Agency - www.cla.co.uk – for information on the CLA, copyright, CLA licences, and an excellent directory of copyright organisations
Her Majesty's Stationery Office – www.hmso.gov.uk – information on crown and parliamentary copyright, the copyright unit, electronic texts of statutory instruments (SI), and publishing/copyright guidance notes
World Intellectual Property Organisation (WIPO) – www.wipo.int – for information on international copyright treaties

Key terms

academic journals, 82
catalogue, 88
citation, 92
conceptual framework, 79
copyright, 73
copyright depository library, 86
database, 85
dissertations, 84
double-blind review, 84
edited volume, 84
evidence, 78
keywords, 88
keyword search, 88
literature, 72
literature review, 74, 91
literature search, 73
magazines, 83
managerial journals, 83

metasearch engine, 90
monograph, 84
newspapers, 83
peer review, 84
periodicals, 82
plagiarism, 92
reference books, 84
reference list, 90
references, 77
research setting, 78
snowball (egocentric) search, 87
specialist libraries, 92
subject librarian, 86
syntax, 88
systematic literature review, 92
textbooks, 84
theses, 84
virtual library, 92

Discussion questions

1. Should you consult the internet or the library first to find out more about the theoretical aspects of your research topic?
2. Can you believe everything you read on the internet?
3. Why is the process of peer review considered so important in scholarly publishing?
4. 'If I am trying to solve a practical problem, reviewing the literature is irrelevant.' Discuss.
5. In quantitative research, is it OK to do your literature review after you've collected and analysed your data?
6. 'A good literature review is one that describes everything ever written on my topic.' Yes or no?
7. Why is knowing how to use citations and references an essential skill for researchers?
8. Is ignorance of your university's rules about plagiarism an adequate defence if you are caught?
9. Is plagiarism a 'victimless crime'?
10. Is anything on the internet 'fair game' as far as research materials go?

Workshop 1

Task

Using the topic area that you identified in Chapter 2 workshop, carry out a basic literature search. You should:

1. Identify the subject area(s) relevant to your topic, and note the main texts for the subject area(s).
2. Check in your library and at online bookstores for specialist books on the area.
3. Carry out a search of newspapers and business periodicals.
4. Identify keywords and do an internet search.
5. Use your library online journal article service to identify potentially relevant articles.
6. Browse through relevant journals in hard copy in your library to identify current views of this general area.
7. Classify the type of publications that you have found using the classifications of books and periodicals from this chapter.
8. Prepare a mind map of the topic area

Workshop 2

Making sense of the literature – avoiding overload

Task

Now you've collected a sizeable stack of printed-out articles or their equivalent in saved PDFs that you need to read for your research project. How do you best make sense of them? We suggest that you use a multi-pass strategy rather than reading through each article word-by-word and taking copious notes on each one.

Step 1. Sorting

Read carefully through the abstract of each article that you've collected, and decide how closely it fits with what you know at the moment about your research topic and proposed research design. After you have read each abstract, triage it into one of the three following groups:

Group 1. 'The Good'. Immediately relevant and likely to be important.

Group 2. 'The Bad'. Not sure how it's likely to be relevant.

Group 3. 'The Maybes'. Could be useful, but not sure how or where.

Step 2. Winnowing

Focus on the articles that you've classified into Group 1. Read carefully through the introduction to each article (in many articles, this is helpfully given the heading 'Introduction', but otherwise it's usually the first section in the main body of the text). We suggest that you use the 'active reading' technique described in the next section, instead of taking separate notes or no notes at all. If you're using PDFs rather than printed-out copies, you may be able to annotate the PDFs

▶

directly if you're using suitable software. If you have many articles in this pile, you should triage them again ... if you can identify five or so articles that you think are really good examples of how to do research on your topic, this is ideal.

Step 3. Detailed reading

We suggest that you now read through your 'core' articles in depth. You've already read through the abstract and introduction once, but read through those two sections and the theoretical background carefully again, using active reading. Go back and forth between each article and your ideas about research topic, problem, questions, conceptual framework, and design. Also skim the research methods, findings and discussion sections (these may have different names), and then read the final section (usually 'Conclusions') carefully, as it will often have suggestions for 'future research'.

Techniques such as mind mapping, Venn diagrams, Post-it notes, etc. are often useful here for brainstorming the relationship between and across articles.

You may find that once you've read through your core articles, you still have gaps. Don't worry! This is where you can go back to those articles that didn't make the core set, and look for the missing pieces, or go back to the literature search and perform a more detailed search for those bits (e.g. a concept that you want to investigate but isn't covered in your core articles).

Active reading

Often the study habits that are useful in one context (e.g. A-levels or bachelor's degree study) aren't those that are most effective in other contexts (research degrees, master's or doctoral level modules).

If you're used to going through an assigned reading and writing down whatever seems like it might be relevant in what you read, you will quickly find yourself either spending way too much time reading, or reading too little.

Study skills experts describe the process of purposefully reading and taking the right notes as 'active reading'. You can think of it as having a conversation with the author(s) through the medium of the article or book, as well as highlighting the key elements and recording your thoughts as you go along.

Key aspects of active reading include understanding the purpose for which you are reading a given text:

1. Are you trying to get a broad overview quickly (covered in the previous section)? or
2. Are you trying to fill a detailed gap?

Active reading is much like the process of 'coding' qualitative data, which we will cover in Chapter 12. The key idea of active reading is that you mark up the reading while you read it, rather than taking notes. Things that you may want to mark include:

a. Definitions, e.g. of key theories and concepts (you can circle the key phrase and underline the definition – Kate even has a specific symbol /// that she uses for definitions);

b. Knowledge claims, e.g. why the research is important and interesting;

c. Weak or missing links in the argument;

Workshop 2 cont'd

d. Critiques of the material;

e. Aspects of the reading that you don't understand;

f. Notes to yourself to follow up, e.g. interesting-looking readings;

g. Links across the material you are reading, e.g. to the article you just read.

Note that active reading is not at all the same as simply 'underlining passages' or 'using highlighters' … active reading requires you to engage with the reading in an active fashion by evaluating key or novel points, taking notes and asking mental questions that make sense of the information as you go along.

Step 4: Summarising what you've read

After you've finished reading the key parts of an article (or book chapter) using the active reading technique we've outlined above, it's a good idea to put it aside for half an hour and then come back and summarise it.

A useful way of summarising an article is on no more than one page using a mind map, spider diagram, judges' notes or Cornell notes.

A *mind map*, as we've seen earlier in this book, starts with a central concept or questions and then links subsidiary concepts, questions or other points to it, spiralling out until all points have been connected.

A spider diagram does the same, except it doesn't necessarily have a (or a single) central 'bubble'.

Rather than visually, judges' notes or Cornell notes are two ways of summarising critically, in words:

- For judges' notes, you divide your page into two. Just as a judge would do in listening to evidence in a trial, you divide what you have read into arguments 'for' a particular position and their supporting evidence, and arguments 'against' that position, and their supporting evidence.

- In Cornell notes, on the other hand, you divide your page into three. The main part of the page is devoted conventionally to your notes on the article. In the second part of the page, you make active notes on this information. At the bottom of the page, you leave space for a brief (one or two sentence) summary of the article.

No matter which method you use out of these four for summarising your reading, make sure that you label it with enough detail so that several months from now you'll be able to connect the notes with the article or other source!

Notes

1. See a recent Association of Business Schools list at https://charteredabs. org/academic-journal-guide-2015/ (accessed 2 August 2016) and a recent *Financial Times* list at www.ft.com/cms/s/2/3405a512-5cbb-11e1-8f1f-00144feabdc0.html#axzz4GAUJqLrQ (accessed 2 August 2016).

2. https://en.wikipedia.org/wiki/Pacific_Northwest_tree_octopus (accessed 2 August 2016).

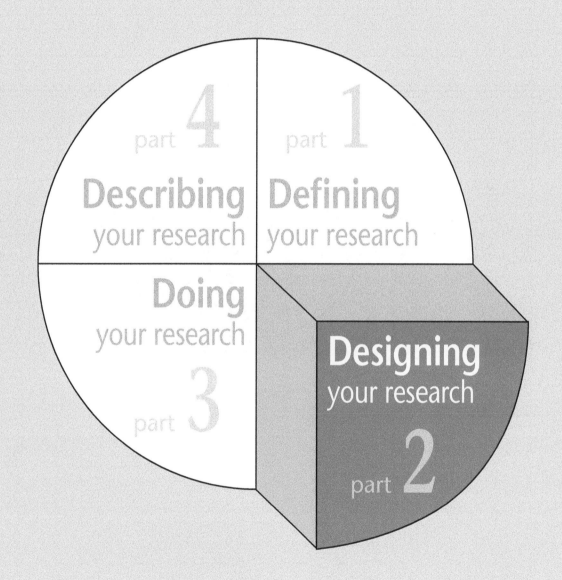

part 4

Describing
your research

part 1

Defining
your research

Doing
your research

part 3

Designing
your research

part 2

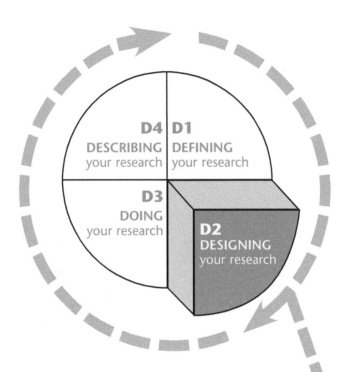

Relevant chapters
13 How do I write up my report?
14 What do I do now?

Key challenges
- Making sense of your findings
- Presenting your research to others
- Reflecting and learning from your research

4

Relevant chapters
1 What is research?
2 What should I study?
3 How do I find information?

Key challenges
- Understanding what academic research is
- Generating and clarifying ideas
- Using sources of information

1

D4
DESCRIBING your research

D1
DEFINING your research

D3
DOING your research

D2
DESIGNING your research

Relevant chapters
9   How do I do field research?
10 What do my quantitative data mean(1)?
11 What do my quantitative data mean(2)?
12 What do my qualitative data mean?

Key challenges
- Practical considerations in doing research
- Describing data using simple statistics
- Carrying out statistical tests
- Interpreting words and actions

3

Relevant chapters
4 What is my research approach?
5 How do I do quantitative research?
6 How do I do qualitative research?
7 How do I do case study research?
8 How do I make sure my research is ethical?

Key challenges
- Choosing a research approach
- Choosing a research design
- Collecting data using quantitative methods
- Collecting data using qualitative methods
- Integrating quantitative and qualitative methods

2

4
chapter

What is my research approach?
Linking research philosophy to research design

 Key questions

- What is meant by research philosophy?
- What is a research approach?
- What are the possible research approaches?
- What are the assumptions underlying each research approach?
- What logic guides how research questions are answered?

 Learning outcomes

At the end of this chapter, you should be able to:

- Describe the relevance of research philosophy to business and management research
- Explain how research philosophy enables us to understand the principles underlying a consistent research approach
- Explain and justify the research design associated with your approach

Contents

Introduction

Philosophy and football

Imagine that you are watching an important international football game. In the last minute of the game, your team's shot at goal rebounds off the underside of the bar (the horizontal strut over the goal) before being cleared by the goalkeeper. The referee decides it is not a goal and orders play to continue. TV replays of the incident subsequently show that the ball had crossed the goal-line, and therefore it should have been a goal.

We can see that there are two equally valid ways of answering whether it was a goal:

- *Objectively* – as presented by multiple images from TV cameras, it was a goal, but...
- *Subjectively* – the referee believed the ball had not crossed the line. This wasn't just a random decision – he did have help from another match official who concurred. As far as that particular match is concerned, this answer counted.

Was this a goal? What is the 'truth' of this incident? Who gets to decide?[1] Both objective and subjective perspectives are equally important ways of knowing things about the world, and each has its role to play in business and management research. For the purposes of research, understanding this distinction between objective and subjective is crucial to how we gather and interpret evidence. Even though two researchers may use the same methods and collect the same data, their interpretation of that data – as shown in the example above – may be completely at odds, yet each interpretation may be equally valid. Furthermore, each has its benefits and limitations.

Research philosophy explains the assumptions that underlie any particular research approach. A research approach describes how you will answer your research questions. In this chapter, we expand on the role of research approach and how it leads to the next stage of your research process – your research design. The research design is the specific techniques or methods you will use to gather, analyse and interpret data.

In **Section 4.1**, we introduce the concept of research philosophy and describe the subjective and objective philosophical positions. We show how these underpin a wide range of research choices. We believe that having some acquaintance with research philosophy will improve your research project. First, understanding these two positions – objective and subjective – will help you to understand why there are so many different ways to do business and management research. This understanding will help you to make better choices about your selection of **research methods**, make them in a justifiable way, and recognise the implications of these choices. If you are using this book to help you to conduct a research project, these choices will affect your research process from this point forward and, as a result, will guide your path through the rest of this book.

In **Section 4.2**, we explain how each position influences the research approach, the timing and sequence of your research tasks, especially the use of theory and the relationship between theory and data in the research process. Each research approach is linked with a different 'theory' of research which influences what research questions you can ask, what methods you can use and what data you can collect.

In **Section 4.3**, we explore the broader implications of each research approach, which include not only the process of your research project but also its content. Understanding the linkage between research philosophy and research approach will help you to assess other people's research, particularly the business and management research you find in your literature search. Your critical understanding will include its strengths and limitations – one key part of the *critique* discussed in **Chapter 3**.

Although this chapter is the only one that focuses on research philosophy, the issues that it introduces will resonate through the rest of this book. **Chapters 5, 10 and 11** will focus on research methods associated with the objective position, while **Chapters 6, 7 and 12** will focus on research methods associated with the subjective position. Both approaches have implications for how you work inside an organisation, as we discuss in **Chapter 9**. How you interpret and report your research, discussed in **Chapter 13**, will depend on which position you choose.

Figure 4.1 shows how the focus in this chapter – research philosophy, research approach and research design – links to the dimensions of topic choice that we have described in previous chapters. We showed the topic choice to comprise the dimensions of theme, context/setting, the discipline/sub-discipline, the problem of interest and the social group to be studied. As this figure shows, underpinning any investigation is your research philosophy and your research approach. We think of it as an iterative relationship between the research approach, research design and the topic dimensions – they have to become aligned for your study to work. Before we explore this alignment further, we will consider the nature of the research approach, research design and philosophical perspective that underpins these.

Before you embark on this chapter, please do bear in mind that this is an overview of a very large and often contentious area. It is neither *the* detailed nor *the* definitive

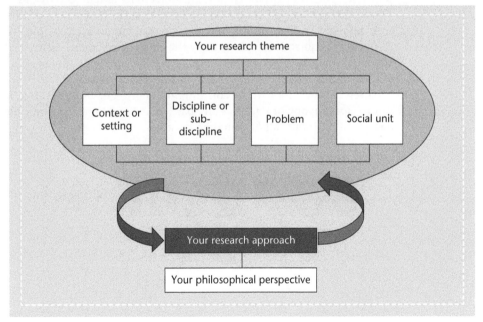

Figure 4.1 Positioning your research

road map. We hope that it provides the opening for a conversation for you about research in general and your research approach in particular.

4.1 What is research philosophy?

Because **research philosophy** explains the assumptions that underlie any particular research approach, we say that it 'describes a theory of research'. These underlying assumptions can be summarised as the two components of research philosophy:

- **ontology**: what is out there to know, the 'nature of reality' and in particular whether it exists independent of the observer.
- **epistemology**: what we can know about it or 'nature of knowledge', how we can create knowledge of reality.

Figure 4.2 shows how research philosophy is linked to your research project. At an abstract level your research philosophy (your position with respect to ontology and epistemology) is reflected in your research approach, which then links to your research design – how you collect and analyse data – and then more concretely into your sources of evidence. *Consistency* between the elements is a critical determinant of the quality of research projects.

How does research philosophy link to research approach?

Figure 4.3 shows that researchers can take a range of ontological and epistemological positions. The two extremes represent subjectivity and objectivity, as described above. Those at the objective extreme view believe that the best way to conduct research is as if **social reality** exists and that research can present an accurate picture of that reality. Those at the subjective extreme deny the existence of social reality and, therefore, for them it is not possible to make a complete and accurate picture of it. The two extremes are essentially *stereotypes* and most business and management researchers position themselves somewhere in the continuum in between. Our intention in this chapter is not to label anyone or reinforce any particular stereotype, but to enable description of a range of positions, all of which have values and limitations for your research.

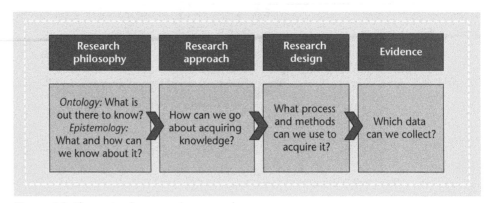

Figure 4.2 Elements of a research approach

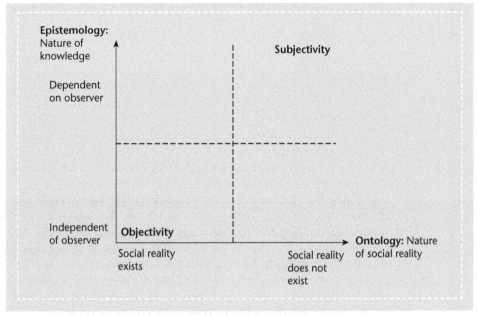

Figure 4.3 Epistemology, ontology, objectivity and subjectivity

The difference between an objective and a subjective perspective is illustrated in the following story as Martina recounts.

> Somebody was saying to Picasso that he ought to make pictures of things the way they are – objective pictures. Picasso mumbled he wasn't quite sure what that would be. The person challenging him produced a photograph of his wife from his wallet and said, 'There, you see, that is a picture of how she really is.' Picasso looked at it and said, 'She is rather small, isn't she? And flat.'
>
> (Ralston 2010: 35)

If you position yourself at the **objective** extreme, you might reasonably treat **social objects** (e.g. organisations, jobs, work roles) as being just as 'real' as physical objects, such as rocks, cars and buildings. However, rocks can be argued to have an objective reality independent of researchers and their understanding; even if you didn't know what a rock was, you would probably recognise it as real if you stubbed your toe on it. Researchers who study physical objects usually find that an objective position suits what they want to research and how they want to research it – they deal with what is physically real and do not consider anything that does not fit in with this 'reality'. As a result, an objective position is usually associated with collecting evidence from observations or measurements.

If you position yourself at the **subjective** extreme, you might recognise that although the person with the work role of 'manager' is a real person, the concept of manager isn't a 'natural' concept – it didn't occur in nature until humans invented it. We say that the idea of a manager has been **socially constructed** – it isn't a physical or tangible idea. The role of the manager has evolved over centuries and different people have different ideas about what a manager is/does, depending, for example, on their national culture, the point in time they are considering and their experience of people who have borne the title 'manager'. Many social researchers argue, therefore, that even though we treat social concepts such as 'manager' or 'organisations' as real in everyday life, it is inappropriate to treat them as objective in the same way that a geologist would a rock. A more subjective position may therefore be more appropriate for studying many business and management phenomena since human behaviour, whether at the level of the individual or the social system, differs significantly from the behaviour of natural objects.

The subjective position accepts that reality is constructed by patterns of behaviour, for instance, with these interpreted by the view of the observer. As a result, someone who adopts this position will generally focus on what people, or whatever social unit they are studying, perceive as 'the truth' about the world.

Our discussion of research philosophy so far has centred on the distinction between two extremes (subjective or objective). Between these extremes there exist many more options for the researcher. Each of these might be considered a 'School of Philosophy' – a particular position that a group of researchers adopts. They are included here in **Table 4.1** with very brief descriptions of how they fit with the philosophies and approaches contained in this chapter in case you come across them in the literature or want to do further reading. Many examples of specialist sources are located in the **Additional resources** at the end of this chapter.

Table 4.1   Schools of Philosophy

School	Research philosophy	Description
Radical Constructivism	Subjective	Knowledge is actively created by the researcher, who tries to find research solutions that fit reality.
Constructivism	Subjective	Focuses on the collective construction of social phenomena.
Interpretivism	Subjective	The goal of research is not to explain human behaviour, but to understand it. A fairly mainstream epistemology for business and management researchers.
Critical realism	Subjective and objective	Acknowledges that management researchers cannot establish a cause-effect relationship between two entities, but they can study the world 'as if' they can – the understanding of that causality can be 'good enough', reconciling both subjective and objective perspectives but recognising the limitations of each.
Realism	Objective	We cannot directly get a perfect model or view of the world, so any model we create is presumed to be good enough until it can be improved by further observation or test. Becoming much more popular.
Positivism	Objective	Business and management phenomena behave as physical systems would and can therefore be understood by working out sets of 'laws'.

In our experience, however, few business and management undergraduate or taught master's projects need go further in exploring research philosophy, especially ontology and epistemology, than we go in this chapter. Indeed, should you wish to go further, we strongly recommend that this is agreed with your supervisor and be part of the requirements of your project. Your philosophical perspective reflects deeper issues about research and your own personal beliefs and values. Unfortunately, there isn't general agreement in the research literature on where these elements fit into any hierarchy, or even what elements belong in the hierarchy (and indeed some deny the existence of any hierarchy!), so the best we can do is *try* to be consistent in our writing.

4.2 What is a research approach?

You need to identify or select your **research approach** before you go any further in your research process. Although you might select any approach to study a given research topic, you might not be able to ask the same research questions. Your research approach will influence how you answer these questions:

- **What research questions can I ask?** – should I focus on *'what'*, *'how much'*, *'why'* or *'how'*?
- **What methods or techniques will I use to collect my data** – methods taken from natural science or social science?
- **What type of data will I be collecting?** – quantitative or qualitative data?
- **How will I analyse my data?** – statistical or thematic analysis?

You do not necessarily need to understand research philosophy to answer these questions. Indeed, if you see your research project as a one-off, or if you are working to a narrowly defined project brief, you can plan your research pragmatically. You may not need to address these questions in your research project, but you should understand whether the decisions you make in the rest of the research process are consistent with your research questions. In the bigger picture, the approach you take will affect what you study, how you study it and why you study it. Understanding research approaches will also help you to read and understand the business and management literature.

As we move from left to right in **Figure 4.2**, we move from your philosophical position (subjective or objective) and now start to consider its linked research approaches – quantitative and qualitative. The **quantitative approach** is influenced by the **logic of research** in the natural sciences and is associated with research projects that focus on quantitative data. It was exemplified in **Chapter 1** by Frederick W. Taylor and the Hawthorne researchers. The **qualitative approach** is influenced by the logic of the social sciences and is associated with research projects that focus on non-quantitative – or qualitative – data. It was exemplified in **Chapter 1** by William Foote Whyte.

We will use the example in **Student research in action 4.1** to explore the quantitative and qualitative approaches to gathering and interpreting research evidence. The rest of the chapter will then detail the approach that underpins any research and examine the associated benefits and limitations.

Student research in action 4.1(a)

IDENTIFY DIFFERENT WAYS TO APPROACH YOUR RESEARCH PROBLEM

A toiletries manufacturer sponsored an undergraduate student project team to find out why sales of their male grooming products had the highest market share among 14–16 year olds but only a miniscule share among 18–22 year olds. The company had already commissioned extensive consumer marketing research that gave it specific details about product usage. The company wanted some more in-depth information before it invested in a revised advertising campaign.

The students started by discussing how they might find out more about this problem. The company could provide the students with access to point-of-sale data from supermarkets, pharmacies and other retail outlets, but it left the students free to choose how to carry out their research.

 Student research in action 4.1(b)

CONSIDER HOW YOU MIGHT COLLECT AND ANALYSE DATA

The students first considered using market research to find out more about attitudes towards the brand among university students. Whilst they did not have the resources to send out an army of market researchers with clipboards or large databases of email address lists to ask male university students a series of questions, they could use focus groups and questionnaires to find out what grooming products the men used and why they used those particular products. They were certain to be able to get enough students to complete the questionnaires to carry out statistical analysis of the questionnaire results. The focus groups would help them understand what questions to ask on the questionnaires.

This type of research, gathering data by asking questions that you have decided in advance, is consistent with what we will describe as '*the objective view and quantitative approach to business and management research*'. Questionnaires, which we will discuss in detail in **Chapter 5**, are a popular method for gathering data that answer specific, well-defined questions, whose answers can be expressed as numbers for statistical analysis. If they chose this approach, the students would need to make sure that they constructed their surveys carefully, selected a representative sample of students, and collected enough data for statistical analysis to be valid. Researchers who prefer this objective and quantitative approach tend to understand what the numbers mean and can take action based on them, for example to advise the company how it could reverse the drop among older consumers by targeting its marketing to likely buyers.

Student research in action 4.1(c)

CONSIDER ALTERNATIVE WAYS TO COLLECT AND ANALYSE DATA

On reflection, however, the students realised that the interesting question for them was not 'who' purchased (or didn't purchase) the company's products, but 'why' the market share changed so emphatically with age group. They decided to study the role that grooming products played in the life of male students – something that market research and POS (point-of-sale) figures could not reveal. They used video diaries, collages and other creative research techniques to find out more about what was going on. This focused their attention on the question of 'what influences what products male university students purchase?', rather than 'who purchases them?' and 'how much do they purchase?'

The use of these video diaries, collages and other creative techniques resulted in data that were mainly impressions, words and pictures, rather than numbers. As you will see in **Chapter 6**, direct observation is a popular way of gathering data that answer questions that cannot be specified in advance and are better represented as words than numbers. To make sense of these data, the students needed to find patterns of common meanings and interpret them as themes, rather than analysing them statistically. This approach to research, gathering data to answer questions that are themselves suggested by the data, is consistent with *'the subjective view and qualitative approach to business and management research.'*

Student research in action 4.1(c) shows how an awareness of the differences between these two approaches led the student project team to radically redefine their project brief and to go on to do an outstanding project, as we show below. It also demonstrates how the research approach influences the choice of research design and the interplay between this and your research questions.

Student research in action 4.1(d)

THE CONTRIBUTION FROM TAKING AN ALTERNATIVE RESEARCH APPROACH

At the end of the project, the students had made some fascinating and revealing findings about male university students and their relationship to male grooming products, including the significant amount of time most male students spent in front of the mirror getting their look just right, the need to have the 'right labels' in their rooms or bathrooms and the widespread sniffing and even borrowing of products among friends. These findings helped the company to understand that the popularity of its products among 14–16 year olds actually created the sales gap when men got to university, in particular when their mothers were no longer buying their toiletries and they made their own choices.

By choosing between quantitative and qualitative approaches, the students were choosing between measuring behaviours and finding meanings associated with those behaviours. Because *measurement* and *meaning* are different aspects of social behaviour, the quantitative and qualitative approaches are (on the whole) associated with different research designs and methods. These are usually employed in separate research designs, although we will discuss case study designs in **Chapter 7** as an approach that often combines the two.

Table 4.2 now contrasts the quantitative and qualitative research approaches, and identifies some of the key characteristics of each approach. The rest of this section will then explore in more detail the characteristics of each approach.

As shown in **Figure 4.2**, your choice of research approach leads to options for your research design. These comprise the process or methodology, and methods for acquiring knowledge. *Methodologies* describe how to translate the research philosophy into a way of studying the world. If research philosophy concerns the 'study of study', then **research methodology** concerns the 'study of how to study'. *Methods* comprise specific techniques and tools, the physical or electronic artefacts associated with particular methods, for example a web survey, a questionnaire or an interview schedule. On the right of **Figure 4.2**, we have evidence – data and theory building or theory testing. Methodologies, designs, methods, data and analysis are the subject of **Section 4.3**.

Table 4.2   Contrasting qualitative and quantitative approaches

Characteristic	Quantitative approach	Qualitative approach
Philosophical position	Predominantly objective	Predominantly subjective
Logic	Natural sciences – the scientific method	Social sciences – the ethnographic method
Examples	F.W. Taylor; Hawthorne studies	Street corner society
Research questions	What, how much, who?	Why, how?
Research process	Predominantly linear sequential, ordered	Predominantly iterative, overlapping
Theory and data	Deductive – data test theory	Inductive – data generate or build theory
Research purpose	Verification, generalising	Discovery, exploration

4.2.1   Research questions

Student research in action 4.1 demonstrated the linkage between research question and research approach. On their first attempt, the students focused on the questions of 'what is happening?', 'how much do sales fall off in the 18–22 age group compared to the 14–16 group?' and 'who purchased (or not) the company's products?' These questions were consistent with their quantitative research approach, but didn't address the question that had been posed to them – '*to find out **why** sales of their male grooming products…*' 'Why' is unlikely to be discovered from using a quantitative approach. This requires a process of discovery or exploration, and is entirely consistent with a qualitative approach.

It is one of the most basic checks that you can make of your intended research approach – to compare your research question with your research approach. In most cases, we find:

- If your question starts with a '*why*' or '*how*' then a qualitative approach is most likely to be suitable.
- If your question starts with a '*what*', '*how much,*' or '*who*', a quantitative approach is most likely to be suitable.

4.2.2   Research process

Whether you choose a qualitative or quantitative approach will have a major influence on your research process. These two approaches have 'alternative starting and concluding points, [and] different steps between these points' (Blaikie 2000: 25).

By choosing the qualitative approach, the students let the precise nature of the observations of male student behaviour and even some of the questions emerge as they were doing their research. In this case, the students decided they needed to closely observe how male students actually used grooming products 'in the wild', so that they could build up a picture of these behaviours rather than trying to identify all the questions and data they would need in advance. They needed some starting point to help them to decide where to look and what to look for, but they didn't do a detailed literature review until they started making sense of the materials they had collected. The data themselves – video images, collages and verbal impressions – are different from survey responses. As you can see, this represents a more *unstructured* approach to doing research. Each stage of the study depended on what emerged from the data they had collected – in particular by analysing the themes they saw.

With the quantitative approach, by contrast, you develop a complete research plan before you start to collect data. If the students in our research in action example had chosen this approach, they would decide exactly what data they wanted to collect to find what was happening with the brand and its customers. Before they started collecting data, they would specify in precise detail what questions they needed to ask to collect those data, so that they could develop a standardised questionnaire to give to a large number of male students. This approach often requires a fairly extensive literature review, in order to make sure that you ask the right questions. By deciding on the questions in advance, you can limit the responses to a simple set of responses or even just numbers (for example 'What hair products do you currently buy?', 'How frequently do you buy them?'). These answers can be quickly transcribed onto a spreadsheet and analysed using statistics to identify patterns of behaviour. This is a highly *structured* approach to doing research: the students could identify each stage in advance and each stage could be carried out relatively independently.

4.2.3   Research logic

Clearly the relationship between theory and data differs significantly in the two approaches. The qualitative approach relies on an inductive logic, where you collect data to *generate* theory. *Inductive* logic (usually associated with a qualitative approach) is associated with research projects that emphasise **theory building**. A stream of projects can be used to test theory by comparing the theoretical arguments generated in each, for instance in different contexts.

The quantitative approach to research relies on a deductive logic – you collect data to *test* theory. *Deductive* logic (usually associated with a quantitative approach) is associated with individual projects that emphasise **theory testing**. A stream of quantitative research projects can be used to build theory by testing, revising and then retesting new theory. However, this does require multiple projects and multiple testing phases, of which a student project could form a small part.

Induction – the logic of the qualitative researcher

The logic of **induction** is that the researcher will generate theory from data. The data can be analysed to identify **patterns**, for instance if there appears to be a pattern that people you meet at the weekend smile more than people you meet during the week, you may conclude that there was something in this. You can generalise these patterns as a conceptual framework or theory, for instance by stating that from your observations, either 'people in general are more happy at the weekend than they are during the week', or that 'the people you associate with at the weekend are generally more happy than those you associate with during the week'. Such general patterns are what we mean by theory. They are different from the kind of grand theory that you have read about during your literature reviews, but can be classed as a theory, nonetheless.

Researchers often rely on induction when they are researching an area without theory to guide the development of hypotheses (and hence which data to collect). In this case, a researcher will want to collect data about as many aspects as possible of what he or she is studying, and induce the theory from the data, as you will see in **Chapter 12**.

Researchers also use induction when studying an area in which they believe that relying on a conceptual framework or even a high-level theory might bias data collection towards evidence that supports (or in some cases contradicts) that framework. For example, ethologists (researchers who study animal behaviour) may go into the field without having studied primate behaviour intensively, so that they do not try to impose existing research frameworks on what they observe, which might prevent them from observing something important. This was one of the characteristics of the approach that came to be known as '**grounded theory**' (this is largely associated with Barney Glaser and Anselm Strauss in social science research, and Kathy Eisenhardt in management research). Whilst we do recognise that there are often surprising patterns in familiar and apparently random behaviours, the requirements of such a radical approach to grounded theory are included as examples and not recommended for bachelor's- or master's-level study.

Deduction – the logic of the quantitative researcher

The purpose of **deduction** is to provide a structured process for testing a general rule or theory using data about a specific instance. Starting with a theory or conceptual framework that may explain a behaviour or a social phenomenon you are interested in studying, you deduce one or more hypotheses from the theory to test, which will guide what data you collect and how. You then analyse your data to see whether they do or do not support the theory. Hypothesis testing in quantitative research usually takes place through the following process:

1. Select a method such as an experiment, survey or secondary data analysis (**Chapter 5**) to collect data.
2. Collect data in the form of numbers or transform them into numbers (**Chapter 10**).
3. Use statistical techniques to analyse these quantitative data (**Chapters 10** and **11**).
4. Decide whether to accept or reject the hypothesis based on the statistical analysis.
5. Decide whether the results challenge or support the theory or conceptual framework from which the hypotheses were generated (**Chapter 10**).
6. Report the results in numbers, tables and charts (**Chapter 13**).

If you are not testing a specific theory or hypothesis (as in the marketing research project described in **Student research in action 4.1**), omit step 4.

We stated that the research methods associated with the natural sciences were typically good for collecting quantitative data. However, as we will see in subsequent chapters, you can also test your hypotheses using qualitative data collected using qualitative methods (Blaikie 2009). For now, though, we will associate quantitative methods with the objective approach.

Using the logic of deduction, going from data back to hypotheses to theory is known as **verification**. You can only show whether your hypothesis is true for the data that you have collected and analysed. If you have done a good job of deducing your hypotheses from your theory, you can make the argument that your theory has been strengthened or weakened by your findings. As you and other researchers test hypotheses in different studies, then theories become stronger or weaker. As theories become weaker, they are replaced by better theories; as theories become stronger, they replace weaker theories. In **Student research in action 4.2**, the student sets out to challenge whether an 'accepted theory' holds in a particular context.

Student research in action 4.2

TESTING A HYPOTHESIS IN A NEW RESEARCH SETTING

Neil was interested in using his research process to investigate SMEs (small to medium enterprises, typically less than 250 employees). He noticed that much of the management literature, in particular the literature on 'best practices', was based on studies conducted on large, often multinational corporations. He wanted to find out how relevant these 'best practices' were to SMEs, and specifically whether his experience that they rarely produced benefits for SMEs – also suggested in the small business literature – was more generally true.

Neil conducted a study to see whether SMEs were adopting 'big business' best practices and whether these practices were associated with performance improvement. His conceptual framework was based on the proposed link between the issues or concepts of 'employing big business best practices' and 'achieving performance improvement'. His hypothesis was 'Employing big business best practices is associated with achieving performance improvement.' This was consistent with the mainstream management literature, but not the small business literature or his own experience, and was what sparked his interest in the project in the first place. He prepared and piloted a questionnaire and then surveyed some small businesses.

Neil discovered that SMEs who had adopted best practices based on big businesses were failing to see any benefits from them. He failed to verify the hypothesis from mainstream management literature and he concluded that these big business ideas were questionable for SMEs. This helped support the small business literature, which argued that a 'one-size-fits-all' approach of using big business ideas in SMEs was inappropriate. Neil's conclusions suggested that researchers should specifically consider the small business context in future research.

The philosopher of science Karl Popper (1959) argued that there is no such thing as objective observation and thus, since theories can never be proven to be true they can only be proven to be false. His classic example to demonstrate this concerned swans. If someone lives in the northern hemisphere and has never visited the southern hemisphere (or a zoo), they might *believe* that all swans are white. No matter how many white swans they saw, however, they would never be able to *prove* this unless they could examine every swan in the world. On the other hand, if they set out to *disprove* the hypothesis that all swans are white, then they could do so by seeing just one non-white swan. Popper's argument was that since a single exception such as one single black swan anywhere would disprove a hypothesis, we should only accept a hypothesis as provisionally true (not disproved) rather than proved. As a result, he recommended that a researcher should set up a hypothesis so that it can be disproved (which he argued was doable) rather than proved (which he argued was impossible).

Choosing one research approach for a project does not commit you to this research approach and associated logic for life! However, it is unlikely that more than one research logic will be used in one undergraduate or master's research project. Where research is phased or consists of multiple independent subprojects, usually as carried out by professional researchers, subsequent phases or subprojects may use different logic. For example, a researcher might use a subjective position for theory-building research, and then follow it up with an objective position for testing the theories through a phase of further research.

4.3 What is a research design?

In this section we will examine a number of characteristics of each research approach, but this time with a view to operationalising your **research design**. We summarise the characteristics of each approach in **Table 4.3**.

4.3.1 Quantitative research

A brief look at the management literature will show the influence that the objective approach has had on the development of the body of knowledge. The workshop in **Chapter 1** discussed Frederick W. Taylor and the Hawthorne experiment researchers

Table 4.3 Characteristics of research design associated with quantitative and qualitative approaches

Characteristic	Quantitative approach	Qualitative approach
Research focus	Measurement of general conditions	Meaning of specific situation
Typically found in	Economics, finance, consumer marketing, operations management, information systems, decision sciences	Human resource management, organisational behaviour, organisational science
Research aims	Testing of theory through hypotheses, replication, extension and comparison	Generating of theory through propositions, understanding situation in depth
Type of system studied	Closed system	Open system
Examples of research approach/designs	Survey Experiments Case-control studies	Case studies Action research Ethnography
Research methods	Database analysis Questionnaires Structured observation	Documentation analysis Interviews Observation Focus group
Research data	Hard, reliable, replicable	Rich, deep, valid
Quality criteria	Statistical significance, generalisability, validity, reliability/repeatability of results	Dependability/repeatability of process, viability

as examples of the objective approach to business and management research, along with Stanley Milgram from psychology.

A fundamental principle of the objective approach is: 'If you can measure it, you can understand it' (Michael Faraday). For example, Taylor was concerned with applying the 'scientific (objective) principles' he had used in experimenting with machining to managing workers. Here, he analysed what the workers did by measuring their movements – the loads, the distances moved and the time that each movement took. By understanding what they did, he was able to redesign the work they undertook and propose better methods for doing tasks. He also proposed extending this logic to how workers should be supervised and managed. This shows an early emphasis on the objective approach and on measurement in business and management research.

We will now discuss some other characteristics of this approach, and the associated worldview and subjects of research.

How do quantitative researchers view the world?

Quantitative approaches originated in the natural sciences, including biology, chemistry and physics, which are mainly concerned with natural objects and phenomena. The approach is based on making observations using our senses or through the use of scientific instruments or other measuring devices. Such research focuses on **measurement** as the way of understanding something of interest. The researcher looks for general patterns, which can be interpreted as theories or 'laws'. Consider Newton's laws of physics, for instance, which predict general properties of matter and motion and are predominantly derived from experimentation and observation. Objective researchers view the natural world as real and capable of being studied objectively; that is, scientists do research 'as if' they can study the world without being influenced by personal opinions or beliefs about what they will find. Whether scientists support a particular political party, religion or football team should not influence what they discover or what they choose to study.

This approach to doing research on the natural world has been adopted by many researchers for doing research on the social world, including business and management research. Instead of looking for physical laws, scientific researchers may seek to develop general principles about how people, organisations or social systems behave. They focus on what these social units have in common, rather than individual differences. For example, the market research carried out by the consumer products firm in **Student research in action 4.1** identified a general problem – that sales of its products dropped as their target consumers aged. But this only identified what happened, not the reasons underlying the drop. Further objective research by the students might have clarified this, but might not have revealed the deeper meaning of the drop in market share.

Who are the 'quantitative researchers' in business and management research?

Business and management researchers who use the quantitative approach in their research often come from subjects that look at physical systems or the general behaviour of people, organisations or other social units. For example, finance research often investigates the behaviour of investors in financial markets, with personal information about these investors being irrelevant. Subjects associated with the objective approach include economics, finance, consumer marketing, operations management, information systems and decision sciences such as operations research and management science. This does not mean that researchers in these areas only take quantitative approaches, but it is the 'prevailing approach' in each of these areas.

The role of theory in developing a research design

In a quantitative approach, an extensive literature review often takes place as part of developing the research design. The concepts and relationships identified in previous research often form the foundation for the present research project. In some cases, the research project itself focuses on collecting data to test a theory or set of propositions put forward by another researcher. Motivations for doing this kind of research include:

- **Replication** – can we duplicate what the original researchers found out?
- **Extension** – can we find similar results in different contexts?
- **Comparison** – which theory (among competing theories) is the most useful to explain or predict the world?

For instance, one student wanted to test whether the Balanced Scorecard (Kaplan and Norton 1992) could be used to motivate employees. The student formally stated the relationship as the hypothesis: '*The level of employee motivation will be higher where the Balanced Scorecard has been adopted than where it has not been adopted.*' He then developed a research project to collect data to test this hypothesis. In this case, he found that the staff reported being more motivated in the departments where the Balanced Scorecard was being used. Whilst this particular research did not prove that adopting the Balanced Scorecard *caused* motivation to be higher, only that the use of the scorecard and higher motivation occurred simultaneously, the data supported some link between the Balanced Scorecard and motivation. As an aside, there is often the concern with such research that the opposite causal link might be also be true – for instance here, it is perfectly reasonable to suggest that more highly motivated teams like to have the Balanced Scorecard as it enables them to track their own performance. The scorecard doesn't cause the high motivation; the high motivation does cause the use of the scorecard.

In a quantitative approach, researchers often use a literature review to develop a **conceptual framework** that describes both the key issues and concepts they are interested in and the relationships they expect to find between them (Blaikie 2009). A conceptual framework or model is often included as part of an academic article that takes this approach. For instance, the student who was studying the relationship between the Balanced Scorecard and employee motivation had a simple conceptual model, derived from the literature, as shown in **Figure 4.4**. It shows the two entities of interest and the + between them indicating that it is expected that the effect will be positive.

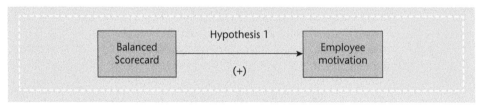

Figure 4.4 A very simple conceptual framework

The scientific method

The approach is derived from a particular way of doing research known as the **scientific method**. It is an idealised model to arrive at what scientists consider to be truth. The key ideals of this model are objective observation and measurement and careful and accurate analysis of data. In applying the scientific method, scientists try to set aside their preconceptions about how the world works and gather data using 'objective' methods such as laboratory experiments, where they are able to *control* conditions and repeat experiments over and over again with only slight variations. Such a **closed system** allows them to rule out alternative explanations for their findings and propose that (at least under certain conditions) one thing is linked to another.

We can only use quantitative methods if we ourselves are objective – this was the important link we identified in **Figure 4.2**. The researcher must be separate from what he or she is studying in order to be objective. This distance may come from physical distance (for example sending out a postal survey), social distance (for example the authority of the researcher as a 'social scientist') or procedure (for example separating the planning and execution of research). This distance (backed up in professional research with external control by peer review – see **Chapter 3**), makes sure that personal bias is minimised.

When the social sciences started to become recognised areas of study, they were highly influenced by the logic and process of scientific research, so they borrowed the scientific method for the social sciences. The scientific model for research has thus significantly influenced social research, both as 'the way to do research' and as 'a way not to do research' – depending on your perspective. Although business and management researchers study different topics and use different methods from natural scientists, many researchers believe that the scientific method is the best way to do research, 'as if' we are natural scientists.

The quantitative approach – a practical example

As described above, if you use the scientific model, you may be able to write nearly all your research report before you ever collect any data. Because this approach is highly structured it is often appropriate for a short project since you know how long each stage will take.

Suppose that you are researching customer satisfaction with an online travel retailer and have decided to use an online questionnaire to gather data about customer satisfaction. Before you start collecting data, you could:

- Come up with a series of research questions and hypotheses to test customer satisfaction, for example: 'Customers who are highly satisfied with their first online purchase are more likely to repurchase from the same retailer.'
- Specify each aspect of your research plan before you start collecting data (this will be covered in detail in **Chapter 5**).
- Design, pre-test and pilot your survey before you start collecting your data.
- Set up a spreadsheet for your data, and even run some statistical analysis with dummy data.
- Calculate the number of responses you need to test your hypotheses.
- Design your research report.

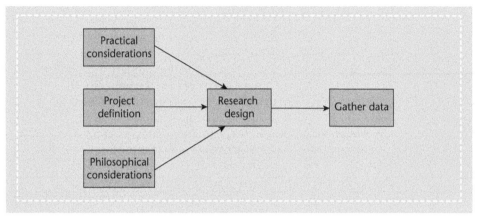

Figure 4.5 Where do I go from here?

As described above and shown in **Figure 4.5**, quantitative research is relatively straightforward once you have decided what research questions you will ask. Although you might have to revisit some issues, once you have decided how you will collect and analyse your data you have made all the major decisions that will affect your research process.

Quality criteria for quantitative research

Quantitative researchers generally agree on the standards for judging whether research is good or not good. The goal of such research is to produce *statistically significant* and *generalisable results*. Statistically significant means that the findings are unlikely to have occurred by chance alone (discussed further in **Chapters 10** and **11**).

The goal of many quantitative studies is **generalisability** – drawing conclusions about a group from a sample. You can only generalise the findings of quantitative research if you can first show that they are valid and reliable.

Validity refers to how accurately we have conducted our research. For instance, if you were trying to measure customer satisfaction, have the measures you used really measured customer satisfaction or a related concept? Also, did you have enough responses to justify the findings you are claiming? If, as the scientific method proposes, the world is objective and knowable, then the main source of error in our data will be our research method.

Reliability means that you or another researcher would get the same findings if you repeated your study. For example, if you studied the relationship between the location of the till and theft from the till in your high street bookstore, you should find the same relationship in the bookstore on any high street. Another way of describing reliability is repeatability. Research findings are only reliable if the world itself is uniform.

4.3.2 Qualitative research

Although the scientific method and the quantitative approach unquestionably influenced the early development of business and management studies, the qualitative approach is *equally* important. Rather than the white-coated laboratory researcher as exemplifying users of the scientific method, those who have used and contributed to the development of the subjective approach are exemplified by the ethnographers. **Ethnography** is concerned with the study of culture and is an important research approach in areas such as anthropology and sociology. Early ethnographic research focused on exotic, faraway people, such as the American Samoans studied by Margaret Mead in the South Pacific. However, many ethnographers today focus on cultures closer to home, such as high-tech workers, Harley-Davidson owners or *Star Trek* fans (Kozinets 2001).

A qualitative researcher is more likely to pick up on differences between cultures if he or she tries to blend in (as the early ethnographers did) and learn from watching rather than walking around with a clipboard and a list of questions. Qualitative study is more open-ended – those early ethnographers started out not knowing exactly what they might find or even how they might get there. Much of the learning will emerge along the way and from the journey itself. Qualitative research is much better at finding out about meaning rather than measurement, through investigating feelings, attitudes, values, perceptions or motivations, and the state, actions and interactions of people, groups and organisations. In interpreting these, researchers consider their properties – hence the association of ethnography with qualitative research.

The study of 'street corner society' by William F. Whyte described briefly in **Chapter 1** is often cited as a classic professional ethnographic study. In a brief student project, it might be impossible to achieve this 'deep hanging out' in a social group, but many placement or sponsored projects offer students a chance to experience life from the perspective, albeit a temporary one, of a member of or a participant in the organisation or social unit being studied. Even if this isn't possible, many student projects can benefit from using the unstructured tools and techniques associated with ethnography, including observation and interviews, as an alternative to the structured tools and techniques associated with the scientific method.

How do qualitative researchers view the world?

Whilst the natural scientists claimed objectivity about what they were researching, ethnographers emphasise the extent to which the world, especially the social world of business and management, is subjective and shaped by our perceptions. If we perceive what we are studying (for example the complex dynamics in employer–employee relations) to be a certain way, there is rarely an instrument that will confirm or deny that view. Any view of what is happening is thus subjective – it depends on your viewpoint. Ethnographers emphasise the extent to which views differ between individuals, and across cultures, so that the extent to which research is actually based on indisputable social 'facts' is limited. For instance, consider a course of study you have undertaken. It is likely that there will be differing views on the success of the course – some people will have enjoyed it, others may not have done so. In evaluating the course, we could compile quantitative measurements describing how students viewed the course that would provide us with data about the course, focusing, for instance, on the average ratings of the lecturer. Under this approach, the perception of each individual matters less than the average. This would fit with an objective approach. We could also investigate satisfaction with the course through different students' perceptions. Here, all views would be considered to be relevant, and reveal more about the expectations of individual students, how their views (or perceptions) of the course

gone

were formed, and why they viewed the course in different ways. This would be a subjective approach. What you learnt about the course would differ significantly between the two different studies.

Who are the 'qualitative researchers' in business and management research?

Qualitative researchers traditionally had backgrounds in subjects concerned with studying people, either individually or collectively, and how they behave – including psychology and sociology. They draw on those disciplines for theory and research methods. In business and management research, these subject areas include human resources management, organisational behaviour and organisational science.

Ethnographic method

In the discussion of the quantitative approach, we saw that researchers are concerned predominantly with trying to uncover general laws or patterns, similar to the laws being investigated by natural scientists. Subjective researchers try to uncover meaning in a specific situation by studying it intensively. This *depth* is characteristic of subjective research.

Wherever possible, researchers using the ethnographic method study issues of interest in their 'natural settings', by involving themselves in the workplace or, in the case of the student project discussed at the start of the chapter, in the lives of the group of people they research. This emphasises fieldwork – being physically present in the setting being studied. Qualitative research thus involves the role of the researcher, the effect of the researcher on what is being studied (you can imagine the impact a loud person may have on the group dynamics of an otherwise quiet group, and the effect this would have on the research if they are concerned with studying group dynamics) and potential sources of bias. Because it takes place in these natural settings, where the researcher cannot control conditions, research takes place within an **open system**.

Subjective researchers point out that all researchers are human and cannot be completely objective, and therefore will inevitably introduce some sort of bias or subjectivity into the research process. Even experimental research, usually held up as a model of objectivity, can be influenced by researchers, as summarised in **Research in action 4.1**.

Research in action 4.1

RESEARCHING THE ROLE OF THE RESEARCHER

Rosenthal and Fode (1963) conducted an experiment to test the effect of experimenter bias, specifically whether experimenters' expectations affected experimental outcomes. Rosenthal and Fode gave student subjects five rats to train to run a maze. Students were told that they had either 'bright' rats, specially bred to run mazes quickly, or 'dull' rats, which were not.

The students found that the 'bright' rats performed significantly better over 50 trials than the 'dull' rats, but the two groups had been actually given rats bred under identical conditions and randomly labelled as either 'bright' or 'dull'.

Just how objective were the experimental results reprinted by the students in this case? Was it not a scientific study carried out in a laboratory environment? Were the conditions not controlled? The students' preconceptions impaired their objectivity in both training and measuring the performance of the rats. This reinforces the ethnographers' belief in subjectivity, and they argue that a challenge in research is recognising your own biases. We will return to this theme later. Natural science researchers argue that objectivity is improved when individual research experiments are designed with controls, such as the 'double-blind' experimental design for conducting medical research, where neither the doctor nor the patient knows whether an active or inactive (placebo) treatment has been administered. They also argue that the scientific community as a whole minimises individual researcher bias through replication. For example, the inability of the scientific community to replicate 'cold fusion' showed that the original study by Fleischmann and Pons (1989) was biased in some way and so disproved its existence.

The qualitative approach – a practical example

Many ethnographers prefer to 'enter the field' (that is, start their data collection in the setting they are investigating) with a completely open mind about what they will find. They will do everything possible to rid themselves of their own biases about the situation into which they are going and prevent other biases developing. For example by reading a critical newspaper article concerning their research setting, they know that, whether consciously or not, they will be led to looking at aspects related to those criticisms. Imagine for yourself doing research on corporate ethics in one of the banks that has been the subject of a major scandal. You cannot but help to be influenced in your views of the organisation and the people. In contrast, the ethnographer will let the data (for example what people tell them) dictate the way they proceed with the study and the findings. This is known as 'being led by the data'. They argue that this minimises the likelihood that what they observe and record in the field will be determined by prior beliefs.

In many instances, though, it is not truly possible to do this; all researchers go into the field with some orienting ideas (e.g. investment banking working on a different ethical basis to other institutions). Thus, many researchers prefer to enter the field with at least some preparation, without developing explicit conceptual frames or instruments such as questionnaires for testing or gathering data, so that the themes (the conceptual framework, as discussed above and in **Chapter 3**) will emerge during the study. This is more typical of student projects and dissertations, where time constraints and other practical considerations (such as people wanting to know what you are going to ask them before they will agree to interviews) are important.

As we have already seen, if you choose a qualitative approach, you will spend less time planning your research, since you can begin collecting data with a relatively broad topic, and more time actually gathering and analysing data. Ethnography as carried out by Whyte may not be the best approach for a short project – it is fundamentally uncertain and we do not recommend this approach, unless you are being closely supervised by an experienced researcher who has specifically selected the research setting and research method and will work with you on making sense of the data as you go along. However, we do suggest that a form of **bounded ethnography** is entirely appropriate – it combines the practicality of the time-limited project with the ethnographic method. In a bounded situation, you may not reach the level of depth that you would if you were able to explore an issue in unlimited depth. However, you need to finish a project report and provide at least limited answers to your research questions. For this reason, we advocate bounded ethnography as an entirely appropriate research approach for student projects.

We can demonstrate this by returning to the earlier example of researching customer satisfaction with an online travel retailer and take a qualitative approach. Rather than setting up hypotheses, an appropriate research question might be: 'How do customers judge the quality of travel websites?' To answer this question, you could decide to use interviews and observation (for example sitting with customers as they try to make enquiries and bookings online) and, consistent with this, only specify the broad outline of your research process before you start collecting data. Once you have started collecting data, you might:

- Change the data you collect and the methods you use to collect it. For example, if it becomes clear, after the first round of interviews and observations, that speed of response/refresh rates are vital for some people, you could investigate why this is so by conducting further targeted interviews. If you wanted to know if different customers rate speed differently, you could revert to a scientific approach and prepare a questionnaire.
- Decide how to analyse and interpret your data – again emergent, so only planned as far as the analysis of your first set of data.

Once you have done the first set of data analysis, you will have identified the main themes emerging from your data and can search the literature for conceptual frameworks to support your findings.

As you can see from this example and **Figure 4.6**, if you choose a qualitative research approach, it will be more *recursive* than the objective approach, i.e. it will be an *iterative* (stages looping back to previous stages) rather than a linear process (one stage following another in sequence). Our four research stages – defining, designing, doing and describing your research – will overlap significantly. As we have seen, your data collection and data analysis strategies might only emerge once you have started doing research. You may start describing your research, as you will see in **Chapters 6** and **12**, before you have finished doing it, and you might identify your detailed conceptual frameworks late in the process.

This messiness is characteristic of subjective research. In some ways, it represents the natural way that we solve problems in real life, compared with the linear process of the objective approach.

A final thought on the practicalities of the qualitative approach to research concerns your own attitudes and preferences. Some researchers are content to live with this messiness and relative lack of structure; others believe that you should do some preliminary research so that you are adequately prepared to observe and record data. If you are the kind of person who might travel alone for the first time by hopping on a plane to the other side of the world with no hotel reservations, no return ticket and no fixed plans, you might find that a completely 'data-led' approach might suit your personal beliefs and preferences. On the other hand, if you are the kind of person who needs to know what you are doing every day, where you will be staying and when you will be coming home, you might find this an unsettling experience.

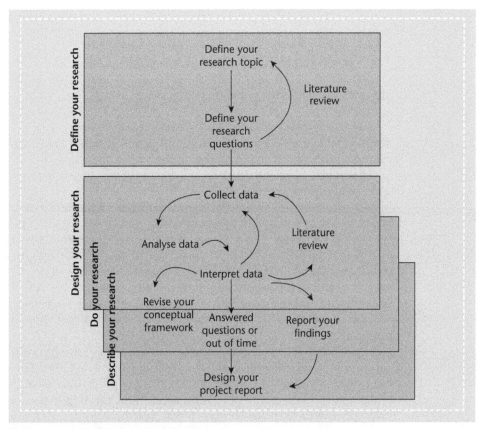

Figure 4.6 A qualitative research process

As we noted above, most business and management researchers prefer to start collecting data with at least some preparation, although they may not develop an explicit conceptual framework or structured approaches to collecting data (**Chapter 6**). This is more likely to lead to success in a student project, since you do not have the luxury of starting over again if things go wrong and you face many practical constraints such as time.

Quality criteria for qualitative research

People take one of two positions on the criteria for assessing the quality of subjective research, depending on where they start. Some researchers, mainly North American, see the goal of such research to be as rigorous as scientific research. They therefore apply the scientific method to data gathered using qualitative research designs, or qualitative data gathered using quantitative research designs such as surveys. This group would be more likely to seek the same qualities in their findings as scientific researchers – validity and generalisability.

Others do not agree, stating that objective criteria are incompatible with the subjective research approach. Most subjective researchers argue that the standards for assessing the quality of qualitative research must differ from those for quantitative research. If the goal of scientific research is statistically significant and generalisable results, then the goal of qualitative research is *valuable*, and *idiographic* or *transferable* results (O'Leary 2013). Either way, subjective researchers need to be as careful as quantitative researchers in reporting how they designed their research and how they collected and interpreted their data; rigour is still a key quality of their research process.

In understanding the further value of the research, the process for analysis of data needs some further discussion. The subjective researcher may rely on intuition to guide the analysis and interpretation of findings, rather than rules or procedures. It is in this uniqueness of the situation and the intuitive analysis that the value arrives. It is valuable because it is original.

Most subjective researchers disagree that researchers can be objective, and even question whether objectivity is a desirable quality in research. Instead, researchers should recognise that all human beings are subjective but that subjectivity can be managed in research. Two ways of managing subjectivity are **neutrality**, developing strategies to avoid unrecognised subjectivity that might bias research findings, and **transparency**, acknowledging subjectivity (O'Leary 2013: 62). Following an agreed procedure for generating theory from data helps to demonstrate neutrality. Explicitly stating your own position helps to demonstrate transparency.

Qualitative research requires the researcher to see through other people's eyes and interpret events from their point of view (Bryman 1988). The researcher may even need to adopt the viewpoint of the people being researched in order to understand what is going on. Think about how you might research business and management in another culture. If you try to study it from your own (native) perspective, you may not really comprehend what is going on. You might need to think as a person from that culture in order to understand the social reality. This is a major concern in international business research – in part it is about resisting the 'Americanisation' of management, in part about the value of differences between cultures.

Whilst a quantitative study should be repeatable (yielding the same findings in subsequent trials), a qualitative study will almost certainly not be – people move, ideas change and culture shifts. For this reason, rather than repeatability, dependability may be a more realistic research goal. **Dependability** refers to the *repeatability of the process* of inducing theory from data, rather than the *repeatability of the findings* themselves.

Some researchers question whether uniform criteria can actually be established for research, since every study will differ on essential criteria. They regard the emphasis on universal standards as trying to promote an artificial and unworkable consensus, in the presence of 'multiple realities'. It has been argued that we should instead look at viability. **Viability** means that the research you have conducted yields some useful insight or 'potential for problem-solving' (see Von Glaserfeld 1995; Kilduff et al. 2011; Huemann 2015).

Generally, your research should:

- Make a contribution to understanding some aspect of social reality
- Be original in some way

Table 4.4   A research profile

	Qualitative			Quantitative
Focus	Meaning		X	Measurement
Definition	Exploring instances and examples		X	Collecting and analysing data
Purpose	Examining individual differences	X		Testing general principles
Research questions	How, why	X		What, how much, who
Theory	Theory-generating		X	Theory-testing
Reasoning	Inductive		X	Deductive
Researcher	Subjective and involved	X		Objective and independent
Data	Words and symbols	X		Numbers and categories
Data collection	Up close and extended		X	Remote or brief
Typical methods	Observation, unstructured interviews	X		Surveys, experiments
Data analysis	Thematic		X	Statistics

- Have been conducted in a consistent manner (see next section), as far as possible, and have had potential sources of bias identified and recognised
- Be both interesting and true.

4.3.3 Auditing your research using a research profile

You can profile your research design and decide whether your plan is consistent or inconsistent. **Table 4.4** shows the **research profile** for one student project. This researcher is mixing elements of research approaches inconsistently.

You might want to build a profile of your research and perhaps the key exemplars you have identified in your literature search. Good research tends to be *consistent* – by consistent we do not mean that every box must be ticked for one or the other approaches, but that there is a logic for any deviation. For example, you could use statistics and inference on data that were collected in qualitative form, but you might want to consider if this is the best method or the best use of your data.

Table 4.5 summarises all the elements of each approach, as constructed through this chapter.

Table 4.5   Summary

Characteristic	Qualitative approach	Quantitative approach
Philosophical perspective	Predominantly subjective	Predominantly objective
Logic	Social sciences – the ethnographic method	Natural sciences – the scientific method
Examples	Street corner society	F.W. Taylor; Hawthorne Studies
Research questions	Why, how?	What, how much, who?
Research process	Predominantly iterative, overlapping	Predominantly linear sequential, ordered
Theory and data	Inductive – data generates or builds theory	Deductive – data test theory
Research purpose	Discovery, exploration	Verification, generalising
Research focus	Meaning of specific situation	Measurement of general conditions
Typically found in	Human resource management, organisational behaviour, organisational science	Economics, finance, consumer marketing, operations management, IS, decision sciences
Research aims	Generating of theory through propositions, understanding situation in depth	Testing of theory through hypotheses, replication, extension and comparison
Type of system studied	Open system	Closed system
Examples of research approach/designs	Case studies Action research Ethnography	Survey Experiments Case-control studies
Research methods	Documentation analysis Interviews Observation Focus group	Database analysis Questionnaires Structured observation
Research data	Rich, deep, valid	Hard, reliable, replicable
Quality criteria	Dependability/repeatability of process, viability	Statistical significance, generalisability, validity, reliability/repeatability of results

Summary

In this chapter, we have presented the two main philosophical perspectives of business and management research and their accompanying research approaches. The objective view favours the logic of scientific enquiry, and uses the scientific method as the model for research endeavour. The research approach is most likely to be quantitative. The subjective view rejects scientific enquiry as inappropriate for studying the social world, and takes the methods of social science, particularly ethnography, as its model. The research approach is most likely to be qualitative.

Quantitative research is relatively linear and predictable once you have decided how you will collect and analyse your data. On the other hand, qualitative research is cyclical and unpredictable – how you will collect and analyse your data emerges as you are actually doing your research.

Research philosophy helps us to understand the differences between the two and make sure that a research design is internally consistent.

Answers to key questions

What is meant by research philosophy?

- The assumptions that underlie any particular research approach.
- It includes ontology (the nature of reality) and epistemology (nature of knowledge).

What is a research approach?

- How a researcher can go about acquiring knowledge.
- How you will answer your research questions.
- The basis of your research design.

What are the possible research approaches?

- Subjective – social reality does not exist, and knowledge is dependent on the observer.
- Objective – social reality exists and knowledge is independent of the observer.

What are the assumptions underlying each research approach?

- Underlying the objective research approach are the assumptions that the world is real and knowable, and all phenomena can be reduced to a set of numbers.
- Underlying the subjective research approach is the prime assumption that the world is complex and only knowable through interaction with the social systems that it contains.

What logic guides how research questions are answered?

- Inductive logic – the logic of the quantitative researcher.
- Deductive logic – the logic of the qualitative researcher.

References

Blaikie, Norman 2000. *Designing Social Research*. Cambridge: Polity Press.

Blaikie, Norman 2009. *Designing Social Research*, 2nd edn. Cambridge: Polity Press.

Bryman, Alan 1988. *Quantity and Quality in Social Research*. London: Routledge.

Fleischmann, Martin and Pons, Stanley 1989. Electrochemically induced nuclear fusion of deuterium, *Journal of Electroanalytical Chemistry and Interfacial Electrochemistry*, 261(2): 301–8.

Huemann, Martina 2015. *Human Resource Management in the Project-Oriented Organization*. Aldershot: Gower.

Kaplan, R.S. and Norton, D.P. 1992. The Balanced Scorecard – Measures that drive performance, *Harvard Business Review*, Jan–Feb: 71–9.

Kilduff, Martin, Mehra, Ajay and Dunn, Mary B. 2011. From blue sky research to problem solving: A philosophy of science theory of new knowledge production. *Academy of Management Review*, 36(2): 297–317.

Kozinets, Robert 2001. Utopian enterprise: Articulating the meanings of Star Trek's culture of consumption, *Journal of Consumer Research*, 28(1): 67–88.

O'Leary, Zina 2013. *The Essential Guide to Doing Research*, 2nd edn. London: Sage.

Popper, Karl 1959. *The Logic of Scientific Discovery*. London: Hutchinson.

Ralston, P. 2010. *The Book of Not Knowing: Exploring the Nature of Self, Mind, and Consciousness*. Berkeley, CA: North Atlantic Books.

Rosenthal, Robert and Fode, Kermit. L. 1963. The effect of experimenter bias on the performance of the albino rat, *Behavioural Science*, 8: 183–9.

Von Glasersfeld, Ernst 1995. *Radical Constructivism: A Way of Knowing and Learning*. London: The Falmer Press.

Additional resources

Benton, Ted and Craib, Ian 2001. *Philosophy of Social Science: The Philosophy of Social Science*. Basingstoke: Palgrave Macmillan.

Cartwright, Nancy and Montuschi, Eleanora (eds) 2014. *Philosophy of Social Science: A New Introduction*. Oxford: Oxford University Press.

Cooper, Donald R. and Schindler, Pamela S. 2001. *Business Research Methods*. International edition. Singapore: McGraw-Hill Book Company.

Crotty, Michel 1998. *The Foundations of Social Research: Meaning and Perspective in the Research Process*. London: Sage.

Easterby-Smith, Mark, Thorpe, Richard and Lowe, Andy 2012. *Management Research: An Introduction*, 4th edn. London: Sage.

Grix, Jonathan 2004. *The Foundations of Research*. Basingstoke: Palgrave Macmillan.

Hacking, Ian 1999. *The Social Construction of What?* Cambridge, MA: Harvard University Press.

Hollis, Martin 1994. *The Philosophy of Social Science: An Introduction*. Cambridge: Cambridge University Press.

Hughes, John 1990. *The Philosophy of Social Research*, 2nd edn. Harlow: Longman Group.

Kaplan, Abraham 1964. *The Conduct of Inquiry: Methodology for Behavioural Science*. San Francisco: Chandler.

Kincaid, Harold 1996. *Philosophical Foundations of the Social Sciences: Analysing Controversies in Social Research*. Cambridge: Cambridge University Press.

Nola, Robert 2003. *Rescuing Reason: A Critique of Anti-Rationalist Views of Science and Knowledge*. Dordrecht: Kluwer Academic Publishers.

Potter, Gary 2000. *The Philosophy of Social Science: New Perspectives*. Harlow: Prentice Hall.

Rosnow, Ralph L. and Rosenthal, Robert 1997. *People Studying People: Artifacts and Ethics in Behavioural Research*. New York: W.H. Freeman.

Schatzki, Theodore R. 1996. *Social Practice: A Wittgensteinian Approach to Human Activity and the Social*. Cambridge: Cambridge University Press.

Schutt, Russell K. 1996. *Social World: The Process and Practice of Research*. Thousand Oaks, CA: Pine Forge Press.

Searle, Clive 1996. *The Quality of Qualitative Research*. London: Allen Lane.

Shermer, Michael 1997. *Why People Believe Weird Things: Pseudoscience, Superstition, and Other Confusions of Our Time*. New York: W.H. Freeman.

Weick, Karl E. 1979. *The Social Psychology of Organising*, 2nd edn. Reading, MA: Addison-Wesley.

Williams, Malcolm and May, Tim 1990. *Introduction to the Philosophy of Social Research*. London: Routledge.

Key terms

bounded ethnography, 121
closed system, 117
conceptual framework, 116
deduction, 112
dependability, 124
epistemology, 104
ethnography, 119
generalisability, 118
grounded theory, 112
induction, 111
logic of research, 107
measurement, 115
neutrality, 124
objective, 105
ontology, 104
open system, 120
patterns, 111
qualitative approach, 107
quantitative approach, 107

reliability, 118
research approach, 107
research design, 114
research methodology, 109
research methods, 102
research philosophy, 104
research profile, 125
scientific method, 117
socially constructed, 105
social objects, 105
social reality, 104
subjective, 105
theory building, 111
theory testing, 111
transparency, 124
validity, 118
verification, 112
viability, 124

Discussion questions

1. Why should you consider research philosophy between the research definition stage and the research design stage?

2. Are there any research methods that can only be used in quantitative research and any that can only be used for qualitative research?

3. If the overall goal of research is to find 'truth', why should we judge qualitative research by the standards of quantitative research, or vice versa?

4. Is it acceptable in quantitative research to develop hypotheses from 'interrogating' a large data set with statistical techniques? What principles might this violate?

5. Why do we need to know about research philosophy?

6. What subject areas within business and management are likely to take a quantitative or qualitative approach?

7. Why should we try to disprove a hypothesis rather than to prove it?

8. What is 'truth' in the context of the research that you have come across? How close to 'the truth' do these research projects come?

Workshop

Task

Review the cases discussed in the **Chapter 1** workshop.

1. Classify each of these projects as having used either a subjective or an objective position, and a qualitative or quantitative research approach.

2. Use the research profile of **Table 4.4** and profile two of these projects. How consistent is the research design in each case (as far as is possible to tell from the descriptions)?

3. Identify your own 'natural' research approach (the one that fits best with your own worldview), using the tables in this chapter. Identify the strengths and weaknesses of this approach.

4. Find someone with a different philosophical position, and compare their approaches with your own.

Note

1. This did happen at the World Cup 2010, Germany vs England.

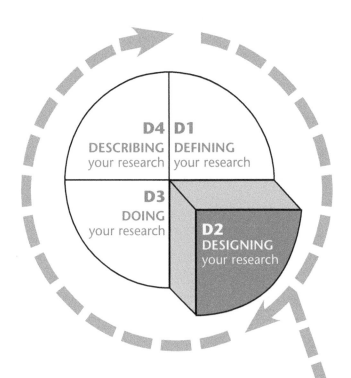

Relevant chapters
4

13 How do I write up my report?
14 What do I do now?

Key challenges
- Making sense of your findings
- Presenting your research to others
- Reflecting and learning from your research

Relevant chapters
1

1 What is research?
2 What should I study?
3 How do I find information?

Key challenges
- Understanding what academic research is
- Generating and clarifying ideas
- Using sources of information

D4
DESCRIBING your research

D1
DEFINING your research

D3
DOING your research

D2
DESIGNING your research

Relevant chapters
3

9 How do I do field research?
10 What do my quantitative data mean(1)?
11 What do my quantitative data mean(2)?
12 What do my qualitative data mean?

Key challenges
- Practical considerations in doing research
- Describing data using simple statistics
- Carrying out statistical tests
- Interpreting words and actions

Relevant chapters
2

4 What is my research approach?
5 **How do I do quantitative research?**
6 How do I do qualitative research?
7 How do I do case study research?
8 How do I make sure my research is ethical?

Key challenges
- Choosing a research approach
- **Choosing a research design**
- Collecting data using quantitative methods
- Collecting data using qualitative methods
- Integrating quantitative and qualitative methods

5 How do I do quantitative research?

chapter

Surveys, experiments and secondary data

 Key questions

- What methods for collecting data are associated with the quantitative research approach?
- How can I conduct a survey, run an experiment or analyse previously collected data?
- What are the particular issues in quantitative research design that I should be aware of?

 Learning outcomes

At the end of this chapter, you should be able to:

- Design a research study using a survey, an experiment or secondary data
- Discuss the strengths and weaknesses of each design
- Identify how the quality of quantitative research is assessed

Contents

Introduction

95% of adults *say* they wash their hands after using the toilet. However, the American Society of Microbiology reports that only 78% of people actually *do* wash their hands after using the toilet. Of those who wash their hands, only half use soap and only half wash for 15–20 seconds. What do you think accounts for the difference in the two figures for handwashing above? How could you collect data to see which figure was more accurate? Would this raise any legal or ethical questions?

After reading **Chapter 4**, you should have an idea about whether you prefer the quantitative approach, with an emphasis on closed-ended research designs and quantitative data, or the qualitative approach, with an emphasis on open-ended research designs and qualitative data, or a mixed-method research design combining both. Quantitative research designs are worth considering if you want your findings to focus on measurement, quantitative data, statistical significance and generalisability, and for your research to be judged by *quality standards* of objectivity, reliability and reproducibility. This chapter presents three **quantitative research designs** – surveys, experiments and secondary analysis – associated with the quantitative research approach. It provides a general overview of these research designs and methods, describes their main strengths and weaknesses, and provides some preliminary guidance for designing a research study using one of them. A simple decision tree for determining the most appropriate design is shown in Fig. 5.1. We will turn to the research designs and methods that are associated with the qualitative research approach in **Chapter 6**.

Section 5.1 focuses on survey designs, which many people view as nearly synonymous with business and management research. Different types of surveys include questionnaires, structured interviews and structured observations. If you decide to use a survey, you might use an existing questionnaire as is, choose pre-existing questions to build your own survey, or develop your own survey from scratch. Survey questions can be asked directly to respondents through face-to-face or voice-to-voice interviews, or indirectly through the post, email or internet. Although surveys are ideal for gathering data from many respondents without requiring face-to-face contact, they require careful thought about sampling and response rates in order to succeed.

Section 5.2 turns to experimental designs, which are often more closely associated with the natural sciences but also have a place in business and management research. Although true laboratory experiments are rare in the social sciences, experiments come closest to the idealised scientific model of research described in **Chapter 4** because they let researchers test cause-and-effect relationships. Many of the assumptions made in quantitative research are implicitly or explicitly based on laboratory experiments, as well as many of the criticisms made of quantitative research, so even if you don't plan to use them, you should understand a number of key aspects. Furthermore, field experiments, quasi-experiments and simulations are common in business and management research, and are based on laboratory experiments.

Section 5.3 describes how you can use data that have already been collected to answer your research questions. Government surveys, proprietary databases, documents, archives or statistical databases may already contain secondary data that you need to answer your research questions. Because they have been created for purposes other than your research project, and you will not need to contact with people or organisations to collect these data, they are known as **secondary data and secondary sources**. While secondary data can reduce difficulties with gaining access to people

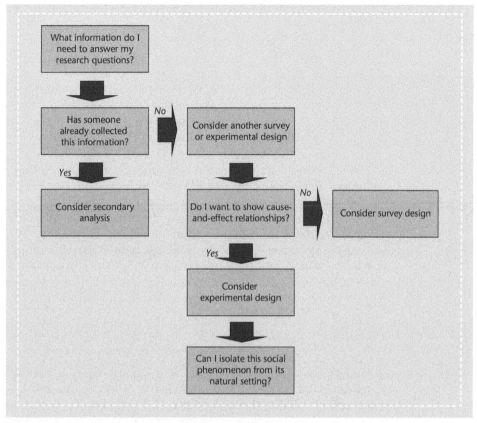

Figure 5.1 A decision tree for quantitative methods

or organisations, it may be difficult to find exactly the data you need to answer your research questions compared with designing and carrying out your own research.

After reading this chapter, you should have a better idea what research methods you might use in a quantitative approach, choose the most appropriate one for your research questions, and get started. (You may need to consult more specialised guides for detailed design.) Even if you don't plan to use one of these methods, these designs are commonly used to collect data in academic research, consulting, and journalism, so you need to understand them to analyse critically the articles you have found in your literature search. **Chapters 10** and **11** will cover basic and advanced statistics that you can use for analysing quantitative data.

5.1 How can I collect quantitative data using a survey?

Researchers often use **surveys** to gather data about organisations and their members (Gray 2004), because the data gathered through structured interviews, questionnaires and structured observations can reveal what people think, believe or do. They are many people's automatic choice for research design because people are used to them as a way of getting information and they provide a quick and inexpensive way to find out information. This can be an important consideration if you don't have time to use an in-depth but long-term qualitative method such as participant observation (see **Chapter 6**). They are especially useful if you are interested in drawing conclusions about groups rather than individuals.

A few basic principles of **survey design and administration** underpin questionnaires, structured interviews, and structured observations, as shown in this section. However, survey design cannot really be taught from books: reading about surveys is not a substitute for hands-on experience. We can only give practical, do-it-yourself information that will point the way out of difficulties (Oppenheimer 1992: 1) and show you how to avoid some obvious pitfalls. We list a number of specialist sources on survey methods in the **Additional resources** at the end of this chapter for more detailed follow-up.

Survey design and administration is surprisingly difficult to get right and most people underestimate how difficult and time consuming it is to design and carry out an effective survey. You may not get the information you need or be able to draw any conclusions. Most novices also underestimate the effort involved in getting enough survey respondents (see **Chapter 9** for a discussion of contacts). We have even seen many new researchers end up discarding all of their survey responses, wasting their time and resources and their respondents' time. The worst-case scenario is getting few – or even no – completed questionnaires back and having to scramble for an alternative source of data to analyse for your research project just before it is due.

5.1.1 What is a survey?

All surveys ask structured questions with defined types of answers across a set of respondents. A survey enables a researcher to collect comparable data from multiple respondents by asking them questions, eliciting anything from specific facts ('How many employees does your company have?') to the survey respondents' attitudes, opinions or behaviours ('Have you ever observed any unethical behaviour by your company's suppliers?'). Specific types of survey discussed in this section include questionnaires, structured interviews and structured observations.

Student research in action 5.1

LIKE THEY DO ON THE DISCOVERY CHANNEL

Five final-year undergraduate students were working on a project sponsored by an animal welfare group, which we will disguise as the Hamsters and Gerbils Conservation Society (HGCS). The organisation raised money in the UK to fund refuges for hamsters and gerbils that had been abandoned or abused by their owners, and for feral colonies of hamsters and gerbils. It also carried out political campaigning to try to strengthen the laws on hamsters and gerbils in the UK and internationally. Some of this it carried out on its own, some of it with similar groups in other countries and some of it with organisations interested in other rodents.

The organisation wanted the group to survey its members to see how satisfied they were with its strategy. The organisation had a list of its members, to whom it sent publications about its activities and requests for funds. It also distributed a monthly newsletter specifically to junior members (memberships were popular as birthday gifts for children aged 12 and under).

The students developed a survey, which the HGCS enclosed with its next newsletter to junior members. The response rate was high, so the students were able to argue that they had a clear picture of what the organisation's current members thought. They would never have been able to capture information from so many respondents through structured interviews or observation.

A survey is normally based on a standard set of questions that may be called an **instrument** or a **schedule**. These can be administered to respondents face to face, through the post, over the telephone, by email, or on the internet. **Structured interviews** are administered by a researcher asking a predetermined series of questions. **Questionnaires** record respondents' answers to a series of questions on paper or electronic forms that can be completed with or without the researcher present (for example store or hotel comment cards). **Structured observations** involve the researcher making a record of people's behaviours, as in work study, rather than verbal responses. Most surveys are one-offs, but they can also repeated at regular (e.g. the national census) or irregular (e.g. service quality interviews with customers) time intervals (e.g. a decennial national census).

When do researchers typically use surveys?

You should consider using a survey if:

- You want to collect data from a large number of respondents;
- You need to collect the same data the same way across a group of people;
- You have limited access or time to collect your data;
- What you are studying is well understood;
- Your respondents can understand and answer your questions with minimal explanation (structured interview) or even without your being physically present (questionnaire);
- You are asking questions that your respondents might find sensitive discussing with someone else or data they might only provide anonymously (questionnaire);
- You want to minimise the impact on people's behaviours by collecting data unobtrusively (structured observation);
- You need a large number of responses to analyse statistically in order to have a complete picture and/or confidence in your findings.

A survey may not be appropriate if:

- It is not clear who might have the answers to your questions;
- You do not know in advance what you want to ask;
- Your questions will evolve during your study;
- You need to explain your questions in detail;
- You need to collect different data from different respondents but you cannot define this in advance.

5.1.2 Survey design and administration

Many students (and university administrators) seem to believe that in an hour or two you can: design a survey, draft a questionnaire using SurveyMonkey and email the 1000 other students in your degree programme to complete a research project. However, survey design and administration is actually rigorous and time intensive. You should go through quite a few rounds drafting and redrafting your questions before you send out your first questionnaire, interview your first respondent or observe people's behaviours.

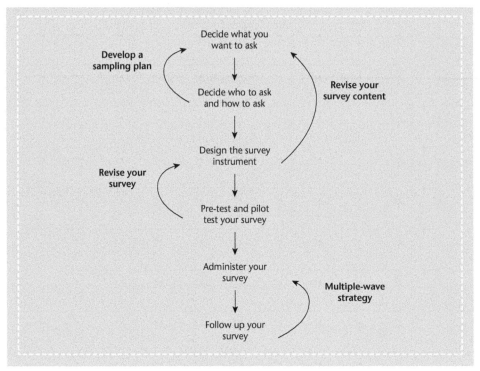

Figure 5.2 An overview of the survey process

We recommend that you follow a structured process to design your survey, as shown in **Figure 5.2**. The backwards loops are especially important in survey design, because you won't have a chance to revise your structured interview schedule or your questionnaire once you launch into full-scale research without losing data you have already collected. We describe the major elements of the process below, and highlight some of the key issues.

Step 1. Before you go any further – is a survey really the best research design?

Students often decide to use a survey because they are familiar with filling out questionnaires, and assume that they will be quick and easy. You need to know whether a survey can actually answer your research questions before you jump right in. Here are some issues you should consider before you go ahead:

1. **What data you need to collect to answer your research questions?** Surveys work best when people have the information that you need, and can articulate it. Can you capture the information you need to answer your research questions using a survey? What are the major concepts and relationships you need to measure? Will you need additional sources of data? Is there a better way to capture this information?

2. **Who has the data that you need?** Surveys only work if you get them to the right people. Can you identify your respondents – the people who have the information you need? Can they provide the correct information? The 'good subject' effect

(discussed in **Section 5.2**) may lead people to give an answer in order to be help-ful, even if they have to guess and give incorrect or made-up information.

3. **Is a survey the best way to get data from these people?** Do your proposed respondents actually have any interest in or incentive to fill out your question-naire, be interviewed, or be observed engaging in the behaviour that you want to observe? You might think that your respondents will want to or have a duty to fill out your questionnaire or talk to you just because you have asked, but a CEO of a Fortune 500 company is extremely unlikely to answer a student's (or even a professor's) unsolicited questionnaire or agree to an interview. You are asking for a substantial commitment of their time, which they might use better in other ways.

Getting enough people to participate is probably most the biggest barrier to using questionnaires, especially if it involves more than minimal effort. Students (includ-ing the authors) usually overestimate how much participation they are likely to get. One of us saw a form letter sent out by a Japanese automotive company's UK site in response to a request to fill out a questionnaire. The company politely explained that it would have to hire at least one full-time employee just to answer requests to fill out questionnaires, because it received so many of them! It might be easier to get other students on your course or in your halls of residence, members of an organisation or society, people you work with and so on to participate because of a shared interest or connection (or an implied social obligation). We will consider this again in this sec-tion when we look at sampling and response rates, and in **Chapter 9**.

Step 2. Decide how you will administer your survey – interview, questionnaire, or structured observation?

How you will administer your survey: face-to-face, voice-to-voice (telephone, Skype), on the web (intranet, hosted website, your own website), leaving them in a physi-cal location such as a shop, posting them to respondents? This has a major effect on what questions you can ask, how many questions you can ask, and many other aspects of the design. Postal surveys are cheap (photocopying and a stamp), but we do not advocate large-scale postal surveys unless you have managed to secure exter-nal funding and sponsorship from an organisation that will give your project the 'stamp of approval' and perhaps even access to a mailing list, as in **Student research in action 5.1**.

Unsolicited surveys typically have low response rates – even as low as 1 in 100. We know of a student group who sent out several hundred questionnaires, includ-ing stamped self-addressed envelopes for the replies, and received just two responses. It doesn't make any sense to use a research design whose strengths are large-scale research and only collect a small set of replies. The cost to the group in time in money per response ended up being much higher than interviews.

Step 3. What questions will you ask, and where will they come from?

Has someone already developed a questionnaire or questions that you could use? Consider whether there are any existing survey instruments and/or questions that you can use before you design your own, which will save you time and improve the qual-ity of your survey. In your literature search (**Chapter 3**), did you find any background readings in which someone used surveys to investigate your research problem? It can be very helpful to build on work already done by experienced researchers who have already tested the questions and saved you considerable work. (If you can't find any examples of surveys in your literature search, question whether it is an appropriate research design.)

Many journal articles and books include key questions – or even the entire survey instrument – or the authors will provide them on request. For example, Zeithaml et al.'s *Delivering Quality Service* (1990) includes a copy of their *Service Quality Questionnaire*. Remember to ask permission to use a survey or a questionnaire unless the author has explicitly given permission for general use. You might also find relevant surveys and questions in question banks – books, online resources, or large-scale social surveys such as the Economic and Social Research Council's (ESRC) Social Survey Question Bank in the Centre for Applied Social Surveys at the University of Surrey.

If you do want to design your own questions, surveys are often associated with closed-ended questions, in which your respondent chooses the best response from a list that you have specified in advance or provides a short answer. For example, in a face-to-face survey, you would read your question and then the list of answers or prompts, and record which one your respondent chooses. In a web-based or postal questionnaire, your respondent records their choice of an answer by clicking on the right one or ticking a box, as shown in **Figure 5.3**. If you are making a structured observation, you will tick the answer corresponding to the behaviour that you have observed. **Closed-ended questions** are best for asking a large number of questions about a large number of respondents.

Since your respondents can only choose from a limited range of answers, you can easily record (or 'code') the answers in a computer spreadsheet and analyse them using statistics. Advantages of closed-ended questions include:

- **Speed** – Answers can be recorded quickly by survey administrators or respondents.
- **Accuracy** – Inappropriate or incorrect answers are less likely to be recorded by survey administrators or respondents.
- **Data entry** – Data can be entered more quickly from an interview schedule or questionnaire, or even automatically downloaded from a web-based instrument.

Surveys may sometimes make use of **open-ended questions**, where your respondent can give any response rather than choosing from your list, as shown in **Figure 5.4**.

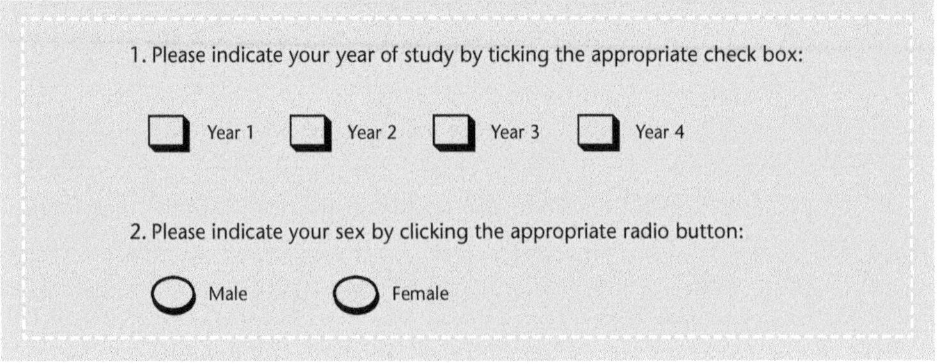

1. Please indicate your year of study by ticking the appropriate check box:

☐ Year 1　☐ Year 2　☐ Year 3　☐ Year 4

2. Please indicate your sex by clicking the appropriate radio button:

○ Male　　○ Female

Figure 5.3　Common formats for closed-ended questions

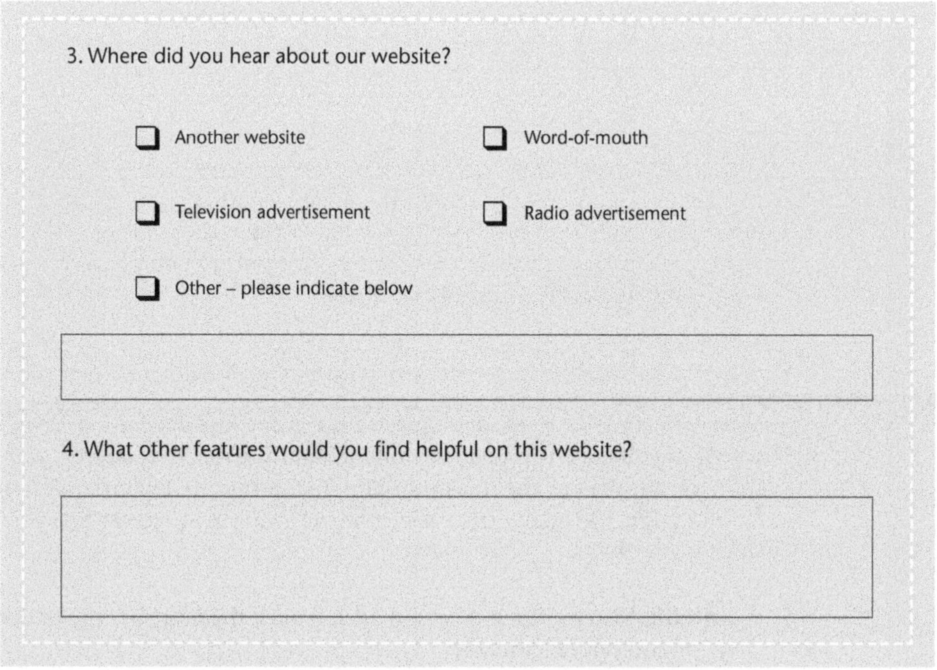
3. Where did you hear about our website?

- ❑ Another website
- ❑ Word-of-mouth
- ❑ Television advertisement
- ❑ Radio advertisement
- ❑ Other – please indicate below

4. What other features would you find helpful on this website?

Figure 5.4 Common formats for open-ended and mixed questions

For the open-ended question 'Who would you say are your top three competitors?', the survey administrator would note the response, or the respondent would fill in the blank on the survey instrument or web-based form. Making this text box long or short can give your respondent a clue as to how long you expect an answer to be. If you do want to mainly ask open-ended questions, where there is no pre-defined answer, you might consider the methods in **Chapter 6** instead.

Whether closed-ended or open-ended, good survey questions are:

1. **Clear** – Structure your responses so that it is clear what each response means instead of making your respondent interpret them. For example, would your respondent know that 'seldom' means less often than 'rarely'? Specify 'Once a month' and 'Once a year' to give a more precise frame. Also spell out (or better yet avoid) avoid technical terms that may be unfamiliar to your respondent: 'Does your manufacturing plant use JIT/TQM/BPR?' might be more intelligible as 'Does your manufacturing plant use just-in-time, total quality management or business process engineering?'.
2. **Simple** – Avoid multiple questions or general questions. If you ask 'How often do you walk or use the bus and train to get to work?' you won't find out about the individual activities. Check to make sure that each question is only a single question, even if multiple questions take up more physical space. You might want to list each of the options separately.
3. **Brief** – Avoid long questions, especially in interviews where it is difficult for your interviewee to remember the entire question and answer it accurately, or in questionnaires because your respondent may lose interest and skip the question.

4. **Unbiased** – Avoid asking leading questions, such as: 'Are you in favour of raising taxes to waste money on able-bodied people who could work but don't?' You are conducting research to find out information, not confirm your own opinions.

Even if your respondent has the relevant information, remember that you might still get inaccurate answers depending on how you ask the questions and whether your respondent actually knows the answer. Rather than asking your respondent to estimate a figure in response to 'How many times did you go to the cinema last year', it might be better to ask 'On average, how often do you go to the cinema' and give a range such as weekly, monthly, and so on.

Step 4. Combine the questions into your survey instrument – first round

Once you get your individual questions right, think about the survey instrument as a whole. If you are letting participants self-administer your survey, you should work on the look and feel of the questionnaire, including the layout and design on the page. Good design will make life easier for you even in structured interviews or observations. Consider:

- **Intelligibility** – the instructions are part of the instrument, so make sure they are clear and understandable.
- **Sequence** – the order you want to present the questions in, which influences your respondent's willingness to answer and the answers themselves.
- **Comprehensibility** – try to look at your instrument from your respondent's perspective – have you actually created something that he or she can and will answer?

We give some pointers on each of these areas below.
   Some tips for smoother flow are:

- Begin with simple questions and put difficult questions at the end of the questionnaire, to keep from putting people off at the beginning.
- Put awkward or potentially embarrassing questions last.
- If your questionnaire is long, or covers different areas, divide the questionnaire into sections to give your respondents a break and avoid 'respondent fatigue'.
- Make sure that you have provided clear and explicit instructions on how to answer the questions, and what to do when the questions have been answered – especially important for self-completion questionnaires!

Step 5. Check the length

Now check to make sure that your interview schedule or questionnaire is not too long or your respondents may end up with survey fatigue, may give incorrect answers, may not complete all the questions, or may even not fill it out at all. You may need to drop some questions, or settle for a lower response rate. Trying to 'trick' respondents with narrow margins or smaller fonts, or breaking a long web-based survey into multiple screens won't fool anyone and will lead to survey fatigue and drop-outs. Many online packages now have a status bar that updates to show respondents how far they have progressed through the survey.

If you absolutely must ask a large number of questions for your research, you might divide your survey into two or more questionnaires for different respondents. The World Class Manufacturing Project included more than 1000 questions for each plant site, but they were broken up into 26 separate questionnaires so that no respondent had to answer more than 100 questions. Each questionnaire could thus be answered in a reasonable amount of time, before the respondent got bored or fatigued. Also consider whether you could collect some of the information yourself, for example from annual reports or industry publications.

Step 6. Lay out your instrument

Once you are happy with the individual questions and their overall sequence, then – and only then – determine the physical design and appearance of your instrument. Getting the content of your survey instrument (your questions) right is more critical than how it looks, even though a crappy format may put respondents off. We receive many questionnaires that look good, but are poorly conceived and designed, with missing or unclear instructions, poor or confusing questionnaire wording and the entire questionnaire being irrelevant because it has been sent to the wrong person.

For informal or small-scale questionnaires, a neatly word-processed and photocopied questionnaire (or a web-based questionnaire you have designed yourself) is usually good enough. Popular survey host sites such as SurveyMonkey have pre-defined formats that make it easier to put up a web-based form. For professional or large-scale questionnaires, or where respondents are of high status, you may need to have them professionally designed. Using software or an app may make designing the instrument and entering the data much simpler, but the trade-off is the time involved in learning to use the package and the temptation to focus on design at the expense of content.

Step 7. Pre-test and pilot your survey

We now move from survey design and question selection to the pilot phase. The next step is to **pilot** or **pre-test** your survey instrument to highlight any mistakes with a 'captive audience', which will help you pick up mistakes, unclear questions and even serious problems before you send it out to your respondent group.

1. Make sure that people know who you are and why you are asking for their help, and that you have dealt with any reservations about providing you with the data (for example, through a statement on confidentiality).
2. Try out your questions – do people understand what the questions mean? Missing or incorrect responses may indicate that people do not understand what you are asking.
3. Time how long it takes for the interview or for your respondents to fill out your questionnaire – too short or too long, and you either miss data or people do not complete the forms.
4. See how they deal with the instructions on the forms, including what to do with the completed form.
5. Enter the data – set up the necessary databases or spreadsheets to feed your data into – how easy is it for you to enter data?

Go back and revise anything that you identified as a problem before you do anything else. If you make major changes, pilot test your survey again before you administer it. Keep doing this for as long as it takes to get it right. Once everything seems to be OK, check it one more time. You will probably find some mistakes or ambiguities you have not previously spotted.

Step 8. Identify your respondents

Except for a census, which is administered to every member of a population (or at least as close as possible), surveys are administered to a **sample** or subset of the whole group or population you want to study. Because you are using your sample to make conclusions about the social units you are studying by selecting units that are representative of your population, sample selection is as important as instrument design.

You first need to understand what **population** – the set that contains all members of the social units you want to study – you want to sample. According to O'Leary (2013), the first step is describing the population in words. Is it all Chinese restaurants in the UK, all university students or all Honda drivers? Your **sample** is the subset you have selected to study: Chinese restaurants in Manchester, students at Loughborough, or Honda drivers in Swindon. See **Section 5.1.3** for strategies and issues in choosing your sample from your population. Your **sampling frame** describes how you select members of your population for studying. This can be tricky – if your population is all of O2's current mobile phone customers, the company's database might include customers who no longer have a mobile phone but who haven't cancelled their accounts, or exclude customers who have signed up in the last week.

Step 9. Administer your survey and track its progress

Now you are ready for questionnaire administration. Once you have started administering your survey, keep returning to the issues described above. If you are using a postal questionnaire, keep track of the response rate to your questionnaires, so that you can take corrective action if necessary. You may need to send out reminder letters after an appropriate period (two to four weeks), and perhaps even send out more surveys to the same sample or a new sample. This might involve following up **nonresponses** with a letter or polite phone call after a reasonable period of time to remind people to respond. If you are conducting structured interviews, are there questions that your respondents find difficult or aren't answering? Try to figure out why this is so.

5.1.3 Key issues in designing and administering surveys

Sampling

A sample must be representative of the population if you want to generalise, i.e. to draw conclusions about your population from your sample, from your sample to your population (Bryman and Bell 2011). If you want to make generalisations, then your sample needs to be representative of your population. Otherwise, your results will be inaccurate because your sample is **biased**, over-representing some members of the population and under-representing others.

You can choose your sample from your population using either probability sampling, where you select the units you study randomly from your population, or nonprobability sampling, where you systematically or purposefully select these units. Differences between your sample and your population create **sampling error**. Using an accurate sampling frame and probability sampling correctly minimises over- or under-sampling, but if people in different subsamples have different response rates, you may still end up with sampling error.

When should I use probability sampling?

The goal of **probability sampling** is to make sure each unit in your population has a known and equal probability of being selected so that your sample represents the entire population. Most probability samples also rely on random selection. Avoid drawing conclusions about household wealth by sampling only footballers' wives.

Four techniques that you can use for probability sampling are illustrated in **Figure 5.5**. In *simple random sampling*, any particular member of the population is equally likely to be selected. In *systematic sampling*, you use a non-random but systematic technique for selecting the members of your subset, for example by selecting every tenth employee on the list (2, 22, 32, ...). In *stratified random sampling*, you subdivide your population according to some criterion (e.g. year of study), and then apply random sampling. Finally, in *cluster sampling*, you select your entire sample from

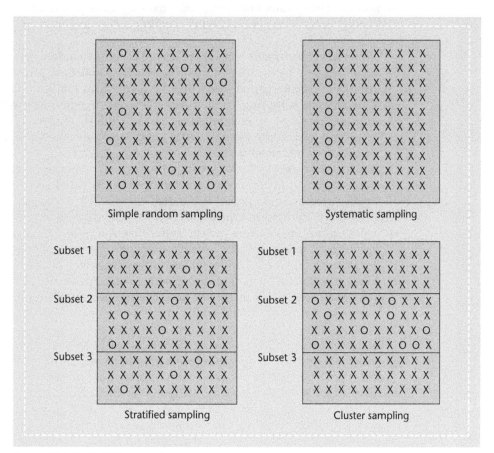

Figure 5.5 Probability sampling

a particular subset, known as a cluster, that is representative of the entire population but not random, e.g. a single hall of residence to represent all first-year student houses.

These four techniques illustrate two important aspects of sampling: (1) random or systematic, and (2) single-stage or multi-stage. Except for simple random sampling, the other three techniques can introduce bias into your sample if not handled carefully.

Student research in action 5.2

UP, UP, AND AWAY

A project group wanted to collect data for a research project on awareness of the environmental effects of low-cost air travel. They planned to stop students outside the student union and ask them a few questions, which they estimated would take about 10 minutes per student. They decided to encourage students to answer their questions by giving each respondent a chocolate bar. Is this a good approach to sampling in order to answer their research question? What issues do you think they should take into account in designing a sampling plan?

When should I use nonprobability sampling?

In **nonprobability sampling**, some units have a greater probability of being selected than other units. Four nonprobability sampling techniques used are:

1. **Volunteer recruitment** –This is unlikely to be a truly random because people who volunteer tend to be different from the general population. Anyone who watches reality or audience participation shows can vouch for that!
2. **Convenience sampling** – Otherwise known as begging one's mates. This may ensure that you get enough responses, but it's unlikely that you can draw any sort of general conclusions from it. Better to use your convenience sample to pre-test or pilot your instruments.
3. **Snowball sampling** – Starting with a single person (or other social unit), expand your sample using additional respondents or units based on contacts known to or suggested by your original respondents (social network). Again, you may have problems with drawing conclusions beyond your sample.
4. **Quota sampling** – Define the categories that you want to study, and then keep recruiting respondents until you have enough representatives of each category. For example, if you want 50 men and 50 women, you would stop sampling men when you reached 50 but keep going with women. This is used in opinion polling for election research, where they need to make the sample representative of the voting public. It may look like random sampling, but is not.

Each of these techniques is non-random in at least one way, so that it is harder to draw general conclusions about the population from the sample. If you don't need to generalise to a population anyway, and the emphasis is on the lessons learnt from the sample, these can be useful ways to sample (O'Leary 2013).

It is important to consider whether your research might over- or under-represent respondents systematically (and unintentionally induce bias). A telephone survey might under-sample young people (who gave up landlines for mobile phones), more affluent people (who tend to be ex-directory), and lower-income people (no or shared landlines). Many elderly people do not have email accounts, which could be a problem if you are recruiting respondents by email and want your sample to represent the general population.

Sample size

Probably the most worrying question for students is 'How many completed surveys do I need?'. Try to get as many high-quality responses as you can, given your time and cost constraints. Consult an expert or a survey guide if this is important to your research. This depends on how confident you want to be that your conclusions accurately represent your sample, and the specific questions you have asked, and how you are going to analyse your data. (We will discuss this in **Chapters 10** and **11**.) As the administrative scientist James March and his colleagues observed, a sample size of one is sufficient, if it's the right one! (March et al. 1991).

In general, the number of responses that you will need will increase when:

1. You plan to use sophisticated statistical methods
2. You plan to test the relationships between two or more variables
3. Your variables can take on more values
4. Your data do not follow a normal distribution
5. You are investigating weaker relationships among your variables.

Calculating the number of responses you will need – and therefore the sample size – is rarely straightforward, since you don't know how many people will actually respond, as shown in **Student research in action 5.3**. Rob and his group needed to estimate the likely response rate to their survey from ex-students (who might not be easy to contact).

 Student research in action 5.3

BACK ON THE CHAIN GANG

Rob and his project group wanted to show that the more hours per week a full-time student worked in paid employment, the less likely they were to get a good degree. They decided to survey past students to see whether the number of hours that students worked in paid employment affected their final degree classification. So, how many questionnaires to send out?

Other factors that might affect the sample size the group needed in this case:

- Not all former students would have worked during their studies;
- How many students got 'good degrees' in the programme. Did 5% or 20% of students receive a first? Does a good degree also include a 2.1?

Response rate

Students are often wildly optimistic when they estimate their likely response rate and therefore underestimate how many surveys they will need to administer in order to get a specific number back. To get 100 surveys back with a 50% response rate, you would need to send out 200; to get the same number back with a 5% response rate, you would need to send out 2000. Most surveys are lucky to achieve a 10–15% return rate; even mandatory surveys such as the National Census achieve a less than 100% return rate. Calculate the ceiling on your response rate based on the survey response rates found in your literature review.

A low response rate may be due just to people's dislike of filling out forms or lack of time, but it can also suggest problems with your study. This is where good survey design, including pilot testing, follow-up and multiple-wave survey designs, can make a difference.

What are the key issues for questionnaires?

How to administer the survey. Although the most familiar survey design is the **self-administered questionnaire** (see for example Oppenheimer 1992; Foddy 1993, and the additional sources listed at the end of this chapter in **Additional resources**), surveys can be administered in many ways: on the *web*, which is often free and has global reach, although there is little control over who answers, how many times they answer, or even if they are who they say they are; by *email*, although sending unsolicited mass emails is **spamming** and should be avoided; by *post*, popular because of its low cost and geographic reach to anywhere in the world that post is delivered; and by *deliver and collect*, handing out the questionnaire or leaving it in a convenient location for the respondents to return.

Questionnaires can be cheaper per respondent than interviews, especially for collecting data from a large number of people. Once a questionnaire has been developed and piloted, the marginal cost of administering one additional questionnaire is very low – the cost of photocopying and postage or hosting the website. By comparison, each additional interview is as expensive as every other interview. Given the low response rate to unsolicited questionnaires, however, you may be sending out 5–20 questionnaires for each one returned, which can add up quickly. However, questionnaires can only capture the answers to the questions you have asked, but in a structured interview you can capture additional information and insights. You are less likely to have missing data problems with interview data, because people often skip questions or leave them half-complete. Interviews can also capture more spontaneous feedback from your respondents, including nonverbal feedback.

Finally, you need to make sure that your respondent can answer the questions on a questionnaire without any help, so your questionnaire design will have to be very clear, whereas you can clarify your questions in an interview. If you make a major design error on a questionnaire, you cannot easily fix it once it has been sent out, and if you do make changes you may not be able to use the early data. Since you usually interview people one at a time rather than simultaneously, you have more of a chance to improve your questions between interviews.

Applying the survey principles to structured interviews

The *structured interview* is very similar to the questionnaire, because you will ask the same questions in the same order to every interviewee. This structured approach makes sure that the data you collect are consistent across interviews. Structured interviews can be conducted face-to-face, over the telephone, over the internet or in writing. The standardised list of questions is known as an **interview schedule**. Rather than just having a list of questions, many researchers prefer to leave space to record the answers directly on the interview schedule, even if they are recording the interview. Even with a list of questions, you may want to probe, ask for further information or explore unexpected answers. Professional survey researchers may use computer-based interview schedules known as **computer-assisted protocols for interviews** (CAPI), especially for large surveys. CAPI allows you to record responses directly on the computer and transfer them to the program you will use to analyse them, reducing errors.

Chapter 6 will discuss how you should behave as an interviewer in more depth. In order not to influence the answers you get by how you conduct your interviews, you should aim to be:

1. **Consistent.** Make sure that you ask questions in exactly the same way and the same order during each interview. If you need to explain a question to your interviewee, make sure that you are consistent with the instrument; building standard **prompts** into your interview schedule may help to maintain this consistency. If you interpret or embellish the question with an example or additional information based on what you think, such as 'Well, I think that this means ...', you may influence the answer you get.
2. **Complete.** Make sure that you have asked every question and not left any out. You may sometimes be tempted ask questions out of order if your interviewee starts talking about a subject you know comes up later in the interview schedule, but besides making it more likely that you will omit questions, this can contribute to a lack of consistency between interviews.
3. **Accurate.** Make sure that you are recording the replies exactly. If you are only recording answers to closed-ended questions, make sure that you are ticking the right boxes. If you are recording answers to open-ended questions, make sure that you are capturing them exactly.
4. **Ethical.** Because interviewing is so often used for commercial research, including consumer marketing and public opinion research, codes of ethics have been developed that address most of the issues you might encounter if you use a structured interview. Obviously, you need to consider ethical issues and **informed consent** if you plan to record a telephone interview. We will discuss this issue further in **Chapter 8**.

Even when using an interviewing schedule, you may have a hard time maintaining consistency across interviews if several people in your project group are conducting interviews. Try to practise interviewing together before you start interviewing respondents. For example, try round-robin interviewing until you achieve consistency across interviewers. In the *International Service Study*, for example, Professor Chris Voss of London Business School flew from the UK to the US to train the American interviewers (Voss et al. 2004). It is also a good idea to hold a refresher session periodically to make sure that variation hasn't crept in.

Applying the survey principles to structured observations?

In *structured observation*, rather than directly asking questions you are observing behaviours and recording the information on a schedule. Frederick Taylor's time-and-motion studies relied on structured observation. *Mystery shoppers* do this in stores when they unobtrusively follow people around and record what merchandise people look at, touch, try on and purchase, as described by Underhill (2000). Structured observation can also be used to collect data indirectly by observing the traces people leave in the physical environment or other natural settings (Webb et al. 1966), a technique described as using **unobtrusive measures** (see **Research in action 5.1**). Since unobtrusive data are collected in the natural setting of organisations and people, the researcher is less likely to cause changes in the behaviour of participants than someone standing there with a clipboard watching them. Lee (2000: 2) gives examples of how creative researchers have used unobtrusive data such as:

- Wear on the floor tiles surrounding a museum exhibits;
- Showing hatching chicks to measure visitor flows (really);
- The size of suits of armour as an indicator of changes in human stature over time; and
- (Tongue in cheek) the relationship between psychologists' hair length and their methodological predilections.

Unobtrusive measures can complement other data especially if you want to collect data about sensitive issues or do not have direct access to respondents, they are unwilling to answer questions or the act of asking questions might affect the answers (Lee 2000: 1). For example, when people are asked questions directly, they tend to over-report behaviours or attitudes they perceive as positive or **socially desirable**, such as recycling and giving to charity, and to under-report undesirable behaviours, such as drinking too much or wasting food.

 Research in action 5.1

IT'S NOT RUBBISH, IT'S RESEARCH … HONESTLY!

In studies of household consumption, people often consciously or unconsciously misreport what and how much they consume of various products. To find out what people actually buy, consume and throw away, many researchers have turned to analysing household waste – finding out what's in people's rubbish bins. This can be used to complement survey data ('what people said they did' versus 'what they actually did') or as a stand-alone research design.

In 1973, the Garbage Project at the University of Arizona started to analyse people's household rubbish using the same techniques that archaeologists use for studying ancient populations. A number of studies have used 'household archaeology' or garbage-ology to study business and management problems. For example, Wallendorf and Nelson (1986: 273) studied the contents of nearly 1600 waste bins to determine whether Americans of European and Mexican backgrounds differed in the use of body care products, including 'personal cleansers, household cleansers, oral hygiene products, odour fighters, hair care products, skin care products, cosmetics, feminine protection products, over-the-counter drugs, and aspirin'. In another project, Reilly and Wallendorf (1987) studied differences between the foods consumed by these two groups based on the contents of their rubbish bins. The data gathered by such methods, it is argued by the researchers, is more reliable than asking people what products they are prepared to tell you that they buy.

5.2 How can I collect quantitative data using an experiment?

The second research design associated with the quantitative approach is the experiment. An **experiment** is a structured process for testing how varying one or more inputs affects one or more outcomes. Experiments are often used in the natural and behavioural sciences, where an experiment can be often carried out on a limited part of the phenomenon or context that is being studied. Experimenters study natural or physical systems by breaking them down into smaller systems or parts that can be studied in isolation from the whole system (*reductionism*). They can study how a car engine works without having to study the entire automobile, or how an artificial hip joint works without having to study the entire human body. Experiments are often conducted in controlled settings such as laboratories that are isolated from the outside world.

Although experiments are associated in the popular imagination with the natural and applied sciences, you are probably already familiar with experiments from everyday life, for example, 'taste tests' or 'trial offers'. You may even have unwittingly participated in quite a few business and management experiments. Fast-food companies often test out new sandwiches in just a few locations before offering them nationwide – the fast-food company McDonald's even has a mock-up of an entire McDonald's restaurant on the campus of McDonald's University, where new menus and new processes can be tried out before they go public (Bradach 1997). Heinz has tried out different colours of ketchup around the world, to see whether total ketchup sales will increase (BBC News 2000). Camden Council in London is experimenting with ways to help residents become more environmentally sustainable.

On the other hand, people who prefer the qualitative approach for doing research often regard the experiment as not all that useful for studying human behaviours and complex organisations because they argue that it is difficult to reduce the social units and systems that we research in business and management to a simple enough system to study in a laboratory. This doesn't mean that you can't use experiments in business and management, but that researchers are seldom able to apply the experimental method in the same way as in the natural sciences. In fact, much of what we know about business and management has been learnt from field experiments, starting with Taylor's scientific management experiments and the Hawthorne experiments. It does mean, however, that the conclusions we can draw from an experiment in business and management research are not necessarily as strongly supported as in scientific research.

5.2.1 Should I consider an experimental design?

Although experiments are less common in business and management research than they are in areas such as psychology, to understand quantitative research it is important to understand the role of design and analysis and experiments. This is because the experiment is the best choice for testing cause-and-effect relationships. A cause-and-effect relationship is hypothesised where a change to one variable (independent variable, cause or input) creates a change in another (**dependent variable**, effect or outcome). You must be able to measure the **independent variable** and to measure the change in the dependent variable with variations in the independent variable, as well as eliminating or measuring any other variables that might explain the change in the dependent variable (alternative explanation), as shown in in **Student research in action 5.4**.

Student research in action 5.4

WAITER, THERE'S A SURVEY IN MY SOUP

Xin decided that he wanted to test David Maister's eight principles for managing service queues in his MSc dissertation. He decided that his summer job in a Chinese restaurant would be a good place to test these principles with real customers. One of Maister's predictions is that 'unexplained waits seem longer than explained waits' (Maister 1985). In order to test whether this was true, one evening he told some groups of customers who were waiting to be seated why they had to wait and told other groups nothing. At the end of the meal, each group of customers was asked to fill out a questionnaire rating their satisfaction with the meal. Xin expected that if Maister's principle was true, those groups who had been informed would be more satisfied with the meal – everything else being equal of course! The findings did show that explaining the wait seemed to help overall satisfaction, but the data was inconsistent and demonstrated that there were other factors at play here.

5.2.2 What are the main types of experiments?

Researchers classify experiments by the relationship between the experimental setting and the natural setting of the system or phenomenon being studied, which affects the amount of control you will have over the variables and participants. The three main types of experiments discussed in this chapter are laboratory experiments, which are held in an artificial setting; field experiments, which are held in a natural setting; and quasi-experiments, which are usually in a natural setting. Computer simulations and mathematical modelling are a type of laboratory experiment.

Laboratory experiments

A **laboratory experiment** takes place in an artificial setting, rather than the setting where the phenomenon or participants would normally be found. This may literally be a laboratory, as in Stanley Milgram's experiment on people's obedience to authority (**Chapter 1**), but it could be a classroom or a mock-up of an office, factory or other business setting. Reality television shows such as *Big Brother* where participants are isolated from the world could also be considered laboratory experiments.

The laboratory setting gives the experimenter the most control over participants, experimental treatments and the experimental setting. As we discuss in **Section 5.2.3**, it is nearly impossible to control every possible factor even in a laboratory setting. However, this leads to criticisms of laboratory experiments as unrepresentative of what actually goes on in organisations, because:

- The laboratory setting can be artificial and simplified compared with the real-world people and settings we are interested in;
- The tasks people are asked to perform may not closely represent actual tasks in organisational settings;
- The experimental participants themselves are often undergraduates or master's-level students, rather than managers.

Laboratory settings are therefore most appropriate when you are investigating basic aspects of how people behave, independently of the setting, rather than complex social and organisational phenomena.

Field experiments

An experiment that takes place in its natural setting is called a **field experiment**. Xin's Chinese restaurant experiment in **Student research in action 5.4** is a field experiment; so were Taylor's experiments in work methods. Natural settings for business and management experiments include the workplace (office, shop, factory), the classroom, the household and public spaces such as shopping malls or public streets. The setting in **Research in action 5.2** is a summer camp. Although field experiments minimise the artificiality of the experimental setting on what you are studying, they offer less control over your participants, experimental treatment and other factors than in a laboratory experiment. While laboratory experiments are high in control, but low in realism; field experiments are low in control, but high in realism.

 Research in action 5.2
THERE WAS THIS ONE TIME AT SUMMER CAMP

Sherif (1956) and Tajfel (1970) both tested whether 'simply being a member of a group was enough to cause people to discriminate against members of another group'. Sherif set up an experiment known as the 'Robber's Cave' in a summer camp, where he allocated boys randomly to different groups and got them to compete on different tasks. Even when the boys in different groups had previously been friends, the rivalries grew so intense that the experiment had to be modified!

Similarly, Tajfel found that when boys were allowed to allocate rewards, they discriminated against members of the other group (the outgroup) in favour of their own group (the ingroup). The ingroup–outgroup hypothesis has been widely used in social psychology and organisational behaviour to explain and predict people's behaviours.

Even field experiments with people in natural settings can have surprisingly misleading outcomes. Soft drink giant Coca-Cola found this out the hard way in the 1980s. The company replaced its successful Coke with New Coke, whose taste customers had preferred in market research blind taste tests. People refused to buy New Coke in the supermarkets, and an embarrassed Coca-Cola was forced to bring back Classic Coke (the original, less-preferred recipe) at enormous expense.

Quasi-experiments

A **quasi-experiment** is not a true experiment because it lacks at least one of the experimental attributes we discuss in **Section 5.2.3**, but is a naturally occurring situation that you are taking advantage of as a researcher to try to illuminate cause-and-effect relationships without being able to test them. Usually, in a quasi-experiment:

- You can only observe what is going on directly or indirectly but not manipulate it;
- You have little control over your participants, the experimental treatment or other experimental conditions.

You might be interested in a quasi-experiment because you can analyse the data using the same logic as a true experiment. **Research in action 5.3** illustrates how useful a quasi-experiment can be for a researcher.

Many naturally occurring quasi-experiments let you collect useful data and apply the logic of experimental design. Suppose you are interested in studying the provision of online shopping by supermarkets, you should be able to identify which supermarkets have adopted online shopping and which haven't, even though you have no influence over which ones do or don't. In this case, you will be observing a quasi-experiment. Your ability to support your hypothesis, though, will be weakened because you cannot randomly assign supermarkets to adopters and non-adopters. Indeed, with most of the major supermarkets being 'adopters', the non-adopters could be regarded as 'outliers' from the start.

We described Xin's research study in **Student research in action 5.4** as an experiment. Do you think his study was closer to a true experiment or a quasi-experiment? How much control do you think he had over:

- Queuing time – long versus short wait to be seated?
- Waiting time – long versus short wait to receive meal?
- Number of people in party – couple to group?
- The atmosphere in the party – was it celebratory or deflated?
- Quality of meal?

The source of data in many quasi-experiments is secondary data, which we discuss in **Section 5.3**.

5.2.3 What are the essential characteristics of an experimental design?

Researchers classify experiments as **true experiments** if all the principles of experimental design – experimental treatment, random assignment, control groups, before-and-after measurement – are met. If one or more of these are lacking, but the general design is experimental, these research studies are known as quasi-experiments.

Cause-and-effect relationships

An experiment is the strongest method for showing a relationship between two or more concepts, especially if you want to show that a change in one causes a change in another – a **cause-and-effect relationship**. Because an experiment allows you to see what effect varying an independent variable has on the dependent variable, holding everything else constant, it is the strongest design for showing a cause-and-effect relationship between concepts. The factor that you can vary (or factors) is known as your **experimental treatment.**

It is difficult in many cases to show cause and effect, because for one factor to cause another, the factor that we argue is the cause must precede the result in time, consistently. If you can eliminate as many other factors as possible – which we will discuss in more detail below – you can be even more confident that you have found a cause-and-effect relationship. But this is not the same as proving that A causes B. What if it is impossible to show that the variation in A happens before the variation in B? In real life, this is difficult, so usually we can only make statements about associations, or correlations, which are much weaker than statements about cause and effect.

In an experiment, we would want to show that our variation in our experimental treatment (A) led to the variation in our outcome (B), as shown in Figure 5.6 as the difference between outcome (B) due to the change in input (A). We would also need to show that it was the variation in A that led to the variation in B, and not some other unobserved variable, C. This is easier to do in laboratory experiments, where the experimenter can control a larger number of the experimental conditions, and more difficult in field experiments or quasi-experiments. You need to identify any other factor (C) or factors that could affect the outcome or the relationship or offer an alternative explanation (see Fig. 5.7).

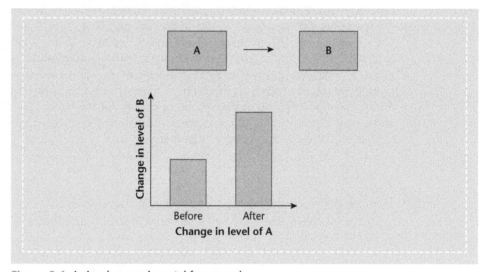

Figure 5.6 A simple experimental framework

These factors might include any other potential causes of changes in the results, difference in the people or organisations being observed or even our own expectations about what the outcome of the experiment should be. For example, a company wants to know why the pay-for-performance programme (P4P) that it implemented didn't result in higher employee performance (EP). We might naively conclude that P4P didn't work, but if we also knew that the company had laid off a significant number of workers during the same period we might instead decide that we need to include other things that are going on.

The need to show that a change in A should cause a change in B, and to rule out alternate causes (C) means that one of the most important steps in experimental design is the step where you are deducing your hypothesis or hypotheses from your theory. If you do not identify all the alternate causes and measure or control them, your experiment will be pointless. An experiment is the best research design if you want to rule out the possibility that any other factors have affected the relationship between the two (or more) factors that you are looking at. If you can systematically examine the relationship between varying your input factor and changes in the output factor you are observing, and you consistently find changes in the outcome, it is easier to propose that 'changes in A lead to changes in B'. Even in a laboratory setting, there may be factors that you are not testing but you can't control. These variations might be *systemic*, recurring in some fashion, or they might be *extraneous*, nonrecurring and random in nature. If you conduct an experiment where your outcome variable is participant performance, the room temperature might be higher in the afternoon sessions than in the morning sessions, and the heat might negatively affect your afternoon participants' performance by putting them to sleep. This would be a **systemic variation**. On the other hand, the noise caused by drilling outside the room might be a one-off and hence extraneous, even though it might still affect the participants. Being able to identify at least one independent variable and one dependent variable is an important aspect of the experimental design, and one that makes it different from secondary analysis and surveys where we may only study relationships between variables.

Ruling out alternate explanations for the relationships between two or more concepts is always difficult, especially when you are doing research with people or organisations rather than natural systems. If you do find that C (or D and so on) has an effect on B or the relationship between A and B, you may need to revise your model or even your theory. You might need to come up with an alternative hypothesis for the role of C. First, A might not really have any effect on B and a variation in the level of C might be causing the change in B rather than A. Second, although A might have an effect, the effect of C might overwhelm or cancel out the effect of A. Alternatively, A and C might both affect B, but it might be difficult to disentangle their relative effects, especially if A and C always occur together.

Experimental treatment and control

Scientists have developed a structured approach to ruling out as many alternate causes or explanations as they can in an experiment in which the experimenter holds constant those factors you want to rule out as causing the changes in the output variable to maximise the certainty that the changes are due to varying your input. A good experimental design will help disentangle whether a change in B is due to a change in A rather than a change in C (as shown in Figure 4.7).

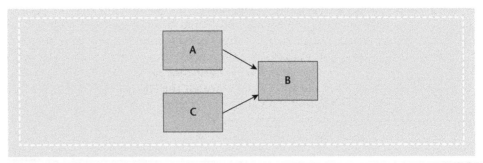

Figure 5.7 Alternate causes

In experimental language, this is known as **control**. Control is essential for examining cause-and-effect relationships. There are four types of variables that you will need to measure and/or control in an experiment:

1. **Experimental variables** are the inputs you intend to vary to see the effects on outcomes, for example varying the drink (water or Red Bull) as the input to see the effects on test performance
2. **Dependent variables** are the outcomes that you predict will vary in response to changes in the experimental variables
3. **Control variables** are any elements of the experiment that you will try to eliminate as potential causes of the variation in outcomes by excluding them from the experiment, holding them constant during the experiment or by randomising some element of the experiment
4. **Uncontrolled variables** are variables you do not know about or are unable to control, which might lead you to make mistakes about concluding there is (or isn't) a cause-and-effect relationship.

You should already realise that it is difficult to control any systems except simple systems, or any human behaviours except basic or readily observable behaviours. Although you might also be able to observe the behaviour and interactions of two people (a dyad), it would be much more difficult to observe the behaviour and interactions in a large group or complex system such as an organisation.

Control group

In an experiment, we also need to make sure that the change in our dependent variable wouldn't have happened anyway because of a change occurring in the people, behaviour, or another phenomenon that we are investigating. If we have two groups – one a **control group** that receives no experimental treatment and the other a **treatment group** – we will be more convinced that our independent variable has created our change in our dependent variable if it only happens to the treatment group and not to the control group. As you can see in **Figure 5.8**, the control group has stayed the same despite the experimental treatment (change in the independent

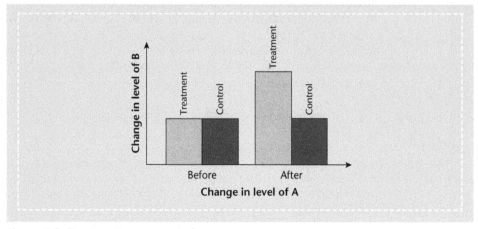

Figure 5.8 Treatment versus control group

variable A), whilst the treatment group has changed. Thus, we are more confident that our experimental treatment has caused the change in the dependent variable.

Random assignment

Even with a control group, the possibility of no cause-and-effect relationship or no alternate cause can only be ruled out if you have randomly assigned the experimental participants to the control and treatment groups to rule out any variations due to differences between the people or organisations assigned to different levels of your experimental treatment. **Random assignment** is the third principle of experimental design, and one that is often difficult to apply in business and management experiments, since people and organisations usually vary significantly one from another, unlike laboratory rats, and it is often difficult to randomly assign participants. If you are able to do random assignment, the principles of probability sampling discussed in **Section 5.1** will be useful to you.

Statistical analysis

Finally, in order to draw valid conclusions from a quantitative research including but not limited to experiments, you want to make sure that the change you have observed in the dependent variable has actually occurred. That is, any difference before and after the treatment is not measurement error or natural fluctuations. Ideally, you should design your experiment so that your experimental data provide the strongest empirical evidence (that is, statistical analysis of data) to support (or overturn) this hypothesis. We will discuss various types of statistical analysis in **Chapters 10 and 11**. You should use statistical tests to make sure that you are not arguing for a cause-and-effect relationship based on a systematic association where this relationship is actually due to change. This is one area where journalism and consulting often fail to measure up to research.

Knowing how to design a statistical test and which statistical test you can use is important to being able to correctly interpret the results of an experiment or other quantitative data. Statistical analysis is important because research shows that people are not very good at actually interpreting results accurately, and without statistical tests they often reach the wrong conclusions. There is an old joke that 'one anecdote is a story, two anecdotes is data'. Without statistical analysis, you might conclude that there is no relationship when one exists, or that there is a relationship when one doesn't exist.

There is considerable research on how people tend to err in understanding data. People often overestimate or underestimate the probability that certain events will occur, or the probability that the distribution of events that have occurred differs significantly from randomness, as shown in the activity below. This is the topic of Nicholas Taleb's popular book, *The Black Swan*, which looks specifically at how people deal with the probability of rare events occurring.

ACTIVITY

If you flip a coin 20 times, you expect on average to get 10 heads and 10 tails, if it is a fair coin. If you get 12 heads and 8 tails, you might not be too surprised. If you get 1 head and 19 tails, though, you would probably begin to suspect that you might not have an average coin or your flipping technique might be biasing the result.

▶

Suppose we asked you to mentally flip a coin 10 times and record the number of times it comes up heads and the number of times it comes up tails. How many times would you expect it to come up with no heads or no tails in 10 tosses? One or fewer? Two or fewer? Record your answers in the table below.

	0	1	2
Heads or tails			

Suppose you did flip the coin 10 times and it came up with zero, one or two heads or tails. Would you think that the coin was dodgy? We flipped a simulated coin 10 times, for 100 trials. The exact distribution is shown in the **Postscript** at the end of this chapter.

If you thought that it was unlikely that a fair coin would come up heads or tails zero times, then you are right – this might happen by chance once in less than 1000 times, and it never occurred in our simulated 1000 trials. Coming up with one head or tail is also unlikely – this might happen as often as 1 in 100 times. Once we get to two heads or two tails, this might occur 1 in 10 times. This is well above the level of 1 in 20 times that is the accepted level for statistical testing.

What you are investigating in an experiment may be much more subtle than flipping a coin. This means that you need to be careful so that you do not draw the wrong conclusions from an experiment (or indeed any other relationship). **Chapters 10 and 11** will help you identify some useful statistical tests.

5.2.4 What are the key issues in experiments?

The principles of experimental design that we described before enable researchers to minimise the risk of mistaking a chance result or spurious cause for the cause-and-effect relationship you are interested in, but other issues might still cause your experiment to lose credibility. These include subtle effects such as experimenter or subject effects.

How do I minimise potential sources of bias?

Although the principles of experimental design rule out some sources of error, you need to be aware of other ones when you are designing and conducting your experiment so that you can minimise them. Social psychologists Rosnow and Rosenthal (1997) identified the major sources of experimental bias as experimenter effects and experimenter expectancies, as well as subject effects. **Experimenter effects** are intentional or unintentional mistakes in how you collect, record, interpret or report your data and findings; or interactions between you and the experimental treatment, participants and/or setting. One source of bias to be especially aware of is **experimenter expectancies** – your expectations about the outcomes of the experiment might influence your design of the experiment to increase the likelihood that that outcome actually occurs. It is sometimes known as a 'self-fulfilling prophecy'. Educational experiments have shown that teachers are more encouraging towards students classified as 'bright', and less encouraging towards those designated 'not bright'. These 'bright' students were actually found to outperform the other students at the end of the year, even though there was no difference between the two groups at the beginning. This is similar to the experiment with 'bright' and 'dull' rats by Rosenthal and Fode (1963) described in **Chapter 4**. This isn't the same as *deliberate fraud* (which has been known to occur in scientific and other experiments).

Another source of experimental bias identified by Rosenthal and Rosnow is **subject effects**, also known as *demand characteristics*. The **good subject** effect occurs when participants change their behaviours to help (or hinder) the experimenter, thus making the experimental results invalid because they do not represent how people usually behave. The **volunteer subject effect** occurs when people who volunteer to participate in studies differ from the general population, and again the experimental results may not represent how people in general (rather than experimental subjects) usually behave. In the behavioural psychology literature, David O. Sears has questioned whether there is a second-year undergraduate effect, since those students are used as experimental subject so often in that field (Sears, 1986).

What are the key ethical issues for experiments?

Although we will discuss ethical considerations in research more specifically in Chapter 8, experiments create a number of specific ethical concerns that we will preview. One element you must absolutely consider in designing an experiment is any **potential harm** that might come to participants – even inadvertently – because of your experiment.

 5.3 How can I identify and acquire quantitative data from secondary sources?

 Research in action 5.4

GOOOOOOOOOOOOOOOOAAAAAAAAAAAAAAAALLLLLLLLLLLLLLLL!!

The economist Robert Metcalfe, one of Kate's colleagues, attracted considerable media attention with a study of the effect of World Cup football on GCSE marks. Rob and his colleagues used a government database of 3.5 million students to show that marks were a quarter-point lower when the World Cup or Euro were held during the summer, with the impact affected by the student's sex and socioeconomic class. It would be difficult to conduct this kind of study with either a survey or an experiment, but the UK already had a vast database of key skills achievement by students that could be used in a quasi-experimental design.

Whether you are taking a scientific or ethnographic approach to research, you will probably find yourself doing some secondary analysis, even if it is not the only method you use for collecting data to answer your research questions. If someone else has collected the right data and you can gain access to it, you should make use of it if you can. People and organisations create large amounts of secondary data as part of their everyday activities, and, some proprietary secondary data sources are even deliberately created and maintained as a source of revenues.

Some researchers find the challenge of archival research or unobtrusive measures exciting because it requires 'thinking outside the box'. If you are a fan of Sherlock Holmes, for example, you may recognise some of the detective's methods in unobtrusive research. If you are interested in historical or longitudinal research, this may be the only way to find out about people and companies.

In this section, we will describe how you can use secondary analysis, analysing previously collected data as your main research design. **Secondary analysis** is used to describe a research design based around collecting (or acquiring) and analysing secondary data, data that you do not directly collect from organisations or people in their natural settings. Secondary analysis includes both reanalysing data that someone else has already analysed and analysing data that you collect indirectly about people and organisations or collected by other people for other purposes or extracted by you from such sources. This section will be helpful if you are considering a research design where you:

- Analyse an existing data set such as a large-scale survey or a commercial database
- Create a data set yourself from published or unpublished materials such as company archives, document analysis, or from observing people or organisations without interacting with them (unobtrusive analysis), as shown in **Research in action 5.5**.

Secondary analysis may be your best research design when:

- Someone else has already collected the data you need, and you can use them to answer your own research questions
- You want to study a social unit that you cannot contact directly because of geographic distance or other access problems
- You want to study the historical activities of social units or social units that no longer exist (historical data), or covering an extended period of time (longitudinal data).

Research in action 5.5
YOU CAN BANK ON IT

Frances and Kate were interested in whether high street banks were responding to pressures for corporate social responsibility (CSR). They decided that one measure of this would be whether the banks had included a statement of their policy regarding diversity on the company website and the content of that policy (if there was one). They collected data from the 25 major banks and building societies in the UK. They also used publicly available information such as reported profits and return on assets to see what influenced these statements. Although this only revealed information about a small part of the banks' CSR activities, it agreed closely with other information about this sector, including market research on customer perceptions and regulatory actions. This secondary analysis gave them some good ideas for doing further research in which they collected information directly from bank customers about their perceptions of their own banks.

Secondary analysis is sometimes classed as a **desk/library research** project, because you do not have direct contact with organisations or people in collecting your data. You should check with your project supervisor and/or business sponsor to see if this meets your project guidelines, because some project guidelines require you to collect **primary data**. If you are working on a sponsored project, you should check to see if secondary data are acceptable to your project stakeholders, as they may want you to collect primary data to support your findings.

5.3.1 What are the advantages and disadvantages of using secondary data?

Analysing secondary data may save you time and effort (although not always money). People collect data in many fields of business and management and make those data available. Some companies, such as Mintel and Gartner, consult and conduct market research, and they publish data and market reports that are available for purchase – sometimes for thousands of pounds.

Some areas of management use secondary analysis as a core research design. Secondary data abound in accounting and finance, because companies have to report their financial performance. For example, many financial studies are based on data from financial databases that have been put together by government or for-profit organisations, such as records of stock prices. Studies of technological innovation may use counts of patents derived from patent databases.

Advantages and disadvantages of secondary analysis are listed in **Table 5.1**. Bryman and Bell (2011) discuss some of these aspects in more depth.

5.3.2 How can I acquire data from existing databases?

Few students consider analysing data already collected for other purposes despite the volume of data available in business and management research (Saunders et al. 2012). However, it may be worth looking to see if someone has already collected data that

Table 5.1   Secondary analysis in perspective

	Advantages	Disadvantages
Effort	Saving money and time in data collection Allowing more time for data analysis	Need to familiarise yourself with the data Need to manage large and complex data sets May be expensive
Analysis	Access to high-quality data Comparing subgroups or subsets within the data sample Comparing subgroups or subsets in other countries Opportunity to analyse data longitudinally	Lack of control over data quality Limited to data already collected May be biased in unobservable ways May not answer your research questions
Contribution	Reinterpret original findings Fully exploit data set	May not be seen as being as rigorous or relevant as purposefully collected data Does not build as many research skills as direct methods

may be relevant to your research problem. If you are lucky, someone has already collected the data you need to answer your research questions, and, if you are especially lucky, they have created an electronic database with the kind of information you need in an appropriate format. If you are inordinately lucky, you can gain access to this information and it will be free.

We have already described library and internet search processes in **Chapter 3** as two ways to find information about your research problem and research setting, an essential part of any research project. You can also use these search processes to identify data to answer your research questions. (Please note however that a literature review as described in **Chapter 3** is *not* a research design and it is not part of your research methods chapter.)

Secondary data are stored in **data archives**, commercial databases, market reports and company archives. Government departments, trade associations, market research organisations, commercial research organisations, academic research units, newspapers, businesses and other organisations all collect and publish information that may be relevant to answering your research questions. This information may be available in printed form, CD-ROMs, online computer databases or internet sites.

Depending on how the data are stored and organised, you may be looking for:

- A **data set**, a set of information collected by academic or professional researchers about one or more social units using a consistent research design or research protocol;
- A **database**, a structured data set, usually a matrix of data that allocates a row to each social unit (for example organisation, household or person) and a column to each variable or other measure related to that social unit.
- An **archive**, a collection of documents, images and other data in unprocessed form, which you might process into a data set or a database.

You are using a secondary analysis research design even if you are collecting data specifically for your research project, but your research design still counts as 'secondary analysis' because you are not directly observing, interviewing or surveying the people or organisations you are studying. The documents you are using as sources have already been produced for another purpose rather than being created specifically for your research project, even though your data do not exist until you 'interrogate' the documents (O'Leary 2013).

If you are considering secondary analysis, some questions you might want to explore early on include:

1. **Do the data cover the organisations and the phenomena you are interested in?** It is unlikely that the people who collected the data originally were interested in exactly the same research questions you want to answer in your research, so they may have omitted some data that are relevant to your research and included irrelevant data. Furthermore, data sets tend to focus on large industrial organisations so the sample may be biased.
2. **Do you have to pay for access to the data?** Some data sets or databases cost hundreds or even thousands of pounds – beyond the reach of most student projects.
3. **Will you have to enter the data yourself?** Many older data sets are only available in printed tables, or sometimes in obsolete computer formats such as punched cards.

4. **Are the data accurate?** Research on commercially produced data sets such as Compustat has shown that the data are not always correct, due to either collection or entry errors. You will sometimes need to spend as much time checking your data as if you had originally collected and entered it yourself.

Where can I find secondary data?

Secondary data can be found everywhere. People and organisations collect information about many aspects of business and management. Governmental and quasi-governmental bodies such as international trade bodies collect and publish statistics about a wide variety of activities, such as trade statistics. Corporations publish annual reports and file information related to stock offerings and other significant activities. Markets such as the New York Stock Exchange are a source of detailed information about transactions such as share prices. Any of these could be used in research. Although it is relatively rare for undergraduate or taught master's research projects compared with postgraduate research projects, sometimes you may be expected to analyse data that have already been collected by your supervisor or your institution.

Social surveys as sources of secondary data

A major source of information about organisations, households and people is **survey data**. The internet has revolutionised researchers' ability to identify and access large-scale survey data for secondary analysis. These survey data include data from **censuses**, surveys that collect data from every member of the group being studied, **repeated surveys**, surveys that collect data continuously or at regular intervals and **ad hoc surveys**, surveys that collect data only once. Since we have discussed survey designs in Section 5.1, in this section we will focus on using survey data rather than how to design and administer a survey.

The UK, in particular, is taking a leading role in making survey information available through the web with the Economic and Social Data Service (ESDS), founded jointly in January 2003 by the Economic and Social Research Council (ESRC) and the Joint Information Systems Committee (JISC). The ESDS coordinates storage and access to data archives, which are repositories for survey data. Four ESDS research centres currently provide access to key economic and social data for secondary analysis:

- The UK Data Archive (UKDA) at the University of Essex
- The Institute for Social and Economic Research (ISER) at the University of Essex
- The Manchester Information and Associated Services (MIMAS) at the University of Manchester
- The Cathie Marsh Centre for Census and Survey Research (CCSR) at the University of Manchester.

If you are studying in the UK, you may be able to access many different kinds of data through these centres, including large-scale government surveys, qualitative data sets, international data sets and longitudinal data sets, as shown in **Table 5.2** and illustrated in **Research in action 5.6**.

Table 5.2   Examples of online data sources provided through ESDS

ESDS Government Surveys	
Labour Force Surveys/Northern Ireland Labour Force Survey	General Household Survey/Continuous Household Survey (Northern Ireland)
Family Expenditure Survey/Northern Ireland Family Expenditure Survey	National Food Survey/Expenditure and Food Survey (new combined National Food Survey and Family Expenditure Survey)
Family Resources Survey	ONS Omnibus Survey
Survey of English Housing	Health Survey for England/Welsh Health Survey/Scottish Health Survey
British Crime Survey/Scottish Crime Survey	British Social Attitudes/Scottish Social Attitudes/Northern Ireland Life and Times Survey (and the former Northern Ireland Social Attitudes)/Young People's Social Attitudes (periodic offshoot of the BSA)
National Travel Survey	Time Use Survey
ESDS Longitudinal British Cohort Study (BCS70)	British Household Panel Survey (BHPS)
Millennium Cohort Study (MCS)	National Child Development Survey (NCDS)
ESDS Qualidata	
The Peter Townsend collection featuring studies on poverty and the life of older people, Family Life of Old People (1955), The Last Refuge (1959) and Poverty in the UK (1979)	The Paul Thompson collection comprising the major life history interview study of The Edwardians (1975)
Stan Cohen's (1967) Folk Devils and Moral Panics focusing on the genesis and development of 'moral panic'	Dennis Marsden and Brian Jackson's research papers, including their data for Education and the Working Class (1962)
Goldthorpe et al. (1962) The Affluent Worker undertaken to test the thesis of working-class embourgeoisement	
ESDS International	
OECD Main Economic Indicators	OECD Main Science and Technology Indicators
OECD Quarterly Labour Force Statistics	OECD Social Expenditure Database
OECD Measuring Globalisation	OECD International Development
OECD International Direct Investment Statistics	OECD International Migration Statistics
NS Time Series Data	UNIDO Industrial Statistics
UNIDO Industrial Demand Supply	IMF Direction of Trade Statistics
IMF International Financial Statistics	IMF Balance of Payment Statistics
World Bank World Development Indicators	World Bank Global Development Finance
United Nations Common Database	Eurobarometers
European Social Survey	International Social Survey Programme
World Values Surveys and European Values Surveys	

Research in action 5.6

BRITAIN AT WORK

Many academic researchers have conducted secondary analysis on the Workplace Employee Relations Survey (WERS) data set (see the webpage at the end of this box). The survey is conducted by the Centre for Social Research (formerly SCPR). It started in 1980 as the quadrennial Workplace Industrial Relations Survey (WIRS), surveying British establishments with 25 or more employees, and was renamed WERS in 1998 and extended to workplaces with 10 or more employees. The survey provides 'statistically reliable, nationally representative data on workplace relations and employment practices'.

Secondary analysis of the data has been conducted by other researchers, who may not have any connection with the project except through the data. (A recent list of research publications is located at WERS n.d.). These secondary analyses include journal articles, master's dissertations and doctoral dissertations.

See, for example: www.gov.uk/government/collections/workplace-employment-relations-study-wers

There are many advantages to using archived survey data as a source of data for a research project. The survey data provide you with access to much larger samples than you could ever hope to collect. Surveys such as these are designed and conducted by teams of experts, so that the quality of the research design, instruments, data collection and data processing is very high.

As well as data from a single source such as WERS, you can also combine data from different sources, as shown in **Research in action 5.7**.

Research in action 5.7

COUNTRY MUSIC, THE MUSIC OF PAIN

To see whether country music and suicide rates were linked, sociologists Steven Stack and Jim Gundlach combined data from the Radio and Records Rating Report, which reported on the size of the country music listening audience in 49 US metropolitan areas, with suicide rates for those areas from the annual Mortality Tapes compiled by the Inter-University Consortium for Social and Political Research at the University of Michigan in the US (Stack and Gundlach 1995). They proposed that the two would be related, because the themes of country music dealt with the same issues that sociologists associate with suicide. This touched off a debate in the journal Social Forces over the link, with other sociologists arguing that divorce, gun ownership, living in the south and poverty accounted for both suicide and listening to 'country radio' (also see Stack and Gundlach 1992, 1994).

To use archived survey data, you first need to find out what surveys exist and then gain access to them, which is not always easy. Projects such as ESDS provide comprehensive listings of the survey data they hold, but you may have to use some of the tools and techniques for searching discussed in **Chapter 3** to find other surveys.

Even if you find a survey or other source whose data may help you answer your research questions, you may not always gain access to that data. Whilst many government and academic research centres make summary results and even raw data from their surveys available to researchers, you may only be able to obtain summary results of surveys conducted by commercial research organisations by paying and they may charge more than most student projects could afford. In some cases, however, they may not want to share this information with anyone else.

How can I acquire data from commercial databases?

Proprietary databases are data sets or databases created to be sold. These are often the best source of access to company financial data. You may have access to some proprietary data sets through your department or library, if they subscribe. **Company-specific** databases give company names, sales, profits, geographic profiles, industry profiles and other useful data. Because these databases are compiled and published by commercial organisations, they typically sell the results or charge for access to them. Popular databases include market research archives such as Mintel, and financial databases such as AMADEUS and FAME. These are based on the financial reports and other data provided by companies to governments, securities overseers and investors. You can use these databases to find company accounts data for public and private companies, and can download selected data to create your own custom database.

Marketing information can be essential for projects involving either consumer or industrial products, especially if you are studying a marketing problem or your research setting is consumer-oriented. **Market research reports** are another type of proprietary information that students find useful for research projects. These reports may be published by commercial market research or consumer research organisations, or trade associations.

Many business schools subscribe to Mintel market reports. **Mintel** is a consultancy company that:

> publishes some 600 reports into European, UK-specific and US consumer markets every year (http://www.mintel.com/sinatra/reports/about/?__cc=1).
> Our specialist team of market analysts scours the globe for trade, industry and government data, which our statisticians then integrate into meaningful sizing models and future value forecasts for thousands of sectors worldwide. (http://www.mintel.com/about-mintel)

For example, if you were studying food consumption, you might want to consult Mintel's reports exploring the yoghurt market in the US or other countries. Other reports listed on the site examine the beer market, book retailing, analgesics and household cleaning products.

Trade associations are another good but often overlooked source of information about the commodity or organisations they represent. The National Hot Dog and Sausage Council's website (www.hot-dog.org) provides extensive information about the sales of 'tube steak' in the US. Information on this site includes:

- General market information (reports on *'The size and scope of the US market for hot dogs'* and *'The size and scope of the US market for sausages'*)
- Consumption by geographic area (reports on the *'Top ten hot dog eating cities'* and *'Top ten sausage eating cities'*)
- Special reports, such as how many hot dogs are eaten at baseball games in the US (a report on *'Major League ballpark consumption'*).

5.3.3   How can I create data from documents and unobtrusive observation?

In the previous section, we described surveys and databases as sources of data for secondary analysis where the data had already been collected and processed for you. If you are interested in secondary research but you can't identify a data set or database that contains the information you want to analyse to answer your research questions, you may want to create your own data set from materials that you collect or that have been collected by organisations or other researchers but not processed and analysed. As we noted above, although you might be the first person to collect and analyse this data, it is still generally considered as secondary analysis because you are relying on data you are not collecting directly from organisations or people. Below, we will describe some features of archival research.

How can I create data from documents and archives?

In some research projects, you may want or need to gather data without any direct contact with organisations or people. You might choose to analyse documents, whether they are company records, publications or other sources.

Research that takes a historical perspective can often only rely on documents and other records for evidence, since the organisations and people being studied no longer exist to be interviewed or studied. These materials may be held in library or company archives, collections of documents or other artefacts that organisations or people create as part of their ongoing activities. Research that uses only secondary data, especially if it focuses on documents, is sometimes called **archival research**, whether the information is actually held in an archive or not, because the same techniques are used for recording and analysing information. Many placement projects involve investigating archival data, as shown in **Research in action 5.8**.

Research in action 5.8

AS EASY AS ABC

As part of a summer job between completing her MBA and starting her PhD, Kate worked on a project for a telecoms manufacturer looking for ways to reduce the costs of materials management. As part of this project, the author and her colleague analysed the purchase orders that had been made over the past year, to identify the items that fell into A*, A, B and C purchase categories. This meant organising and sorting through tens of thousands of purchase orders (historical data), using data downloaded from the division's mainframe into a format viewable in a spreadsheet program. This allowed the organisation to identify the costs associated with purchase orders and thereby assess whether electronic purchasing would be cost-effective.

Secondary data can provide otherwise lost insights into management decisions outside any respondent's living memory, so business history and management history tends to focus largely on archival research. A company's **archives** can be a rich source of data, since it may contain detailed information that has never been made public and hence never analysed. Company archives may contain catalogues, reports, records of transactions and minutes of meetings, all of which tell us what happened in the past. Researchers may also use other archival materials such as images (photographs, film, video), sounds and other non-written materials in doing their research.

Archival records can show what people actually (recorded as) thought or did at the time, since organisational members have not reinterpreted archival records through hindsight – as the saying goes, 'Success has many fathers but failure is an orphan.' On the other hand, archives typically only capture a small part of what goes on in an organisation, because they cannot capture informal and verbal interactions.

Some organisational researchers have used archival research to look at how change unfolds over decades, rather than the few months or years that a particular research project would normally take. They may even span centuries, as illustrated in **Research in action 5.9.**

Research in action 5.9

BOTTOMS UP

Glenn Carroll and Anand Swaminathan (2000) were interested in how the emergence of microbreweries contradicted a long trend towards greater concentration in the beer brewing industry. Carroll and Swaminathan used archival sources to identify the companies that entered and exited the brewing industry in the US over a long period. They used archival sources to construct life histories of 2251 breweries in the country, including microbreweries, brewpubs, contract brewers and mass producers. To identify all the brewers, they relied on industry histories, trade publications and web pages, rather than collecting information directly from existing firms. This is something that would have been, practically, almost impossible to achieve by direct measurement – not just in terms of the logistics of visiting all the firms, but also the relative availability of data on firms that no longer existed.

You can also analyse 'texts' that are not words, such as films, television commercials and programmes, magazines advertisements, advertising coupons or bumper stickers. This kind of research can be extremely creative. Even though it is unlikely that you could find a database or a data set of, let's say, how commercials portray people drinking coffee, you could gather these materials and create your own data set to analyse. Consumer researchers, for example, have reported studies in the *Journal of Consumer Research* based on materials as diverse as comic books, romance novels, television commercials and popular television programmes. These are all artefacts created by organisations and used by people.

You might only want to use archival materials as a source of descriptive information, such as names, to create a record of key events in a company's history or as a source of illustrations, but you can also use them in a much more structured way to generate information you can analyse statistically. Various techniques are available for **structured content analysis** to find and count how often concepts, ideas or other 'meaning units' occur within documents or other texts. There are various computer programs you can use to make this task easier.

Major issues in archival research are similar to issues in large-scale survey data archives:

1. **How do you find out what archives exist?** Public organisations such as the government, charities, trade associations and universities may make information available about their archives and even provide public access to those archives, but company archives are usually private, closely controlled, and difficult to find

out about and access. Additionally, corporate and other business records may disappear when those businesses disappear through merger, acquisition, bankruptcy or dissolution.

2. **How do you gain access to these archives?** Access to most archives, especially those in private hands, is usually tightly controlled. You may need to use some of the tips for gaining access to people to gain access to archives (see section 9.1).

3. **What data do I need and how should I structure them?** Since you are not working with data in a predefined data set or database as for survey or proprietary databases, you will need to make these decisions yourself. It may take two or more passes through the data to collect all the information you need.

4. **How much time will it take?** Archival research is often time consuming and open-ended. Archival research is usually slow compared with the other kinds of data gathering described in this chapter and the next, since you will have to go through many documents, and you may not be able to make photocopies or even take notes by hand if there are restrictions because of confidentiality or the condition of the materials. Therefore, extensive archival research may not be appropriate for short- or medium-length research projects, since the time needed to identify, access and collect data may be longer than the time you have available.

5. **Is there another way to get these data?** Can you interrogate any company sources or databases to get the same information? Archival data may be the only records relating to long-ago events or defunct organisations.

 Summary

In this chapter, we have considered three quantitative research designs. **Section 5.1** discussed a familiar research design, the survey, which includes interviews and questionnaires. Surveys can be used to gather information about a sample that can be generalised to the population from which it comes. Survey design needs care and experience, so you should first see whether there is an existing survey or question bank related to your research topic before you decide to design your own survey and questions. You should also think about the trade-off between the cost of information and the quality of information, especially with postal or online questionnaires.

Section 5.2 explained how you can use experiments to investigate cause-and-effect relationships. Laboratory experiments are seldom used in most areas of business and management, but field experiments and quasi-experiments are common designs. In designing experiments, you should try to minimise experimenter and participant effects, and be mindful of ethical issues that you may need to address before you do your experiment.

Section 5.3 introduced the secondary analysis of data as a research design. Secondary analysis can be used to analyse data that have already been collected, and sometimes analysed, by other people. The sources of this secondary data include archived surveys and proprietary databases. Secondary analysis can also be used to analyse data that you collect yourself from indirect sources, including documents and other artefacts or unobtrusive observation. Although nearly all research projects involve some secondary data, they are underused as a research design when the potential sources of high-quality data are considered.

 ## Answers to key questions

What methods for collecting data are associated with the quantitative research approach?

- A secondary analysis, a survey or an experimental research design for social measurement all provide ways to capture quantitative data.

How can I conduct a survey, run an experiment or analyse previously collected data?

- By understanding the advantages and disadvantages of the methods presented in this chapter, I can choose between:
  - A survey to capture structured information about a sample by asking the same questions of all respondents in a face-to-face or other contact situation, or at a distance from the researcher.
  - An experiment such as a true experiment or a quasi-experiment in a natural setting – field experiments; or an artificial experiment – laboratory experiments.
  - Secondary analysis to analyse data that other researchers have already captured, to analyse data from documents and other artefacts produced for purposes other than research by individuals and organisations, or to capture information about distant or historical activities.

What are the particular issues in quantitative research design that I should be aware of?

- Can I answer my research questions using quantitative research methods?
- Can I identify enough respondents to participate in my research?
- Will I be able to draw inferences about the relationships that I am investigating?

 ## References

BBC News. 2000, 11 July. Heinz to launch green ketchup. Available at: http://news.bbc.co.uk/1/hi/uk/828847.stm (accessed 14 September 2016).

Bradach, Jeffrey L. 1997. Using the plural form in the management of restaurant chains, *Administrative Science Quarterly*, 42(2): 276–303.

Bryman, Alan and Bell, Emma 2011 *Business Research Methods*, 3rd edn. Oxford: Oxford University Press.

Carroll, Glenn R. and Swaminathan, Anand 2000. Why the microbrewery movement? Organizational dynamics of resource partitioning in the US brewing industry, *American Journal of Sociology*, 106(3): 715–60.

Foddy, William 1993. *Constructing Questions for Interviews and Questionnaires: Theory and Practice in Social Research*. Cambridge: Cambridge University Press.

Gray, David E. 2004. *Doing Research in the Real World*. London: Sage.

Lee, R.M. 2000. *Unobtrusive Methods in Social Research*. Maidenhead: Open University Press.

Maister, D. 1985. The psychology of waiting lines. In J.A. Czepiel, M.R. Solomon and C.F. Surprenant (eds), *The Service Encounter: Managing Employee/Customer Interaction in Service Businesses*. Lexington, MA: D.C. Heath and Company, Lexington Books.

March, James G., Sproull, Lee S. and Tamuz, Michal 1991. Learning from samples of one or fewer, *Organization Science*, 2(1): 58–70.

McDavid, John 1965. Approval-seeking motivation and the volunteer subject, *Journal of Personality and Social Psychology*, 2(1), 115–117.

Meyer, Alan D. 1982. Adapting to environmental jolts, *Administrative Science Quarterly*, 27(4): 515–37.

Oppenheimer, A.N. 1992. *Questionnaire Design, Interviewing, and Attitude Measurement*, new edn. London: Continuum.

O'Leary, Zina. 2013. *The Essential Guide to Doing Research*, 2nd edn. London: Sage.

Reilly, Michael D. and Wallendorf, Melanie 1987. A comparison of group differences in food consumption using household refuse, *Journal of Consumer Research*, 14(2): 289–94.

Rosenthal, R. and Fode, K.L. 1963. The effect of experimenter bias on the performance of the albino rat, *Behavioural Science*, 8: 183–9.

Rosnow, R.L. and Rosenthal, R. 1997. *People Studying People: Artifacts and Ethics in Behavioural Research*. New York: W.H. Freeman.

Saunders, Mark, Lewis, Phillip and Thornhill, Adrian 2012. *Research Methods for Business Students*, 6th edn. Harlow: Financial Times/Prentice Hall.

Sears, D.O. 1986. College sophomores in the laboratory: Influences of a narrow database on social psychology's view of human nature, *Journal of Personality and Social Psychology*, 51: 515–30.

Sherif, M. 1956. Experiments in group conflict, *Scientific American*, 195: 54–8.

Stack, Steven and Gundlach, James 1992. The effect of country music on suicide, *Social Forces*, 70(5): 211–18.

Stack, Steven and Gundlach, Jim 1994. Country music and suicide: A reply to Maguire and Snipes, *Social Forces*, 72(4): 1245–8.

Stack, Steven and Gundlach, James 1995. Country music and suicide – individual, indirect, and interaction effects: A reply to Snipes and Maguire, *Social Forces*, 74(1): 331–5.

Tajfel, H. 1970. Experiments in intergroup discrimination, *Scientific American*, 223: 96–102.

Underhill, Paco 2000. *Why We Buy: The Science of Shopping*. Knutsford: Texere.

Voss, Christopher A., Roth, Aleda V., Rosenzweig, Eve D., Blackmon, Kate and Chase, Richard B. 2004. A tale of two countries: Conservatism, service quality, and feedback on customer satisfaction, *Journal of Service Research*, 6(3): 212–40.

Wallendorf, Melanie and Nelson, Daniel 1986. An archaeological examination of ethnic differences in body care rituals, *Psychology and Marketing*, 3(4): 273–99.

Webb, E.J., Campbell, D.T., Schwartz, R.D. and Sechrest, L. 1966. *Unobtrusive Measures: Nonreactive Research in the Social Sciences*. Chicago: Rand McNally.

WERS (The Workplace Employment Relations Study). n.d. *Bibliography of Research*. Available at: www.wers2011.info/download/i/mark_dl/u/4012959824/4628195566/WERS%20bibliography%20(17%20May%202016).pdf (accessed 4 August 2016).

Zeithaml, Valarie A., Parasuraman, A. and Berry, Leonard L. 1990. *Delivering Quality Service: Balancing Customer Perceptions and Expectations*. New York: Free Press.

Additional resources

Aldridge, A. and Levine, K. 2001. *Surveying the Social World: Principles and Practice in Survey Research*. Maidenhead: Open University Press.

Bell, Judith and Opie, Clive 2002. *Learning from Research: Getting More from Your Data*. Maindenhead: Open University Press.

Blaikie, Norman 2009. *Designing Social Research*, 2nd edn. Cambridge: Polity Press.

Boone, Christopher, Carroll, Glenn R. and van Witteloostuijn, Arjen 2004. Size, differentiation and the performance of Dutch daily newspapers, *Industrial and Corporate Change*, 13(1): 117–48.

Braun, V. and Clarke, V. 2006. Using thematic analysis in psychology, *Qualitative Research in Psychology*, 3(2): 77–101.

Dobrev, Stanislav D., Tai-Young Kim and Carroll, Glenn R. 2003. Shifting gears, shifting niches: Organizational inertia and change in the evolution of the US automobile industry, 1885–1981, *Organization Science*, 14(3): 264–82.

Easterby-Smith, Mark, Thorpe, Richard and Lowe, Andy 2002. *Management Research: An Introduction*, 2nd edn. London: Sage.

Johnson, Roxanne T. 2000. In search of E.I. DuPont de Nemours and Company: The perils of archival research, *Accounting, Business and Financial History*, 10(2): 129–68.

Maguire, Edward R. and Snipes, Jeffrey B. 1994. Reassessing the link between country music and suicide, *Social Forces*, 72(4): 1239–43.

Mauk, Gary W. and Taylor, Matthew J. 1994. Comments on Stack and Gundlach's 'The effect of country music on suicide: An Achy Breaky Heart' *Social Forces*, 72(4): 1249–55.

McKendrick, David G. and Carroll, Glenn R. 2001. On the genesis of organizational forms: Evidence from the market for disk arrays. *Organization Science*, 12(6): 661–82.

Oliver, Paul 2003. *The Student's Guide to Research Ethics*. Maidenhead: Open University Press.

Parry, Vivienne 2004, 29 June. The panic button. *Guardian*, G2: 16.

Rubin, H.J. and Rubin, I.S. 2011. *Qualitative Interviewing: The Art of Hearing Data*. Thousand Oaks, CA: Sage.

Snipes, Jeffrey B. and Maguire, Edward R. 1995. Country music, suicide, and spuriousness, *Social Forces*, 74(1): 327–9.

Webb, E. and Weick, K.E. 1979. Unobtrusive measures in organisational theory: A reminder. *Administrative Science Quarterly*, 24(4): 650–9.

 Key terms

ad hoc surveys, 164
archival research, 168
archive, 163
archives, 168
biased, 144
cause-and-effect relationship, 154
censuses, 164
closed-ended question, 140
company-specific databases, 167
computer-assisted protocols for interviews, 149
control, 157

control group, 157
data archives, 163
database, 163
data set, 163
dependent variable, 151
desk/library research, 161
experiment, 150
experimental treatment, 155
experimenter effects, 159
experimenter expectancies, 159
field experiment, 153
good subject effect, 160

Researching Business and Management

Discussion questions

1. What research designs are associated with the quantitative approach?

2. What is secondary analysis?

3. How can I use secondary data to answer my research questions?

4. What are the main advantages and disadvantages of secondary analysis?

5. Does secondary analysis always mean quantitative data and hypothesis testing?

6. What reliability and validity issues does secondary analysis present?

7. From a research methods point of view, what might be wrong with the statement, 'I haven't decided what to look at yet, but I will be using a questionnaire'?

8. What are good practices in setting up a survey?

9. How do laboratory experiments, field experiments and quasi-experiments differ?

10. Sherif's experiment (Research in action 5.2) was set in a summer camp – literally a field experiment. Although he could control the random assignment of boys to groups, and the boys competed on similar tasks in a similar environment, Sherif couldn't control the boys' interactions with other campers, the weather and so on. What do you think would have been different if the experiment had taken place in a laboratory setting (for example, choosing the group from students in a classroom)?

Workshop

This workshop will give students practice in gathering data using a scientific approach.

Background

Capacity is often a problem for frontline service operations because demand tends to be higher in certain parts of the data and lower in others. For example, a coffee shop, cafeteria, restaurant or other food service facility will probably experience peaks and troughs of demand during the day. The operation needs to collect information on these variations in demand so that it can set service levels and decide how many service operatives it needs to deploy at a given time.

Task

Form into teams of no more than three people. Each team should pick a food service facility to observe and set aside several hours to complete the activity.

1. Decide how you would collect data to determine the number of customers arriving at the facility, how long each customer had to wait before being served, and any other information that you think would be relevant.

2. Decide how you would record and analyse these data.

3. Collect these data. (It is a good idea for each team member to collect data independently for at least part of this exercise, so that you can see how accurately people can collect data.)

4. Analyse the data and present the results to your instructor.

5. Hold on to these data for the workshops at the end of **Chapters 11 and 12**.

Postscript to activity on coin flipping (pp. 158–9)

Heads	0	1	2	3	4	5	6	7	8	9	10
Tails	0	9	45	131	187	244	223	97	51	13	0

Relevant chapters

4   How do I write up my report?
14 What do I do now?

Key challenges

- Making sense of your findings
- Presenting your research to others
- Reflecting and learning from your research

4

Relevant chapters

1   What is research?
2   What should I study?
3   How do I find information?

Key challenges

- Understanding what academic research is
- Generating and clarifying ideas
- Using sources of information

1

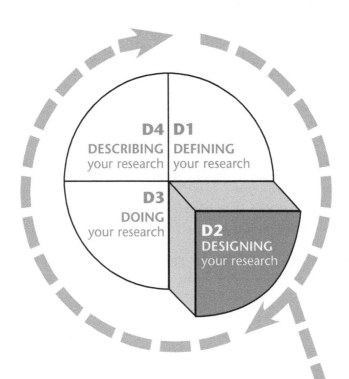

Relevant chapters

9   How do I do field research?
10 What do my quantitative data mean(1)?
11 What do my quantitative data mean(2)?
12 What do my qualitative data mean?

Key challenges

- Practical considerations in doing research
- Describing data using simple statistics
- Carrying out statistical tests
- Interpreting words and actions

3

Relevant chapters

4   What is my research approach?
5   How do I do quantitative research?
6   **How do I do qualitative research?**
7   How do I do case study research?
8   How do I make sure my research is ethical?

Key challenges

- Choosing a research approach
- Choosing a research design
- **Collecting data using quantitative methods**
- Collecting data using qualitative methods
- Integrating quantitative and qualitative methods

2

6 How do I do qualitative research?
chapter

Remote data collection, observation and interviews

 Key questions

- What methods for collecting data are associated with the qualitative research approach?
- How can I conduct remote data collection, observation and interviews?
- What are the particular issues in qualitative research design that I should be aware of?

 Learning outcomes

At the end of this chapter, you should be able to:

- Design a qualitative research process appropriate for your research
- Select appropriate qualitative research methods for your research approach
- Evaluate the relative practical challenges associated with each qualitative research method

Contents

⊕ Introduction

> Words are merely utterances: noises that stand for feelings, thoughts and experi-
> ence. They are symbols. Signs. Insignias. They are not Truth. They are not the
> real thing. Words may help you understand something. Experience allows you to
> know. Yet there are some things that you cannot experience. So I have given you
> other tools of knowing. And these are called feelings. And so too thoughts.
>
> (Walsch 1995: 4)

In **Chapter 4**, we introduced the possibility of using a qualitative approach to your research, depending on your research questions and on your research philosophy. Many influential business and management academics have used qualitative research to study people and organisations. Even in areas we usually think of as mostly quantitative, such as consumer marketing, taking a qualitative approach can help us ask and answer questions about how and why people, both individually and collectively, behave in certain ways.

Qualitative research is often what we call '*exploratory*' – its purpose is to allow you to explore of a particular issue or context. Qualitative research approaches tend to be taken when the research field is less explored or where the elements that could form part of your conceptual model are not well understood. If your research questions ask 'how?' or 'why?' rather than 'what?' you should consider using a qualitative approach.

How and why kinds of questions are asked in many business and management research projects. For example, why do people take up extreme sports such as skydiving? Why has there been a revival of cycling among middle-aged accountants and other professionals – the Mamils (middle-aged men in Lycra)? How does office gossip influence team behaviour? How does chatting during surgical operations on the part of the operating team reduce medical errors such as leaving surgical instruments inside patients? How do older managers interface with social media?

This chapter will give you an overview of qualitative research designs, show you how to design a qualitative research project, and outline some potential research methods supported by guidelines, practical tips and tricks. As with quantitative research, you can justify a number of different research methods to use in a qualitative research project. We will also show how qualitative methods for acquiring and handling data differ from the quantitative methods and data discussed in **Chapter 5**.

If you decide to use a qualitative design after reading this chapter, please make sure you read **Chapter 12** on analysing qualitative data before you start collecting data as data gathering and data analysis often run in parallel in qualitative research. You should also be aware of some issues that commonly arise in doing qualitative research.

Why should we use qualitative research in business and management research?

As the opening passage in this chapter indicates, organisations are both **social systems** and the setting for **social behaviour**. Since people construct and maintain social systems, researchers are interested not only with organisations but also with the people in them. Because people ascribe meanings, thoughts and feelings to the situation in which they find themselves, research on people differs from research on the physical objects and systems that are studied in the natural sciences. Qualitative methods are therefore as important in business and management research as quantitative methods. In qualitative research, your research questions will typically be focused on answering 'why?' or 'how?' questions by increasing your understanding of an issue within the context of a particular social system.

What qualitative research methods can I use?

Although there many different methods you can use as part of a qualitative research design, in this chapter we will concentrate on the main ones you might use for your project. **Figure 6.1** arranges the main qualitative designs by how involved the researcher is with the subject of the investigation. At the left-hand end of the scale, there is little involvement, the researcher is predominantly an observer. In **Section 6.1**, we will first look at indirect research methods with which you can collect data remotely from the context of interest – focusing on the left-hand side of **Figure 6.1**. Remote data collection, as you will see, is close to the surveys, experiments and secondary research designs that we explored in **Chapter 5**.

As your design moves to the right, you increasingly become part of whatever context or organisation you are researching. In **Section 6.2** and **Section 6.3**, we will discuss direct data collection and the methods associated with interviews, focus groups and workshops. As with quantitative research, you can be creative in your research design. You can combine different qualitative methods, and even combine quantitative and qualitative methods if you apply a mixed-methods approach.

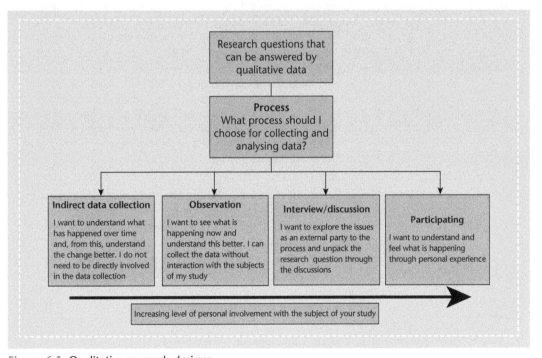

Figure 6.1 Qualitative research designs

How do qualitative designs differ from quantitative designs?

Research on organisations as social systems leads to three important characteristics of qualitative research:

- It is **multidimensional** – rather than focus on a single narrow concept, it allows the context to be explored more fully.
- It is **iterative** – research progresses in cycles rather than as a linear series of activities.
- It is **subjective** – rather than being independent of the researcher, qualitative research relies on how the data is perceived by the researcher.

Each of these justifies some further explanation.

Qualitative research is multidimensional First, qualitative research is multidimensional because social systems are multidimensional (see, for example, Giddens 1984; Bourdieu 1990; Vaara and Whittington 2012). As shown in **Student research in action 6.1**, you may draw on multiple qualitative research methods to explore different dimensions of social systems.

Student research in action 6.1

SEEING THE ORGANISATION AS A SOCIAL SYSTEM: SUSTAINABLE DEVELOPMENT

Dora wanted to research whether the sustainable development (SD) strategies being espoused by organisations would influence the decisions that a particular organisation was taking on a daily basis. For instance, where an organisation had an initiative to reduce carbon emissions, how would this strategy be reflected in the array of decisions that might impact the carbon footprint? Dora defined her research question as 'How do SD strategies influence the operational decisions on energy usage in [the organisation that was sponsoring her studies]?'

Because this was a 'how' question, she decided to use a qualitative research approach, to allow her to explore how the people who made these day-to-day decisions understood the SD strategy of the organisation. The single organisation became her 'case study' and she was able to collect data using both document analysis and personal interviews. What she found was that rather than having a consistent view of both the particular strategy and SD in general, there was huge variation in its recognition and understanding, and no consistency at all in its application around the organisation.

Qualitative research is iterative Second, the process of research design in qualitative research is likely to be iterative: you will revise your research design according to what you find out in your investigation as it proceeds. **Figure 6.2** shows a generic qualitative research project as an iterative process. The activities follow a cycle of generation of propositions, data collection, interpretation and reflection into new or improved propositions. Each cycle is integrated with a search for relevant literature as part of the reflection stage. By contrast, in quantitative research you are likely to be able to specify all of the aspects of the research process early on in the project lifecycle.

Student research in action 6.1 illustrated an iterative qualitative research process. Dora found out based on her initial analysis of the content of company documents that there was a lack of common practice in how the organisation followed its carbon reduction strategy. This allowed her to begin generating *propositions*. Her early

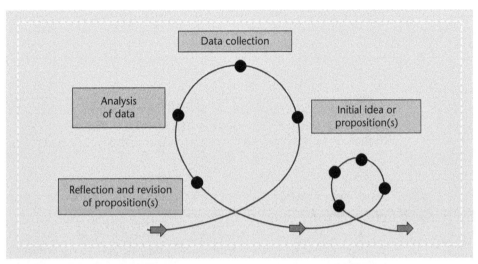

Figure 6.2 Iterative research process

analysis resulted in a tentative proposition: 'The firm is not following its own strategy here.' She was then able to explore this by going back into the company to collect further data to see if this was really happening, and if so why. Dora began to explore *why* this was happening as she subsequently carried out interviews. Her further data, and the subsequent analysis, allowed her to refine her proposition into: 'At an operational level, managers in the firm do not appear to understand the sustainable development strategy of the firm and what it means for them.'

Qualitative research is subjective   Finally, in qualitative research the researcher is subjective and interacts with the research setting. Qualitative research designs allow you to collect very rich data. The researcher brings his or her own mental models which influence the collection and interpretation of these data. Whilst quantitative research emphasises the need for objectivity and independence of the researcher, qualitative research relies on the opinion or impression of the researcher and on the researcher becoming involved or having at least some connection with the setting in which the research is taking place. This may be, for instance, through meeting people from that setting and being able to discuss particular issues with them.

   This subjectivity will influence what you are able to see and what is important to you in a certain situation. We use the analogy of a jazz band playing at a pier to illustrate this subjectivity.

A man and a woman are standing at that pier observing the scenery. The man looks at the ocean and has a closer look at the waves and the sound the wind makes. He estimates the strength of the wind and the direction it comes from. He appreciates the smell of the sea and looks for sailing boats on the horizon. The jazz music he finds rather annoying and too loud as the wind blows it in his direction. The woman observes the musicians and how they use their instruments. She is particularly interested in the saxophone player and tries to see what kind of saxophone he is using as the sound has a soft undertone. She appreciates the performance of the band and sees the difficult circumstances for the musicians because of the wind blowing. It is not hard to guess which of them is the passionate sailor and which the musician. Both of their observations are likely to be accurate but what has each of them taken from the same setting? This is crucial to determining the criteria for each iteration of your data gathering and analysis: what are you looking at?

To be a good qualitative researcher you must be continually reflective about how you gather and interpret data and whether, to use the analogy, you are watching the jazz or the sea. Lastly, you must be open to ideas that were not on your original schedule.

6.1 How can I collect qualitative data using remote data collection?

To answer your research questions, you may be able to use **indirect** or **remote data collection**. This approach has many similarities with secondary analysis, which we described in **Chapter 5**. However, our focus in that chapter was on data that were already in the form of numbers (for example official statistics or computer databases) or that could be transformed into numbers (e.g. questionnaire responses on a 1–5 scale), whilst in this chapter our focus is on non-numeric data, including words, pictures, sounds and other qualitative data. Collecting data by Skype, for instance, does not fall under this category, as it is collecting data directly from a first-hand source.

Remote data collection may be your only option if you are studying an historical phenomenon. For instance, a student was investigating the spending patterns of people in post-war Europe. He was not able to travel back in time to directly observe people's behaviour, so he had to rely instead on contemporary accounts that people had recorded in their diaries. Another student's project used historical documents to provide data to investigate the impact of the 'McDonaldization of society' (Ritzer 2015), which he contrasted with contemporary accounts from the present day.

We present documentation analysis as an example of a research method associated with qualitative research not least because it is an approach we have often seen used in the research projects of master's students. Documentation analysis can be used as a research method in its own right. It can also be used as a supporting research method to gain a better understanding of the context. This then provides a basic model or set of propositions to be able to ask appropriate questions in an interview or to guide the preparation for an observation.

Four steps in a research project using documentation analysis are:

- **Planning**: defining the purpose, sources and types of documents you would like and defining the analysis criteria;
- **Preparing**: collecting the documents;
- **Performing**: based on the analysis criteria;
- **Documenting**: writing up the results and preparing for further data collection.

Planning considers the purpose of the documentation analysis and identifies sources and types of documents. These may include public documents or web pages, or company internal documents such as procedures, plans, emails, minutes of meetings etc.

Your challenge here is to identify potential sources of secondary data and gather data from them.

For example, suppose you were studying decision making and in particular the history of a particular kind of decision. Because the decision-making process is usually both confidential and sensitive, you might have difficulty in getting 'real-time' access to observe a decision being made within an organisation. However, an organisation might agree to provide you with access to its archives, for example to see copies of reports and correspondence on past decisions. You could then track the organisation's decision processes over time.

It is important to remember that while documents such as minutes of meetings can provide valuable data, especially about the timing of issues and decisions, these are not 'the truth' – they are merely somebody's record of their impressions of it. It is always worth checking in such a case that 'approving the minutes of the previous meeting' is the first item on the agenda of the subsequent meeting, standard practice for many organisations. If it is, you can have some confidence in their accuracy. Similar concerns apply to all organisational records.

We always recommend that you discuss the nature of the data you require with a company representative, and ask them to provide the specific sources or names of the relevant documents. Be very clear what kind of documents you want. Such a discussion is vital as whilst sometimes the documentation you receive is very limited, other times it can be overwhelming. It is quite normal that terminology differs between organisations. Much of the world, for instance, uses project management offices – administrative support functions to provide professional services to project teams. If you were researching these and went to Royal Dutch Shell, they don't use this term and instead call the function 'Project Services.' Similarly, *change management* is concerned with organisational change in some organisations, whilst in others it is concerned with how changes to the requirements of a particular project are coordinated and managed. It is important then to plan for your documents and analysis criteria so that you are able to get a useful amount of data for analysis, and on the topic of interest.

The analysis criteria are related to the objectives of the documentation analysis – what is it that you are trying to understand better? **Student research in action 6.2** illustrates the use of analysis criteria.

 Student research in action 6.2

AUDREY'S AUDIT

Audrey wanted to analyse how managers used the formal mechanisms of an organisation's project management processes. These, if followed, should be reflected in the project management plans and related documents. She therefore planned her analysis and identified the documents that she needed from each project to include the project charter, its governance structure, the bar chart, resource plan, risk log and the minutes of project board meetings.

She then defined analysis criteria for the 'quality' of these documents. These criteria included not only the extent of the relevant plans, but also their content (how logically consistent were they were). Content-related criteria to analyse the project management quality of the plans were: Is the plan logical? Is it complete? Can I understand it? Are the timelines realistic? Process-related quality criteria were: How have the plans been prepared? Was the project team involved in the preparation (as evidenced by minutes of meetings)? All of these data were available and, given the number of projects, were not overwhelming.

Whilst in some instances, such analysis may by itself be sufficient, in others you may need to supplement it with interviews or observations to generate a more comprehensive understanding.

For the purposes of writing up your research, it is important that you formally note as you progress the decisions that you took in planning, preparing, performing and documenting your research. It is far more difficult to try to write it up at the end of your research process.

6.2 How can I collect data using observation?

We now explore three commonly used methods for data collection: observation, interviews and focus groups. These differ from the indirect data because they are collected first-hand, and usually by the researcher. This juxtaposition of data collector and analyst (they are one and the same person) is a strength of the qualitative approach.

In practice, observation requires decisions regarding:

- **What to observe**: the purpose, content and the observation criteria (what are you looking for?);
- **When to observe**: the setting, and when the observation starts and ends. For instance, a series of team meetings, or observing the behaviour of potential customers in a shop;
- **How to observe**: documenting all of this in an observation protocol;
- **How to analyse**: what is it that is going to be measured, counted, interpreted?

Table 6.1 shows some of the characteristics of observation as a research method, and some of the decisions associated with each characteristic.

Table 6.1   Characteristics of observations

Characteristic	Decision
Degree of formality	Formal – you have agreement with those being observed to observe them under a structured arrangement (e.g. in a meeting)
	Less formal – no agreement exists (e.g. observations conducted in an open or public space)
Form	Open – it is clear that you are carrying out observation and this is understood by those being observed
	Covert – those being observed do not know it (see important note below)
Number of observers	One – you alone are responsible for gathering the data
	Several – responsibility split allowing different aspects or times to be observed, or multiple interpretations of the same observed data
Role of observer	External observation – you are looking in from the outside
	Participant – you are part of the group
Setting	Natural – this is how, for instance, work is carried out normally
	Experimental – a particular designed situation is created

Student research in action 6.3

CENTRAL PERK — AND WAIT

For a coursework assignment, a student project group decided to investigate service quality in a local service operation. The group wanted to see how the varying workload caused by changes in customer demand over time affected a local coffee shop. In particular, they wanted to see how customers and staff responded to the queues that built up at peak times.

The students observed that first thing in the morning customers were able to get a seat easily once they had collected their coffee and cakes. Customers seemed happy to sit for a while in the café and enjoy the experience. As the day progressed, particularly at lunchtime, customers had to queue to get served and then were unable to get a seat. Not only was customer satisfaction dropping off, with customers becoming frustrated by trying to get seated whilst balancing their coffee and shopping bags, but the shop also was losing business to less crowded neighbours.

On several Saturdays, the students recorded how customers reacted to the different queue lengths during the day, including counting the number of people who walked in, looked around and then walked out again. They used this as a measure of the business that the shop could have captured, if only it had had the capacity. The study identified the likely 'tolerance' of potential customers to waiting, its cost and its effect on customer satisfaction. As a result, the researchers were able to recommend how the coffee shop should change its layout and process for serving customers.

Observation can also be carried out using secondary materials. As well as observing people's behaviour and actions in person, some researchers are able to take advantage of the proliferation of cameras in public areas. Town planners and store designers frequently use film and time-lapse photography as a research tool, for instance to see how people move (speed, direction or what causes them to change direction).

If you have an opportunity to use such material, you should think carefully about the ethical implications for your participants. It is usually OK to observe people in public settings such as streets or fast-food restaurants, and take notes, but recording them may raise ethical issues. You should always seek such permission from people you are observing if you can, especially if it might affect them. If you have obtained permission to film participants as part of a research project, the discussion in a focus group for instance, then it is certainly appropriate to use these recordings as a source of data for that particular research project. Research ethics is discussed further in **Chapter 8**.

We recommend that you do not use **covert observation** using surveillance technology, or observation in semi-private or private settings. **Student research in action 6.4** illustrates an example from one of our students who forgot to check that it was OK to observe people. Even though we are used to being observed (there are CCTV cameras recording the movements of people throughout many cities) and there are television shows that use such footage, it is not acceptable to observe anyone at any time. This is likely to contravene the ethical guidelines for your project and may even be illegal in some countries. You should avoid this approach and consider other methods of obtaining the data you need. There is, after all, plenty of choice.

Student research in action 6.4
HOW TO WIN FRIENDS AND INFLUENCE PEOPLE (NOT)

A student was undertaking a placement project at a large car factory. As part of his work, he was asked to investigate the practices associated with the assembly of a car door. Taking the initiative, he took his clipboard, stopwatch and white coat, and headed out to the factory floor. He then started observing the work of the people who were assembling the doors, noting the tasks they were doing and the times that each task took.

When the union convenor saw the student and his stopwatch, he jumped to the conclusion that the student was retiming the jobs that people were doing on behalf of the organisation. This was a perennially sensitive issue, as the timing of a job determined an individual's rate of pay, and any retiming had to be pre-agreed with the unions. Since no such agreement was currently in force, the union ordered all work in the factory to stop. Needless to say, our student was not too popular with the factory management after that.

6.2.1 The process of observation

As with document analysis, we find in practice that worthwhile research comes with the researcher making good choices of the observation setting and with a well-defined set of observation criteria, tightly linked to research questions. This doesn't mean that they don't evolve with your findings at each stage in your process, but that at each stage they are re-evaluated.

A process of observing includes:

- **Planning the observation**: the setting, the observation criteria, deciding how to record and analyse the data;
- **Preparing and performing the observation**;
- **Analysing and documenting the results, preparing for further data collection**;
- **Final analysis and documentation**.

An example of a well-planned observation is given in **Student research in action 6.5**.

 Student research in action 6.5(a)
SO, HOW'S IT GOING?

Julia, a student in an MSc programme, was interested in how teams construct their realities and generate a shared opinion on the status of the progress of their work. She conducted a series of observations of team meetings and supervisor meetings within one particular IT firm over a period of six months. Before she started her observations, she made sure to get both company permission and ethical approval, which required the signing of a non-disclosure agreement.

When Julia first came to the meeting room, she was introduced by the manager, who was her contact person and the leader of the meeting. Julia briefly explained the purpose of her being there and what she was interested in observing. She also explained that she would not be giving the team feedback based on her observations at the end of the meeting, nor share any of the data or observations which would directly identify any of the participants.

▶

Julia took a seat away from the meeting table where the team sat. Whilst at the beginning of the meeting she had the feeling that some meeting participants were really aware that she was in the room, after 10 minutes she seemed to be forgotten. In subsequent meetings she was able to just take her seat in the corner of the room and observe.

As shown in **Student research in action 6.5(a)**, having an observer sitting in your meeting is not a natural situation, so you need to plan your introduction to the setting as the observer carefully to be acceptable for the people being observed. In this case, Julia explained in a couple of sentences why she was observing the meeting. In addition, she made it clear that this was not an assessment and she would not be judging anyone's performance or potential.

If you use observation as research method, you should be very clear on the observation criteria you are using. Observation criteria can be drawn from the literature, either from a model or theory you base your research on or you are further developing.

Student research in action 6.5(b)
SO, HOW'S IT GOING? (CONTINUED): OBSERVATION CRITERIA

Julia was observing the team meetings to find out how the team 'constructed' the status of the progress of their work. To do this, she used a set of observation criteria. Some were process related, some were content related. She had done some initial literature study, and identified that power, the nature of conflict and agreement, the level of commitment and the roles of formal plans and documents were important in how people report status. These elements were therefore included in the observation criteria.

Process-related observation criteria:

- Who leads the process? What power do they have and how is it used?
- Are there any conflicting opinions on the status?
- Are any differences taken seriously?
- How is information exchanged?
- Does the leader seek to create commitment in the team to its objectives?
- Does the leader have a plan for communication within and outside the team?
- Does the leader refer to the last status meeting?

Content-related observation criteria:

- What is the status of the work, and how has it changed compared to the previous meeting?
- What is the outcome of the meeting?

Observation criteria must be relevant to your research question if you are to be able to collect the adequate data for your particular research. If for instance, Julia had found that the project manager possessed very low power, she might continue on to investigate who was really running the project. Qualitative research requires both a plan and an awareness of factors that will change that plan. It is an awareness that you will see in common with the other methods discussed in this chapter.

6.2.2 Participant observation

Participant observation is appropriate where you are part of a group and you record your observations either at key times (e.g. as a participant in certain meetings) or on an ongoing basis. This is the basis of many studies in the field of social anthropology and the methods associated with it are well established. Typically, though, the process for carrying out your research looks very similar to the other methods we have covered in this chapter. The process involves:

- **Gaining access**: if you are not already part of the group you wish to observe, how are you going to gain access to them?
- **Establishing rapport**: following the characterisation of **Figure 6.1**, this is a highly involved approach. Therefore, you will need to get to know the people, 'immersing yourself' in the activities of the group, and becoming accepted by them;
- **Recording data and observations**: typically through keeping a reflective diary. You may ask others in the group to do likewise, to provide a useful counterpoint to your own observations;
- **Analysing the data you have collected.**

There is much to recommend participant observation as a research method, provided you can manage the risks involved. This method is often a natural fit with placements or sponsored projects where you are carrying out work for the organisation as well as doing research on it. You can take advantage of this access and the insights gained in doing your research, which would be difficult if not impossible to gain through other types of research. We will cover some other relevant issues such as honesty and confidentiality in **Chapter 8**.

6.2.3 Action research

Action research is participant observation with a twist. An essential aspect of this approach is that you are trying to change the organisation in some way through your involvement as a researcher, not just analysing and reporting the situation. In action research, you are involved in making a change and participating in and observing the consequences. For instance, you might use this approach if you were investigating a system for handling customer complaints. Your recommendations for changes are implemented, and you then spend time with the team working in the new system. A danger is 'going native' and letting the participation and action aspect overwhelm the research aspect. It also raises some ethical questions, especially if you are participating in an organisation or a context that has legal or moral aspects.

Finally, in action research you must deal with your split role of researcher and participant, and retain some **critical distance** about the situation. You should not become so involved with the situation that you are unable to carry out the reflection necessary for it to be a useful piece of research. When you fail to maintain some separation, you have 'gone native', and your research may only reflect what the organisation thinks and believes. This happened to a student project group that spent one day per week for most of a year in their sponsoring organisation (the Hamsters and

Gerbils Conservation Society mentioned in **Chapter 5**). They lost any critical perspective and, as a result, turned in a poor piece of work. However, there are many other examples from our experience where student projects have had a significant and positive impact on their organisation.

6.3 How can I collect qualitative data using interviews and focus groups?

Interviews are one of the most widely used research methods in student projects, not least because they draw on familiar skills of finding out things by asking questions. An interview undertaken as part of a qualitative data gathering process is characterised as oral and personal, non-standardised, using predominantly open questions, and with the interviewer focused on mediating and investigating the responses of the interviewee. **Table 6.2** provides an overview of different types of interviews.

Individual or group interviews create different opportunities and challenges for the researcher. You should also decide whether you should carry out your interviews singly or in pairs. **Table 6.3** summarises some of the strengths and weakness of the various combinations of interviewers and interviewees.

Table 6.2   Characteristics of interviews

Characteristic	Decision
Degree of standardisation	Structured Partly structured Not structured
Form of contact/medium	Direct, personal By phone In writing, on-line
Number of interviewees	One-to-one/individual interview Group interview/focus group
Number of interviewer	One interviewer Two interviewers Interview panel
Purpose	Investigating Mediating
Interviewer behaviour	Soft Neutral Hard

Table 6.3   Types of qualitative interviews

	One interviewee	Several interviewees
One interviewer	Single interview Advantages: Relatively easy to arrange Most appropriate for confidential and sensitive topics Most appropriate if interviewer only has a short duration time available Disadvantages: Danger of misunderstanding/ misinterpretation Dealing with contradictions of different interviewees in several interviews	Group interview/focus group Advantages: Can generate a lot of data Can be also found interesting by interviewers as they might learn from others Clarifications of different opinions/ perceptions in group possible Allows for observing group dynamics as additional source Disadvantages: Very challenging to lead for inexperienced interviewer Group dynamics might be difficult to manage Less likely to be useful for sensitive topics and in-depth explorations
Two or more interviewers	Panel interview Advantages: Reduces the potential for bias resulting from having a single interviewer Good for building the confidence of novice interviewers Can make sure that all points are covered Disadvantages: May be intimidating for interviewee if there is a power differential (unlikely with students as interviewers) Role distribution of interviewers on panel must be clear	Group interview/group discussion Advantages: Can generate a lot of data Clarifications of different opinions/ perceptions in group possible. Allows for observing group dynamics as additional source. Two or more interviewers may raise quality Disadvantages: Role distribution between interviewers must be clear, one must take the lead. Group may be difficult to manage. Remains challenging for inexperienced interviewers

The **focus group** is a particular type of group interview that enables researchers to gather broad data from multiple parties. A focus group is carried out in a group setting and involves different participants who, it is hoped, will provide different perceptions on a topic and engage in reflection on the topic (D. Morgan 1997). The focus group can be positioned as a method between the group interview/discussion and participatory observation. It can provide more comprehensive data than group interviews, due to the workshop format being more interactive.

Focus groups can also be used to observe group interactions around a specific topic. In a focus group workshop the researcher moderates the workshop, and may provide both topic input and some influence on how the discussion moves.

6.3.1 The interview process

The quality of interviewing is determined by the choice of interviewees, the questions asked and the skill of the interviewer in obtaining data relevant to the research questions. A transparent and carefully planned process can help to ensure the quality. The process of interviewing includes:

- **Planning and preparing the interview**: the interviewees, arranging times for the interviews, the types of interviews and setting, the interview guide, and planning for analysing data;
- **Performing the interview**: from personal introduction to final checks on the data gathered;
- **Documenting results**: analysing and preparing for further interviews;
- Reflection and revision of plan for subsequent interviews.

6.3.2 Planning and preparing the interviewing

Planning and preparing identifying interviewees, gaining access (no trivial task), defining an interview guide, and planning for the analysis of the data. Key to selection of your interviewees is that they will provide a range of views. This is illustrated in **Student research in action 6.7**.

Student research in action 6.7
IT'S ALL ABOUT COMMITMENT...

Ash was interested in investigating how managers create commitment to key tasks in their teams. He interviewed a number of managers, who all were able to demonstrate how they really were expert in the creating of commitment in their teams. However, there were such differences in the accounts that he decided there was more to the study than he had first thought. He decided to ask team members how they perceived the levels of commitment within their teams and how successfully team commitment was created.

After Ash had returned to the teams and completed his interviews, it became clear that his research was still incomplete. So, he went further and asked the bosses of those managers about how they perceived the levels of commitment in those managers' teams. Ash found cases where the 'stories' told by the team, the managers and their bosses all aligned, but also cases where there was a considerable dissonance between the different accounts. The discussion he produced explored insights into the difference between the aligned and dissonant teams.

The decision on who to interview is comparable with the issues discussed in **Chapter 5** as **sampling**. Quantitative research designs emphasised random sampling as a key to being able to generalise results based on statistics. For qualitative research design, instead of random sampling you should try to select your sample so that it *represents the concepts* (those likely to be involved or have a view on your area of interest), rather than being *representative of the population*. In qualitative research, we use either **theoretical** or **purposive sampling**. So instead of choosing interviewees based on how well they represent the group you are studying, you will select them to generate the maximum variety in their responses – your data.

If you can use theoretical or purposive sampling, your interviews will provide a range of views about the issue being researched, rather than what any particular group thinks. This is not a drawback. The standards by which you will assess the quality of qualitative research are different from those for quantitative research, which we will discuss further in **Chapters 10** and **11**.

You will also need to gain access to the potential interviewees. This access needs to be arranged in advance. Gaining physical access to your subjects – agreeing to meet or interview them by some other means – is important. Ideally, you could decide exactly who you will see and for how long. In most projects, you are using goodwill to gain you the interview, so you are at their mercy. You should tell people in advance what you expect to talk to them about, how long it will take and what they might hope to gain from it. It is often tempting to promise a full report to the organisation of your findings. The rule here is that you should always exceed your promises – a good compromise might be to agree to provide some up-to-date references to articles on the topic you are researching.

As well as physical access, getting your interviewees to agree to provide information is important. Having arranged all the logistics of the interviews, you will sometimes find that you will not be given full information. These two factors – physical access and incompleteness – will affect how many people you should plan to interview.

An essential part of the planning is preparing of the questions you will ask in the interview in order to be able to lead the interview. In structuring your interviews, beyond the type of questions you use, consider how you intend them to progress. The extremes of your choices are shown in **Figure 6.3**.

If you are asking exploratory research questions, you will probably find it more natural to use the unstructured approach, although an interview doesn't have to be entirely structured or unstructured. In an unstructured interview, you direct your interviewee to the general area you want to discuss, and then allow the issues to emerge from the conversation.

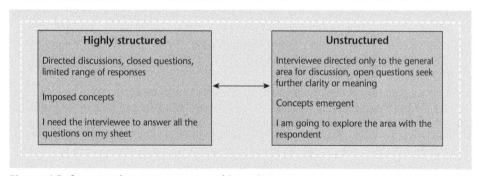

Figure 6.3 Structured versus unstructured interviews

Getting this to happen is a skill that you have to hone over time. If you reflect on the interview process as you go along by analysing your recordings or transcripts, this will greatly help you to improve. You also need to think about precisely how you will elicit information and opinions from your interviewees; indeed a practice interview that you record and then playback is always valuable, but usually more than a little disconcerting. In carrying out your interviews you have to work with a tension: having a completely unstructured discussion can lead to a most pleasant hour and some interesting comments, but little by way of useful data. Conversely, imposing your concepts through the questions you ask is contrary to the spirit of qualitative research. As Whyte (1978: 111) notes, there is a tension between these two positions:

> The interview structure is not fixed by predetermined questions, as it is in the questionnaire, but is designed to provide the informant with the freedom to introduce materials that were not anticipated by the interviewer … [however] a genuinely non-directive interviewing approach simply is not appropriate for research. Far from putting informants at their ease, it actually seems to stir anxieties.

A totally unstructured approach is unlikely to be appropriate in a professional setting, such as when you are interviewing managers, as without evidence of prior preparation some will question whether you are respecting their time.

This suggests that, at least in opening the interview, you will need some structure so that you can develop a rapport with the interviewee and establish mutual credibility. You will need to vary your degree of *directness* (guiding the respondent in the type of answer) and *restrictiveness* (guiding the respondent in the length of answer).

Qualitative interviewing, then, is different from quantitative interviewing. It does raise the criticism that unstructured data gathering is 'unscientific' because the content *emerges* as you progress the interview. However, where your objective is to build your understanding, this continual evolution is to be expected. Eisenhardt (1989: 539) warned researchers that:

> This flexibility is not a licence to be unsystematic. Rather, this flexibility is controlled opportunism in which researchers take advantage of the uniqueness of a specific case and the emergence of new themes to improve resultant theory.

That controlled opportunism is part of the skill set that you will develop as you use the methods – it takes practice and reflection to make this happen. Your interview guide or *protocol* should contain questions set out with suitable levels of structuring, which will help you to get out of the interview what you need. It is vital that this is mutually agreed in advance if you split the work in a student group, where you might use the interview guide to ensure broadly similar data is collected. Still these can be qualitative interviews, with open questions and the interviews can emerge. An example of an interview guide is provided in **Chapter 12**.

6.3.3 Performing the interview

In carrying out qualitative interviews, we have found it helpful to use the *7-I structure* shown below:

1. **Introduce** – state who you are, who you represent, your purpose in seeing that person or people and how long you will be (see note on time below). Reassure them about

the confidentiality of the information you hope they will give you. Gain agreement to use any recording equipment you intend to use (also see below). Introduce who is taking which role: if you are more than one interviewer, one might concentrate on the questions, the other might document and make sure that all points are covered.

2. **Icebreak** – start to establish rapport with the person or people you are interviewing. Don't forget that they might not have a clear idea why you want to talk to them. It is also worthwhile to start with some easy questions to get the ball rolling. Show an interest in what they are doing. Ensure that you appear relaxed about the discussion – people pick up on anxiety very easily.

3. **Increase the intensity of the questioning** – ask the questions either as pre-structured or as the discussion leads (see the example below on motivation).

4. **Intervene** – when a discussion goes off track, you may need to intervene. You lead the interview. If you need to be focused because of time constraints, you should politely but firmly refer the person back to the original question. Some interviewees will have pre-prepared speeches of their own, and will 'play their tape' whether it answers your question or not. You might go with it for a short while, but when you absolutely must collect specific information and time is limited, letting someone ramble on about their hot topic may be cathartic for them but of limited use to you. A more extreme experience – but thankfully rare – is described in **Research in action 6.1**. You should think about how you might handle an awkward interviewee – perhaps to thank them graciously for their time and cut your losses and run.

 Research in action 6.1

I'LL NEVER BE YOUR BEAST OF BURDEN

Having arranged an interview with the research director of a large multinational company, I went excited about the good material I hoped the interview would yield for my project. The discussion started with the interviewee asking me about the research I was doing. That was OK, until he stated that this was, of course, 'missing the point'. He then proceeded to tell me what my research should have been about. His opinion was that whilst what I was asking about was interesting, it was all stuff that had been done 10 years previously, and was already well documented. He then patted me on the head as I left and said that he hoped his contribution would be recognised in my thesis. Given that I had carried out an extensive literature review that showed that the work hadn't been done, I found this quite ironic. It could very well happen to you, so please don't feel so bad about it when it does!

5. **In conclusion** – wrap up the session at the end and thank the interviewee for their time. As a final question you may ask if there was anything they think is important to you for understanding the topic which you had not asked. Sometimes you get a new perspective on the area of interest that you hadn't previously considered. You need to agree on follow-ups, for example if your interview partner wants to see the interview protocol, or if the interview partner promised you some documents to make an issue and provide evidence for a point he/she made in the interview. Check details such as how to get out of the building. Attempting an exit through the broom cupboard at this stage, as one of the authors has done, is going to blow any credibility you had with the interviewees!

6. **In case** – always request that you can get back to the person you have just spoken with to clarify any points. This is vital for when you start your analysis. You cannot always cover everything you need to in one session and there will be some

areas that you will have missed altogether. Don't count on being able to follow up any missed material, though.

7. **Interpret your data** soon after the interview, at worst within hours of the event. Otherwise, it is easy to forget that critical point that you didn't note down, or be unable to interpret some ambiguous and cryptic notes you have made to yourself. Start amending your plan for the coming interview based on the increased knowledge you have now.

Chapter 5 provided examples of open-ended and closed-ended questions. Even though qualitative research focuses more on open-ended questions, we suggest that you start out with some closed-ended questions, where you provide your interviewee with a limited set of prescribed answers to encourage the start of the conversation. For instance, you might start out a discussion on motivation by asking:

Q: Can you identify a point in the past 12 months where you would say that your motivation level was high?

You could follow this up with an open-ended question to elicit more detail:

Q: Why was your level of motivation high at this point?

Open-ended questions are more exploratory in nature and can lead to many other questions that cannot always be determined in advance. You may also use them to clarify or probe an issue more deeply, such as:

Q: To what extent does your work environment determine your level of motivation?

Q: Are there external factors that affect your motivation at work?

As you develop rapport with the person or people you are interviewing, seek confirmation or further discussion of key points. This should then lead to your most in-depth questions, but only after the people are comfortable with what you are doing. Even when you have interviewed that person before, start gently and allow the flow of information to be established.

Three tips from our experience in doing interviews:

1. **Respect the time of the people you are interviewing**. More than once, after someone has told me repeatedly they are so busy they can only give me 10 minutes, I have offered to close the meeting after 10 minutes only to be told that it is fine for me to continue. The important issue here is that if they say 10 minutes, it is your responsibility to watch the clock. After that time, offer to go. It is rare that an interview that is going somewhere will be terminated, but your courtesy will be respected.
2. **Check before you go into the interview that your phone is turned off**. If your mobile phone goes off during an interview, it can totally ruin the interview. Even the buzzing of a vibrating phone can be a trigger to an interviewee that reminds them of something more important that they should be doing.
3. **Where possible, try to arrange the interview in a neutral location where you are less likely to be interrupted**. When you are interviewing managers, any disruption can prove fatal to the process. If the interview is in someone's office, a ringing telephone or other interruption can cause a break in the flow that makes it difficult to restart the interview afterwards.

You should also consider some other issues in interviewing:

- **Don't** impose your own preconceptions or ideas by the language you use. In discussing the uncertainty caused by a merger of two large companies, an interviewer was trying to determine its effects on workforce morale. If he were to ask the question 'How angry do you feel about the possibility of being made redundant?' he would clearly be imposing *anger* and *redundancy* into the discussion. If the interviewee has not previously mentioned these two ideas, this might well bias the resulting discussion.

- **Do** use the interviewees' language. If they are talking about something you don't understand, clarify what they mean and then use their language. (The technical term for this is 'native categories'.) In most organisations, people have their own codes, or even TLAs (three-letter abbreviations), for most things.

6.3.4 Documenting the interview

The best method to ensure that you faithfully capture your qualitative data is to record your interviews, wherever possible, and **transcribe** them word for word later on. This is a painstaking process, but it has significant benefits, as we show in **Student research in action 6.8**.

⊕ *Student research in action 6.8*
THE BEST MAN FOR THE JOB?

As mentioned in **Student research in action 2.11**, Anjali was investigating the criteria by which managers were selected for particular jobs. Despite her discussions with both managers and various human resource professionals, she never felt she was making any real progress in finding out the criteria or how decisions were made. She had started out looking for a formal, identifiable process, but felt frustrated by the answers she was getting. Going back to the recordings of her interviews, she noticed that when she looked for evidence of a rational selection process, the HR interviewees became more careful and frequently tried to change the subject.

This provided the evidence for one of her findings – there was little to suggest that rational selection processes were taking place in the firms she was investigating, and that whilst they might think this undesirable, it was with the consent of the HR professionals. This was quite a surprise, but one that could not be proved directly in the position she was in – an outsider with the interviews only proceeding out of goodwill. Being seen in that context to be implicitly critical of the interviewees was not going to help her to carry out the project. Instead, she was able to rely on other non-verbal communication signals which she noted as the interview progressed.

You should never assume that recording replaces **taking notes**. During the interview, you should note down any issues that might be worth returning to during the interview, should any topics need probing or if the conversation needs more direction. In a quantitative design where you have a structured interview schedule and mainly closed-ended questions, recording short answers on your interview scripts may be good enough. When you are using mainly open-ended questions, however, to summarise responses you will have to filter the data – decide what is important and what is not. This is definitely something you should avoid: whatever you don't write down you won't have available to analyse, and you could lose important data because you only realise its significance later on. Furthermore, no matter how fast you can write, you also need to listen to what the person is saying, so that you can seek clarification where necessary or be ready with the next question. Very few people manage both simultaneously. This alone is a good reason to interview in pairs if you are allowed only to take notes.

Some tips for recording your interviews:

- **Do** get permission to record the interview.
- **Do** reassure your interviewees about confidentiality.
- **Do** make sure that whatever device you are using as a recorder is working, including testing in the actual situation to ensure that you can hear what you have recorded. Background noise often makes the conversation inaudible and some workplaces do not allow mobile phones on site.
- **Do** have a system worked out for keeping files and give audio files names that make them easily identifiable.

The usual stage between notes or recording and analysis is *transcription*, where you convert the spoken word into written text which then becomes your raw data for analysis. Transforming verbal data into written form makes it relatively simple to work through and perform the analysis. Also, transcribed data, if you manage the process carefully, will allow you to trace particular themes or issues back to particular people you have interviewed. As a rough rule, it will take at least three to four hours of transcription work for each hour of interviews, and may take as much as six to eight hours. Professional typists can work faster, but this does get expensive quickly. You should check your transcripts as soon as possible, especially for key points, against your recordings to make sure that they have been faithfully reproduced. This will be useful as the first stage of the analysis process – you can use it to re-familiarise yourself with the material you have collected. Try not to summarise or filter your data here. Do not discount any material at this stage, just because it may appear to be out of line with other material. You should wait until the analysis stage to look for the reasons as to why it was different.

What should you do if you can't get permission to record your interviews?

If there is more than one interviewer, one person may ask questions and the other take notes. If there is just one interviewer, then jotting down notes will help, but as soon as you have finished the interview, go and write down as complete an account as you possibly can. If you are unable to take any notes, it's especially important to write down everything you remember, as soon as you can, even if it means doing this in the car park, a café, or even in the WC.

 ## Summary

This chapter addresses the key question: 'How do I do qualitative research?' You can choose from a range of methods, depending on your research question and the practicalities of your available time and places to carry out your research. We discussed possible difficulties with access early in the chapter, but this is an issue that is central to all research methods, not just those described here.

We classified qualitative methods according to the level of involvement you would have in each with the subject of your research. You can carry out observation remotely, and collect data about what people do. Remote observation is the least involved of the methods and can be either direct or indirect. More involved methods included direct interviews. These are very common and there is much to guide the practices you use to make your study highly effective. You can achieve even higher levels of involvement under the heading of participant observation – there are well-formulated research designs for both this and action research. Furthermore, you do not have to use any of these methods in isolation, as one method can provide further evidence to support or question the findings of another method.

We have introduced you to the main methods of qualitative research which include remote data collection, observations or interviews and focus groups. These can be used as standalone, for example conducting a series of 40 qualitative interviews with managers, a series of observations of decision-making meetings or five focus group workshops to have sales managers discuss the status of their occupation.

In business and management, the application of qualitative research approaches has become increasingly popular with academics over the past 30 years, to the point today that there are a well-established range of methods available, and plenty of examples of good work to demonstrate the value of this approach.

 ## Answers to key questions

What methods for collecting data are associated with the qualitative research approach?

- Remote data collection, including document analysis.
- Observation, including remote and participant observation.
- Interviews and focus groups.

How can I conduct remote data collection, observation and interviews?

- Each of these approaches relies on the same set of characteristics of qualitative research, namely that it is multidimensional, iterative and subjective.
- Remote data collection will involve gathering data from documents including diaries of individuals and organisational documents such as minutes of meetings.
- Observation can be undertaken either covertly or directly. We recommend you stick with direct observation, whether this is passive or active. Active observation, otherwise called participant observation and including action research, requires the researcher to become part of the research.
- Interviews can be conducted by one or multiple researchers, talking to one or multiple respondents. Where multiple respondents are chosen, these can be pulled together into a focus group. The researcher has to choose carefully the mixture of closed and open questions to allow that balance between structure and flexibility to accommodate concepts not previously considered.

What are the particular issues in qualitative research design that I should be aware of?

- The purpose of qualitative research is to understand how participants view the social world. This is by nature subjective, as is your interpretation of their views. This brings a richness to the data that you don't get in quantitative research.

- The process of data collection and analysis is iterative, requiring that analysis is carried out without waiting for all data to be collected.
- Each of the designs has well-established detailed methods for data collection and analysis. Whilst broad in outlook and subjective, it does not mean that rigour in the process can be ignored.

References

Bourdieu, P. 1990. *The Logic of Practice*. Cambridge: Polity Press.
Eisenhardt, Kathleen M. 1989. Building theories from case study research, *Academy of Management Review*, 14(4): 532–50.
Giddens, A. 1984. *The Constitution of Society*. Oxford: Oxford Polity Press.
Ritzer, George 2015. *The McDonaldization of Society*, 8th edn. Thousand Oaks, CA: Sage Publications Inc.
Morgan, David L. 1997. *Focus Groups as Qualitative Research*. Thousand Oaks, CA: Sage.
Vaara, Eero and Whittington, Richard 2012. Strategy-as-practice: taking social practices seriously, *The Academy of Management Annals*, 6(1): 285–336.
Walsch, Neale D. 1995. *Conversations with God: Book One*. London: Hodder & Stoughton.
Whyte, William F. 1978. Interviewing in field research. In R.G. Burgess (ed.), *Field Research: A Source-book and Field Manual*. New York: Allen & Unwin.

Additional resources

Charmaz, Kathy 2014. *Constructing Grounded Theory*, 2nd edn. Thousand Oaks, CA: Sage.
Creswell, John W. 1998. *Qualitative Inquiry and Research Design: Choosing Among Five Traditions*. Thousand Oaks, CA: Sage.
Denzin, Norman K. and Lincoln, Yvonne S. (eds.) 2000. *Handbook of Qualitative Research*, 2nd edn. Thousand Oaks, CA: Sage. See particularly Fontana, A. and Frey, J.H., Chapter 22, Interviewing – the art of science, pp. 361–76.
DeWalt, Kathleen, and DeWalt, Billie 2010. *Participant Observation: A Guide for Fieldworkers*, 2nd edn. Walnut Creek, CA: AltaMira Press.
Dirks, Melanie and Mills, Jane 2011. *Grounded Theory: A Practical Guide*. London: Sage.
Glaser, B. and Strauss, A. 1967 *The Discovery of Grounded Theory: Strategies of Qualitative Research*. London: Wiedenfeld & Nicholson.
Gummesson, Evert 2000. *Qualitative Methods in Management Research*, 2nd edn. Thousand Oaks, CA: Sage.
Lawson, Hal A., Caringi, James C., Pyles, Loretta, Jurkowski, Janine M. and Bozlak, Christine T. 2015. *Participatory Action Research*. Oxford: Oxford University Press.
Lee, R.M. 2000. *Unobtrusive Methods in Social Research*. Milton Keynes: Open University Press.
Locke, Karen 2001. *Grounded Theory in Management Research*. London: Sage.
May, Tim (ed.). 2002. *Qualitative Research in Action*. London: Sage.
Morgan, Gareth 1997. *Images of Organisation*. Revised edition. Thousand Oaks, CA: Sage.
Mintzberg, Henry 1979. An emerging strategy of 'direct' research, *Administrative Science Quarterly*, 24: 582–9.
Phillips, Brenda D. 2014. *Qualitative Disaster Research: Understanding Qualitative Research*. Oxford: Oxford University Press.
Rathje, William and Murphy, Cullen 1992. *Rubbish! The Archaeology of Garbage*. New York: HarperCollins.

Reason, Peter and Bradbury, Hilary (eds) 2000. *Handbook of Action Research: Participative Inquiry and Practice*. Thousand Oaks, CA: Sage.

Richardson, S.A., Dohrenwend, B.S. and Klein, D. 1965. *Interviewing: Its Forms and Functions*. New York: Basic Books.

Richie, Donald A. 2015. *Doing Oral History*, 3rd edn. Oxford: Oxford University Press.

Rosen, M. 1991. Coming to terms with the field: Understanding and doing organisational ethnography, *Journal of Management Studies*, 28(1): 1–24.

Saldana, Johnny 2012. *The Coding Manual for Qualitative Researchers*, 2nd edn. London: Sage.

Strauss, Anselm L. and Corbin, Juliet 2007. *Basics of Qualitative Research: Techniques and Procedures for Developing Grounded Theory*, 3rd edn. London: Sage.

Symon, Gillian and Cassell, Catherine (eds) 1998. *Qualitative Methods and Analysis in Organisational Research: A Practical Guide*. Thousand Oaks, CA: Sage.

Urquhart, Cathy 2012. *Grounded Theory for Qualitative Research: A Practical Guide Paperback*. London: Sage.

Van Maanen, John 1982. Fieldwork on the beat. In J. Von Maanen, J.M. Dabbs Jr. and R.R. Faulkner (eds), *Varieties of Qualitative Research*. Thousand Oaks, CA: Sage.

Van Maanen, John 1988. *Tales of the Field: On Writing Ethnography*. Chicago, IL: University of Chicago Press.

Whyte, William F. 1955. *Street Corner Society*. Chicago, IL: University of Chicago Press.

Key terms

action research, 188
covert observation, 185
critical distance, 188
focus group, 191
indirect data collection, 182
interviews, 189
participant observation, 188
qualitative interviewing, 193

remote data collection, 182
sampling, 192
social behaviour, 178
social systems, 178
taking notes, 196
theoretical or purposive sampling, 192
transcribe, 196

Discussion questions

1. What are the main methods associated with a qualitative research design?
2. How can an interview be used in both quantitative and qualitative designs?
3. Think of three examples of data that could be collected by remote observation. What would be the main method of actually gathering the data in each case?
4. Why is it a good idea to tape record unstructured interviews?
5. What is the role of the interview schedule and how does this compare with a questionnaire?
6. How is ethnographic research different from nonparticipant observation?
7. What are the risks involved with participant observation?
8. Why is it a good idea for you to transcribe your own data? What are the drawbacks of this?
9. Are verbal statements really data?
10. What forms of data, other than words, could you collect as part of a qualitative research study?

Workshop

This workshop focuses on how to use unstructured interviews to find out information. At the end of the workshop, you should have a better understanding of what it is like to be both interviewer and interviewee, by playing both roles.

Background

People have to make significant changes in their lives when they go into higher education. To assist in this process, we need to understand the nature of these changes better.

Task

Conduct interviews in pairs – not necessarily from the same subgroup.

1. Set-up – Two-minute individual preparation (silence) to think about the issues involved.

2. Interview – Spend five minutes with one person interviewing the other on the subject of their experiences of moving into higher education (all aspects of the change – not just educational). The interviewer is responsible for recording the interview – take notes, tape or video record it if possible – it will be used again in the **Chapter 12** workshop.

3. Debrief – what types of questions were asked (open/closed, structured/loose) and what was the role of the interviewer (how much did they impose their own views on the interviewee, intervene and so on)?

4. Now change roles – those that were interviewing now become the interviewee – again a five-minute interview and the interviewer is responsible for taking a record of the interview.

5. Debrief – what questions were asked this time, how were they put and how did the interviewer ensure that they did not impose their view on the situation? What form did your record of the interview take? What did you write down – everything they said or just what appeared important (to you)?

6. Break into subgroups (four or more usually works well, the key is to have no more than five or six students per group), collate the information using thematic groupings – combine your interviews with your own experiences in the group. It is suggested that a mind map display may be appropriate here.

7. Debrief the rest of the group – one-minute 'show and tell' of what you found about the subject and the process of carrying out unstructured or semi-structured interviews (such as how much of what was said you were able to capture using notes).

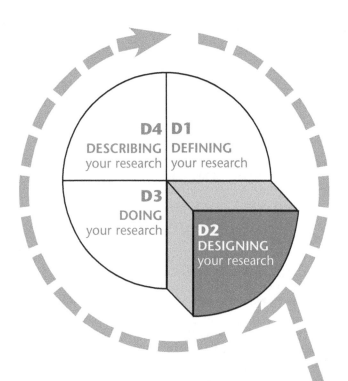

Relevant chapters
13 How do I write up my report?
14 What do I do now?

Key challenges
- Making sense of your findings
- Presenting your research to others
- Reflecting and learning from your research

4

Relevant chapters
1 What is research?
2 What should I study?
3 How do I find information?

Key challenges
- Understanding what academic research is
- Generating and clarifying ideas
- Using sources of information

1

D4
DESCRIBING your research

D1
DEFINING your research

D3
DOING your research

D2
DESIGNING your research

Relevant chapters
9 How do I do field research?
10 What do my quantitative data mean(1)?
11 What do my quantitative data mean(2)?
12 What do my qualitative data mean?

Key challenges
- Practical considerations in doing research
- Describing data using simple statistics
- Carrying out statistical tests
- Interpreting words and actions

3

Relevant chapters
4 What is my research approach?
5 How do I do quantitative research?
6 How do I do qualitative research?
7 **How do I do case study research?**
8 How do I make sure my research is ethical?

Key challenges
- Choosing a research approach
- Choosing a research design
- Collecting data using quantitative methods
- **Collecting data using qualitative methods**
- Integrating quantitative and qualitative methods

2

7
chapter

How do I do case study research?

 Key questions

- Why would I use a case study design in my research?
- How can I design a case study?
- What does a good case study look like?
- Can I combine both qualitative and quantitative methods in a single research design?

 Learning outcomes

By the time that you have completed this chapter, you should be able to:

- Decide whether a case study design is appropriate for your research project
- Select suitable methods for your case study design
- Identify suitable case studies for your research
- Recognise the benefits and limitations of mixed-method research designs

Contents

Introduction

Chapters 5 and 6 introduced you to some common quantitative and qualitative research designs and methods for business and management research. **Section 7.1** will introduce the **case study**, an important research design that is commonly used in business and management research, as well as social research, including psychology, sociology, education and economics. As a research design, the case study is defined by *what* you collect data about, rather than *how* you collect your data.

Case study designs, because they focus on a 'natural' unit of observation such as a business unit or a charitable organisation, are popular for student research projects. Although the 'case' you study in business and management research will often be an organisation or an organisational subunit (a division or department, for instance), the case you can study ranges from an individual to an industry. William Foote Whyte (1955) studied a particular group of people in society in *Street Corner Society*; Philip Selznick (1949) studied the Tennessee Valley Authority; and Alfred Chandler (1962) studied the historical development of American business. Such designs enable you to investigate a phenomenon in its real-life setting, particularly the dynamics that take place in this setting. This focus on context rather than methods is particularly useful when you're not sure what data you will need to collect, how to collect them, or what you will find out.

Section 7.2 will discuss the use of multiple methods for use in case study research. Organising your research around a social unit such as an organisation will make your data collection and therefore your research manageable. For example, you might collect data about the organisation sponsoring your project, using as many different methods as you find appropriate to find information. Being able to draw on different methods and data sources makes the case study one of the most powerful, yet challenging, research designs in business and management.

One advantages of the case study as a research design is that a researcher can combine both qualitative and quantitative methods. This is not a requirement for case research, but an opportunity. **Section 7.3** will introduce multiple-method research designs more generally as a way of improving the quality of your research project. We show how you can combine multiple research methods, respondents, data sources, measures or investigators in a single research study.

After you have read this chapter, you should be able to decide whether you want to use a case study approach or another multiple-method approach in your own research project. You might want to go back to **Chapters 5** and **6** to review the methods we have presented, and to see which might be appropriate for your design.

One source of confusion to avoid is between teaching case studies, which you may have encountered in your classes, and the case study discussed here, which is a research design. Case studies are generally more complex than teaching case studies in textbooks and in classes, because teaching case studies have usually been simplified to illustrate part of a situation for specific teaching purposes (even if they are based on case study research). It is important to choose the right model for investigating and/or writing up your research.

7.1 What is a case study research design?

Creswell (2013) describes a **case** as a *single, bounded entity, studied in detail*.[1] The 'single bounded entity', or unit of analysis, defines your *case study*. It could be a person, a project, a group, a 'group of groups' (a trade association, for instance) a company or an organisation. Although every research design involves the study of 'cases' in a sense, the case study design is defined by the case being the focus of the research design. You can collect data for a case study using any of many different research methods discussed in **Chapter 5** and **Chapter 6** (and beyond), but it will still be a case study. (By comparison, a project that uses participant observation will not be a survey.)

A case study approach often suits group projects because each person can conduct site visits in pairs or teams, and then the group can compare and contrast its experiences, gaining insights from multiple perspectives. Each person may pick up aspects of the case that the others have missed.

Table 7.1 provides an overview of the different types of case studies based on the decisions that you make in the research design process.

7.1.1 What is the case that I'm studying?

A key difference between case study research and the research design that we encountered in earlier chapters is that you start with identifying the case (or cases) that you will study, and only then identify the research methods that you will use. This is the

Table 7.1 Varieties of case studies

Characteristic	Decisions
Case study unit	Person Group Organisation Industry Society
Purpose	Exploratory Explanatory Descriptive
Number of case studies	Single Multiple
Duration	Short term Longitudinal
Time	Real time Retrospective Mixed

opposite of the research designs presented in **Chapter 5** and **Chapter 6**, where you will select the sample after the methods.

Thus, the most important step in research design will be to define the case that you are going to study, as shown in **Student research in action 7.1**. Although defining a case sounds simple, it may be more difficult in practice. If you are doing a placement or sponsored project, then your sponsor may determine your case, but you will still need to decide what the boundaries of the case will be. Is it your work group, department, business unit, organisation or industry? If you are free to choose the context of your research, this gives you both more freedom but also less guidance than for a research project linked to a particular business sponsor.

Case studies often start with a description of the 'entity' and its 'boundaries'. For example, if your case is your work group, you may need to describe the department you are working in so that your reader understands the context of your work group. So does the department or the work group define the boundaries of your case? The boundaries of the case determine what is relevant and what is not to your research.

7.1.2 Why am I using a case study?

Good case study research, like surveys, takes careful planning and execution. If you choose a case study as your research design, you need to make sure that it is the best way to answer your research questions, design how you will carry out your research and demonstrate how you will analyse and interpret what you find out. You can use a case study to explain, describe, illustrate, explore or evaluate the phenomenon you are interested in (Yin 2014). A case study can answer exploratory and descriptive 'how' and 'why' research questions or analytic research questions.

So when do researchers choose to use case studies? A case study is particularly useful for:

- Studying an organisation or phenomenon that you cannot study directly but about which you can collect secondary or archival data;
- Conducting a limited or exploratory study, especially if you are conducting an individual research project and you have a limited budget and limited time (Blaikie 2009);
- When you have no control over the events you are interested in studying *and* the phenomenon takes place at least partly during the period you are doing your research.

Quantitative and qualitative researchers may also define cases differently (see **Chapter 4**). From a *quantitative* perspective, cases exist 'out there', independently of the researcher, and hence their boundaries are pre-defined. Cases will use pre-existing categories based on general or conventional social units such as individuals, teams, families, organisations, cities and nations, and therefore they will have identifiable boundaries set by the social unit. For example, there would be a clear boundary between a company and its industry as part of the case, although the industry may be relevant as part of the research context and so on.

On the other hand, from a *qualitative* perspective, cases are theoretical constructs created by investigators, are specific to a piece of research, and are developed during the research itself. Ragin and Becker (1992: 6) suggest that 'A researcher probably will not know what their cases are until the research, including … writing up the results, is virtually completed'. The boundaries of the case are not set by the selection of the case and do not exist until you have defined them, for example, the 'type A personality' or the 'newly developing country', because they emerge as evidence accumulates. Therefore, you not only identify and investigate cases, but also to bring them into being.

While this may sound fuzzy, case study research designs are just as valid and rigorous as the research methods and designs we described in **Chapters 5 and 6**. As Yin (2014: 6) explains:

> Many social scientists still deeply believe that case studies were only appropriate for the exploratory phase of an investigation, that surveys and histories were appropriate for the descriptive phase, and that experiments are the only way of doing explanatory or causal inquiries. [This] view reinforced the idea that case studies are only an exploratory tool and could not be used to describe or test propositions. This … view, however, is incorrect. Experiments with an exploratory motive have always existed. … case studies are far from being only an exploratory strategy. Some of the best and most famous case studies have been both descriptive (for example, Whyte's *Street Corner Society* 1943/1955) and explanatory (see Allison's *Essence of Decision: Explaining the Cuban Missile Crisis*, 1971).

7.1.3 Should I study one or more cases?

An important issue in designing case study research is choosing how many cases you will study. **Student research in action examples 7.1 to 7.4** illustrate student projects that used different forms of case study design. For example, you may decide to study a single case or multiple cases. A **single case study** focuses on a single unit of analysis, such as a corporation. It may occur naturally when you are studying something that is unique – such as the credit crisis – or when you are using your company as a research setting. Single case studies are low on generalisability (but high on realism). If you are taking a quantitative approach, then a 'sample size of one' might seem to be at odds with our discussion in **Chapter 5**, but, as we have noted above, many classic examples in business and management research have been single case studies. As the eminent organisational scholar James March points out, a sample size of one is sufficient *if it's the right one*.

Student research in action 7.1
EXAMPLES OF SINGLE CASE STUDY DESIGN: STRATEGY IMPLEMENTATION

Gerhart was working for a large German bank, and was interested in how the bank implemented its stated corporate strategy. Specifically, his research question concerned how the bank controlled the many activities that were concerned with this strategy implementation. This is an example of a single case approach – he considered many examples of the activities within the one organisation without focusing on any specific activity, group or part of the organisation. He mixed his insights as a manager in this organisation with some survey work of the organisation and interviews with individual senior managers to provide a rich picture of this issue in the organisation.

Whether you study one or several cases in your case study also requires you to think about whether you are more interested in depth or breadth. **Multiple case studies** are more powerful because of what is called *replication* – looking at the same phenomenon in more than one setting; and because you can identify similarities and differences across cases, you can develop a more 'complete' picture. However, you will have less time and effort to spend on each case than if you were doing a single case study because you can investigate each case in less depth than a single case study. Quantitative researchers therefore often conduct *multiple case studies* in order to avoid the drawbacks of single case studies.

The two main multiple case study designs are (1) more than one (independent) case and (2) an in-depth case that includes more than one related 'sub-case'. You can build *multiple independent cases* by choosing cases from unrelated case settings. For example, instead of studying just one case of supply chain management implementation by an automobile manufacturer, you could study cases in three different automobile manufacturers. You might decide, for example, to study the credit crisis by doing case studies on Iceland, Greece and Cyprus.

Student research in action 7.2

EXAMPLES OF MULTIPLE CASE STUDY DESIGNS: ORGANISATIONAL CHANGE

Liz was working with a large public sector organisation, looking at how they implemented organisational change. The total number of initiatives carried out at any one time was over 100, so she decided to consider some key cases that would illustrate her research question – 'What would constitute "best practice" in such an organisation?' Specifically, she considered a small number of cases that had been successful and some that had failed. The key aspects of the successful could then be compared with those aspects of the failed initiatives, and allow further comparison with the best practice literature in the area. This is a good example of an embedded case study, because she sampled more than one case from the same organisation.

An **embedded case study** might involve the study of multiple divisions within a single company, or multiple project teams within new product development. By holding the setting or context constant, you eliminate external sources of variation and focus on systematically identifying patterns of actions, behaviours or practices. You can also use an embedded case study to investigate multiple hierarchical levels within a single study, for example industry, firm and division level as in **Student research in action 7.3**. For example, in a study of management coaching you might collect data about *embedded case studies* through:

- Each individual person coached as a case,
- A coach and person being coached, with each pair as a case,
- The coach and all of the people he or she coaches as a case,
- A team of coaches as a case, or
- The entire organisation as a case.

Student research in action 7.3

EXAMPLES OF MULTIPLE CASE STUDY DESIGNS: COUNTY COUNCIL SERVICE DELIVERY

Ian's project was set in a county council where there had been some problems – notably that it had been audited and labelled as a failing council. A key aspect of this failure concerned its ability to deliver services and make changes. Ian's project was to consider the way the council managed capacity and capability – literally to find whether it had the workforce or ability to deliver all that it was required to do. He soon found that nobody really knew how much work the organisation was capable of doing in total. The result was that the organisation regularly took on far more work than it could handle, resulting in chaos. Having spent the majority of his available research time with the council exploring the project in depth and identifying his key findings, he then contacted local organisations from both the public and private sectors to provide contrasting cases – and explored each of his key issues at those organisations. In this way, he was able to gain insights into those specific issues of importance. This is an example of a multiple case study, because Ian's other cases came from outside his original case study site (compare with Liz's selection of cases in **Student research in action 7.2**).

Student research in action 7.4

EXAMPLES OF MULTIPLE CASE STUDY DESIGNS: EMPOWERMENT

Ann's study of empowerment practices in the construction sector investigated the research question, 'What is the policy and reality of empowerment in the construction sector today?' In answering this research question, she looked at the overall patterns of empowerment, as cited in various reports on the sector. She then looked at one firm thought to be 'typical' of the sector. Here she considered the firm's policies on empowerment and how these fitted with the overall managerial philosophy of the firm. She also considered what really happened in the enactment of that policy, by considering examples from a division within the firm – again through management statements such as policy statements, and then particular projects – and by short site visits conducting interviews of site personnel. This multi-level approach was particularly good at providing a contrast between policy and practice in empowerment – as she did find that there was considerable variation between the views at different levels. This is another example of an embedded case study, where the cases are selected 'vertically' (i.e. as a series of vertical slices through the organisational chart) rather than horizontally (across the organisational chart) as in **Student research in action 7.2**.

It's not always clear whether a case study is a single case study, a multiple case study conducted within a single setting, or a multiple case study conducted within multiple settings. The multiple-case, single-setting design described in **Student research in action 7.2** is an *embedded case study*.

Compare **Student research in action 7.2** and **Student research in action 7.3** with **Student research in action 7.1** and **Student research in action 7.4**. Identifying common patterns, as in **Student research in action 7.1**, will help you show that your findings are valid and reliable. This does not mean that the quantitative approach to the case was necessarily better than that adopted in the other examples – which were more qualitative – it just answered a different type of research question.

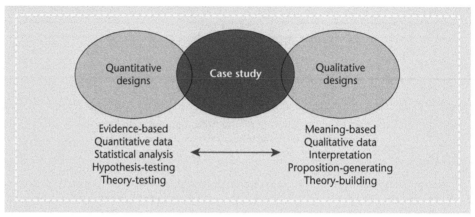

Figure 7.1 Case study as research design

Figure 7.1 illustrates how the case study as a design integrates aspects of both quantitative and qualitative designs. Whether the case study is approached from more of a quantitative or qualitative perspective depends on the philosophical perspectives of the investigators, as well as practical considerations.

Grounded case study designs

You may find that you can best capture the evolving insights and determine your evolving research design using a grounded research approach, where data collection and data analysis overlap. The procedure for grounded case study research presented by Kathleen Eisenhardt (1989) has been widely used by business and management researchers. This approach is different from the deductive (theory determines what data you collect) and the inductive (data determine what theory you develop) logics that we described in **Chapter 4**: 'grounded' refers to an repeatedly 'weaving' back and forth between theory and data.

Using a grounded approach can be extremely helpful when you haven't started with a particular theory (or conceptual model), and you are trying to bring together your theoretical insights and your observations. If you are examining a phenomenon that no one else has studied before, it may not be clear before you start your research either what models are relevant or what data you need to collect. For instance, you might be the first person to do research in a particular type of firm, or on a particular practice, so you might not be able to identify what sorts of things you need to be looking for, or even what sorts of things you might expect to find. This grounded approach will help you to capture both theoretical and empirical insights from your data.

Eisenhardt (1989) presents an extremely useful road map for using a **grounded case study** research approach to build theories from case study research. This road map is appropriate for research that combines both quantitative and qualitative approaches. The steps she suggests are as follows:

1. **Getting started** – problem definition
2. **Selecting cases** – theoretical sampling
3. **Crafting instruments and protocols** – preparing multiple data collection methods
4. **Entering the field** – collecting data
5. **Analysing data** – within-case analysis followed by cross-case analysis

6. **Shaping hypotheses** – building evidence and explanation
7. **Enfolding literature** – comparing findings with the literature
8. **Reaching closure** – knowing when to stop.

Steps 1–4 of the grounded case study design are common to all case study research. However, whilst you can use the same methods to collect data for a grounded case study and a case study from the scientific approach, typically you will need much more time to interpret the data and understand what they mean.

Steps 5–8 are worth looking at in more detail. Teh-Yuan's project given in **Student research in action 7.6** illustrates the relationship between within-case and cross-case analysis in data analysis. Teh-Yuan first analysed each of his UK cases and Taiwanese cases using a within-case logic; that is, separately and without trying to bring together insights across the different cases. Next, he compared pairs of similar cases using cross-case analysis, based on the case's background (for example size of project, type of technology being worked on (predominantly biotechnology) and stage in the research (basic research or commercial development). In this step, he did try to look for patterns across the cases.

Teh-Yuan could then use speculations about the differences between cases that he found in his cross-case analysis to develop his propositions about whether how the research process was managed affected its outcome. He found that a key difference between the projects was the presence of a scientist-manager – someone with the specific remit to manage the project – which led him to propose that 'the presence of a scientist-manager in such research projects is associated with higher productivity'. This proposition was reasonable based on his case study data – but he did not need to generalise it to cases outside of his research. This proposition would then give him something to add to his section on 'areas for future work' in his final research report, and a point for discussion and comparison with the literature.

Once a researcher has analysed and speculated from the cases, he or she can now turn to the literature to find vital points of reference and comparison. This is where Eisenhardt's Step 7, **enfolding the literature**, comes in. For example, Teh-Yuan could go back to his literature review to find support for his proposition about the importance of the role of the scientist-manager. He could also conduct a mini-literature review to find relevant research. This step can be used to reinforce key findings and provide evidence for the need for research to be carried out to explore the areas of difference further.

Step 8 – **closure** – comes when you are confident that if you stop gathering data you will not miss anything new. This is a powerful reason for closely linking your data collection and your data analysis. You will have reached what we term *conceptual saturation* when relatively few new concepts or insights are coming out of your cases. You may need to return to the field later to collect specific data about issues that have emerged from your work, and check that the scope of the work you had envisaged has or has not changed. We will describe these approaches further in **Chapter 12**.

7.2 How should I do my case study research?

Now that we have described the use of case studies and demonstrated their popularity for student research projects, we will consider some additional issues that you should consider when you are designing a case study. As you will see, there are few restrictions on choice, and so it is worth also considering how the quality of a piece of case study research will be assessed.

7.2.1 What data should I collect and how should I collect it?

As we noted earlier in the chapter, case study research designs may draw on both qualitative and quantitative methods for collecting data. The use of different methods increases the richness of your data, as does the use of different sources. If you achieve the same findings using different methods, you will have more confidence in them. (We discuss triangulation in **Section 7.3**.)

Nearly all case studies rely on some archival or indirect methods of collecting information, although this may be primarily for describing the case and its context. Some only use this kind of data, but most go on to use various direct methods, including interviews and observation.

How should I select the cases that I will study?

As part of your case study research design, you will need to think about how you will choose your cases, especially if you plan to use multiple cases. There are two ways to select your research cases based on:

- **Replication** – choosing similar cases, e.g. companies in the same industry or managers in a particular situation, and looking for similarities and differences across cases;
- **Variation** – choosing cases that vary along the main variable you are interested in researching, and looking for systematic variation linked to that variable.

If you take a replication approach, you will select cases that are similar to each other and look for differences and what causes those differences. For example, you could select two small companies to investigate that use similar marketing strategies. You could then try to tease out differences in their approaches to marketing, and then repeat this for two medium and two larger firms – as shown in **Figure 7.2**. You should think of replication as repeating studies rather than increasing sample size (if this were an experimental design, you would be conducting a new experiment with the same parameters rather than recruiting more participants to the same study).

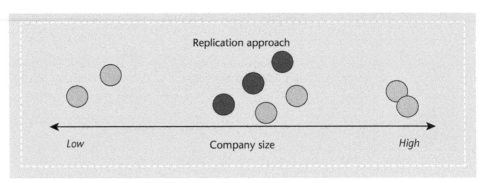

Figure 7.2 Case study design: Replication

If you are taking a *quantitative* approach to your case study design, you are likely to use a replication strategy, while if you are taking a *qualitative* approach, you are likely to take the variation strategy. The variation comes from what is known as *theoretical sampling* (sometimes called *purposive sampling*), which allows you to study or develop propositions and draw some conclusions.

Student research in action 7.5

SELECTING CASES ON THE VARIABLE OF INTEREST: ENGLISH BIOTECH

Rebecca wanted to do her MSc dissertation on why English biotech firms survived or failed. Since she only had three months to design, conduct and write up her research and she didn't already have access to any biotech firms, she decided to do a comparative case study of two firms – one which had survived and one which had failed – to see if she could identify factors that contributed to these outcomes. She selected her two cases to create the maximum contrast between firm success in the biotech field; she could thus explore differences between the two and show that factors, for example early venture capitalist involvement and influential people sitting on the corporate board, were present in the successful firm but had not been part of the one that failed. Similar factors had already been demonstrated in the literature on technology start-up firms. As she explored the biotech firms further, she uncovered some interesting differences with technology firms.

Effective designs may be to choose (1) one case that represents an extreme (for example a 'best practice' or 'worst practice' company), as shown in **Figure 7.3**; or (2) two (or more) cases that vary widely on one or more aspects that you wish to investigate, as shown in **Figure 7.4**. **Student research in action 7.5** illustrates the variation strategy. For instance, if your research question was: 'Does marketing effort depend on firm size?', you may wish to select one small, one medium-sized and one large company as cases, and investigate how marketing activities vary across the three firms. Firm size is the dimension on which firms vary. At the end of your study, you could propose something about the relationship between size and marketing.

Students often want to know how many cases 'are enough' in a multiple case study design, especially the 'grounded case study' (Eisenhardt 1989) that we discuss in **Section 7.1.3**. Given the constraints of student research, we find in practice that it is hard to do more than eight case studies to an adequate depth. As we will discuss in **Chapter 12**, the logic of multiple case studies is more like the logic of qualitative

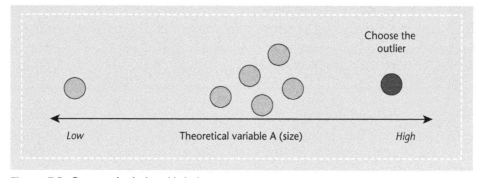

Figure 7.3 Case study design: Variation at one extreme

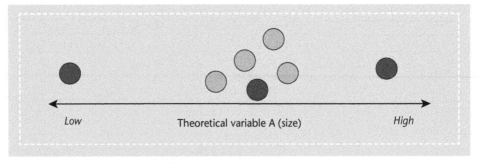

Figure 7.4 Case study design: Variation at both extremes

research than the logic of quantitative research: you are trying to reach '**theoretical saturation**' rather than generalise to a population (remember that each case study is a 'new' design rather than another unit within a quantitative sample). If you need to provide depth *and* breadth, for example on the case identified by your project sponsor, you might consider doing one single in-depth case study as your main study, and then collecting a number of shallower and smaller **comparison case studies**.

If you are conducting an open-ended number of cases, you should review the contribution each new case is making, rather than wait to the end of your study to note that the findings were the same in all cases. Once you start finding the same results each time, you can stop adding more cases. If the findings are more consistent than you expected (e.g. very different contexts yielding very similar results), you should investigate the reasons behind this consistency. In this kind of situation, the case study approach can be evolutionary.

ACTIVITY

Fast-food corporations have a choice between franchising new units and opening these units themselves. This decision has obvious financial implications. A less obvious implication is the opportunity to use a company-owned site for getting closer to customers and creating learning, and trying out different policies and procedures and new products.

Suppose you were interested in how a fast-food corporation changed its advertising and product offerings in response to government initiatives on obesity, and changes in public opinion due to anti-fast-food films and campaigns. How might you develop a case study to investigate this? Try to think about how you would:

● Define the case and its boundaries.

● Decide how many cases and what sort of sampling logic to use to select cases.

How would these decisions affect what you find out in your research? Develop three options and explore whether it does make a difference.

A word of warning here. If you are using a multiple case study design and you want to compare your within-case findings across cases, you need to make sure that you collect *comparable* data across the cases. For example, if you are using interviews, an interview guide helps you to make sure you cover all the questions you have (Creswell 2013). This comparability means you have a common basis for analysis, rather than ending up with multiple irreconcilable data sets.

How can I gain access to organisations?

One of the biggest challenges in case study research is that it can be difficult to gain access for in-depth case study research, especially if you are not already connected with the organisation. (This is why the case study is more popular with sponsored case study research.) **Chapter 9** will discuss strategies for gaining access to organisations. Furthermore, even if you have strong access to an organisation you will need to explain to people what your proposed case study research is about and justify the value of the research.

7.2.2 How should I analyse my case study data?

The first step in case study research is to develop a coherent narrative about your case (or about each case) that tells your *story*. You should write a detailed case study for each case, for example each plant site you have visited. This is usually a descriptive write-up, although you can also provide quantitative information such as graphs and tables to illustrate your case.

The first step is to identify which of the many possible themes around which you could organise your story, and to select the one that is the best for your research project These include chronologically, around actors (such as people, groups or organisations) or around processes (such as work activities or technologies). The most common way that student projects report case study research is to arrange the narrative around a timeline. At the end, your reader should understand the detailed and unique features of each case by itself.

Tracy Kidder's *The Soul of a New Machine* (1981) describes how Data General developed the Eclipse computer by telling it as a story in more or less chronological order from the founding of the company through to the introduction of the new computer. This is often the easiest way to organise your narrative, especially if you are telling the story of a company or a person.

Analysing individual cases

Whether you have researched a single or multiple cases, the first stage of any case study analysis is **within-case analysis**. Here, you focus on each individual case, without trying to bring in the findings or lessons from any other cases you might have been investigating. This is important as it allows the richness of the data from each case to be harnessed, unconstrained by other cases. The tools of this level of analysis are described in Chapter 12.

Research in action 7.1 shows how qualitative data were turned into quantitative data, as a pragmatic approach to dealing with a large data set with many observations. Whilst larger than would be expected from an undergraduate or master's level student research project, it does illustrate this particular research design well.

Research in action 7.1

TURNING OBSERVATIONS INTO QUANTITATIVE DATA: OFFICE PRODUCTS

Pär Åhlström spent several years when he was a doctoral student researching a company that made office products. Par made notes of every conversation or meeting he observed on the days he was present at the company. At the end of his observation period, he had over 6000 observations saved on his computer. This was too much data to analyse as raw data. Instead he used what is termed 'content analysis' (see **Chapter 12**) which helped him to identify key themes in his data. He was then able to go back to the data and plot the frequency with which those themes appeared over time. This mixed method worked very well – the qualitative analysis to identify the themes and then the quantitative analysis to identify patterns in the occurrence of those themes (see Åhlström 1997).

Cross-case analysis

When you have conducted within-case analysis on each of your cases, then you should analyse all the cases simultaneously, your **cross-case analysis**. This aims to find common patterns or significant variations across your cases. In the next stage, when you have conducted multiple cases or have used an embedded case design, you should search for patterns across cases. This process is to conduct within-case analysis, followed by cross-case analysis if you have multiple cases.

One way of doing this cross-case analysis is to select a number of categories and see how each case fits into that category. Are different cases more similar or more different? Another way to do this is to identify common themes across all the cases, and then see which individual case best illustrates each of those themes. In *Microsoft Secrets*, for example, Michael Cusumano and Richard Selby (1995) organise their story around the key themes they identified in their study of Microsoft:

- Organising and managing the company
- Managing creative people and technical skills
- Competing with products and standards
- Defining products and development processes
- Developing and shipping products
- Building a learning organisation.

They then bring in different aspects of the organisation to illustrate each of them.

You can also analyse multiple cases using a **paired-case analysis**, where you list the similarities and differences between pairs of cases. This can help you to identify new concepts and categories from the data. People who feel more comfortable with the quantitative approach may find the paired-case analysis a more natural way to analyse their findings, because it draws more on the scientific reasoning described in **Chapter 4**. We return to Teh-Yuan's research in **Student research in action 7.6**.

Student research in action 7.6

WHY CAN'T WE BE FRIENDS?

Teh-Yuan's project was concerned with the management of science and scientists in collaborative biotechnology ventures. He wanted to establish how such ventures could be managed well, in particular focusing on the exploitation of the knowledge produced during basic research. His work was to take place partly in the UK and partly in his home country – Taiwan. He chose two cases – one in each country.

Initially he noted the difference in productivity between UK and Taiwanese researchers in terms of their key outputs – specifically papers in scientific journals, where UK researchers were at least twice as productive (in terms of papers per researcher) as their Taiwanese counterparts. The difference in terms of patents registered was similar, with the UK researchers being more than twice as productive.

His paired-case analysis would establish some of the differences in the way that scientists worked – by looking at comparable cases from the UK and Taiwan. His work showed that there were many similarities in the motivations of scientists, but that the need to 'publish or perish' was much stronger in the UK. It became clear that the UK researchers were given more time for this activity and when they didn't get it as part of their working hours they would put in more of their own time to complete the writing tasks.

Presenting your case study

Even if you take a quantitative approach to your case study, designing and presenting a case study can require more thought than projects based on research methods such as experiments or surveys, and the challenges are closer to qualitative research. There is no 'one best way' to present a case study. Remember that as well as using the literature to support your findings, you can also use the literature to show how your findings have filled a gap in the existing literature or how they challenge existing theoretical explanations. During your literature review, look at how case studies are presented in the literature on your research topic, and see which examples you are more comfortable with. For instance, if your evidence is mainly:

1. **Questionnaire or other quantitative data** – present the case study evidence as statistical summaries and tables, using the case study detail to illustrate or explain the findings
2. **Archival** – present the case study evidence as a narrative, often in chronological order
3. **Interview** – present the case study evidence around themes, illustrated with quotes
4. **Ethnographic** – present the study as a narrative, often around themes, illustrated with quotes.

In quantitative research designs such as surveys, reporting your findings is usually straightforward, as we show in **Chapters 10** and **11**. You can analyse your data statistically and then present them in tables and charts, and structure your discussion around these exhibits. If you have taken more of a quantitative approach in your case study, you should try to be consistent with the style and content of a scientific analysis and report.

If you have taken a more qualitative approach to your case study, you should present your research more in line with the style and content of an ethnographic analysis and report. In many areas of business and management this is the dominant approach to case studies. If your case study is more qualitative in orientation, you will draw mostly on the methods for analysing qualitative data in **Chapter 12**.

The following example illustrates how one student chose to present his work at this stage.

Table 7.2   Sam's findings

Issue	Theory/best practice	Case findings
Use and deployment of risk management systems	If you use a formalised risk management process, it is likely that you will avoid costly problems during the project	Despite the use of formalised risk management systems, problems emerged, particularly during the early stages of the development
Technical complexity	Even complex technical work can succeed if appropriate risk management is used	Clear evidence that managers underestimated risk and complexity so there was no clear view of what the product really entailed
Organisational structure not aligned with purpose	Inappropriate organisation design will cause misalignments between those working on the team	It did have serious consequences
Senior management interference	Senior management intervention should be minimal once work has started	Senior management interfered and continually made changes
Reporting of 'bad news'	Communication channels should be open and used with a 'no-blame system'	People afraid of passing on bad news as management and customers tended to 'shoot the messenger'
Proactive risk management	Formal risk management minimises risk exposure	Risk management seen as secondary and not implemented effectively – many risks were identified and then ignored
Attitudes to risk	Attitudes towards risk should be based on individual experience and training	Attitudes to risk based on over-optimism and wild guesses
Risk deferral	Effective risk management avoids crisis management	Management almost always by crisis, but could have been avoided if addressed early

7.2.3 Assessing the quality of a case study

The criteria that may be used to judge your case study include:

1. Have you conducted your research in a systematic way?
2. Does the story that you tell make sense?
3. Does your evidence support your story?
4. Is there any other story that could equally well be told?
5. Have you shown something new, insightful or interesting?

These are generic quality criteria for research; however, we find the open nature of the research process can give the impression that they are less important in case study work. Whilst we will elaborate in future chapters, these are worth having front and centre in your mind as you progress.

7.3 What are other multiple-method research designs?

The case study is probably the most well-known example of a research design where you employ multiple methods for collecting and analysing your data, but it is not the only example of a **multiple-method research design**. Marketing research often combines focus groups, interviews and questionnaires in a single research design. A focus group (or groups) is initially used to capture what respondents think are the most important issues or aspects of an issue, usually in a fairly non-directive way. These issues or aspects can then be used to shape structured interviews as the next stage of the research process. Finally, a large-scale survey can be used to validate the findings of the previous two stages.

7.3.1 Advantages and disadvantages of multiple-method research

When might you want to use multiple methods in your research project? First, a single method may not be able to capture all the information you want to find out. For example, if you are looking at current or recent new product introductions, you might be able to interview current managers about decisions they are making now. On the other hand, if you need to find out historical information about past new product introductions, where no one has the relevant knowledge, you may need to rely on secondary sources such as company archives. Different methods enable you to investigate the same kind of decisions at multiple points in time, where a single method would be insufficient.

Second, when you find out different answers depending on what method you use, and no one method reveals 'the truth' you want to get at, you may want to use different methods to capture these. In the garbage study described in **Chapter 5**, what people reported they had consumed in their weekly surveys differed significantly from what they discarded in their rubbish, but researchers were interested in whether people accurately reported their use of packaged foods so they needed to use multiple methods. Using different methods to collect information on the same phenomenon, rather than on different phenomena, is known as **triangulation**, and it is so important for doing research that we will give more attention to it below. Even if your answers from the different methods are not identical, then you should have more faith in the conclusions you draw. If you found that consumers in neighbourhoods with an active recycling programme discarded less waste than those in other neighbourhoods, even if the amounts discarded in the rubbish varied among different methods you would be more confident in arguing that recycling programmes were effective in promoting desirable behaviours.

You might also consider using different methods when you are asking people to recall or estimate behaviours where their memory may not be accurate. Perhaps the people in the 'garbology' study weren't trying to mislead the researchers, but they did not have accurate recall of how much they discarded (how much attention do you actually pay to your rubbish?). Here, the more methods that you can bring to bear, the more chance you have at finding a reliable set of answers.

Third, you may use multiple methods when you are asking sensitive questions where people may be unable or unwilling to respond frankly. People will often give the answers they think are socially appropriate in face-to-face interviews, they are slightly more likely to be honest in telephone interviews, since they can't be seen, and much more likely to be honest in anonymous surveys or computer-based questionnaires. We have already mentioned the differences between people's reports on how often they wash their hands after going to the loo and direct observation. You may be interested or appalled to find out that socially desirable responding makes it difficult for toilet paper manufacturers to find out how people actually use toilet paper – fold or crumple – despite significant consumer research budgets.

If you have the time and resources, you may want to experiment with different methods to find out how the methods that you are using affect the evidence that you collect. You can then select the best method – or combine information from the different methods – in answering your research questions. You can capture information about the same issue or aspects of that issue using different methods to see if the information is consistent or inconsistent.

A final reason for using more than one method in your research project is when you want to conduct your research in stages and different methods are appropriate for each stage of your research. This would actually be a series of linked mini-research projects examining the same research question. For example, you might identify a general topic and conduct a few pilot case studies to identify the important characteristics of the topic. The outcomes of the case study analysis could be used as the input to research that uses interviews, and the outcomes of interviews as input to research that uses surveys. Over time, the research methods could be used to converge progressively on more detailed refinements of your investigation.

If there are so many advantages to doing mixed-method research, why don't all researchers use mixed-method research in every research project? Some of the reasons include:

- You must invest more time and other resources in doing mixed-method research
- You may have difficulty in reconciling the answers from different methods
- Different methods may not give you additional information
- Only a single method (or narrow set of methods) may be considered appropriate in your research area or subject
- Different methods may reflect different and incompatible research approaches (at the process and worldview levels).

Despite these potential disadvantages, however, we suggest that you consider a mixed-method design if you have the time and resources to carry one out. The advantages that you will gain in terms of confidence in your data, your interpretation and your conclusions may well make a mixed-method approach worth the extra investment in carrying out your research.

7.3.2 What is triangulation?

The goal of *triangulation* is to investigate what you are researching from many different angles, and include multiple explanations for what you have found. This increases the confidence in your results. **Figure 7.5** summarises our discussion of triangulation.

Some of the different approaches to triangulating your research include:

1. Multiple methods
2. Multiple sources of data
3. Multiple measures
4. Multiple viewpoints.

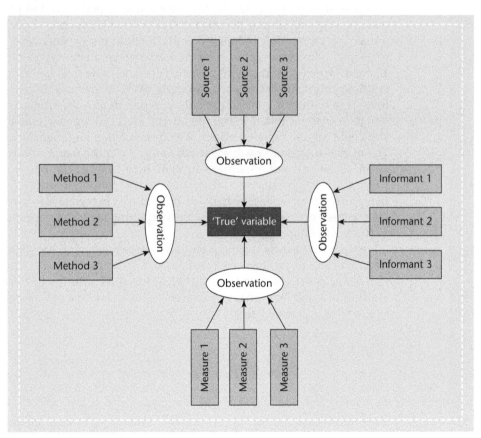

Figure 7.5 Triangulation

Multiple methods

Multiple methods are particularly useful when what you find out using one method conflicts with another method, or where you can't capture the information you want using a single method.

Multiple sources of data

Data can be inherently unreliable. This may be either as a result of error (wrongly recorded price data, for instance) or even deception (this is the story I want to give you, not what really happened). If you collect data about the same thing from different sources, you are more likely to spot data that are unreliable. To take a trivial example, imagine reading the same news story in a tabloid, a conservative broadsheet and a liberal broadsheet. How many of the facts and opinions will be consistent? How many of the facts and/or interpretations will differ?

Multiple informants

Many research projects rely on just one person – a single informant – as the source of data about an organisation, work group, household or other group of individuals. This person may or may not be the person who is best placed to provide the information! Single-informant designs have been widely criticised, especially in strategy research (for example Van Bruggen et al. 2002). In our experience, if you ask a range of people in an organisation what the corporate strategy is, you will get a range of answers – when presumably there is just one corporate strategy being pursued. With multiple-informant designs you are more likely to reveal a diversity of opinion, if there is one, than if you sample only one person and take their response as representative of the whole. For example, if you are studying new product introduction, you could ask the same questions of both marketing and manufacturing managers. The marketing manager will see it differently from the manufacturing manager and so on. If the different responses converge, then you can have more confidence that you have the right answer – at least for that organisation and set of respondents. Indeed, in our experience, when you do find that everyone is 'on message' and telling the same story, this is in itself, worth exploring further (see e.g. Brady and Maylor 2010 for an example of this).

Multiple informants can be especially useful when you are asking questions for which there is no 'right answer', especially when you are asking opinion or other subjective questions. Opinion polls, especially electoral polls, go to great lengths to get multiple informants so that the answers to the questions they ask are as representative of the whole population as they can possibly be.

Multiple measures

You may also improve the quality of your research if for each significant concept (or aspect of an issue) you are investigating you collect evidence using multiple measures, rather than a single measure. In attempting to assess, for instance, the level of motivation of a group of employees, you could think of many different measures that can be applied. For instance, you could assess the amount of their own time they were prepared to invest in their work, the level of excitement they felt on a Monday morning going to work and the number of sick days they took off when they weren't really ill. As with multiple informants, you are trying to get convergence, and divergence between the measures may signal problems with the concept you are trying to capture.

It is easy to assume that different measures are capturing the same concept, but you might well be measuring different concepts. For example, absenteeism might reflect employee motivation but lateness to work might reflect extra-work responsibilities that have nothing to do with motivation. If you are taking a scientific approach to measuring intangible aspects such as emotions or beliefs, you may need some expert help in devising multiple measures for the same emotion or belief. You may want to read ahead about measurement scales, which contain a number of different items that (at least in theory) measure the same underlying aspect, in **Chapter 11**.

7.3.3 Multiple researchers

If you are doing an individual research project, it may help to discuss your research and findings with someone else, to make sure that it is making sense. If you have kept a research diary along the way, as we recommend, go back and read through your emerging thoughts. Have you left out some promising insights by focusing on the major themes, which you can recapture now? It might also be useful to try to see your research from a different perspective – how would this look to me if I were a scientist/ ethnographer?

If you are doing a group project, multiple viewpoints may come naturally. Try to make sure that your group is receptive to these different perspectives, and that 'groupthink' or premature convergence doesn't keep you from being as creative as you can be.

If you are doing a placement or sponsored project, you may find it helpful to have a discussion with your co-workers or your manager to get different perspectives and make sure you haven't missed anything out. Of course, if you get agreement, you need to make sure that you have not gone native – you might try consulting with someone outside the company, within the limits of confidentiality. You should also try to make sure that the received 'company line' does not overwhelm your own findings if they are not what the company wants to hear. You might want to read ahead in **Chapter 9** if this seems to be happening.

7.3.4 Multiple-method versus mixed-method approaches

It is important to understand the difference between using multiple methods within a single research approach and using different research approaches. We recommend that you stick to using methods from a single research approach in your research project; for example, we would not recommend combining a laboratory experiment with participant observation in the same project. This is because the different research approaches, as shown in **Chapter 4**, draw on very different conceptions of the world and how to do research. It should be obvious that you cannot conduct a research study using the scientific and the ethnographic approach simultaneously, because you cannot let theory determine your observations without selecting a theory, or data determine your theory if you haven't collected data. Quantitative research emphasises deduction, where you draw on theory to determine what data you collect, whilst qualitative research emphasises the role of data in guiding what theory you choose to explain your observations. (The grounded research approach described in **Section 7.1.3** is a way of 'bootstrapping' your way if you want to choose the middle ground – you are going back and forth between theory and data.)

On the other hand, many research methods are flexible enough to be used in either research approach, so you could use a questionnaire to collect unstructured verbal data about why people attend *Star Trek* conventions, or use observation to collect detailed measurements on how people navigate through particular websites.

This also ties into our discussion in **Chapter 4** on the underlying worldviews associated with quantitative and qualitative research. It would be quite a juggling act to believe that we can simultaneously research the social world as real, objective and independent of us, and constructed, subjective and dependent on us. We do sometimes observe multiple approaches when you look across researchers, or at the stream of research projects conducted by an individual researcher. The methods that people use to investigate a particular topic or phenomenon vary over time across different research projects in predictable fashion. This reflects the way that research methods change as a topic moves from being new and not well understood to being established and fairly well understood. Some researchers even argue that there is a hierarchy, or natural cycle of methods, starting with case studies and ending up with large-scale surveys. However, this has been argued to be a quantitative way of thinking: from a qualitative viewpoint, it may be that any sequence of methods might be valid in investigating a phenomenon.

Summary

This chapter presented some guidelines on how to design and execute a case study. The case study design combines both quantitative and qualitative research designs, whilst remaining unique. We briefly reviewed the grounded case study approach proposed by Eisenhardt.

The case study is only one type of research design to use multiple methods. The logic of using multiple methods is explained in **Section 7.2**.

Triangulation explains how you can combine quantitative and qualitative data, techniques, methods or approaches with multiple methods and other approaches to strengthen your findings. Triangulation, whether you use multiple informants, researchers, sources of data, techniques, methods or approaches, can increase your insights and the credibility of your research.

Answers to key questions

Why would I use a case study design in my research?

- Case studies allow the application of multiple methods in the design, collection and analysis of data.
- Multiple methods can be used at different times and on different aspects of a case.

How can I design a case study?

- Cases can use predefined issues or take a grounded approach.
- Case studies can be single cases, multiple cases, embedded cases and paired cases.
- Different methods can be combined to answer different parts of a research question and provide different insights into a research problem.

What does a good case study look like?

- A good case presents what you are studying accurately.
- A good case has a clear and justifiable design, including the number and selection of cases.
- A good case is consistent with the underlying quantitative or qualitative orientation in methods, analysis and presentation.

Can I combine both qualitative and quantitative methods in a single research design?

- Both qualitative and quantitative research methods can be used in the same case study.
- Advantages include the generation of a greater insight into the phenomenon being studied.
- Disadvantages include more work and the need to reconcile often conflicting data.

References

Åhlström, Pär 1997. Sequences in the Process of Adopting Lean Production, Stockholm School of Economics. Dissertation submitted for the degree of PhD.

Allison, Graham 1971. *Essence of Decision: Explaining the Cuban Missile Crisis*, 1st edn. Boston: Little Brown.

Blaikie, Norman 2009. *Designing Social Research*, 2nd edn. Cambridge: Polity Press.

Brady, T., & Maylor, H. 2010. *The improvement paradox in project contexts*: A clue to the way forward?. International journal of project management, 28(8), 787–795.

Chandler, Alfred D. 1962. *Strategy and Structure: Chapters in the History of the American Industrial Enterprise*. Boston: MIT Press.

Creswell, John W. 2013. *Research Design: Qualitative and Quantitative Approaches*, 4th edn. Thousand Oaks, CA: Sage.

Cusumano, Michael A. and Selby, Richard W. 1995. *Microsoft Secrets: How the World's Most Powerful Software Company Creates Technology, Shapes Markets, and Manages People*. London: HarperCollins Business.

Eisenhardt, Kathleen M. 1989. Building theories from case study research, *Academy of Management Review*, 14(4): 532–50.

Kidder, Tracy 1981. *The Soul of a New Machine*. New York: Avon Books.

March, James G., Sproull, Lee S. and Tamuz, Michal. 1991. Learning from samples of one or fewer, *Organization Science*, 2(1): 1–13. doi: 10.1287/orsc.2.1.1.

Ragin, Charles and Becker, Howard S. (eds). 1992. *What is a Case?* Cambridge: Cambridge University Press.

Selznick, P. 1949. *TVA and the Grass Roots*. Berkeley: University of California Press.

Van Bruggen, Gerrit H., Lilien, Gary L. and Kacker, Manish 2002. Informants in organizational marketing research: Why use multiple informants and how to aggregate responses, *Journal of Marketing Research*, 39(4): 469–78.

Whyte, William Foote 1955. *Street Corner Society*. Chicago: University of Chicago Press.

Yin, Robert K. 2014. *Case Study Research: Design and Methods*, 5th edn. Thousand Oaks, CA: Sage.

Additional resources

Bryman, Alan and Bell, Emma 2011. *Business Research Methods*, 3rd edn. Oxford: Oxford University Press.

Drejer, Anders, Blackmon, Kate and Voss, Christopher A. 2000. Worlds apart? – A look at the operations management area in the US, UK and Scandinavia, *Scandinavian Journal of Management*, 16 (1): 45–66.

Eisenhardt, Kathleen M. 1991. Better stories and better constructs: The case for rigor and comparative logic, *Academy of Management Review*, 16(3): 620–7.

Glaser, Barney G. and Strauss, Anselm L. 1967. *The Discovery of Grounded Theory: Strategies of Qualitative Research*. London: Weidenfeld & Nicholson.

Gomm, Roger, Hammersley, Martyn and Foster, Peter (eds) 2000. *Case Study Method: Key Issues, Key Texts*. London: Sage.

Jick, Todd 1979. Mixing qualitative and quantitative methods: Triangulation in action, *Administrative Science Quarterly*, 24: 602–11.

Kanter, R.M. 1983. *The Changemasters*. New York: Simon & Schuster.

Karlsson, Christer and Åhlström Pär. 1996. Assessing changes towards lean production. *International Journal of Operations and Production Management*, 16(2): 2–41.

McClintock, C., Brannon, D. and Maynard-Moody, S. 1979. Applying the logic of sample surveys to qualitative case studies: The case cluster method. *Administrative Science Quarterly*, 24(4), 612–29.

Miles, Matthew B., Huberman, A. Michael and Saldana, Jonny. 2013. *Qualitative Data Analysis*, 3rd edn. Beverly Hills, CA: Sage.

Schroeder, R.G. and Flynn, Barbara B. 2001. *High Performance Manufacturing: Global Perspectives*. New York: John Wiley & Sons.

Stake, Robert E. 1995. *The Art of Case Study Research*. London: Sage.

Strauss, Anselm L. and Corbin, Juliet 2007. *Basics of Qualitative Research: Techniques and Procedures for Developing Grounded Theory*, 3rd edn. London: Sage.

Travers, Max 2001. *Qualitative Research Through Case Studies*. London: Sage.

Key terms

Discussion questions

1. What is a case study?
2. Why are case studies so popular among student research projects?
3. What are the different forms of case research?
4. How many cases are enough?
5. Can you use questionnaires and ethnography in the data collection of one case study?
6. What does triangulation mean and how might it be applied in other (non-case) areas of research?
7. 'Surely cases are just like journalism and consulting?' Discuss.
8. How can having multiple researchers be helpful to the quality of your research?
9. How do you know when to stop collecting data?
10. Can you do a case study on an organisation without visiting it?

Workshop 1

Task

You have been asked to demonstrate how you would use a case or multi-method research design in the project to find the changes that people experience as they move into higher education. Using the results of the previous workshops on this, or starting afresh, identify:

1. Opportunities for using cases – what questions might cases be good at answering? What types of case analysis could you use here, for example would an embedded multiple case design be appropriate?
2. Opportunities for using triangulation – again, what questions might such an approach be good at answering?
3. Choose a main research question from this work and construct a research design that will enable you to answer this in detail.

Workshop 2

Read the following case studies prepared by students and presented here in summary form.

Case 1: New Product Development at Big Car Company

Background

Big Car Company (BCC) is one of Europe's larger mass producers of vehicles. The decision was taken in 2000 that it would belatedly enter the market for mini MPVs (multi-purpose vehicles), and this case refers to events surrounding the development of the powertrain for this vehicle. Powertrain development includes the design and alignment of the engine, transmission, exhaust, cooling, mounts, air induction, clutch and drivelines. The product was launched late in 2003, three months behind schedule.

The process

The overall time frame for a development project from concept to mass production within the car industry is between 18 and 42 months. The duration is set at the beginning of the project. Powertrain is just one of the divisions involved in the process – the others being responsible for other systems that go to make up the car.

The first stage in the process for the powertrain people is agreeing the basic parameters of the powertrain design, including engine power, transmission options (for example manual, auto, steptronic, constantly variable transmission), vehicle weight and likely sales volume. The budget for the development is also fixed at this stage and often has to go through several iterations, as specification issues impact sales projections, and marketing requirements influence design issues. As one manager commented on this process:

> Price, target and volume assumptions for the new product directly depend on the powertrain line-up. Adding or deleting one powertrain line (for example by changing the choice of engines available) will affect the price of each component, as the production is very sensitive to any volume or complexity changes. This negotiation is a time-consuming process. Over and over again, current assumptions about required design, projected component quantities, product targets and programme budget are rejected. In many projects it can be observed that this iterative loop becomes a never-ending process. Given that this time is part of the already fixed development time, time lost today will cause losses on cost and/or quality at the other end of the programme.

Even once agreement is reached internally at BCC, each of the teams then has to do its own negotiation on pricing, design and volume with various suppliers. These in turn have a similar process to go through with their suppliers. The theoretical procedure versus the reality is illustrated in **Figure 7.6**.

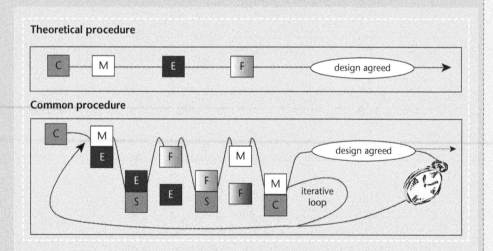

Figure 7.6 Theoretical versus common procedure

Workshop 2 cont'd

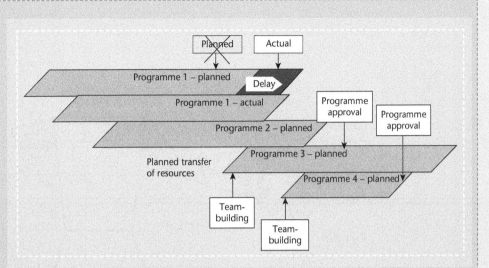

Figure 7.7 A resource profile

The overall effect of the above was that BCC did launch three months late. This meant that they lost three months at 500 vehicles per day of sales. The firm does recognise that a lost sale is a lost customer to the organisation for many years. The losses were huge and the knock-on effects to other programmes have been significant.

The resourcing profile on this project is shown in **Figure 7.7.**

Case 2: Workplace ergonomics at Small Engineering Firm

Two students carried out a study of the working conditions of the staff at a small firm, as the firm were interested in the potential impacts on productivity. They were asked to prepare a report on what they found. Their most interesting finding though was rather challenging; one of the machines in the workshop was particularly difficult to operate. Indeed it could have been argued that it was unsafe.

Given the problems associated with redesigning the machines and the view that their report would be rejected as flawed by the management (they were told that this was an inevitable response), the students decided they had no other option but to rework the job description for the operators. This, in effect, redesigned the operator. The result is shown in **Figure 7.8**. This stroke of genius saved the day – the managers did not reject the report as only a brief outline was presented to them, focusing on the benefits of such a change, and with such a conclusion they had little choice but to act on it, but it was seen as a benefit, rather than 'holding a gun to their heads'. Indeed, the management committee made a commitment on the basis of the project to replace the machines and for other amendments to be made as a matter of urgency. The full, anonymised report was presented to the students' assessors at the university.

Workshop 2 cont'd

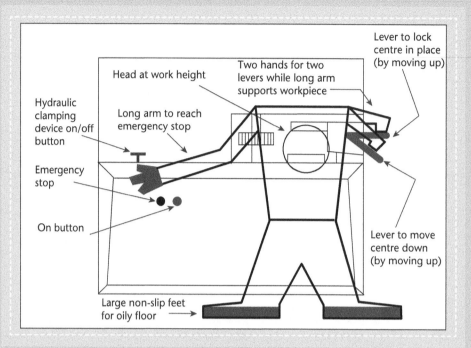

Figure 7.8 The ideal maxicut operator
Source: Courtesy of Wendy Bourne and Susan Myers

Discussion questions

1. What type of case studies are these?
2. What data collection methods were used in each case?
3. What practical and ethical concerns would you have about researching each case?
4. Should the findings of either or both cases be made public?

Note

1. In professional business and management case study research, you will frequently see reference to the work of two researchers in particular, Robert Yin and Kathleen Eisenhardt. We will be drawing on their work extensively in this chapter.

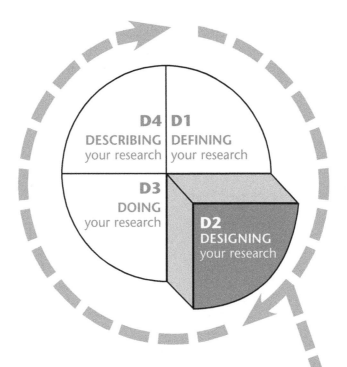

Relevant chapters
4   What is my research approach?
5   How do I do quantitative research?
6   How do I do qualitative research?
7   How do I do case study research?
8   **How do I make sure my research is ethical?**

Relevant chapters
13   How do I write up my report?
14   What do I do now?

Key challenges
- Making sense of your findings
- Presenting your research to others
- Reflecting and learning from your research

4

Relevant chapters
1   What is research?
2   What should I study?
3   How do I find information?

Key challenges
- Understanding what academic research is
- Generating and clarifying ideas
- Using sources of information

1

D4
DESCRIBING
your research

D1
DEFINING
your research

D3
DOING
your research

D2
DESIGNING
your research

Relevant chapters
9   How do I do field research?
10   What do my quantitative data mean(1)?
11   What do my quantitative data mean(2)?
12   What do my qualitative data mean?

Key challenges
- Practical considerations in doing research
- Describing data using simple statistics
- Carrying out statistical tests
- Interpreting words and actions

3

Relevant chapters
4   What is my research approach?
5   How do I do quantitative research?
6   How do I do qualitative research?
7   How do I do case study research?
8   **How do I make sure my research is ethical?**

Key challenges
- Choosing a research approach
- Choosing a research design
- Collecting data using quantitative methods
- Collecting data using qualitative methods
- **Integrating quantitative and qualitative methods**

2

8 How do I make sure my research is ethical?

chapter

 Key questions

- What are ethics in the context of research?
- What are the requirements for conducting ethical research?
- What implications do ethics have for my research?

 Learning outcomes

By the time that you have completed this chapter, you should be able to:

- Recognise potential ethical issues for business and management researchers in general
- Identify potential ethical issues for your research
- Demonstrate how you will ensure that your research is ethically sound

Contents

Introduction

This chapter discusses ethical issues that you should know about as you begin your research in business and management studies. Compared with medical sciences, business and management research has traditionally not exposed human participants to significant risk, and does not always even involve human participants. However, as research directly involving human subjects such as interviews, surveys and case studies proliferates, we need to consider research ethics. As direct involvement with human participants increases, the probability of making ethical errors with unwanted consequences also increases.

This is especially true of field-based methods such as ethnography or case study research, which require more interaction with human participants. As a researcher you should therefore be aware of and manage ethical issues in the research process. Ethical mistakes involving people can be costly, as shown in **Research in action 8.1**.

Research in action 8.1
A CAUTIONARY TALE

Imagine that you are the manager at a fancy restaurant in New York City. You receive a letter from a customer who claims to have contracted food poisoning whilst dining at the restaurant with his wife for their anniversary dinner. The letter writer gives graphic details of the illness and even mentions that he is considering the possibility of alerting the regulatory authorities. What would you do?

Restaurants receive letters of complaint every day, and customers undoubtedly do contract food poisoning. But after receiving such a letter, many New York restaurants took drastic action, including searching for the (fictitious) customer, throwing out food supplies and having their restaurants professionally cleaned. Owners went through credit card receipts and reservations to try to identify the meal that had caused the food poisoning. They also tried to trace the customer to apologise, send flowers, offer a replacement meal, or gather further information. Some restaurant employees even had to undergo personal health checks, when the New York City Department of Health investigated the allegation.

How would you feel once you learned that your restaurant was one of 240 restaurants in New York City who received similar letters? The letters were sent by an assistant professor of management at [Ivy League University] (name and university disguised) in September 2001. He intended to use his research to test whether the status of a complainant affected how the restaurant responded: in some letters, he claimed be a trainee manager at The Gap, and in others he used his own status and wrote on Ivy League University letterhead.

Was this a good research design? The researcher signed his own name, so he wasn't deceiving the restaurants as to who he was. Yet, the research had unforeseen consequences for both the restaurants and the researcher.

Some restaurant owners reported the fictitious complaint to the university. Apologies were sent from both the dean of the school and the researcher. The assistant professor (as quoted in the *New York Times*) said that his first letter:

> was fabricated to help collect data for a research study that I designed concerning vendor response to consumer complaints... The study was of my own doing and not that of the business school or of the university.... None of the data collected for the study will be used for publication, and I will not conduct similar studies in the future.

▶

Despite this, the university was held responsible for the breach of research ethics. Even though it had in place a policy that required ethical approval for any research involving human participants, the researcher had sent out the letters without any oversight or approval. Moreover, despite the letters of apology and promises not to repeat the research, 10 restaurants sued the university for $100 million, alleging libel, negligent and intentional infliction of emotional distress and negligent misrepresentation (Kaplin and Lee 2006). Although some charges and the application for punitive damages were dismissed, the restaurants won the lawsuit and appeal against it and set a legal precedent for tort damages from research (as well as winning a substantial sum for the restaurants in damages).

Overview

Universities increasingly require any researcher whose research involves human participants to gain informal or formal approval before they start collecting data. This **research approval** requires institutional approval and protocols for reporting how ethical principles will be applied early on in the research process, before students start collecting data. As a result, most students engaged in business and management research will need to consider ethical issues early on in their research design.

In this chapter we set out some basic ethical principles and standards, and how these are important for you and your work. As we have shown in so many examples so far, research has huge potential to provide great insights and benefits. However, as we saw in **Research in action 8.1**, it can also create considerable harm. In this chapter, we want to raise your awareness of ethical issues for research both in your own research and more generally. We set out some basic principles and standards which will need to be put alongside the requirements of your own institution.

Section 8.1 begins with a broad overview of research ethics and the need for ethical awareness in field-based research. We present a further example that illustrates the **cost of ethical mistakes** involving human participants to participants, researchers, researchers' institutions and other stakeholders. Iphofen (2009) points out, 'All human participant research interferes to some extent with the lives of other human beings.' The section will give some background to research ethics and will identify the main ethical principles of research involving human participants, and how they might be applied in the context of field-based research.

As research methods involving human participants become more popular in business and management, researchers face more ethical choices related to human participants. Researchers should be aware of the ethical standards and principles in **Section 8.2** when they develop research designs and protocols for doing field-based research. These include risk of harm, harm-benefit analysis, informed consent, voluntary participation and confidentiality. Moreover, students can draw on principles and practices designed to protect participants and ensure research integrity from the behavioural experiments that were developed for laboratory experiments, following the well-known experiments by Asch on conformity to peer pressure and Milgram on conformity to authority (Rosnow and Rosenthal 1997).

University regulations increasingly require students to submit their proposed research to a review committee before they begin any research involving human participants.

Section 8.2 explains the role of human-subjects review committees and the importance of institutional oversight, and suggests how you can increase your chances of having your research approved quickly. Although getting your research proposal approved can reduce errors, it cannot eliminate them, and even if processes are in place, they are only effective if you follow them. Any research involving human participants poses the risk of ethical failures, which can result in harm to those participants and to other stakeholders (Bozeman et al. 2009).

Even without oversight requirements, ethics is central to good research. Medical researchers may inflict harm on participants in clinical trials of new medicines. Psychologists may cause stress to participants in behavioural experiments. Educational researchers may be in direct contact with schoolchildren below the age of consent, whilst criminologists come into contact with convicted and suspected criminals. Sociologists and anthropologists may conduct participant observation among disadvantaged or stigmatised groups, or even criminal ones such as gangs or drug smugglers.

Section 8.3 discusses two issues related to ethical behaviour by researchers, namely plagiarism and other forms of intellectual property theft such as copyright violation.

8.1 What is ethics in research and why is it important?

In considering how to design and conduct business and management research, we need to distinguish between what is moral, what is ethical and what is legal to do. Ethics concerns what we ought to do (or ought not to do), based on principles of human dignity and integrity, whilst morality often leads to similar conclusions but is based on belief systems. For instance, in most countries tax avoidance is legal, but it is considered by some to be neither moral nor ethical. **Morality** *concerns 'what is good'*; **ethics** *concerns 'what is right'*; *and* **legality** *concerns 'what is within the law'*. In research, deceiving participants about the goals of an experiment may be legal, but is neither moral nor ethical.

Another example illustrates more subtle potential dangers of field research for researchers and participants, and suggests that the ethics of research involving human participants deserves careful attention in business and management even when research seems completely unproblematic at first glance.

Research in action 8.2

THE CASE OF THE FICTITIOUS VISITOR

Imagine the following scenario. You are a lecturer in business and management studies. You receive an email from an unfamiliar sender, a potential PhD student, who is asking to meet with you later that day. You see that you have a free 10 minutes, and fire off a response giving the student a time and place to meet. Almost immediately, you get back an email saying that you have just been part of an experiment, that the email is from researchers, and that there never has been any PhD student.

How would you feel? Suppose that later on you read a blog about the research and find out more about the experiment. Lots of other lecturers have been asked to respond. And, as well as one experimental condition that varies the meeting request between the same day and a week later, there is another experimental condition that varies the name of the fictitious student, to see whether you have shown racial bias in your responses.

▶

The Chronicle of Higher Education reported in May 2010 that two faculty members at top US business schools had conducted just such an experiment (Basken 2010)

They sent emails in the US pretending to be a potential PhD student to 6300 faculty members. The emails asked for a 10-minute meeting, either the same day the email was sent or a week later. Anyone who responded to the false request was sent an email that explained the identity of the researchers and the purpose of the study, and cancelled the meeting.

Some people might justify the research design on the basis that the research drew on natural behaviours and took very little respondent time. Most of us get dozens, if not hundreds, of emails every day. We can read and respond to them very quickly. It could also be argued that evidence about racial bias is difficult to collect in more overt ways. Few people would respond affirmatively to a survey question asking 'Are you racially biased?'

However, on finding out about the deception, many recipients complained vigorously, either on blogs or directly to the researchers. One person who responded to the survey, but who did not see the follow-up email cancelling the appointment and explaining the research, spent an hour waiting for the fictitious student to show up. As comments in *The Chronicle of Higher Education* pointed out, the study was not only deceptive but also used everyone's time without compensation. Some people asked for an apology. Others suggested compensation of $10 for their time and inconvenience.

As one blogger commented (Institutional Review Blog 2010):

> Even if each of the 6300 recipients averaged only five minutes to read the email, check their calendar, make a decision, and respond (and I spent considerably more time, as did many others, lining up resources from administrators and lab operators), then the total time wasted comes out to more than one dozen full work weeks. All in service to the selfish interests of these researchers.

Commenters disagreed as to whether the email study had violated ethical principles, for example, 'doing no harm to participants' (see **Section 8.2**). Although some people believed that the research, particularly the use of deception, had been unethical, the research project was reported to have received approval from both researchers' institutional review boards. Nevertheless, there were many negative comments on the ethical conduct of business researchers, and on the low quality of business research in general. Few thought that the research was valuable or indeed even worth doing.

8.1.1 Is there a duty for business and management research to be ethical?

Ethics is the branch of moral philosophy that guides decisions about which course of action to take in order to do the right thing (Warnock 1998). Iphofen (2009: 1) defines ethics as 'careful consideration and regular attention' in one's behaviour, whilst Gregory (2003) suggests that ethical and moral are interchangeable. Ethics therefore covers many topics in business and management, from business ethics to professional ethics to research ethics. **Business ethics** concerns what is not only legal but is morally right to do in business (e.g. De Cremer et al. 2011). Many people argue that business and management should be more concerned with ethical issues than it currently is. Business activities have a significant impact on the environment, from the extraction of raw materials to the disposal of waste products, and transfer wealth between individuals and across national boundaries. Accounting practices enrich stakeholders and affect government revenues. Employment practices affect millions of workers every day. The location of supermarkets creates food deserts, and mega-discount stores denude the high street of small independent suppliers. Television advertisements push fast food and toys towards toddlers and infants.

Professional ethics, on the other hand, concerns how to behave as a member of one's discipline and community of practice, whether occupational or academic. Professional researchers must know how to conduct themselves in a variety of roles, including researcher, teacher, administrator, consultant, supervisor, writer, reviewer and editor. The main social sciences fields have developed national or international codes of ethics, including the Academy of Management, which has an explicit Code of Ethics (www.aomonline.org/governanceandethics/aomrevisedcodeofethics.pdf) that sets out a number of principles for management research, and professional and personal conduct.

Research ethics more specifically concerns the choices that researchers face in translating a research problem and questions into a research protocol that specifies how data will be collected and analysed, from whom, and how they will manage unforeseen ethical choices that arise whilst they are actually conducting the research (Gregory 2003). As shown above, even seemingly innocuous survey research can create unintended consequences, not only for respondents but also a variety of stakeholders. Key ethical principles for business and management researchers to consider in field-based research include **risk of harm**, **harm-benefit analysis**, **informed consent**, **voluntary participation** and **confidentiality**. Even deciding what to research – the research problem and questions – carries significant ethical implications (Gregory 2003).

Whilst new research methods and the emphasis on open-ended and qualitative research approaches have greatly enriched business and management research, they have created new ethical challenges related to research ethics. Researchers who were trained in simulation or mathematical methods may have had little exposure to social research methods, and hence less awareness of and experience with these methods, creating a knowledge gap in their own application of these methods and their supervision of students. From personal experience, many researchers do not see research ethics as applicable to their own empirical research, because the possibility of harm to participants or to themselves is not as obvious as the classic social sciences experiments such as Milgram. However, any kind of research involving human participants, directly or indirectly, raises the possibility of harm: laboratory and field experiments and quasi-experiments, interviews, postal and web surveys, multi-method case studies, unobtrusive, nonparticipant and participant observation, extended ethnography and other forms of field research all involve human participants.

Researchers need to be aware of general principles of research ethics and how they apply to field-based research methods such as interviews, surveys and observational methods. Based on our experiences, students find research ethics troublesome when:

1. They don't understand that research ethics applies to business and management research as well as medical and behavioural research;
2. They understand that research ethics applies to research such as experiments, but not that it applies to field research such as surveys or case studies;
3. They know that research ethics applies to field research, but they are not sure how to apply it.

The following sections are intended to help avoid such troubles in your work.

8.2 What are the ethical implications of conducting research with human participants?

Given specific examples to work with, most people can apply **ethical principles** correctly, even without any formal ethical training. When we teach on research ethics, everyone who sees the food poisoning letter (**Research in action 8.1**) can see where the researcher went wrong and what might have been done to prevent it. Beyond this case though, we provide some of the key principles of ethical research. These are set out in **Figure 8.1**.

Principle 1. Always minimise foreseeable risks to participants, researchers and other stakeholders
Principle 2. The benefits of the research must be considered as well as the risks.
Principle 3. Participants engage in the research without coercion, and are free to withdraw at any time.
Principle 4. Research participants should consent to being part of your research study.
Principle 5. Safeguard the rights of vulnerable participants.
Principle 6. Avoid unnecessary deception.
Principle 7. Data about participants should be kept confidential and their privacy should be respected.
Principle 8. Participants should be fairly compensated for their time.

Figure 8.1 Principles of ethical research

8.2.1 How do I minimise the risk of harm from my research?

Principle 1. Always minimise foreseeable risks to participants, researchers and other stakeholders.

As a researcher, you have a legal, ethical and moral duty to not do **harm** (Rosnow and Rosenthal 1997), including to direct participants, researchers and society as a whole. Although the risks of physical or psychological harm are generally low in business and management research, they are not negligible. The researcher in the first example was held liable in the subsequent court case for the psychological distress caused to the restaurant chefs and owners, as well as the economic damage because he failed to consider the serious impact that a report of food poisoning, whether suspected or proven, would have on a restaurant's operations and reputation, but this could have been anticipated.

So, researchers should consider carefully the intended and unintended potential effects of their research on stakeholders, as well as the magnitude and the likelihood of their occurring, and, wherever possible, mitigate the effects of any anticipated risk. For example, discussing your research design and thinking through possible consequences of asking sensitive or potentially distressing questions is a critical phase in your research. Such a check on your protocols is not optional for reducing risks in research today.

Risk to human participants

In general, research participants face the most direct risk from research. Biomedical research creates a risk of **physical harm** to participants, whether through the treatment and its side effects or the lack of treatment to a control group, even if the experiment goes as intended. Whilst there is a low risk of physical harm to participants, behavioural research creates a risk of **psychological harm**.

Some of the questions or issues raised by researchers may cause intellectual or emotional effects, and induce *stress or other negative effects* in participants. Participants may feel compelled to participate in research because of pressure from superiors, even though they might not wish to. Questions may remind participants of current or past unpleasant experiences. Participants may experience conflict between what they think and what they think is the right answer, leading to cognitive dissonance associated with internal pressures to give socially desirable responses. Answering questions may itself be stressful.

Research also presents a risk of *economic harm* to participants, even if only the cost of the time spent participating. Research, particularly if it focuses on practices and their link to performance efficiency, may present a *risk to employment* to participants. The results of a study could be used as a reason to reduce the number of people involved in a process, and hence cause unemployment. Individuals, as well as organisations, may also suffer a *risk to reputation*, especially if principles relating to privacy, including confidentiality and anonymity, are mishandled.

It is clearly wrong to put your research participants in a position where they are worse off than if they had not participated in your research, for example by failing to maintain confidentiality and jeopardising their employment.

Risk to researchers

The second group of participants who might suffer harm is researchers themselves. Certainly, business and management research has traditionally presented lower levels of direct risk of physical or psychological harm to researchers compared with fields such as anthropology, sociology or criminology that study criminal, deviant or anti-social behaviour. Some of the risks to researchers that Kate has reviewed (in other fields) has included 'being burnt as a witch by villagers', 'being eaten by lions or snakes', and 'being put in prison by the local government'. One PhD student whose thesis Harvey examined has survived being shot at, two explosions and a flood that killed 120 people during his fieldwork. Suffering a paper cut while collating surveys on financial management is probably not life-threatening.

However, field research *can* be risky, especially when you are doing research in unfamiliar surroundings. Some principles to keep in mind include:

1. **Take reasonable precautions.** Work in pairs if you can, especially in risky situations. Make sure to leave the details of where you are going and when you expect to be back with someone who will check to make sure you have returned. Carry a phone, identification, money, etc.. Be aware of local conditions and accepted cultural differences.

2. **Be aware of possible risks to your personal safety** – Some researchers collect data in countries or areas where there may be a high level of crime (e.g. Nigeria, Russia), or health risks (e.g. exposure to the AIDS virus). Researchers may also become stressed or distressed through working with vulnerable people, such as asylum seekers or prisoners, and need to have recourse to supervisors or counsellors. Researchers may also suffer stress or referred stress, particularly related to the economic crisis.

3. **Consider whether you will be exposed to illegal or potentially illegal activities.** Whilst generally business and management research is generally pro-social or neutral, just by being in real-world organisations or other settings may expose you to anti-social activities. For example, researching labour practices in Chinese supply chains (Jiang 2009; Jiang et al. 2009) potentially exposed researchers to criminal or potentially criminal activities where workers are being underpaid, exploited or abused. Research on overseas supply chains may also expose researchers to child labour or other coerced work, or other forms of deceitful practices such as piracy, counterfeiting or adulteration.

4. Researchers may also be incidentally exposed to illegal or potentially illegal activities simply through exposure to human participants in their **natural settings**. There is a legal responsibility to report even suspicion of some crimes (e.g. child abuse, child pornography). If a participant admits being the perpetrator or the victim of a crime, the researcher may need to report it to the authorities. This has been a long-time topic of concern in anthropology, where researchers use ethnographic methods to study illegal or quasi-illegal activities, for example, drug users or gangs.

5. **Be aware of possible risks to your reputation** – Doing poor-quality research is certainly a risk to your reputation, but not the only one. Researchers may study a topic or population that is stigmatised, and acquire a 'courtesy stigma'.

Risks to other stakeholders

Even if research is not harmful to participants or researchers, it can still cause harm to stakeholders such as your institution, other researchers or society as a whole. Some researchers consider research that takes up people's time, but is so poorly designed that it will not answer the research questions, a form of active harm.

The research ethics literature is starting to focus on the risks of bad or unnecessary research, which includes harm to other researchers (now or in the future). These include 'muddying the water', making research difficult for future researchers. The effects of poorly designed or poorly executed research projects may be reflected in the continuing decline in response rates noted by many researchers. Publishing misleading or nonsignificant research studies may make the public less willing to believe in significant results, and, as various examples in this chapter illustrate, can damage the collective reputation of the research community.

Whilst there is an overriding injunction against doing harm, research must also do good; that is, it should do **positive good** (Iphofen 2009). Beneficence may be difficult to identify or to quantify, especially in student research. However, if there is little benefit to the research study beyond the researcher, through career or promotion rewards, self-interest should be taken into account. Hence, several social research ethicists have suggested that there should be less primary research and more secondary and archival research. They also suggest that, because of self-interest, third-party review of research protocols is necessary, as neither participants nor researchers are free of self-interest. This leads to:

Principle 2. The benefits of the research must be considered as well as the risks.

8.2.2 What are the rights of my participants?

Voluntary participation

Participants have the right to choose whether to participate in a research study, and to withdraw at any point. (Iphofen (2009) argues that consent is an ongoing process, rather than an act, in this regard.) Some researchers consider the act of consent to be sufficient to imply voluntary participation. However, there are often power and status differences between researchers and participants, and participants may feel coerced to engage in the research directly or indirectly, especially if the researcher or another stakeholder such as a manager has greater relative power than participants.

Principle 3. Participants engage in the research without coercion, and are free to withdraw at any time.

Participants need not be directly pressured into participating for Principle 3 to be violated. A prisoner may participate in a study to demonstrate good behaviour for eventual release. A student may hope to gain the good opinion of the instructor, and hence a higher grade, whether through class participation points, extra credit or general good will. The use of students – on whom much behavioural research relies (Sears 1986) – has been questioned under this principle. Requiring a student to participate in a research study as part of class requirements or an assessment is debated: students may participate for pedagogical purposes, but they must be allowed not to participate or to withdraw without penalty.

Informed consent

Principle 4. Research participants should consent to being part of your research study.

The principle of *informed consent* holds that research participants should be given the essential facts about a research study before they agree to participate in it, and sign a written consent form attesting this (Rosnow and Rosenthal 1997; Gregory 2003). The 'gold standard' for research involving human participants is for them to sign a formal, written, consent form that gives them information about the study's purpose, procedures, risks, benefits, and whom to ask for further information or to make a complaint (e.g. Creswell 2013).

In many disciplines, and research designs such as ethnography, **informed written consent** is an ideal rather than an absolute. Although participation in a survey is usually clear cut, who participants are in other field-based research methods such as observation or ethnography is problematic. Whilst an underlying assumption of informed consent in the medical or behavioural experiment is that a research study is bounded in time, space, and people, this is not always true in field settings. A researcher may visit an office to conduct a face-to-face interview with the office manager, but come into contact with supervisors, workers, support staff, contractors, suppliers, other visitors and so on. Although the primary contact may give written informed consent, it may be difficult to gain such consent from everyone with whom the researcher comes into contact.

In some circumstances, researchers may give full information and gain **verbal consent** from participants, but find it awkward to ask for written consent. This may seem insulting or confrontational, particularly in elite interviewing where corporate officers or senior managers are of equal or superior status to the interviewer. Historians, political scientists and other researchers have argued that consent that is implicit and verbal, for example by agreeing to an interview, may be sufficient for low-risk research. Rosnow and Rosenthal (1997) report that the process of gaining informed consent can create experimental artefacts including lower participation and second-guessing experimental hypotheses.

The requirement for informed consent is a significant challenge to informal, spontaneous, or what anthropologists call 'at home' research (references), which includes non-participant or unobtrusive observation. Observing customers queuing in a fast-food restaurant may not intervene in people's lives, but may conflict with their desires to conduct their activities without being observed. A notice saying that people will be observed by visual or electronic means may suffice, so that people can opt out of being observed during a particular time period. Somewhat paradoxically, there are at present no similar restrictions on similar recording in public spaces for the preparation of radio, television or cinematic films, or on the collection of images through CCTV.

If you are not using formal written consent forms, you should develop some way of showing that you have explained that you are a researcher and given an overview of your research to participants. This may be through keeping copies of emails and other correspondence through which you have gained access to participants, or through keeping a research notebook in which you contemporaneously record your having gained verbal consent from a participant.

Give extra protection to vulnerable participants

Principle 5. Safeguard the rights of vulnerable participants.

Some categories of research participants, called **vulnerable populations**, may be legally incapable of giving informed consent, including children, people with developmental or mental health problems, prisoners or asylum seekers. Participants who fall into one or more of these categories may still participate in research but consent from parents, carers or other responsible adults and additional safeguards may be required.

If members of vulnerable populations are present at your research site, even if you are not collecting data from or about them, this may lead to additional complexity. Conducting a study in a UK school now generally requires approval from the Disclosure and Barring Service to ensure that the researcher does not present a danger to children. There may also be restrictions on making any audio or video recordings in which children may appear, and you may be required to blur or otherwise obscure their faces.

Finally, although it is less common in business and management research, some research participants cannot give written informed consent because they cannot read or write.

Minimise the use of deception

> *Principle 6. Avoid unnecessary deception.*

Grix (2004) defines **deception** as deliberately giving false information in order to get a particular response. Deception conflicts with Principle 4, informed consent about all research aspects. Detailed guidance on when deception may be considered is given by the American Psychological Association's Code of Ethics (www.apa.org/ethics/code/index.aspx). Where deception is acceptable, compensating mechanisms such as the debriefing of participants may be required.

Deception is often used outside of academic research, notably in journalism and law enforcement. Deception may be accepted in some disciplines as a way of capturing natural behaviours, for example, mystery shopping in marketing, false job applications in personnel research, or research on sensitive topics such as racism, or anti-social topics such as criminality. Deception may reduce harm, as Stanley Milgram's famous 'obedience to authority' experiment, where research participants thought that they were giving serious or even fatal electric shocks to the confederates (who they mistakenly thought were fellow participants); it is hard to argue that the shocks ought to have been real. However, the use of unnecessary deception should be avoided, and any deception needs to be justified explicitly by the benefits and risks of the research, not the convenience of the researcher.

Safeguard the privacy of research participants

> *Principle 7. Data about participants should be kept confidential and their privacy should be respected.*

Anonymity and confidentiality are related, but distinct, topics. Researchers may withhold or disguise the identity of individual respondents. They may also not disclose information. Under some conditions, researchers may be compelled to break confidentiality, including when participants were at risk of harm, or involved in illegal activities (Wiles et al. 2008), but this should be disclosed in advance. Researchers should also manage data so that identity and data are neither accidentally nor deliberately disclosed in research or publication.

Researchers in the UK and many other countries have a legal duty to follow data protection regulations such as the **Data Protection Act**, which applies to data protection, storage and collection, before starting field research. Any computer files containing personal data should, at a minimum, be password protected, and any physical files should be locked up when not being consulted. Data key pens are easily lost, and may not be secure enough for storing sensitive information. Data should be held locally and not on a computer server. Cloud computing presents a new challenge: although it is convenient, it probably does not meet the gold standard for file storage.

Researchers should also consider how long to hold data and how to dispose of them at the end of the research project life cycle. Paper files containing personal information should be shredded; storage media should be erased. Special care should be taken that when selling, recycling, or trashing laptops or desktop computers, storage devices, or other technological devices, any files have been securely erased.

Incentives and fair compensation

Principle 8. Participants should be fairly compensated for their time.

Should you then provide an incentive to participants to take part in your research? This is a contentious issue for both professional and student researchers (Head 2009). Incentives in business and management research are often token or *ex gratia* (a chocolate bar) or a chance to win a moderate sum of money. However, some believe they are unnecessary: people in organisations are already being remunerated for their time. There is another issue though that you need to consider. Whilst incentives are believed to increase participation rates, incentives create what we call **experimental artefacts** as volunteers represent a different population than non-volunteers (Rosnow and Rosenthal 1997). We discuss this further in the following chapters, and whilst we recognise that for some people they need to know 'what's in it for me', most student projects require no additional compensation for people to take part.

8.2.3 What do I need to do to get my research approved?

Since we published the first edition of this book in 2005, formal procedures for research oversight have become much more widespread and more stringent. If you are doing research with human participants, you will most likely need to submit a draft of your proposed research to your supervisor, your department and your university. This next session briefly reviews why we need a research oversight system, and the key stages in research approval.

Generally, review consists of three stages, which are increasingly detailed and more closely scrutinised:

1. **Self-completion checklist.** The researcher completes a checklist comprising general questions about the research design and methods. If no items in the 'grey boxes' are ticked, then no further ethical approval is required.

2. **First-level review**. If the principal investigator has ticked any items that suggest the research needs to be approved, the entire form should be completed and submitted to the appropriate committee for desk review.
3. **Second-level review**. If the first-level review identifies the need for more rigorous ethical scrutiny (for example, research with vulnerable populations or research that endangers the researcher), then a more detailed second-level review form is completed and submitted to the appropriate committee for committee review.

The approvals committee may be given the power to approve your research project, to disapprove it, to request changes in your research procedures or to ask for additional information about what you plan to do. However, in practice, if a proposal is unsatisfactory, the researcher would be asked to provide further information or to amend the proposed research design or instruments (for example, to clarify a consent form). A summary of the likely ethical considerations for different research methods is shown in **Table 8.1** (see end of chapter).

 ## How can I avoid unethical behaviour?

We have covered the main research ethics issues that will arise in carrying out your research. However, the consideration cannot be limited to the execution of your research only. As a researcher, you have other legal, ethical and moral responsibilities in the entire research process. Some of these, such as the duty to avoid plagiarism, are part of your more general responsibility as a student, whilst others, such as the duty to avoid copyright infringement, are generally associated with doing research. Because you are using other people's ideas and words, of which they have intellectual if not legal ownership, this stage of your research can raise technical and ethical issues that may be new to you. You absolutely must avoid plagiarism. You do this by **citing** your sources. You should also be wary of copyright violations, which you may commit even if you do give credit to other people.

Plagiarism

Plagiarism, not giving appropriate credit to other people for their ideas, is an increasingly serious concern for researchers, who should avoid committing it, and examiners, who hope to avoid seeing it. Booth et al. (2003: 167) put it bluntly:

> You plagiarise when, intentionally or not, you use someone else's words or ideas but fail to credit that person. You plagiarise even when you do credit the author but use his exact words without so indicating with quotation marks or block indentation. You also plagiarise when you use words so close to those in your source, that if you placed your work next to the source, you would see that you could not have written what you did without the source at your elbow.

Most universities now have strict policies against plagiarising. Whether you plagiarise deliberately or accidentally, because it is stealing, if you are caught you will be punished. You could face penalties ranging from failing the piece of work in which plagiarism was committed to failing the unit for which the work was submitted and even expulsion from the degree course. Since there is no statute of limitations on plagiarism, you could be risking your degree even if you think you have got away with it: if plagiarism is detected some years later, your degree could still be rescinded.

8.3.1 Citing other people's words and ideas in your text

Most universities now give students extensive training in avoiding plagiarism, and use anti-plagiarism software such as Turnitin to detect plagiarism in submitted work. To avoid plagiarising, each time you refer directly or indirectly to someone else's words and/or ideas, you should give credit to the originator.

The basics of citation and referencing are covered in many different places, including style manuals, essay writing guides, and so on. Publishing houses, such as Harvard Business School Press and journals, such as the *Academy of Management Journal,* generally set and publish their own standards for citations. Professional editors and authors can use the *Oxford Style Manual* (Ritter 2002) in the UK, and *The Chicago Manual of Style* (University of Chicago 2003) or Turabian (1996) in the United States. International and national standards have even been developed for citing published and unpublished sources, including the International Organization for Standardization (ISO) (ISO 690:1987 *'Information and documentation – Bibliographic references – Content, form and structure'* and ISO 690–2:1997, *'Information and documentation – Bibliographic references – Part 2: Electronic documents or parts thereof') and* the British Standards Institution (BSI) (BSI 1629, *'Recommendations'*; BSI 5605, *'Recommendations for citing and referencing published materials'*; and BSI 6371, *'Citations to unpublished documents').*

Give credit to other people's words and ideas

Making sure that you give other people appropriate credit is a key research skill. Whatever system you are using, you must give credit to other people's words and ideas whenever you quote someone's words directly or indirectly by paraphrasing them and whenever you quote someone's ideas, directly or indirectly. Your project requirements should give you specific instructions about how to format citations and set up your reference list. If not, consult your project supervisor, project coordinator or librarian to see what to do. Pay attention. From personal experience, we can say that if you are instructed to use a certain system or your tutor has asked you to use a particular system, we will be mightily annoyed if you don't use it! As discussed in **Chapter 3**, in order to give credit you need to know where your information comes from in the first place. You need to understand the principles involved, take careful notes and refer back to these notes when you are writing.

The three common systems for doing citations in academic writing are **Harvard**, using parenthetical references to the author and date and a complete set of references at the end; **Vancouver**, using parenthetical numbers to refer to a numbered list of references at the end; and **Chicago**, using footnotes or endnotes, with or without a reference list at the end. If you haven't been instructed to use a specific citation system, we recommend that you use the Harvard author–date system for citations and references, because it is the most common system in business and management, along with many other social sciences. 'You know immediately whose work has been referred to and when it appeared', suggests Baker (2000: 227). 'It saves space and delivers a cleaner and simpler text than do notes of any kind' (Dunleavy 2003: 126).

In the Harvard system, you cite the source of anyone else's words or ideas that you are generally referring to in the text of your project report by giving their name and the date of the published (or unpublished) material. The author–date combination is usually enough to make sure that each reference has a unique citation, but some authors are prolific enough to publish more than one article in a year. Add the page number if you are referring to specific ideas, words, images, or other content. We cannot emphasise this enough: when you are *directly quoting* or *paraphrasing* someone else's words or a specific idea, to avoid plagiarism, you *must* refer to the page you found the words or idea on, and set those words so that it is clear they are not yours. You set off quoted material in one of two ways:

- for short quotations or paraphrases, enclose the words in quotation marks
- for longer quotations or paraphrases, block indent the entire set of words.

Table 8.2 gives examples for many common situations, but you should consult a technical guide for comprehensive and precise directions for citations and references.

Table 8.2   Examples of Harvard author–date citations and references

	Single author	Two authors	Three to six authors
Entry in reference list	Pentland, B.T. 1992. Organizing moves in software support hot lines, *Administrative Science Quarterly*, 37(4): 527–48.	Sutton, R.I. and Hargadon, A. 1996. Brainstorming groups in context: Effectiveness in a product design firm, *Administrative Science Quarterly*, 41(4): 685–718.	Voss, C.A., Roth, A.V., Rosenzweig, E.D., Blackmon, K. and Chase, R.B. 2004. A tale of two countries' conservatism, service quality, and feedback on customer satisfaction, *Journal of Service Research*, 6(3): 212–40.
Making reference to ideas but not quoting or paraphrasing:			
Direct reference	Pentland (1992)	Sutton and Hargadon (1996)	First reference:* Voss, Roth, Rosenzweig, Blackmon and Chase (2004) Second and subsequent references: Voss et al. (2004)
Indirect reference	(Pentland 1992)	(Sutton and Hargadon 1996)	First reference:* (Voss, Roth, Rosenzweig, Blackmon and Chase 2004) Second and subsequent references: (Voss et al. 2004)
Quoting or paraphrasing the author's words:			
Direct reference	Pentland (1992: 529)	Sutton and Hargadon (1996: 690)	First reference:* Voss, Roth, Rosenzweig, Blackmon and Chase (2004: 221) Second and subsequent references: Voss et al. (2004: 221)
Indirect reference	(Pentland 1992: 529)	(Sutton and Hargadon 1996: 690)	First reference:* (Voss, Roth, Rosenzweig, Blackmon and Chase 2004: 221) Second and subsequent references: (Voss et al. 2004: 221)

* Many publishers use et al. even for the first reference

In this case, you should add a letter of the alphabet to the year (Bloggs 1997a, Bloggs 1997b), to make sure that each source has a unique citation.

Even if you give credit to other people for their words and ideas, you may be presenting an overall misleading impression of your intellectual input in, say, your literature review, if all you are doing is joining up other people's words and ideas without providing any insight or ideas of your own. Check your work to make sure that you have added something of your own to your work.

A good way to check this as you are developing a draft is to cross out every sentence or phrase that simply summarises someone else's work that you have read. Then read what is left uncrossed. Does it tell its own story, or does it simply link up the other bits?

Referencing

When you write your project report, you will need to provide a reference list of the sources you have cited, usually at the end of your paper after the conclusions and before any appendices or other such material. (We will discuss where in your project report your reference list will go in **Chapter 13**.) The main thing to remember is that the reference list entry must provide complete enough information that your reader (who may well be marking your work, remember!) can go straight from that entry to the source that you cited. (And the citation in the text must provide specific enough information so that the reader can go straight from there to the reference list entry.) Table 8.3 summarises the information that you need to include by the type of publication to which you are referring.

You can find technical guidance on preparing a reference list in your project guidelines and the books listed in the **Additional resources** at the end of the chapter. Many business schools and universities have a standard set of guidelines for students. Your project guidelines will usually give you more specific information about how to

Table 8.3   General principles for information that should appear in a reference list

Publication type	Author	Date	Title	Source
Book	Author(s)	Publication date	Book title	Place of publication and publisher
Edited book chapter	Author(s)	Publication date	Chapter title	Complete reference to book (as above), with editors as author, page numbers
Academic journal	Author(s)	Publication date	Article title	Journal name, volume, and issue number, page numbers
Managerial publication	Author(s)	Publication date	Article title	Magazine name, issue date, page numbers
Newspaper article	Author(s)	Publication date	Article title	Newspaper name, page numbers
Web page	Author (if known)	Publication date (if known)	Page title (if known)	Web address, date accessed for your research.

construct your reference list. Your supervisor may also have strong preferences for or against a certain format.

You may find slight differences between different formats, such as whether to use quotation marks around journal article titles, how to capitalise titles, whether to enclose date references in parentheses and so on. If you make sure that you have all the information you need to hand, you will save yourself a lot of work. Once you have the complete list of references, you should put it in alphabetical order by author's last name. If the work you are referencing has just one author, use that author's name for list order; if you are referencing more than one work by that single author, list each work separately in ascending order by date; for example Smith, J.C. (1992) followed by Smith, J.C. (1993).

If a work has more than one author, use the first author to determine the order in the list (as listed in the publication or the citation record – do not put the authors in alphabetical order, which sounds crazy but we have seen it done). Single-authored publications always come before multiple-authored publications with that author as first author. If the first author appears in more than one multiple-authored publication, then they go in order by the second author's name, not the publication date.

If the author of a work that you are referencing is not a person (or persons), then you will usually treat the organisation or institution as the author. For example, you should treat the authorship of an unsigned editorial in the *Guardian* newspaper as if it had been written by a person named 'Guardian' in your reference list and citations will be to the Guardian (date); the OECD (date), etc..

You should combine all of your references in a single alphabetised list unless your project requirements tell you to separate them. That is, do not include a reference lists for books, a reference list for articles, newspaper, web references and so on.

Avoiding last-minute panic

Many students submit project reports with incomplete or erratic citations and reference lists because they run out of time, have not recorded their sources or do not think that the reference list is important. But, your reference list may well be the first place that an experienced examiners looks (Rugg and Petre 2010). An incomplete, poorly formatted, thoroughly inadequate reference list gives your reader the impression that you have carried out the rest of your research in an equally shoddy manner. If you misspell, mis-cite, or otherwise mangle something that your reader, your reader's supervisor or your reader's best mate has written, you can be sure that this jumps right off the page at them! And be assured that it will be the one citation for which you have failed to provide a reference (usually because it is obscure and you can't find it again) that your reader will flip to your reference list to find.

Citing your sources and preparing your reference list will be much easier when you are writing up your research if you have kept a comprehensive list of the sources you have consulted. Even if you think you will end up using only some of the sources, try to record everything you have consulted systematically. Otherwise, no matter how hard you look, if you later want to find some information that you half-remember reading but haven't recorded where you found it, it will take you a lot of time in the library or on the computer trying to track it down. You will never be able to find one or two key references again, and you will have to leave them out of your report. We know from bitter personal experience that the number of references you are missing will be directly related to the closeness of your project end date!

If you record details of each source in the format required for your reference list or bibliography as you consult them, you will spend less time formatting your references during the critical writing up period. This record might be as simple as a running list in a Word document or Excel spreadsheet; the 'Manage Sources' in recent versions of Word; a web-based browser add-on such as Zotero; or a custom referencing software program such as EndNote or Reference Manager.

8.3.2 Cut-and-paste and other forms of completely unacceptable behaviour

When you are doing research, you are expected to know how to use citations and references lists correctly because that is part of your professional responsibilities as a researcher. Not doing so is one form of plagiarism. There is another form of plagiarism: presenting work that is not your own as being yours, either through deliberately omitting the citations, or through wholesale incorporation of other people's work. Although the penalties are often the same, we distinguish between inadvertent plagiarism through being incompetent with citations and references, and intentional plagiarism, which is plagiarism with the intent to deceive. Whether you think that plagiarism is acceptable or not, given the risk of getting caught and the severity of the punishment, the amount of effort that it would take you to plagiarise successfully is probably more than the effort it would take to give credit appropriately. You might also consider whether plagiarism is compatible with learning.

Despite the enormous rise in the cases of plagiarism reported today, students are probably no more predisposed to intentional plagiarism than past generations: new computer and communications technologies have vastly facilitated plagiarism, so that the effort required to cut-and-paste a sentence or an entire document has become much less. It is easy to use the web to search for information and copy or download it in text form, tempting students to copy large amounts of material and *deliberately* plagiarise by incorporating this material without changing or acknowledging it, or only thinly rephrasing it. When you take notes and compose drafts directly on the computer, careless note-taking and drafting can lead to *inadvertent* plagiarism by making it difficult to remember which are other people's words and which are the students' own. Even professional writers who should know better have been found plagiarising: several popular historians have been severely embarrassed recently when plagiarism was detected in their books and widely publicised.

It has been argued that international students are at a disadvantage because the ground rules about plagiarism are different in different cultures, especially at undergraduate level. There is no cultural relativism in plagiarism. Despite the standards applied in your own culture, you will be judged by the rules that apply where you are taking your degree. 'Ignorance of the law is no excuse.' You should review your student handbook and/or code of ethics to make sure that you are complying with them.

Universities, especially those that teach large class sections, have started using software programs such as Turnitin that can detect probable plagiarism by checking submitted material against a database of published and unpublished work. Although software is very efficient at finding the plagiarised source by comparing it with printed texts, however, most experienced markers don't need it to tell whether a student is plagiarising. Most plagiarism is so obvious that it can be spotted right away: plagiarised text seldom sounds the same as text the student has written. (Of course, if the student has plagiarised the entire document and the examiner has never read anything else by this student, this won't apply.) Examples of practices we have experienced are in **Student research in action 8.1.**

Student research in action 8.1

ROGER, COPY THAT

A lecturer gave a student a copy of a paper he had written. Later, he was surprised to find large sections of the paper repeated word for word in the student's thesis.

Another student plagiarised three entire pages, word for word, from Geert Hofstede – probably the best-known author on international management culture. This did not impress his examiner with his academic integrity.

Kate received a master's thesis to examine as the final requirement for a research degree. When she turned to the second chapter, the literature review, it was in a different font than the other chapters, and was written in a different style. A quick Google for key words and phrases didn't turn up any likely suspects for wholesale copying, but then a quick trip next door to the library revealed that the student had copied the literature review from a course text, including the grammatical errors and things that couldn't possibly have been true for the student's work. Kate reported the plagiarism, and eventually the student was failed and did not receive his degree.

8.3.3 Avoiding copyright infringement

Beyond plagiarism, the use of other people's work has ethical implications in the area of what you are actually allowed to photocopy, download, copy or quote. Before the web and virtual library resources, our ability to record information was limited to taking notes on index cards, or the cost and availability of photocopying. Today, we can print out or photocopy printed material, such as articles and books, free or cheaply. This makes it easy, in most cases, to photocopy or download enough published material for a specific project or even more. We can also download images, sounds and other media from the internet with the click of a mouse. **Student research in action 8.2** shows how what can appear relatively straightforward procedurally may not be acceptable practice.

Student research in action 8.2

JUST NOT FUNNY...

Corey wanted to study how humour was used in office settings to defuse tense situations. He decided that he would analyse the British television series *The Office* as part of his summer research project. Since he had box sets of three series of the programme, he planned to use these as the basis for his research. He also planned to illustrate his research using images from the show's website and some fan websites, and quote some of the dialogue in his report. As long as he acknowledged the source of the material, he figured, it would be OK. A casual conversation with one of this book's authors, who was writing this chapter at the time, alerted him to potential problems. When he brought this up with his supervisor, they both agreed that he needed to investigate this much more carefully.

In contrast to how easy it is to print out or photocopy material or download files, our permission to use materials created by other people is becoming more limited. Other people's work is generally protected by **copyright**, whether it is published or unpublished (for example a thesis), for a long period of time (often up to 70 years after the author's death). Materials that are covered by copyright include:

- Literary, dramatic, musical and artistic works (for example books, plays, musical scores and paintings)
- Computer-generated works, databases, sound recordings, films, broadcasts and cable programmes.

Even if something you want to quote, photocopy or reproduce electronically does not have the © symbol and a copyright statement, it is still copyrighted as long as it is an original work in material form. (It is, however, good practice to include a statement such as '© 2005 University of Swindon. All rights reserved' on anything you publish in written or electronic form to remind other people.)

In the UK, the Copyright Licensing Authority (CLA) licenses universities, libraries, museums and other educational institutions to photocopy extracts from magazines, journals and books. A notice from the CLA should be next to any photocopying machine you use, which tells you what you are and aren't allowed to copy.

If you plan to use material from the internet in your research or project report, you should make sure that you understand the current copyright restrictions that apply to electronic works, such as web pages, including the text, images, data and other materials you may find. At the time of writing, the principle of **fair dealing** does not apply to electronic works: you may be allowed to print out a copy of a web page for personal use, but that is all. If you want to quote text from a website, you need copyright permission from the author (or copyright holder, if not the same), unless the web page explicitly gives you permission. This means that you need explicit permission from the author or copyright holder, rather than just acknowledging the source of the material as for traditional publications. The Joint Information Systems Committee (JISC) and the Publishers Association have published a code of conduct that you may want to consult.

Copyright law may also prevent you from using unpublished material without explicit permission from its author. This currently includes student theses and dissertations, student projects and unpublished company reports, such as memoranda or minutes of meetings.

Knowing what you can and cannot use can be tricky. Materials used in essays and research reports that have only been produced for examination, such as doctoral theses, have traditionally been considered 'fair dealing', and thus OK to quote or reference. Downloaded cartoons (for example Dilbert) and images from web pages, which frequently show up in student reports and presentations, are not currently considered 'fair dealing', and thus not OK to use. Most material that is produced for commercial purposes cannot be downloaded and used without permission from the copyright owner: that nifty picture of Barbie or an iPad you download from the internet to illustrate your report or presentation on advertising to children may not fall under fair dealing.

Surprisingly, even quoting text from a web page has not been covered by fair dealing. Given that it may take up to a year to get copyright permission, and most student projects are considerably shorter than a year, you should be careful about keeping to 'best practice' when doing your research and writing up your findings and/or recommendations. If you are looking for material for illustrations, you may want to look at Copyright Commons.

To make matters even more complicated, if you are using the internet to access material in other countries, you are restricted by:

- The copyright law of the country where the website is hosted
- The country in which you are downloading or using material
- International law.

As well as understanding how copyright applies to other people's work, you should make sure that you understand how copyright applies to your own research project, including your written report and any electronic publications such as web pages. In some cases, your university may own the copyright to your work. If you have been sponsored by a business or organisation, they may own the copyright to your work, even if they have only provided access or sponsorship. As with all of the issues we have raised here, you should check this explicitly rather than assuming anything.

 ## Summary

As researchers, we need to be aware of ethical issues in our research designs to avoid committing ethical errors such as those described in the opening two cases. Many of the principles for research ethics are derived from medical or psychological experiments where there was a significant risk to participants' physical or mental well-being.

Although ethical violations in business and management research are typically less serious than breaches in biomedical or psychological research, as the two examples in **Research in action 8.1** and **Research in action 8.2** demonstrated they do have the potential to cause harm to participants (emotional and financial distress), their universities (grants and costs of better internal regulation) and the researchers themselves. At a minimum, researchers should report how they have considered, applied and managed each of these aspects when reporting field research.

Whilst it may not be surprising that business and management research has paid less attention to ethical issues than social psychology and the behavioural sciences, even economics and operations research/management science (OR/MS) have had more extended discussions of research ethics, including a 2009 special issue of *Omega* co-edited by Le Menestrel and Van Wassenhove (2009).

Ultimately, ethical mistakes can harm the wider community of practice, even if there is no harm to participants, because unethical research wastes people's time, produces unsound knowledge, and contaminates the research field for future research (Iphofen 2009).

 ## Answers to key questions

What are ethics in the context of research?

- Ethics are the set of beliefs or values that require, as a minimum, that our research does no harm, and more positively that says we have to 'do it right.' 'Right' refers to the way that we work with those who are involved in our research (human participants), or could be affected by it.

What are the requirements for conducting ethical research?

- Ethics cannot be ignored: an unethical study will fail, or worse.

What implications do ethics have for my research?

- We distilled eight principles for ethical research which should be considered as part of your research design.
- It is your responsibility to consider the general principles we have identified here alongside the requirements for your organisation and to ensure that your research design meets these requirements.

References

Baker, Michael J. 2000. Writing a literature review, *Marketing Review*, 1(2): 219–47.

Basken, Paul 2010, 9 May. Academe hath no fury like a fellow professor deceived. *The Chronicle of Higher Education*. Available at: http://chronicle.com/article/Academe-Hath-No-Fury-Like-a/65466 (accessed 3 August 2016).

Booth, Wayne C., Colomb, Gregory G. and Williams, Joseph M. 2003. *The Craft of Research*, 2nd edn. Chicago, IL: University of Chicago Press.

Bozeman, Barry, Slade, Catherine and Hirsch, Paul 2009. Ethics in research and practice, *American Journal of Public Health*, 99(9): 1549–56.

Creswell, John W. 2013. *Research Design: Qualitative and Quantitative Approaches*, 4th edn. Thousand Oaks, CA: Sage.

Iphofen, Ron. 2009. *Ethical Decision-Making in Social Research*. Basingstoke: Palgrave Macmillan.

De Cremer, David, van Dick, Rolf, Tenbrunsel, Ann, Pillutla, Madan and Murnighan, Keith 2011. Understanding ethical behavior and decision making in management: A behavioural business ethics approach, *British Journal of Management*, 22(S1): S1–S4.

Dunleavy, Patrick 2003. *Authoring a PhD: How to Plan, Draft, Write and Finish a Doctoral Thesis or Dissertation*. Basingstoke: Palgrave Macmillan.

Gregory, Ian 2003. *Ethics in Research*. London: Continuum.

Grix, Jonathan 2004. *The Foundations of Research*. Basingstoke: Palgrave Macmillan.

Head, Emma 2009. The ethics and implications of paying participants in qualitative research, *International Journal of Social Research Methodology*, 12(4): 335–44.

Institutional Review Blog 2010. Researchers deceive thousands of professors. Available at: www.institutionalreviewblog.com/2010/05/researchers-deceive-thousands-of.html (accessed 3 August 2016).

Jiang, Bin. 2009. The effects of interorganizational governance on supplier's compliance with SCC: An empirical examination of compliant and non-compliant suppliers, *Journal of Operations Management*, 27(4): 267–80.

Jiang, Bin, Baker, Revenor C. and Frazier, Gregory V. 2009. An analysis of job dissatisfaction and turnover to reduce global supply chain risk: Evidence from China, *Journal of Operations Management*, 27(2): 169–84.

Kaplin, William and Lee, Barbara, 2006. *The Law of Higher Education*, NY: Jossey Bass.

Le Menestrel, Marc and Van Wassenhove, Luk N. 2009. Ethics in operations research and management sciences: A never-ending effort to combine rigor and passion, *Omega*, 37(6): 1039–43.

Ritter, Robert M. 2002. *The Oxford Style Manual*. Oxford: Oxford University Press.

Rosnow, Ralph L. and Rosenthal, Robert 1997. *People Studying People: Artifacts and Ethics in Behavioural Research*. New York: W.H. Freeman & Co.

Rugg, Gordon and Petre, Marian 2010. *The Unwritten Rules of PhD Research*, 2nd edn. Maidenhead: Open University Press.

Sears, D.O. 1986. College sophomores in the laboratory: Influences of a narrow data-base on social psychology's view of human nature, *Journal of Personality and Social Psychology*, 51: 515–30.

Turabian, Kate L. 1996. *A Manual for Writers of Term Papers, Theses and Dissertations*, 6th edn. Chicago: University of Chicago Press.

University of Chicago 2003. *The Chicago Manual of Style: For Authors, Editors and Copywriters*, 15th edn. Chicago: University of Chicago Press.

Warnock, Mary 1998. *An Intelligent Person's Guide to Ethics*. London: Duckworth.

Wiles, Rose, Crow, Graham, Heath, Sue and Charles, Vikki 2008. The management of confidentiality and anonymity in social research, *International Journal of Social Research Methodology*, 11(5): 417–28.

Additional resources

Alcadipani, Rafael and Hodgson, Damian 2009. By any means necessary? Ethnographic access, ethics and the critical researcher, *TAMARA: Journal of Critical Postmodern Organization Science*, 7(3/4): 127–46.

Becker, Howard S. 1972. A school is a lousy place to learn anything in, *American Behavioral Scientist*, 16(1): 85–105.

Bell, Robert 1992. *Impure Science: Fraud, Compromise, and Political Influence in Scientific Research*. New York: John Wiley & Sons.

Bogdan, Robert and Taylor, Stephen J. 1984. *Introduction to Qualitative Research Methods: The Search for Meanings*. New York: John Wiley & Sons.

Booth, Wayne C., Colomb, Gregory G. and Williams, Joseph M. 2008. *The Craft of Research*, 3rd edn. Chicago, IL: University of Chicago Press.

Calvey, David 2008. The art and politics of covert research: Doing 'situated ethics' in the field, *Sociology*, 42(5): 905–18.

Cooper, Anthony K., Ittman, Hans W., Stylianides, Theo and Schmitz, Peter M.U. 2009. Ethical issues in tracing cellular phones at an event, *Omega* 37(6), 1063–72.

Cooper, Donald R. and Schindler, Pamela 2001. *Business Research Methods*. New York: Irwin.

Fisher, D. and Hanstock, T. 1998. *Citing References*. Oxford: Blackwell.

Haney, C., Banks, W.C. and Zimbardo, P.G. 1973. A study of prisoners and guards in a simulated prison. *Naval Research Review*, 30: 4–17.

Hart, Chris 1998. *Doing a Literature Review: Releasing the Social Science Research Imagination*. London: Sage.

Hart, Chris 2001. *Doing a Literature Search: A Comprehensive Guide for the Social Sciences*. London: Sage.

Hedgecoe, Adam 2008. Research ethics review and the sociological research relationship, *Sociology*, 42(5): 873–86.

Locke, Lawrence F., Silverman, Stephen J. and Spirduso, Waneen W. 2004. *Reading and Understanding Research*, 2nd edn. Thousand Oaks, CA: Sage.

Munro, Emily R. 2008. Research governance, ethics and access: A case study illustrating the new challenges facing social researchers, *International Journal of Social Research Methodology*, 11(5): 429–39.

Nairn, Agnes 2009. Research ethics in the virtual world, *International Journal of Market Research*, 51(2): 276–78.

O'Dochartaigh, N. 2001. *The Internet Research Handbook*. London: Sage.

Oliver, Paul 2003. *The Student's Guide to Research Ethics*. Maidenhead, Open University Press.

Richardson, Sue and McMullan, Miriam 2007. Research ethics in the UK: What can sociology learn from health? *Sociology*, 41(6): 1115–32.

Key terms

Discussion questions

1. Why should a student project require the consideration of research ethics?

2. What do you understand by 'research ethics?

3. Look at the Academy of Management Code of Research Ethics. Why do you think such well-developed requirements have been created?

4. Why is it of interest to your institution that you do ethical research?

5. Look at the cases in **Research in action 8.1 and 8.2**. What ethical standards or principles do you believe they have breached?

6. How would you compare the ethical considerations of a database study with those of a series of interviews in a case organisation?

7. How much could you legitimately copy and paste from this book before it becomes plagiarism?

8. What is the difference between *ethical business* and *ethical research into business*?

9. 'Ethics? That's just more paperwork for the researcher.' Discuss.

10. What are the ethical requirements that your organisation imposes on your research? How do they relate to the principles mapped out in this chapter?

Workshop

Individually, prepare an outline proposal setting out the methods you are intending to use in your research. Then, using Table 8.1 as a reference, outline your plan to make sure that the work is carried out under the ethical principles discussed here and in the requirements of your organisation. As a group, carry out an analysis of the ethical challenges presented by each other's research. Do you notice any patterns emerging in the ethical challenges presented by certain types of research?

▶

Workshop cont'd

Table 8.1   General ethical principles

Research method	Risk of harm	Risk-benefit analysis	Informed consent	Voluntary participation	Deception	Privacy and confidentiality	Data protection	Fair compensation
Mathematical modelling	X	X						
Computer simulation	X	X						
Survey	X	X	X	X	X	X	X	X
Interview	X	X	X	X	X	X	X	X
Unobtrusive observation	X	X	X	X	X	X	(X)	
Non-participant observation	X	X	X	X	X	X	(X)	
Participant observation	X	X	X	X	X	X	X	
Extended ethnography	X	X	X	X	X	X	X	
Case studies	X	X	X	X	X	X	X	
Secondary research	(x)	X	(x)	(x)		X	X	
Archival research	(x)	X	(x)	(x)		X	X	

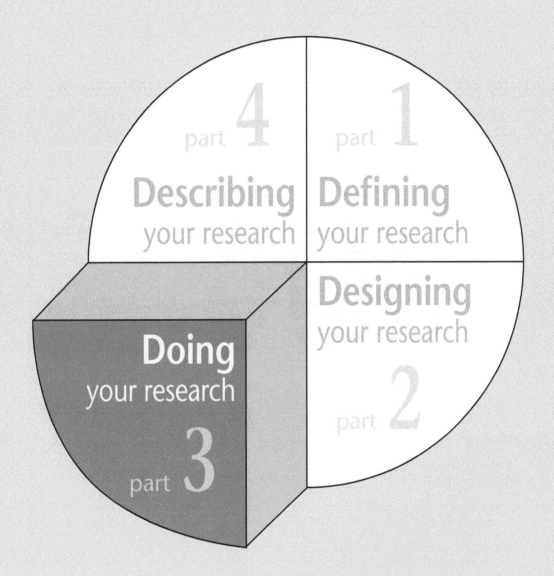

part 4
Describing your research

part 1
Defining your research

Designing your research
part 2

Doing your research
part 3

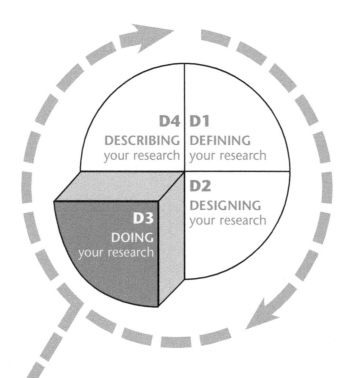

Relevant chapters
13 How do I write up my report?
14 What do I do now?

Key challenges
- Making sense of your findings
- Presenting your research to others
- Reflecting and learning from your research

4

Relevant chapters
1 What is research?
2 What should I study?
3 How do I find information?

Key challenges
- Understanding what academic research is
- Generating and clarifying ideas
- Using sources of information

1

D4
DESCRIBING
your research

D1
DEFINING
your research

D2
DESIGNING
your research

D3
DOING
your research

Relevant chapters
9 **How do I do field research?**
10 What do my quantitative data mean(1)?
11 What do my quantitative data mean(2)?
12 What do my qualitative data mean?

Key challenges
- **Practical considerations in doing research**
- Describing data using simple statistics
- Carrying out statistical tests
- Interpreting words and actions

3

Relevant chapters
4 What is my research approach?
5 How do I do quantitative research?
6 How do I do qualitative research?
7 How do I do case study research?
8 How do I make sure my research is ethical?

Key challenges
- Choosing a research approach
- Choosing a research design
- Collecting data using quantitative methods
- Collecting data using qualitative methods
- Integrating quantitative and qualitative methods

2

chapter

9

How do I do field research?

 Key questions

- How can I gain access to the organisations and people I want to study?
- How can I manage the expectations of different project stakeholders?
- How can I balance academic research and consultancy in a sponsored project?
- What practical issues should I consider in managing my project?

 Learning outcomes

At the end of this chapter, you should be able to:

- Identify strategies for gaining access to organisations and people
- Balance the different aims of research and consulting
- Identify the practical issues concerned with carrying out field research including preparing a plan, measuring progress and working with groups

Contents

Introduction
9.1 Gaining access to organisations and people
9.2 How do I manage competing demands in sponsored research?
9.3 What are the practical considerations in executing my research design?
Summary
Answers to key questions
References
Additional resources
Key terms
Discussion questions

Introduction

We begin the third stage of your project and the third part of our book – 'Doing your research project' – with this chapter. You have now made your hardest decisions, defining and designing your research. You should be on track for collecting and analysing your data to answer your research questions.

Although the rest of your research project can be straightforward, we have found as supervisors that many tricky questions may arise during data collection and analysis, especially for students in extended contact with organisations or the people in them. Unless you plan to obtain your data only from the library and the internet, you will need to gain indirect or direct access to people and/or organisations. You will generally be responsible for making your contacts and arranging access for collecting data. Even if access has been arranged by your university or project sponsor, you will still need to establish your credibility as a researcher and the credibility of your research project through how you approach contacts.

In this chapter, we will offer you some tips and strategies for doing **field research**. Some of the golden rules for doing field research include:

1. **Put your project requirements first.** Work-based projects are only attractive when they allow you to pursue the qualification you have been working for.
2. **Don't leave your success in other people's hands.** Particularly when it comes to gaining access or data, make sure you get agreements in writing. This can be just writing down what has been agreed and getting people to initial it, confirming that this is what has been agreed, or a formal agreement. Some business schools have their own forms, especially for placement students or sponsored projects, which formally commit the organisation to providing access and data for the purposes of the project. Some organisations have their own forms, which specify what you will and will not be able to do. Always investigate this before you commit too much time or resources to a particular project design.
3. **Don't promise more than you can deliver to get a project approved.** You must always follow the highest ethical and legal standards when you design and do your research project. (More about this in **Section 9.2** when we discuss how to manage competing demands.) It is better to under-promise and over-deliver than the opposite.

Many students find one of the biggest hurdles in doing research is getting access. **Section 9.1** presents some strategies you can use to gain access to organisations and people in them. Even experienced researchers often find this challenging. We suggest that using your personal and academic contacts can be much more effective than trying to cold-contact potential participants.

Just being in direct contact with organisations and the people in them while you are working for or with an organisation presents further challenges. **Section 9.2** focuses on conflicts that may arise between the organisation's goals and expectations and your own for your research project. These may pull you in many directions – not least between your academic supervisor and your business sponsor or manager. You will need to actively manage your roles as *researcher, consultant and/or employee* without letting the business concerns dictate the direction of your research.

You may want to revisit your research design after you have read this section to make sure that you have thought about these issues before you go into the field so that you can deal with any unexpected or difficult problems you find. Some especially tricky issues may come up if you are researching your own organisation, whether you are permanently employed there while you are studying or are on a temporary internship or an academic placement. Students who 'go native' seldom produce good research projects, because they have lost the ability to see the organisation and issues from a critical perspective. These issues can threaten your project's success, but they can also present unexpected possibilities. We discuss some ways that you can manage 'insider' research effectively.

Practical issues of planning and controlling your project and work with a group are discussed in **Section 9.3**. What is written here is not complicated in principle, and so difficulty in practice can catch students off guard. We set out some techniques and approaches that we have observed in our supervisory practice that are fundamental to success.

9.1 Gaining access to organisations and people

There is no one best way to get access to the organisations or people you want to study. In the best of all possible worlds, you will approach an organisation with a simple expression of an interest in working with them, an interesting project idea, a well-worked proposal stating exactly what you intend to do, and a summary of your project guidelines, and they will agree to work with you. In our experience, though, calling up an organisation and asking to be put in contact with 'that person who knows about ...' just leads to frustration and few good leads. We suggest a number of strategies that are generally more effective.

9.1.1 Gaining access – leveraging your contacts

Given the large number of requests that firms receive to become involved in different types of research, and the difficulty of contacting the right people in organisations, you may need someone to vouch for you, sponsor or champion your project for it to go ahead.

You should cultivate your personal contacts or networks to find such a champion. The type of network that you can build to try to get your main contacts is shown in **Figure 9.1**. Even though networking is promoted actively in business and management, if you are starting your project you may not find advice such as 'you should always be developing your networks' very useful. However, think about the many **personal networks** you already have:

- Your **family, friends and work colleagues**. Don't underestimate these, as in our experience, they are the *prime source* for collaborative projects.
- Any other **social groups** that you belong to, including sports teams, clubs, or a church/temple/mosque, for instance, where you can make social contacts outside of students or work colleagues.
- **Former students** or **alumni networks** of your academic institution may be friendly towards approaches by current students, especially if you have been sent by your tutor or project supervisor. Most institutions have become far more aware of the potential of their alumni in recent years and may be able to give you some relevant names.

- **Professional associations** related to your area of interest or the trade association of particular organisations. Many are keen to gain student members and to be seen to be assisting in the development of the professional community.
- People attending speaker's evenings, research talks, networking meetings or other relevant **public events** related to your research setting. These are great places to meet people face to face, rather than 'cold-calling' them. The business cards you collect here can be a valuable source of contacts.

Your best starting point is a **warm contact**, someone you already have a connection with who knows you (or at least knows of you) and will probably find the time to pass you on to the right person to talk to in the organisation. Even if you don't have any warm contacts in the organisation that you want to study, your warm contacts may know people in those organisations. These 'friends of friends' can be a great source of contact with organisations that would otherwise ignore or turn down your request out of hand.

Negotiating access through **cold contacts**, people who do not know you personally and with whom you have nothing in common, is the hardest way to gain access, but it still worth trying. At least a cold contact is a name within the company, and a person who may be willing to give you details of more promising contacts. Mentioning the name of the person who gave you the name of the cold contact might help warm them up a bit.

We cannot over-emphasise how important personal networks will be in getting access to organisations, people and data. The sociologist Mark Granovetter found that our close friends tend to know more or less the same information and people that we do, but their friends (and the friends of their friends) have a lot more variety in what and whom they know (Granovetter 1973). Travers and Milgram found that there were on average

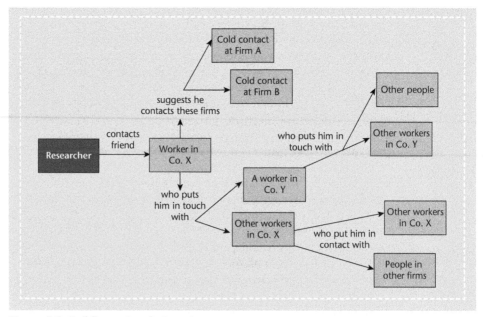

Figure 9.1 Building networks to gain access

six links or fewer between any two people; more recently it has been shown that any two random people on Facebook can be joined up through links of five friends, which you can test yourself on http://phys.org/news/2011-08-facebook-yahoo-degrees.html (Travers and Milgram 1969). Your personal networks can give you access to the entire world if you use them well.

9.1.2 Making contact

Contacts and networks are only useful if they agree to give you access to people and data, as shown in **Student research in action 9.1**. You are more likely to be successful if you can show what you want to do and convince them of your project's potential benefits for them and why you deserve access to their organisation.

 Student research in action 9.1

A FRIEND IN NEED

Bill was due to start a project on customer relationship management (CRM) practices in fast-moving consumer goods (FMCG) firms. He knew someone who worked for the marketing department of a large FMCG firm, so Bill asked him to arrange for him to interview appropriate people in the organisation. He gave his friend a brief verbal outline of the project and waited for his call. Nothing happened for weeks. When Bill called his friend to find out what was happening, he was told that the firm had decided not to implement any more software solutions for the rest of the year, due to a freeze on IT spending, and therefore nobody was interested in talking to him.

This seemed bizarre to Bill, who had only mentioned IT in passing as a potential enabler of CRM – IT was not central to the project, yet this is what his friend had focused on. If Bill had put together a short written proposal for his friend spelling out that he wanted to focus on CRM in his research project, his friend might have had a better idea of what he wanted to research and the firm might have been interested in his work. Instead, as a result of this contact falling through, he ended up changing his project.

One way to 'sell' your project is to provide a copy of your project proposal or a one-page précis of your research. Highlight any key 'selling points' of your research. As well as deciding what information you will give to contacts about your study, you need to make sure that it is available promptly when it is needed. Have it ready, just in case. Once you have managed to gain entrée through a contact, your potential project sponsor will typically want to know:

- What are you investigating?
- How many people do you need to speak to?
- How long will you need to speak to them?
- Can you guarantee confidentiality?
- How much time do you plan to spend in the organisation?
- What facilities will you need to do the work?
- What is it going to cost?
- What's in it for the firm?

Make sure that you can answer all these questions and have your CV ready too.

Gaining deeper access

Whether you need entry to an organisation for an hour or several months, the starting point for your research will be the same. In some situations, however, you will want to arrange deeper access to an organisation, perhaps by doing a paid or unpaid internship, or to your own organisation if you are already working there (or involved in some other way). This is especially critical if you intend to use an ethnographic approach or other form of **embedded research**.

Students often ask whether they should go to an organisation with a well-worked-out strategy, or approach it with something looser and try to find areas of mutual interest for a project. The best answer is most likely to be 'both' – the more ways you try to gain access to different organisations and the more organisations you try, the luckier you will get. If you hope to study or work in an organisation for an extended period, or to do research in your own organisation, you will probably need to provide more information about your research project, and why the organisation should give you permission to do it, than in the project brief or proposal described above.

You should have an initial discussion with the person in the firm who makes the decision to set your project parameters and decide what you can reasonably ask for. What you cost the organisation is not trivial, whether you are asking the organisation to be paid a salary, to be reimbursed for expenses or simply to do an unpaid internship for the period of your research, particularly if someone has to justify it. If you find out that the person you are talking to doesn't have the authority to make this decision or perhaps to make any commitments, you are not talking to the right person to get the project rolling, so check to see to whom you should be talking, and set up a meeting or phone call.

In any meeting with potential sponsors, you should take notes. Afterwards, you should summarise the meeting, and, provided that you have received a positive response, put your understanding of your project and the organisation's commitment in writing. It also provides some momentum to your project, always helpful if you want it to proceed. Levels of access have been discussed in **Chapter 7**. This is where the network approach to research really comes into its own.

9.2 How do I manage competing demands in sponsored research?

In most student projects, two main clients for embedded research have competing claims on your project: your academic supervisor or institution, and your business sponsor. You will need to manage each set of relationships and each set of expectations for your research project process and outcomes, and these are likely to diverge significantly. Understanding the tension between the two parties and managing both parties to the process is the first step towards successful field research. You should be visualising how you will satisfy your particular requirements long before you start writing up your research. It might be useful here to reflect on what your different stakeholders might be expecting from your project (see **Chapter 1**). For instance, does your institution assessment emphasise theoretical or practical research? If you must demonstrate the application of theory to a particular context, you will have to put academic rigour first; whereas if you must 'demonstrate knowledge and ability to design a study, collect appropriate data, analyse that data and present suitable recommendations', you can focus more on practice-focused research. An organisation sponsoring a project is more likely to be interested in solving a particular practical problem than creating new management knowledge. It will be more concerned with your recommendations rather than how you get there, although it will need to be confident that you have got there the right way.

As supervisors, we have found this tension to be core to the experience of research for so many students.

If you think you have resolved the tension without having discussed it with your supervisor, all we can say is you are probably heading for disaster. If so, you could shortcut straight to **Chapter 14**, when we describe the most common reasons that projects fail.

9.2.1   Managing scope in an ongoing project

The first step in managing the expectations for your project is to define the scope of your project clearly. **Project scope** describes 'what is included in the project and what is excluded'. The three different aspects of project scope that you need to manage actively are:

1. **Initiation**: identifying your starting assumptions and constraints
2. **Planning**: providing a statement for agreement of your work
3. **Change control**: seeing how changes made to the scope either deliberately or through circumstances will affect the end result.

Initiation

During the initial stages of your project, you should set out clearly what you plan to study, how you plan to study it, and any assumptions that you are making that could affect the outcomes of your research project. Pay attention to constraints such as the availability of resources and particularly data, the lack of which could affect your project's success. If you assume too much, you risk having to change your project, as **Student research in action 9.2** shows.

 Student research in action 9.2

WHAT THE HECK IS GOING ON?

Paul wanted to study whether what the people of a company spent their time doing and the corporate strategy were related. He assumed that the data he was interested in already existed or that he would be able to collect data about what diverse groups of people (the firm was spread over 30 locations) spent their day doing. He also assumed that there was an explicit statement of corporate strategy that would allow him to compare what people did with the corporate strategy.

Paul's assumptions went unchallenged until a few weeks into the project, when it became clear that neither assumption held. Fortunately, he was able to look at what type of data he might collect and how to construct a data collection system, and start to implement it. This changed the focus of the project, but was not fatal in this instance.

Gaining early commitment from key individuals is a vital part of success in projects being undertaken in organisational settings. If sponsored, you should always get a signed, written agreement from your project sponsor (preferably the person who will be paying for it and the person who will be making sure that you get your work done). To do this, generate a written **scope document** that describes what is included in the project and what is excluded. Usually one page of description will do. This statement becomes a vital tool for managing expectations, since it clarifies what the organisation should expect from you. **Student research in action 9.3** demonstrates the effective use of such agreements in making a project successful.

Student research in action 9.3

HOW GREEN WAS MY VALLEY

A large energy company asked a group of undergraduates to assess the market for green power in the UK so that the firm could start to tap this market. The brief provided by the firm was contained in an email. Wisely, before going any further with the project, the group interpreted this brief in the form of a scope statement that:

● Defined the terms to be used – including how they understood the concept of 'green power'.

● Set out that they would be prepared to carry out primary research with existing customers of the firm, provided they were given details of relevant contacts and meetings were arranged through the firm. Expenses would be provided for such visits and any wider-scale survey of firms was outside the scope of the work.

● Confined the project to the commercial energy sector, as this was the implied area of interest in the original brief. They could exclude the domestic sector from consideration.

● Agreed to carry out case-based analysis of firms and also investigate the regulatory aspects of a green power company. They would not be responsible for starting to 'build a brand' around the concept of green power.

The group presented this scope statement in one page describing what they would do and received the necessary signatures to allow them to move the project to the first stage. By interpreting the brief in their own words and limiting what they would do, the students found that the project, which had originally looked too large for them, became far more manageable. Moreover, they found out through this scoping process that two key players in the firm wanted different things from the project. By identifying this conflict in advance, they were able to resolve what would otherwise have been an inevitable problem for their research project.

In addition, you can use the scoping process to set out what the firm and, in particular, key individuals are prepared to do. You should secure written agreement early on for the time and access necessary to do your work. As **Student research in action 9.4** illustrates, you should always get a scope statement agreed with your sponsor.

Student research in action 9.4

SCANTY BRIEFS!

Saiyyid gained sponsorship for a project with a large financial institution who gave him a verbal brief for the project. Based on his notes during the original discussions, Saiyyid interpreted his brief for the university and the project started well.

▶

His first meetings with the sponsor responsible for his project went less well. The sponsor was always late or simply agreed to meet with him in the presence of others at lunch. Promised data were not forthcoming and contacts and meetings that had been suggested never materialised. He was left with a fairly 'thin' project, but one that he could salvage into a report for the university that met all the necessary criteria.

Unhappy, the firm threatened court action if its criteria (which Saiyyid had never seen but which differed significantly from the brief as he understood it) were not met. He had little choice but to go back to the firm after the project was supposedly completed and to provide extra work for them to meet these criteria.

Saiyyid could have averted this fiasco if he and the organisation had agreed on the project scope. As he reflected later: 'I wish that I had put in place all the CYB [cover your back] stuff, it would not have taken long and would have saved a whole pile of trouble later on.'

We want to make it clear that project disasters such as Saiyyid's in **Student research in action 9.4** are mercifully rare. However, Saiyyid would have had a much better chance of preventing this one from happening if he had spent a few minutes documenting the scope at the outset, and regularly reviewed it as he went. If this is not forthcoming from your partner, you can demonstrate how they have not met their side of the bargain.

Change control: Limiting project creep

Even if you have followed the scoping process outlined above and have gained commitment from key participants, since research is an unfolding and emergent process you can never spell out all of the eventualities that could affect your research. There is always a danger of **project creep**, which occurs when you are asked to accommodate changes to the project. These changes are often innocently disguised as 'just do this bit as well'. 'Just this bit' usually turns out to be a large piece of work that takes up valuable time, usually at the end of the project when you can least afford it.

You can also use your statement of project scope to limit changes that will cause you extra work without adding to the quality of your research project or its outcomes. The logic is simple. Until the project is complete, if any work is added, a corresponding amount of work must be taken away. It is here that you need to actively manage the situation. Borrowing from the service quality literature, we cite David Maister's first law of customer service (Maister 1993), which states that:

$$\text{Satisfaction} = \text{perceptions} - \text{expectations}$$

– that is, the level of customer satisfaction is determined by the difference between what the organisation expected and what you delivered. You must manage both the expectations and perceptions of the people you will be working with. In our experience, students who have created expectations that they cannot meet are the major cause of dissatisfied project sponsors. They promise an elephant and deliver a mouse.

Sponsors and coercion

Sponsors can make your job difficult if you start to diverge from their plan for your project, whether this is inadvertent or deliberate and manipulative. There is always risk involved when you are working with people, and a key skill is recognising this and learning how to deal with it. People agree to sponsor a research project for many reasons, but often they will have an agenda – personal, political or other – they want to promote through your research project. They may try in different ways to influence your research to fit this agenda, including trying to control your research question, limiting your access to sources of information (for instance limiting the people you could talk to) and systematically controlling your findings, including limiting your report's content and scope. Early warning signs include not disclosing why the study is being undertaken or explanations that don't appear to make sense.

Sponsors who do this are behaving unethically and inappropriately. If you think this is happening in your research project, you should immediately get advice from your academic supervisor about what to do. You might need to consider withdrawing from the study. This is part of the challenge of real-world research. You still need to manage your dual roles as researcher and insider, and part of your write-up should reflect any influence the sponsor has had. Ignoring this, or getting it wrong, can have disastrous consequences, as demonstrated by **Student research** in action 9.5.

Student research in action 9.5

A BUNCH OF COMPLETE BANKERS

Jie, a very determined student, had several options open to her in considering subjects for her master's project. She identified two attractive projects: one was on human resource management policies in her native China (her preferred choice) and the other was a paid project looking at investment policies for a bank in the City of London. Jie chose the banking project.

The bank was paying her very well, but also demanding that she fulfil a significant operational role within the organisation. Right from the start, though, her supervisor was concerned about the amount of time that she could give to her project. She ended up working nearly 60 hours a week, leaving little or no time or energy for her project. The bank also reneged on promised data to enable her to complete her project. In the end she was unable to submit a piece of coursework of sufficient quality to enable her to complete her course.

Doing research is rarely dull; people are certain not to do what you expect. All you can do is to be mindful of what is going on and make sure that you work to the best standards.

9.2.2 Research versus consultancy

Any field research can lead to conflicts between academic and practical expectations, but when you are employed by an organisation specifically to conduct your research and feedback the findings, they are inevitable. **Chapter 1 defined** consultancy as being employed to give advice to an organisation. Many researchers conduct consultancy projects for organisations, and many consultants engage in research projects. You need to be clear on the difference between your role as a researcher and your role as a consultant.

Research and consultancy are distinguished by a number of characteristics, as shown in **Table 9.1**. As we noted in **Chapter 1**, research projects and consultancy projects are often conducted for different purposes, even if the same person is doing

Table 9.1   Differences between research and consultancy

Issue	Research	Consultancy
Strategic purpose	Investigate an area of interest	Solve a problem
Motivation	Personal interest in the area	Improve the organisation in some way
Research object	As defined by the research questions in the study	Usually a bounded problem
Research question viewpoint	Ontology defined explicitly	Functional standpoint more relevant
Subject originality	Some element of novelty usually required	Rarely totally original; perceived novelty to the organisation important
Quality control	Process control through use of recognised and appropriate methodology executed in recognised ways	Little on the process, focused on the outcomes
Assumptions	All assumptions, including those of your research approach, must be clear from the outset	Usually focused on the assumptions of the prevailing 'business model'
Research audience	Assessors and possibly wider community	People from the organisation
Idea, pedigree, information basis	Based on identification of needs through analysis of extant literature	Based on perceived needs
Resource–quality trade-off	More likely to be quality-focused	More likely to be resource-focused
Presentation style	Formal academic, focused on the process and discussion	Formal, business-speak, focused on the 'bottom line'

the research. The consultant looks for solutions to a particular practical problem, and the researcher is more interested in finding out more about the area they are looking at. They are fundamentally different, not least because the consultant may be far less involved in 'pure' research.

Company-sponsored field research projects fall between research and pure consultancy, as shown in **Figure 9.2**. The starting point for research and consulting differs, with the consultant defining and bounding the areas for investigation at an early stage. This is vital, as the discussion on scope management has shown.

The consultant's role

A consultant can take one or more of the following roles:

● A **resource provider** – facilitating tasks to be carried out that people from within the organisation claim they do not have the time or capability to do (certain documentation activities or specialist technical knowledge).

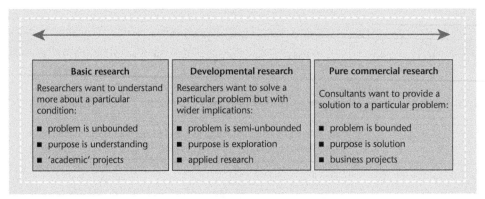

Figure 9.2 Differences between research and consulting projects

- An **inspector** – inspecting the way in which the process is being carried out.
- A **trainer** – rather than doing the job for the organisation, imparting the knowledge to the members of the organisation through training.
- An **integrator** – taking responsibility for a particular piece of work that needs inputs from people from different parts of the organisation.
- A **knowledge provider** – providing expertise in one or more specific areas or techniques.
- A **change agent** – providing the focus for activities, while keeping an overview of what is happening. People working within an organisation can be more inclined to accept the views of an outsider on changes than to move from entrenched positions at the behest of a colleague. As importantly, such a solution may allow individuals to 'save face'.
- An **honesty broker** – providing an external 'independent' viewpoint on a situation, which can be immensely beneficial. As one consultant commented, 'Sometimes people get too close to the coal face to see the wood for the trees!'

Students can take any of these roles, although the role of trainer is less common when there is a research objective. Each role comes with its own challenges. Thinking through this list is useful when discussing with an organisation which they expect you to take (see Block 1981 for further description of the roles of consultants).

If you run through the list above, none of these roles involves generating knowledge specifically. This is one of the ways in which not explicitly managing your dual roles as researcher and consultant can get you into trouble – you can get so involved in the consultant role that the researcher role falls by the wayside.

Organisations will clearly have different expectations as to how you would conduct yourself during a student project and how a professional consultant would behave. If the people in an organisation see your role as consultant rather than researcher, you will need to establish your credibility and that of your project extra carefully. A student will not necessarily have all the answers, but should know either where to get them or when to say that there are not answers. As demonstrated by **Student research in action 9.6**, you will also occasionally have to say 'no' to organisations.

Whilst you should always maintain the general ethical standards discussed in **Chapter 8**, there are also particular codes for consulting, such as those available through the Management Consultancies Association and the Institute of Management Consultants (see www.mca.org.uk or www.iconsulting.org.uk) in the UK. The effort of the student-consultant is only one part of the puzzle, however. A 1995 UK government report cited by Lynch (2001) concluded that 'it is difficult to do good work for a bad client, and it is difficult to do bad work for a good client' (Lynch 2001). The organisation therefore has to take part of the responsibility for the outcome of the work. In particular, the discussion in **Section 9.2.1** on sponsors who have a secret agenda may be worth reviewing.

9.2.3 Doing research in your own organisation

Extended research is tricky, but what if you are doing research in an organisation that you belong to permanently? Many postgraduates nowadays are sponsored on their degree programmes and in return are expected to do research projects of immediate benefit to their organisations; they may be limited by commercial confidentiality from gaining access to other organisations in their field of interest, or they simply do not have time or interest to look for data and access beyond their own work setting. Other students may use organisations in which they are members as a research setting, for example the University of Oxford Morris Dancing Society (strange but true).

Costley and her colleagues identify some issues facing 'insider researchers' in their own organisations (Costley et al. 2010), including:

- The impact of the organisational/professional context on what research can be done and how it can be done;
- The impact on the researcher's professional career and university degree;
- The need to consider power relationships with colleagues, managers and subordinates, and whether other organisational members can 'freely consent' to participating;
- Who actually owns the research.

It can be difficult for students to maintain **critical subjectivity** when they are doing research on their own organisations (employer or voluntary). They must keep a balance between the subjectivity required of being part of that organisation, and the critical thinking necessary to do research. Where critical thinking is missing, researchers simply describe the practices of that organisation as 'excellent', despite any evidence to the contrary. Insights for good studies come from a balance of 'this is good' and 'but this could be so much better.' This is because most organisations do not want to be considered as truly awful at what they do, whilst most managers can recognise that things are not perfect and could be improved.

9.3 What are the practical considerations in executing my research design?

In this section, we will consider three tasks which are fundamental to achieving your objectives for your research project. The first is that you will need to have a plan. The second is that you will need to assess your progress against that plan. The third is that – if you are working in a group – you will need to manage the group process as well as the plan.

9.3.1 How do I plan my research?

You should have a plan for your research project. It doesn't have to be complicated, but does need to be a realistic interpretation of what you think is going to happen and when, and how you will deal with inevitable problems. The main benefit is in the planning process, not in the outcome. 'The plan is nothing. Planning is everything.'

Drawing up an activity list

'Start the journey of a thousand miles with a single step.' To begin your journey, list out the main *milestones* (start date, meetings, submissions, approvals points, presentations) and, what you will have to do to get to each milestone (stages such as initial proposal, literature review, research design, data collection, data analysis, writing up, preparing report). Each is a mini-project that can itself be broken down into smaller activities taking no more than a few days each. This is your activity list. After identifying the activities, estimate how long each activity will take, and in what order you need to carry out these activities. Mark any activities where you need to complete one before starting another (e.g. initial proposal to be completed and approved before major work on literature review starts).

Estimating time to complete activities

Students tend to be either over-optimistic in estimating activity times ('I will be able to write a 100-page report in two days') or overly generous ('I will allow myself a week to write letters to companies, just in case'). *Over-optimism* creates problems during the entire project, since you will always be behind schedule, whilst *over-generosity* misleads you into thinking you are making good progress when you are making no real progress ('I wrote two sentences today – since the plan was only to write one sentence, I am a whole day ahead!').

You should estimate how much time it will take to complete an activity if you are equally likely to finish it early or late – the finishing time, in other words, where 50% of the time it will take less time to complete and 50% of the time it will take more time.

We do this because your overall objective is to finish the entire research project on time, not each individual activity. It doesn't matter if you finish almost every individual activity on time, if, in the end, you hand in your project report late because the last activity – writing up – took longer than you thought. You can use any time saved in completing an individual activity early by immediately starting on another activity. This may make a big difference at the end of the project, when you need it most.

You may want to write up your activity list, as shown in **Table 9.2**.

Table 9.2   An activity list for David's project

	Activity	Estimated time (days)	Dependency
	Defining		
A	Define project	10	--
B	Investigate literature and write literature review	20	A
	Designing		
C	Negotiate company access	2	B
D	Develop questionnaire	5	C
E	Pilot test questionnaire	2	D
F	Revise questionnaire	1	E
	Doing		
G	Distribute questionnaires	2	F
H	Collect questionnaires	3	G
I	Enter data from questionnaires into spreadsheet	2	H
J	Analyse questionnaire data	3	I
	Describing		
K	Write up results of data analysis	2	J
L	Produce first draft of project report	10	K
M	Give draft to supervisor for comments	4	L
N	Revise report into final draft	2	M
O	Print out and proofread project report	2	N
P	Copy and bind report	2	O
	Total time required	**72**	

There are a couple of behaviours that we have seen as supervisors, and that as researchers we also inevitably demonstrate (!). That doesn't make them any less dangerous for your project. One of the most dangerous is 'leaving things until the last minute'. We discuss procrastination with respect to writing your project report in **Chapter 14**, so you may want to peek ahead at that chapter.

With that in mind, now that you have prepared your preliminary project plan, there is one final step you need to take: analyse the project plan and revise it. The purpose of planning is to allow basic analysis to be carried out. The most basic project analysis will answer questions including:

- How long will the project take?
- Can I complete it on time?
- Do I need to add or remove any activities to make the project fit the time available?
- What happens if one or more elements of the project is delayed?

Drawing a Gantt chart

Although some people can analyse complex projects armed with only an activity list, most people find it easier to construct a *Gantt chart*. (These are named after Henry Gantt, who popularised them during the early 20th century for use in production planning.) Project managers often use Gantt charts for presenting project plans in a simple visual form. On a Gantt chart, time runs from left to right on the horizontal axis. Activities are represented by horizontal bars (see **Figure 9.3**) whose lengths are proportional to the amount of time involved, whilst milestones are indicated by diamonds (lozenges). The chart for **Table 9.2** is shown in **Figure 9.3**.

You can use a Gantt chart to see how long a project will take overall. Once you have marked each of your project activities, it is easy to see which activities could overlap

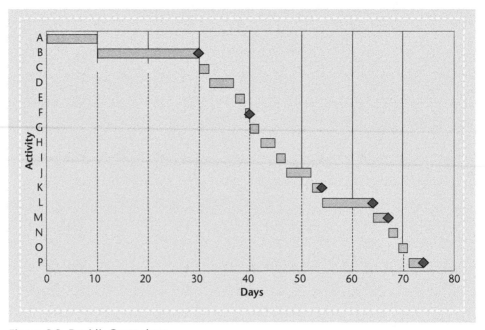

Figure 9.3 David's Gantt chart

if you need to shorten the project. The process of constructing the chart is itself beneficial (you will ask yourself lots of questions in preparing it).

You can easily draw Gantt charts using a specialised software package (e.g. Microsoft Project) or using a spreadsheet. We find that you cannot beat starting off with a piece of flipchart paper and some post-it notes. Put the paper landscape and mark out the time you have available (today on the left, the completion date on the right). Then break up the months and weeks between the two. The Post-its become the activities from your list. Mark any dependencies with an arrow.

Risk and opportunity

Every research project has a certain degree of uncertainty and generally you cannot determine what this will be in advance. Uncertainty creates both risk and opportunity for you as a researcher.

Risk is the downside of uncertainty. Put simply, it is what could go wrong in your project. **Student research in action 9.4** illustrates how risk can affect project outcomes. We recommend you consider the main risks to your project and what actions you will take to remove their causes or effects.

Finally, to respond to risks, always leave a **buffer** – at least a week at the end of your project as a 'safety zone' between when you finish your last activity and submission of any documents. As we will discuss, do not be tempted to use this for any other purpose such as 'completing write-up' – it is there for the inevitable uncertainties that will emerge.

9.3.2 Monitoring your project's progress

During your research project, you should frequently (if not constantly) check your progress by comparing how much work you have completed against the plan. Make sure to update your project plan, and check to see the effects of any changes (they always happen!). Most importantly, you should count an activity as complete only when it is 100% complete, finished and delivered. Not before! Professional project managers have found that a project spends 90% of its time 90% complete.

As well as monitoring your own progress, you should use regular meetings with your supervisor and/or project sponsor to report honestly what you have (and have not) managed to get done since your last meeting. Other people can only give you good advice if you are completely honest about your progress. Experienced supervisors often develop an uncanny ability to interpret what students actually mean when they are asked about their progress. For example, 'I'm almost finished' means 'I'm just getting started', and, as in **Student research in action 9.7**, 'Everything's going fine' can mean anything but that.

Student research in action 9.7
IT'S GOING WELL – HONESTLY

Martha's project proposal sounded good – investigate how the US retailer Wal-Mart was gaining competitive advantage through the use of its IT and operations capabilities, and whether this posed a threat to European retailers through Wal-Mart's European operations. The project was

▶

undoubtedly current, topical and researchable. Many books and articles had been written on Wal-Mart. Martha even had contacts with one of Wal-Mart's competitors to enable her to collect data.

In her first meeting with the supervisor, research questions and the relevant literature were agreed. Martha enthusiastically spent the next few months reading everything she could find about Wal-Mart, including popular business books, plus lots of newspaper and magazine stories about the company downloaded from the web. She had lots of information about Wal-Mart, little of which could be used to answer the research questions, and not much of it reliable enough to be used in a master's dissertation. Overwhelmed by the sheer amount of material on Wal-Mart, she decided to concentrate on finding out what computer hardware systems Wal-Mart was using.

As the summer went on, Martha's supervisor kept asking for information about the progress of the research project, and when he would be able to see a draft of the project report. She kept reporting that everything was 'fine, honestly', although no written work was forthcoming. On the day that dissertations were due, Martha turned in a project report that rehashed the Wal-Mart story with information everyone knew, but didn't shed any light on competitive advantage or Wal-Mart's effect on European retail competition. The project was a resounding failure.

Managing safety/buffer time

You can use a safety margin or buffer to make sure that if problems do occur – anything from illness to a computer crashing or losing pieces of research data – your overall project completion will not be delayed. Suppose that you reach your first milestone – a completed draft of your literature review – two days early. You might be tempted to take some time off after spending a few weeks working on your research project, particularly if you are ahead of schedule. We suggest not – you will lose two days' buffer that you could use later to offset a late activity finish, when it really starts to matter.

Our final issue for progress is the inevitable changes that will occur as you progress through your research. This is illustrated by **Student research in action 9.8**.

Student research in action 9.8

THE DEUX JOHNS

John and Jon were investigating the motivation levels of key managers and how this was or could be monitored by human resource (HR) managers over time for an MBA project. During the project, they established what they believed to be a managerial ability of managers, which they called 'dynamic criticality'. This was the ability to discern well within a situation; to identify, from a mass of data, the elements of importance; to act on these elements, ignoring more spurious elements or noise; and to change this focus as the reality changed. They believed that this ability was under-utilised in the selection criteria most firms used when choosing managers. Indeed, in their interviews with general managers, this ability appeared to be one of the most needed, but in interviews with a group of HR managers, this factor was not recognised.

John and Jon focused their work on developing a profile of dynamic criticality and were contemplating putting together a series of exercises to test the strength of this factor in an individual. This would have taken a considerable amount of time leaving them with little time to complete their main work. Further, dynamic criticality did not actually address the research questions in their project. They needed to decide whether to continue developing a model and testing for dynamic criticality, which might not even be possible and which their supervisor believed had been tried already, or refocus on their original project, and pursue the new idea at a later date.

Imagine that, like John and Jon in **Student research in action 9.8**, you have a 'blinding insight' into what you believe is vitally important, but it is not directly connected to your research questions. This is a great opportunity. Should you:

- Pursue it – ditch everything else and go with the new idea? After all, research is about being creative, isn't it?
- File it for later – it sounds good now, but will it sound so good in a few months' time? Park it somewhere safe (for example write a one-page summary of your idea), and if you have time, explore it when the main work is complete.
- Ignore it completely – you'll soon forget it anyway, and concentrate all your efforts on the main work. There'll be another great idea coming along anytime now.

If you decide to pursue an opportunity that arises after you have defined your research project, you risk having to discard all the work you have done up to that point, for example any data you have already collected. This is highly risky in a short project, because you may not have enough time to change direction and complete your study, as illustrated by **Student research in action 9.9**.

 Student research in action 9.9
SLEEPERS AWAKE

Whilst investigating a large bed manufacturer's distribution and marketing system in order to identify opportunities for cost savings, Juanita became interested in how the company introduced new products. It was an interesting process, with what appeared to be huge opportunities for improvement. Indeed, as the investigation progressed, she spent more and more time looking at new products and less looking at the distribution and marketing systems. This deviation from her original research question was not noticed until she submitted her project report to her university supervisor. Neither the company nor her supervisor was impressed with the change, which had not been sanctioned by either side, despite the opportunity for the organisation that the new project presented.

If you have a well-defined project plan and have made good progress, you might be able to risk a limited exploration of the new insight rather than discarding what you have done so far. Check out what is known about the area or ask the opinions of some knowledgeable experts such as your project advisor. You should be able to decide fairly quickly whether the insight adds value to your project, and whether you can build on your original research plan.

Finally, even though pursuing or postponing your insight may create extra work for your project, you may lose out if you ignore it completely. Insights are gems. You should keep track of them even if their time has not come, and even if you have to adapt, combine or otherwise modify them to use them – whatever you do, don't lose them.

9.3.3 Working as part of a project team

Students increasingly work together on research projects in pairs or groups for both educational and practical reasons. Employers value graduates who can work effectively with other people, whilst the expansion of higher education generally creates pressures for fewer individual assessments. Either way, working as part of a **project team** or group means that you will need to manage the interpersonal as well as the personal and research process.

Our experiences in supervising students working together raise some intriguing questions. Why do some research project teams work really well together, whilst others end up not speaking to, hating or even wanting to physically harm each other? Why do some project teams produce highly creative results, whilst others, despite the inclusion of some very creative people, produce mediocre work?

Working on your research project with other people increases both risk and opportunities. Team dynamics can significantly affect the research process and outcome: just as uncertainty created both risks and opportunities, teamwork can create either synergy – better results than the individuals could create working alone – or disruption – worse results than working alone. Synergy is more rare than people assume and it will only occur under certain circumstances. It isn't automatically created when people work together. Since group dynamics is taught in most business and management courses, we recommend that you review your course materials and/ or discuss this with course tutors if you do have significant problems. Organisational researchers have studied group and team performance for a long time, and knowledge of group processes can be useful. In order to understand group processes, you could review group process models, for example 'storming, norming, performing' (Hackman 2002), or 'collection, entrenchment, resolution, synergy and decline' (Maylor 2017). Many students have found it useful to look at group role descriptions, such as Belbin (1993), to see how to make the best use of each person in the group.

Larson and Lafasto (1989) have identified the following characteristics of highly effective groups:

- They have a clear, elevating goal – a sense of mission must be created through the development of an objective which is understood, important, worthwhile and personally or collectively challenging
- The responsibilities of each group member are worked out and communicated, and each person is held accountable to the group for the discharge of these responsibilities
- They have an active communications strategy, based around face-to-face meetings but also encompassing the use of emails, text messaging and so on
- They have competent team members, with a balance between personal and technical competence
- They foster a collaborative climate – encouraging reliance on others within the team, and where good work is performed, it is recognised
- They set high standards – through individual standards, team pressure and knowledge of the consequences of failure
- They deal with conflict as and when it arises.

You may want to devote some time during your first team meeting establishing how you will handle the group process, and use these points to help establish some goals for managing, and the principles. In particular, we have found it effective to manage the initial project start-up, group meetings and communication, and allocation of group responsibilities, which are particular leverage points for establishing good group practices.

Managing group meetings

Although there is no way you can escape *group meetings* completely, if not carefully managed they often take up a good deal of time relative to what they actually accomplish. You are more likely to get things accomplished if you try to manage meetings as systematically as the rest of your research process. In this section, we provide a few suggestions about good practice, so you can make the most of the time you and your group spend on your research project:

1. **Always meet with a specific purpose**. Your project group needs a specific reason to get together. A meeting should not be held just for social interaction, because you have a regular meeting scheduled or to give everyone a warm fuzzy feeling of progress. Each meeting should have a clear purpose, for example to update weekly progress, compile data or plan the project report.
2. **Prepare before the meeting**. Circulate in advance the location and timing, agenda and any background on the items to be discussed. The agenda should tell team members what information they will be expected to update during the meeting and what critical issues they may need to discuss. You should also take into account that most people's attention declines to zero after 20 minutes, and after two hours you are unlikely to make any constructive progress: people will agree to anything at this point simply to get out of the meeting.
3. **Manage the meeting**. Nominate someone to chair the meeting, whose role it is to facilitate constructive debate while limiting the scope of discussion to the matter in hand. Unless the group agrees otherwise, the role of chair should rotate between meetings. The chair should make sure that the discussion moves forward, rather than getting stuck debating the same points, prevent any one member from dominating the discussions and regularly summarise progress and ask for conclusions to be drawn based on the discussions. A skilful chair will be able to steer the group towards consensus and away from majority rule. This makes sure that everyone has bought in to a decision, and makes carrying it out far easier than if there is dissent.
4. **Follow up the meeting**. Nominate someone to record the minutes of the meeting, and then send copies of the minutes with action points and responsibilities listed against each (see the example in **Table 9.3**). A meeting's conclusions and action points should fit on one side of A4 paper so that they are read rather than filed or thrown away. These minutes and action points then form the basis of the next meeting's agenda, so that the person who said they would carry out a task has a natural responsibility to the group to do it. They also know that should they fail to carry out an action, this will be identified at the next meeting.

Managing group communication

You may be able to use email (or texting) to substitute for face-to-face meetings and other forms of contact. However, when things start to go wrong, relying on email can quickly make them much worse. Because email lacks the cues such as body language that we use in interpreting what other people mean, as compared with what they say, we can easily misinterpret what an email says. This can lead to unnecessary friction in a group.

Table 9.3   Sample of minutes of group project meeting

Date and time: 21 February, 10.30p.m., All Bar One
Present: Chloe, Andre, Felia, Yee Ping
Apologies: Bill (emailed 20 February to say in hospital after hang-gliding accident)
Agreed and signed the minutes of the last meeting prepared by Felia.
During this meeting we discussed our creative strategy and the budget. Everyone was happy
with progress but Yee Ping had had difficulties getting the information she needed about
billboard costs.

Main outstanding issues	Action
Chloe to help Yee Ping with budget information (to be ready for next meeting on 28th)	C & YP
Felia to complete mock up of life-size orange kangaroo (bring to meeting on 28th)	F
Andre to liaise with Chloe and Yee Ping to finalise budget spreadsheet (during the week)	A
Bill to get himself out of hospital as quickly as possible to edit the report (28th)	B
Next meeting 28 February, 5p.m., Saracen's Head. Minutes prepared by Andre	All

Source: Adapted from Nairn (2003)

Managing responsibilities

In an individual project, it is clear that you are responsible for each and every activity. In a team project, you must clarify the responsibilities of each member and the entire group. This is much simpler if you have already prepared a well-defined project breakdown and activity list. **Table 9.4** shows how each activity has been allocated to one or more team members, when activities need to be completed and any dependencies between them (in the notes column). You should prepare an updated activity table for each team meeting.

An activity table will work better when the way you assign responsibilities takes account of each team member's skills and preferences. Some people may prefer to work only on activities that make use of their existing competences (for example volunteering to analyse data after doing well in statistics), whilst others may want to try out new activities to develop new skills (for example volunteering as an editor to learn how to edit). Not everyone needs to be a technical specialist but not everyone has to learn how to do everything. Support and tolerance are more important.

Dealing with conflict

Working with other people can be stressful – naming one of the group process phases 'storming' or 'entrenchment' in the group dynamics literature attests to that. Whilst managing the teamwork process to minimise potential sources of conflict is a pre-emptive strategy, you should also think about how you will handle conflict when it does arise. This is especially useful when conflicts occur due to differences in people's expectations and perceptions of what is happening.

Table 9.4 Activity table

Activity	When	Who	Notes
Write outline of Chapter 4	Mon a.m.	All	
Write section 4.1	Mon p.m.	HT & MR	
Complete graphics for Chapter 3	Mon p.m.	WF	
Complete telephone interviews	Mon p.m.	KR	
Write section 4.2	Tues a.m.	HT & WF	Relies on 4.1 being complete
Outline presentation	Tues a.m.	MR	
Write section 4.3	Tues p.m.	HT & WF	Relies on 4.2 being complete
Transcribe telephone interview data	Tues p.m.	KR & MR	Relies on interviews being complete
Analyse interview data	Wed a.m.	KR & WF	Relies on transcription being complete
Write section 4.4	Wed a.m.	HT & MR	Relies on section 4.3 being complete
Write conclusion to Chapter 4	Wed p.m.	HT & MR	Needs all 4 sections complete
Outline Chapter 5 – data analysis	Thurs a.m.	All	Relies on chapter 4 and the data analysis being complete
Write up data analysis	Thurs p.m.	KR & MR	
Extract key findings into presentation	Thurs p.m.	HT & WF	
Prepare graphics for Chapter 5 and presentation	Fri a.m.	WF	
Compile report and check flow	Fri a.m.	HT, KR & MR	Needs all sections complete, graphics to be inserted for Chapter 5 later
Integrate Chapter 5 graphics and print report	Fri p.m.	All	
Practise presentation	Fri p.m.	All	

Three principles for managing conflict, especially between two team members, are:

- Deal directly with the person concerned, wherever possible
- 'Seek first to understand, then be understood'
- Assume that people are acting from good intentions until proven otherwise.

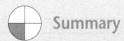

Summary

In this chapter, we have considered issues that arise when doing field research, where you are collecting data from organisations and/or individuals in their natural setting. These issues included how to gain access to organisations, balancing requirements and the practicalities of planning, progressing and working with groups in research projects. Although it is possible to gain access to organisations by presenting them with a project proposal, you will often need to gain access through the agency of a person, including your personal contacts and/or the contacts of people in your personal networks. Organisations will expect you to provide them with information about your project, and about yourself, so that you have credibility.

When you have responsibilities to both your academic institution and your project sponsor, there is usually some tension between the objectives of each. These may be particularly difficult if your project sponsor has a hidden agenda and tries to influence your research. Some research is closer to consultancy than to research, in that the organisation expects you to give it advice, rather than simply reporting on a state of affairs. In this case, you should behave ethically and professionally, but remember your academic responsibilities.

We then considered the practicalities of executing a research design. A plan is essential, and the benefit of that plan is in the understanding gained in the process of its production rather than the multi-coloured print-out. Without this, the second consideration is impossible – being able to monitor progress against that plan. Lastly, working in groups is increasingly commonplace, and not without its own problems. There are many opportunities to ensure that the process remains constructive.

Answers to key questions

How can I gain access to the organisations and people I want to study?

- Warm contacts are usually more successful than cold contacts for gaining access, but either can yield the access that you require.
- Personal networks are usually most effective in gaining initial points of entry to organisations, and from there to find the relevant people to talk to.
- You will need to be prepared, with project ideas and CVs ready, and flexible to find avenues that will yield benefits for both you and the organisation.

How can I manage the expectations of different project stakeholders?

- We advocate putting your academic requirements as the highest priority in your research.
- A managed scope statement will greatly assist in providing the basis on which expectations of your work will be set.

How can I balance academic research and consultancy in a sponsored project?

- Give explicit thought up-front to which roles you are playing and manage those roles carefully.
- As part of your research design, recognise that research is the opportunity to investigate a topic of interest, whereas consultancy is giving advice to an

organisation. You will need to have elements of both in your work and manage expectations accordingly.

What practical issues should I consider in managing my project?

- Prepare a task list, then a visual plan and then analyse it to see what could go wrong and how you will prevent this from happening.

- Monitor progress against the plan. Where there are deviations, changes should be made to the plan. Be honest in reporting progress.

- Work with your group – start out by managing expectations and agreeing behaviours. Use efficient meetings and clear documentation to provide clear responsibilities and accountabilities.

 ## References

Belbin, R.M. 1993. *Team Roles at Work*. Oxford: Butterworth Heinemann.

Block, P. 1981. *Flawless Consulting*. Austin, TX: Learning Concepts.

Costley, Carol, Elliott, Geoffrey and Gibbs, Paul. 2010. *Doing Work Based Research: Approaches to Enquiry for Insider-Researchers*. Los Angeles: Sage.

Granovetter, Mark S. 1973. The strength of weak ties, *American Journal of Sociology*, 78 (6): 1360–80.

Hackman, J. Richard 2002. *Leading Teams: Setting the Stage for Great Performances*. Harvard, MA: HBS Press.

Larson, C.E. and Lafasto, F.M.J. 1989. *Teamwork*. London: Sage.

Lynch, P. 2001. Professionalism and ethics. In S. Sadler (ed.), *Management Consultancy*, 2nd edn. London: Kogan Page, pp. 60–80.

Maister, David H. 1993. *Managing the Professional Service Firm*. New York: Free Press.

Maylor, Harvey 2017. *Project Management*, 5th edn. London: Prentice Hall.

Travers, Jeffrey and Milgram, Stanley 1969. An experimental study of the small world problem, *Sociometry*, 32(4): 425–43.

 ## Additional resources

Buchanan, D., Boddy, D. and McCalman, J. 1988. Getting in, getting on, getting out and getting back. In A. Bryman (ed.), *Doing Research in Organisations*. London: Routledge.

Russ-Eft, D., Burns, J.Z., Dean, P.J., Hatcher, T., Otte, F.L. and Preskill, H. 1999. *Standards on Ethics and Integrity*. Baton Rouge, LA: Academy of Human Resource Development

 ## Key terms

Discussion questions

1. What is the difference in the nature of the activities you will be doing in D3, compared to the other phases of the project?

2. What problems would you expect in gaining access to individuals and organisations for the purpose of carrying out your research?

3. A friend has suggested that you join a marketing project, looking at the marketing strategies of Virgin, The Body Shop and Apple. The project requires you to have access to the organisations. Do you envisage any problems with this?

4. Investigate the ethical requirements of your organisation. How do they compare with the general principles set out in this chapter? How do they compare with the requirements of one of the organisations listed (for example the American Psychological Association)?

5. Would it be ethical for you to do a research project with a tobacco company? Would a financial incentive help you to make the decision?

6. You have been working in a team within an organisation, looking at how it has adapted to new hours and methods of working over a period of several months. During an interview with the plant manager, you see a note on her desk that has asked her to nominate groups who could be eligible for redundancy under a new cost-cutting drive. She has pencilled in the name of the team you have been working with. Do you tell them?

7. What are the ethical challenges that your project is likely to face?

8. Who are the customers of your project? What are the requirements of each and how will you go about managing them?

9. Imagine you were taking the role of consultant in one project and researcher in another. What differences would you expect in the way you would carry out the work? Are there any inherent conflicts between these two roles?

10. You are carrying out a project in an organisation in order to obtain an academic qualification. How would you resolve the conflicts between the requirements of the organisation and your academic institution?

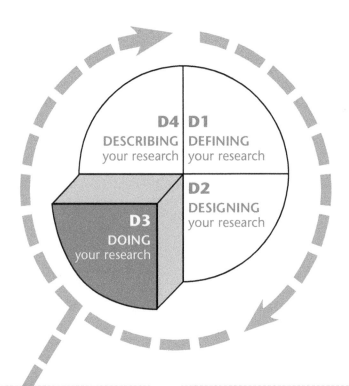

Relevant chapters
13 How do I write up my report?
14 What do I do now?

Key challenges
- Making sense of your findings
- Presenting your research to others
- Reflecting and learning from your research

4

Relevant chapters
1 What is research?
2 What should I study?
3 How do I find information?

Key challenges
- Understanding what academic research is
- Generating and clarifying ideas
- Using sources of information

1

D4
DESCRIBING
your research

D1
DEFINING
your research

D2
DESIGNING
your research

D3
DOING
your research

Relevant chapters
9 How do I do field research?
10 What do my quantitative data mean(1)?
11 What do my quantitative data mean(2)?
12 What do my qualitative data mean?

Key challenges
- Practical considerations in doing research
- **Describing data using simple statistics**
- Carrying out statistical tests
- Interpreting words and actions

3

Relevant chapters
4 What is my research approach?
5 How do I do quantitative research?
6 How do I do qualitative research?
7 How do I do case study research?
8 How do I make sure my research is ethical?

Key challenges
- Choosing a research approach
- Choosing a research design
- Collecting data using quantitative methods
- Collecting data using qualitative methods
- Integrating quantitative and qualitative methods

2

10

chapter

What do my quantitative data mean(1)?

Basic statistical analysis

 Key questions

- How can I record and manage quantitative data?
- How can I describe my quantitative data using statistics?
- What computer programs can I use to analyse quantitative data?
- How can I test relationships between variables or differences between groups using statistics?
- How can I interpret my data?

 Learning outcomes

At the end of this chapter, you should be able to:
- Record quantitative data in a data matrix
- Describe the distribution of variables using statistics
- Analyse relationships between pairs or variables using statistics

Contents

Introduction

If you have taken a quantitative or mixed-method approach to data collection, you will end up with some quantitative data in the form of numbers to analyse, especially if you have used a survey, experiment or secondary analysis, to see whether your evidence supports your hypotheses and to answer your research questions. This chapter and the next will introduce you to some basic statistical methods for describing your data and testing relationships between concepts. You will also be introduced to some ways of understanding how much confidence you should have in your findings.

Chapter 4 and **Chapter 5** described an essential feature of quantitative research as the extensive planning that goes on before you start collecting data, including being able to decide what data to collect, how to collect it, how to analyse it and how to present it in your project report even before you start collecting data. Before you analyse your data, you can also decide how to record your data in a format you can use for analysis and check for any errors and missing data.

Although the qualitative approach puts relatively low emphasis on quantitative measurement and statistical testing, having a feel for numbers can still be helpful. Ethnographers still formally or informally apply some sort of quantitative yardstick to their data, even if just terms such as 'most' or 'usually'. Even if you have not planned to do statistical analysis, the emergent nature of qualitative or mixed-method research designs means that some opportunities may arise. Being able to verify that your statements are true can be useful even for ethnographers.

Section 10.1 reviews how to record your quantitative data and prepare them for further analysis. This may be using common spreadsheet programs such as Microsoft Excel or powerful statistical programs such as Minitab and SPSS, or even by hand if you prefer.

Once you have processed your raw data, you will want to understand them better. **Section 10.2** will show you how to summarise and describe your data using simple statistics such as measures of frequency, measures of central tendency and measures of dispersion. Because simple statistics can be effective for analysing and presenting data from small-scale social research (Denscombe 2003: 236), we focus on statistical analysis that you can do in a spreadsheet such as Excel or with a calculator. The section will also describe how you can understand which statistical tests are appropriate, given the type of design you have used.

If you have taken a quantitative approach, you will also want to examine relationships between variables. **Section 10.3** presents some simple statistics – inferential statistics – that you can use to measure the relationships between pairs of variables, such as chi-square tests, t-tests, analysis of variance (ANOVA) and simple linear regression as ways of testing hypotheses and drawing conclusions about the population based on your measures of a sample. It also briefly discusses the effect of the normal distribution on your selection of appropriate statistical test.

Section 10.4 explains how you can interpret these statistical tests to see whether you have answered your research questions. We describe some useful ways to present your data and your statistical analysis to support your interpretation. We point out some common errors in interpreting statistics you should try to avoid. We also discuss the criteria by which the quality of quantitative research is judged.

Whether you plan to analyse your data using statistics or using thematic analysis, which we discuss in **Chapter 12**, after you have finished this chapter you should be

able to analyse quantitative data using simple statistical tests. You should also understand which tests are appropriate for a particular type of data.

Moreover, no matter what research problem you are investigating or which research
strategy you have selected, you will probably collect some quantitative data as part of
your research project, or read other people's research findings that have been based
on them. Reading about these techniques will help you to make sense of qualitative
and quantitative research findings and judge the findings of other people's research
as well as journalism and consulting.

10.1 Managing your quantitative data

If you feel comfortable with the deductive – or scientific – approach, you may also feel
comfortable with numbers and statistical analysis, and already have some practice
and skills in working with numbers. Even if you prefer the ethnographic approach
and feel a bit apprehensive about statistical analysis, computer technology has made
it painless to record, organise and analyse numerical data. It is even possible to collect and analyse your data completely on your computer – using techniques such as
computer-assisted interviewing (CAI). There are many cookbook-type guides – and
even some computer programs – that let the most confirmed number-phobe do simple statistics.

One of the most comprehensive guides to statistics we know is *Multivariate Data
Analysis* by Hair, Black, Babin and Anderson, now in its seventh edition. Alternatively,
for those of you who have decided to use SPSS for data management and statistical
analysis, Andy Field's third edition of *Discovering Statistics Using SPSS* provides excellent guidance. It will – if followed – take you from complete novice to (relative!)
expert and provides an overview of the different types of analysis available to you
depending on what you are examining.

10.1.1 A systematic approach to quantitative data

Before you can use the data you have gathered, you need to process them so that
you can use them to answer your research questions. The first step is to write them
down or enter them electronically so that they are in the same place and in the same
format.

A key success factor in analysing quantitative data is to think about how you will
record, manage and analyse your data before you start collecting them:

- Decide what variables and what characteristics of your respondents (the social
  units you are studying) you will capture as data.
- Decide what you will measure for each variable or characteristic. A variable could
  be as simple as age or gender or could be a psychometric scale sourced from the
  literature.
- Decide how you will record each measure.

The process is shown in **Figure 10.1**.

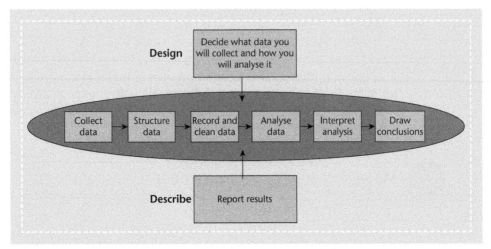

Figure 10.1 A structured approach for analysing quantitative data

10.1.2 Recording and managing your data

You will usually need to process your data in their original form, or **raw data**, before you can use them in any analysis. This processing includes coding the data, entering the data into a format you can analyse and checking for errors or missing data.

Depending on the research design you select for quantitative research, your data may be recorded in the form of survey responses, experimental data or secondary data (see **Chapter 5**). Your first step is to develop some sort of system for capturing your raw data, which may be numbers or words or even pictures or sounds. You need to decide how to end up with numbers.

Your first step is to combine the raw data from your individual records into a single, common format. We recommend that you develop the format for recording your raw data early in the research process, especially if you are collecting data from a large number of respondents or on a large number of variables. If possible, you should also have a dry run of entering your data into your spreadsheet before you start collecting them, and analysing your data using the statistical tests you plan to use but with 'made-up' data. Doing this will reveal many design problems while you can still fix them.

Once you have collected your data, we recommend that you spend some time getting to know them, even if you have collected your data electronically. As in **Student research in action 10.1**, understanding your data thoroughly before you start analysing it can be key to success. There is no substitute for a creative and intuitive feel for your data rather than just 'number-crunching' (O'Leary 2004: 184).

 Student research in action 10.1
METROSEXUAL

Charles was working on a placement project in which he needed to analyse data from every station in the Paris Metro. Before getting too deep into the technical details of how he would analyse the data, he looked at creating a database to hold the details of each station – which had never before

▶

been combined in a single place. As he set up the database, it became obvious that the same information was not available for each station and the accuracy of the data varied wildly. This ruled out some methods for analysing the data, so he didn't waste a lot of time chasing down blind alleys by choosing the wrong methods.

10.1.3 Organising your data

Before you analyse your data, you must put your raw data, however you have collected and recorded them, into a format suitable for analysis. Depending on how much data you plan to collect and how you plan to analyse them, you can tabulate your data:

- By hand
- In a table in a word-processing document such as Microsoft Word
- In a spreadsheet such as Microsoft Excel
- In a specialised program such as Minitab, SPSS or SNAP. We come across SPSS far more than other programs.

Two factors you may want to consider when you decide which to use are:

1. How much data will you collect? Multiply the number of respondents by the number of measures to get a rough idea of the size of your data set. Some computer packages have limitations as to how much data can be stored.
2. How do you plan to analyse the data? Unless you are going to use advanced statistics to analyse your data (more about this in **Chapter 11**), you may find that learning a specialised statistical program may cost you too much time and effort. **Student research in action 10.2(a)** introduces an example that we will return to several times during this chapter.

Student research in action 10.2(a)

NATALIA'S HEAVENLY DELIGHTS

Natalia was investigating whether women entrepreneurs from South Asian backgrounds found it difficult to get financing from high street banks. She decided to interview a number of women about their experiences in starting up businesses, which ranged from florists to nurseries. She also collected data from a number of banks about their lending policies. After several months, Natalia had enough data to start her analysis. She decided to use a spreadsheet to record and analyse the data she had collected, since that would help her get to know the data and see whether she was ready to stop collecting more and get on with the final parts of her research.

By hand

Most people find it easiest to use a table, or **data matrix**, for this. A simple format for a data matrix is to use rows to represent your cases (each separate organisation, household, individual or other social unit) and columns to represent each variable or characteristic of the case you have recorded. **Table 10.1** shows an example data matrix.

Table 10.1 A data matrix for respondents

Student	Date	Sex	Age	Course	Bank	Credit cards	Overdraft
John White	10/9	Male	19	ENGR	HSBC	No	No
Sara Jones	10/9	Female	20	SOC	HBOS	Yes	No
Amit Chaudhari	11/9	Male	19	BUS	Abbey	No	Yes
Om Puri	11/9	Male	21	ENGR	NatWest	No	Yes
Saffi Walden	12/9	Female	28	BUS	IF	Yes	No

If you only have a small quantitative data set, you could draw a simple data matrix by hand and fill in your responses, which you can analyse by hand or with a calculator. This is unlikely if you have a large sample or many questions, but it might be true if you have a small sample or are analysing only a small part of your data quantitatively. An advantage of this method is that you understand your data much better. You might find this useful when you are developing your research design (for example what will the data matrix for the data I collect in this field experiment look like?), or when you are recording your first few cases. A slightly more sophisticated version of this is recording your data using a word-processing program such as Microsoft Word.

Spreadsheets

Whilst recording data by hand is a good way to start organising your raw data, and may be all that you need if you have fairly simple questions and few responses, you will usually need to use more sophisticated methods if you have more than a little data to record and analyse. Doing it by hand gets tedious and if you make a mistake, you need to tippex it out or start over again.

Most students are already familiar with a computer spreadsheet program such as Microsoft Excel, a logical step up from hand tabulation. A spreadsheet allows you to enter both quantitative and qualitative responses (verbal data or observation) which is useful if you have included open-ended questions or responses, as shown in **Student research in action 10.2(b)**. A spreadsheet can deal with a large number of responses and a large number of variables, although some large social surveys would exceed a spreadsheet's capabilities.

Student research in action 10.2(b)

NATALIA'S HEAVENLY DELIGHTS (CONTINUED)

Natalia set up one spreadsheet so that she had a row for each person she had interviewed and a column for each variable or other issue she had collected data on. She set up another spreadsheet so that she had a row for each high street bank and a column for each aspect of its lending policy. She carefully labelled each column with a name for the variable, a description of the units (if any) that the measure had been collected in, and a brief explanation of the variable. Then she entered

▶

the data in the form of numbers or words as appropriate. For example, in the column Age (years at last birthday), she entered the appropriate figure. In the column Reason for starting own business (early experience), Natalia summarised any critical incidents that the women entrepreneurs had mentioned from their own childhoods. She carefully entered the data from each interview until the spreadsheet was complete.

Coding your data

Like Natalia, you may find it convenient to use a row for each respondent and a column for each question, although you can also use a row for each question and a column for each respondent instead. **Table 10.2** shows the first few rows of a sample data matrix.

Something that you might note in **Table 10.2** is how compact the data entry is when you represent qualitative data using numbers compared with recording qualitative data. In the table, we used a numerical code to represent each possible response to each question. Your codes should be complete (one for every response) and unique (each code is assigned to only one response).

Substituting numbers for words, as shown in **Figure 10.2**, makes data entry much quicker (and potentially more accurate), for example instead of typing in 'strongly agree' each time it has been circled by your respondent, you can type in '1'. This, of course assumes that 1 relates to strongly agree! Assigning numbers to verbal responses is known as **coding**, and, somewhat confusingly, entering the codes associated with responses is also often called coding. (Coding is also used for one of the main steps in thematic analysis of qualitative data, but in that sense it refers to processing words (or images) into other words. We will clarify this in **Chapter 12**.)

If you decided on a coding scheme when you designed your questionnaire or other data collection instrument, you will be well ahead at this point. Experienced

Table 10.2 A data matrix for responses

Respondent	Library	Residential	Catering	Parking	Social	Sports
001	3	4	4	2	4	5
002	2	5	3	2	3	3
003	4	4	3	3	4	4
004	2	3	2	2	1	3

4. Sex: ☐ Male [1] ☐ Female [2]

5. Country: ☐ Denmark [1] ☐ Finland [2] ☐ Norway [3] ☐ Sweden [4]

Figure 10.2 Examples of a coding scheme

researchers often design questionnaires or interview schedules to show the codes as well as the responses, as in **Figure 10.2**.

Recording open-ended questions and blank responses

You will seldom collect data using only closed-ended questions: you will usually provide some opportunities for open-ended responses. It is up to you whether you record the answers to open-ended questions in your data table. In some cases, it may be useful to list all the responses to an open-ended question or response (such as 'other – please specify') and then convert the most frequent responses to numerical codes. In other cases, you might want to use the techniques for qualitative data analysis presented in **Chapter 12** instead.

Items that respondents have skipped or incorrectly answered present more of a problem. There are several ways to deal with blank responses. In some cases, it might be possible to follow up with the respondent and obtain the correct data. Obviously, if you have not obtained permission to follow up a questionnaire or interview, or have used anonymous respondents, this won't be possible.

In other cases, other pieces of data may help you to predict what the response probably would be. For example, if someone omits to answer whether he/she is single or has a partner, but later responds to a question that asks for information about his/her partner, you might be able to go back and enter data for the earlier question.

If you get more than a few blank responses, this often signals problems with your sample or instrument or protocol. Missing data can create significant problems, especially when you have a smallish data set and are trying to use advanced statistical techniques. You may want to consult the research methods literature for ways to assign values for missing data, if they would substantially reduce your effective sample size. You should always analyse both your questionnaires and raw data to look for patterns in nonresponses. If many respondents are only filling out the first part of a questionnaire and leaving the rest blank, it's probably too long. If many respondents refuse to answer a particular question, you may be asking for information they don't have, or it may be too sensitive to answer. If the omissions are intentional rather than inadvertent, this might bias your findings.

In any case, if there is a clear pattern of missing data, you may run into problems later on. If an individual respondent has omitted to answer many items in a questionnaire (for example answered the first page and no more), it's probably best to omit that whole questionnaire. If there are many nonresponses to a questionnaire item, you may have to omit that item from further analysis, as they usually indicate a serious problem with that item. Either way, this will reduce your sample size, but increase the quality of your findings.

Types of quantitative data

Getting to know your raw data requires understanding what type of measures each type of data you have collected belongs to, before you start focusing on the magnitude and patterns in the numbers. There are four types of quantitative data, and understanding the differences between these is important, because it affects what they mean and what you can do with them.

The first type is **nominal**, or 'in name only'. Any number you assign to a nominal variable is arbitrary, rather than an essential aspect of that variable. Many qualitative variables are converted to nominal values in scientific research. For example, you might record the sex of a respondent as a 1 if your respondent is a man and 2 if a woman. The choice of 1 and 2 is arbitrary. You could choose 0 and 1 instead without affecting your data. The number is for convenience in data reduction. Similarly, in measuring customer satisfaction, you could represent 'satisfied' as a 1 or a 100.

The second type is **ordinal**, or 'in order from high to low [or vice versa]'. Again, you are representing a variable as a number, but rather than the number being arbitrary, it represents more or less of some quality that can be placed in some order. For example, you might assign numbers to your respondent's level in the organisation: 1 = plant manager, 2 = supervisor, 3 = direct labour. This does not imply that a direct labour employee has three times as much 'levelness' as a plant manager, or that a supervisor has exactly half the 'levelness' of the other two, but that you can rank them in some consistent order. However, we cannot do familiar types of arithmetic, such as calculate averages, on ordinal measures. (We will discuss other issues related to ordinal measures in **Chapter 11**.)

Ordinal measures are often associated with attitude measures, such as the familiar ranked-order responses illustrated by two items shown in **Table 10.3**. Even though the numbers only represent moreness or lessness, rather than a definite quantity, this often tempts even experienced researchers who know better into making mistakes. Someone who circles 5 (strongly agree) is not 5 times as satisfied as someone who circles 1 (strongly disagree), and the distance between 3 (neutral) and 1 or 5 is not necessarily the same.

The third type of quantitative measure is **interval**, where the interval (or distance) between numbers is constant and corresponds to the numerical difference between the numbers. Examples of interval measures include the year and the temperature in degrees Fahrenheit (or Celsius). Here, the distance is constant and corresponds to the numbers we have assigned. In the ordinal example above, we could not say that the distance between 'strongly disagree' and 'disagree' is the same as the distance between 'agree' and 'strongly agree', but we can make this argument for interval measures. The difference between 32°C and 40°C is the same as the difference between 40°C and 48°C. Hence, we can perform familiar arithmetic such as addition and subtraction on interval measures. However, we cannot do all arithmetic operations on interval measures, because they do not include an absolute 'zero' point. We cannot argue that 64°F is twice as warm as 32°F, because 0°F (or 0°C for that matter) has been arbitrarily chosen.

You may also be familiar with being asked to tick one of a series of responses such as 'Strongly disagree'/'Disagree'/'Neutral'/'Agree'/'Strongly agree'. Because the responses

Table 10.3 Ordinal measures

Please circle the number that best represents your response	Strongly disagree	Disagree	Neutral	Agree	Strongly agree
1. I am satisfied with the university's library facilities	1	2	3	4	5
2. I am satisfied with the university's residential facilities	1	2	3	4	5

are arranged in order (e.g. negative to positive), they are technically known as graded-response or ranked-response items. And, because these are often used in psychometric testing of the type pioneered by Rensis Likert (which allowed adding up the responses to a number of these items), you may see them called Likert or Likert-type scales.

You can see that the intervals are not unitary (equal to one) and that the responses doesn't really translate into 1-2-3-4-5, and that the distance between 'Disagree' and 'Neutral' might not be the same as between 'Agree' and 'Strongly agree'. However, this is an area where we behave 'as if' they do. Even if different respondents have different underlying conceptions of the responses (one person's disagree might be another's strongly disagree), we analyse the data 'as if' everyone's 'disagree' represents the same disagreement. This is neither wrong nor right – it enables researchers to be able to collect data on complex phenomena such as personality traits, for example, in an organised and efficient way. It does mean that developing questions (usually called items in this context) is time consuming and very expensive.

Given the more than a century of work with psychometric tests, researchers who study research methods have strong opinions on 'the best way' to construct the items and psychometric texts. For example, there is a 'big end' versus 'small end' debate on whether there should be an odd number of responses, or an even number (to keep people from choosing the 'Neutral' option.) Five- and seven-point responses are the most common, whilst three or nine are pretty rare.

Two examples of Likert items and the related questions are shown below in **Figure 10.3**. One scale goes from positive (i.e. 'Fully agree') to negative (i.e. 'Fully disagree'), and one that goes from 'Not at all' to 'Fully'.

The final type of quantitative measure is **ratio**. Ratio measures have all the properties of interval measures, plus a zero point. An example of a ratio measure is salary or number of employees of an organisation. We could argue that £20,000 is half the salary of £40,000, or that 500 employees is twice as many as 250 employees. We can thus perform any reasonable mathematical operation on ratio measures.

So why do you need to know that there are four types of quantitative measure? This is essential because it determines how you can analyse or interpret your data. The key point to remember is that even though you can stick any number into any statistical analysis and get an answer, those that you can use appropriately will depend on measurement properties.

To what degree do you agree with the following statement? Excellent companies will perform the service right the first time.

Fully disagree			Neither agree nor disagree			Fully agree
○	○	○	○	○	○	○

To what extent does your organisation return customer queries within 24 hours?

Not at all									Fully
○	○	○	○	○	○	○	○	○	○

Figure 10.3 Ranked-response items – some examples

Statistical programs

We recommend you enter your data into a spreadsheet, since most of the data analysis and statistical tests described in this chapter can easily be done in a spreadsheet, and a spreadsheet can usually be read by a statistical program if you want to do more sophisticated tests. However, you can also enter your data directly into many specialised statistical programs.

Many statistical analysis programs, such as SNAP and SPSS, even use a spreadsheet format for data entry, usually rows for respondents and columns for questions, but they may represent blank data in different ways than a spreadsheet. These programs do vary in their ability to record qualitative data (that is, data presented as words), so you might want to consider the balance between quantitative and qualitative data that you want to capture. However, both spreadsheets and statistical programs make it easy to manipulate or transform the data, such as recoding it.

If you aren't familiar with statistical software or don't need its advanced statistical analysis and graphical presentation capabilities, you might choose a spreadsheet program such as Excel. Most statistical software packages will let you import data from popular formats such as Excel. Spreadsheets such as Microsoft Excel offer a variety of built-in statistical functions, but if you know you will be using advanced statistics or have an extremely large data set, you may want to enter your data directly into an advanced statistical software program.

10.1.4 Cleaning your data

Finding and correcting any errors that have occurred in collecting or entering your data is known as cleaning the data. This could include 'out of range' errors such as someone's age being given as 147, or improbable responses such as head of household being given as 'Spot'. (Religion = 'Pastafarian' is not an error, however.) If you are using a spreadsheet or statistical program, you may be able to use a formula to highlight 'out of range' errors, for example where age is less than zero or greater than 100, or responses greater than 5 on a 1–5 point scale.

It can be helpful for different people to enter data and to check it. You might start by randomly checking to see how many errors you have made during data entry, for example working in pairs to check every tenth response. Depending on the number of errors you detect, you may want to check more thoroughly. The quality of your analysis can never be better than the quality of the raw data.

10.2 Descriptive statistics: Summarising and presenting raw data

Once you have recorded and cleaned your data, you can start to analyse them. You can analyse your quantitative data:

1. by hand/eye
2. using a general purpose program such as Microsoft Excel
3. using a specialised statistical software program.

You should start by looking at your individual measures. This will help you to get a good feel for your data and identify any potential problems or unexpected findings.

10.2.1 Frequency counts

Once you have created your data tables and are ready to start making sense of your data, a good place to begin is by summarising the raw data question by question. You can compute a frequency count for the individual responses to each question. A **frequency count** is a total for each individual response to a question. Frequency counts are a compact way of presenting the information from a questionnaire or structured interview in summary form, and anyone reading the table can start to draw some conclusions from the summarised raw data.

Hand tabulation

Hand tabulation is often appropriate for small or simple data sets. All you need is a sheet of paper and a pen or pencil, hardly high-tech, but quick, dependable and reliable. It does give you an excellent feel for your data, especially nominal and ordinal data, but not ratio data. On the other hand, it does get tedious, especially where there could be many possible responses to a question, for example annual income.

To tabulate data by hand, set up a data matrix with a single row for each respondent and a column for each possible response to that question. For example, from **Table 10.1**, you might want to hand tabulate which courses our student respondents were studying and whether they had an overdraft. The result looks like **Table 10.4**. As you go through each of your responses, record it in the appropriate category, as shown in **Table 10.5**. Once you have recorded all your responses, sum the numbers

Table 10.4   A simple data matrix – Step 1

Course		ENGR	SOC	BUS
Overdraft	NO			
	YES			

Table 10.5   A simple data matrix – Step 2

Course		ENGR	SOC	BUS
Overdraft	NO	xx	x	x
	YES	xx	xx	

Table 10.6 A simple data matrix – Step 3

Course		ENGR	SOC	BUS	TOTAL
Overdraft	NO	xxxxx	xx	xxxxx x	
	TOTAL	5	2	6	13
	YES	xxxxx xx	xxxxx x		
	TOTAL	7	6	0	13

Table 10.7 Relationship between credit cards and overdraft

	Overdraft		
Credit cards	YES	NO	TOTAL
YES	11	4	15
NO	2	9	11
TOTAL	13	13	26

for each category and total them. This is shown in **Table 10.6**. You could do the same for the ordinal data in **Table 10.3**. Here, this hand tabulation would let you start to see some patterns immediately.

However, this makes it hard to see whether there are any relationships between variables (which we will discuss in **Section 10.3)**, for example if there is a relationship between whether a student has a credit card and an overdraft. Cross-tabulating the data, as shown in **Table 10.7**, suggests there might be a relationship that wouldn't be obvious from hand tabulating credit cards and overdrafts alone. However, cross-tabulating every pair of measures would get old pretty soon!

Spreadsheets and statistical programs can make your life simpler because they can compute frequency counts and cross-tabulations automatically. They may also summarise frequencies as percentages. These tables are then ready to be incorporated into your project report or presentation if necessary, as discussed in **Chapter 13**. Both frequency counts and **histograms** provide an overall perspective on your data, for example details of the individuals and/or organisations you studied. You can also present this information in graphical form such as a pie chart or a histogram as in **Figure 10.4**, as charts are easier to read and interpret than frequency tables.

10.2.2   Measures of central tendency

The next step after computing frequency counts to summarise your data is *descriptive statistics*. **Measures of central tendency** describe the central point of a measure, for example mean, mode and average. **Measures of dispersion,** for example standard deviation and variance, describe how widely your data spread around this central point. Whilst you can compute these by hand, it is much easier to use your spreadsheet or statistical program's statistical functions. Just two numbers – mean and standard deviation – provide a wealth of descriptive information about each variable. (By adding correlation, a measure of the relationship between two variables, we can complete the circle.)

Take, for example, the number of women sitting on each board of directors of 500 companies. We could describe the number of boards with a given number of women using the frequency distribution shown in **Table 10.8.** You could also compute how many number of women sit on a typical board in your data set in one of three ways. The **mean** is the arithmetic average (the sum of values divided by the number of observations) of the values in a data set, and is what is commonly meant by the 'average'. The mean for the data in **Table 10.8** would be 2523/500 or 5.046. You can see in the table that the 'centre' of the data is probably around 5 or 6.

Many kinds of data have a central point roughly halfway between the minimum and maximum values, for example the average temperature in London. However, there is no reason that this central point has to be there; more data may lie to the left or the right of the arithmetic mean. If so, the mean may give a misleading estimate of the central point of the data. The **median** describes the midpoint of a data set; that is, the place where an equal number of values lie above and below that value. For example, if in Natalia's sample (**Student research in action 10.2(a) and 10.2(b)**), 95% of the women entrepreneurs were aged between 35 and 40, but two were aged over 60, these two women would shift the mean – perhaps misleadingly – towards the right. A more accurate measure of central tendency here would be the median. A spreadsheet calculates the median by ordering all 500 responses (1 to 10) and then picking the middle response. Going back to women's board membership, the median is 5, again which you could predict from the frequency counts. You cannot decide this without looking at the symmetry in your data set.

The mean and the median are not necessarily always the same. Let's look at the histogram for our numbers in **Figure 10.4** to see why the mean here is above the median. Although the distribution of responses (number of women on the board) is more or less symmetrical, the responses are slightly weighted towards those above 10,

Table 10.8   Frequency distribution – Board membership by women

Number of women on board	1	2	3	4	5	6	7	8	9	10	
Number of companies	3	18	67	96	120	107	61	23	4	1	500
Total women on boards	3	36	181	384	600	642	427	184	36	10	2523

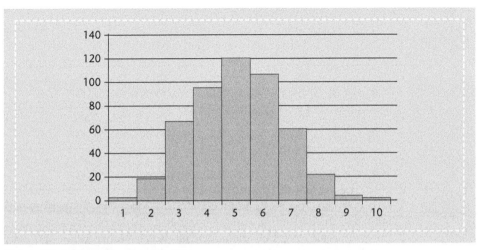

Figure 10.4 Women on boards (1)

so the mean is greater than the mode and median. When the distribution of data is not skewed, for example in a normal distribution, the mean and the median will be the same.

Suppose that your responses had been distributed according to the histogram in **Figure 10.5**. The median is still 5, and the mode is still 5, but the mean is less than 5 because there are more responses in the lower numbers (towards the left). Thus, the mean is not always the best measure of central tendency, because it can disguise this asymmetry.

The mean and the median both measure a single central tendency of the data. However, your data need not be distributed so that there is only one most frequently occurring answer. A third measure of central tendency, the **mode**, indicates the

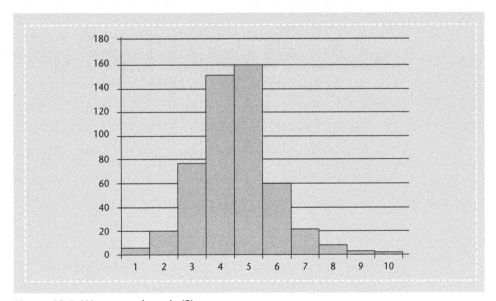

Figure 10.5 Women on boards (2)

most frequently occurring value or values within a data set. The mode describes the answer(s) given the most frequently, which can be seen in your frequency count or histogram. This can be at the centre or shifted above or below the centre. Here, the median is 5, which we can see from the frequency counts, but it is not necessarily so. You can even have more than one mode – some data are bimodal, with more than one peak in the data. For example, a fast-food restaurant might serve more customers between 12 and 2 and 6 and 8.

The normal distribution

The mean, median and mode will all be the same in data that are normally distributed. The **normal distribution** is sometimes called the 'bell curve', because its shape resembles the cross-section of a church bell. More data lie halfway between the maximum and the minimum, and are symmetrically distributed around that point, so that the mean is also the median and the mode (see **Figure 10.6**). Many data are normally distributed, for example the time it takes to serve customers at a supermarket till. (On the other hand, not every data set will follow a normal distribution, for instance the time between customer arrivals does not usually follow a normal distribution.)

To see if your data are normally distributed, start by looking at the frequency distribution or histogram. Are the data symmetrically distributed on both sides of the mean? If your data are asymmetrically distributed, or **skewed**, more data will lie below the mean if they are negatively skewed, and more data will lie above the mean if they are positively skewed.

So why is it critical to know whether your data are normally distributed? This information is required in order to use many common statistical tests. Tests that assume your data have a certain distribution such as normally distributed are known as **parametric tests** (in some cases they assume other distributions). If your data are not normally distributed, you may need to use **nonparametric tests**. You can check to see whether your data are normally distributed using a spreadsheet or statistical program.

When you examine bivariate relationships, you need to make sure that your data meet the assumptions about normality of the test you want to use. For bivariate tests, this usually means that each variable must be at least interval and normally distributed, and your two variables are jointly normally distributed. You should ask your project supervisor or consult a statistics book if you need further guidance. If you

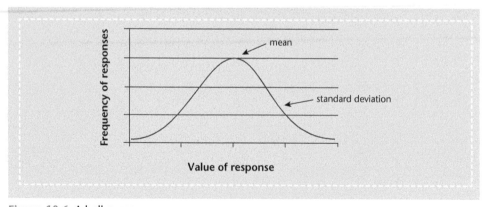

Figure 10.6 A bell curve

want to test relationships between variables that are nominal or ordinal, or that are not normally distributed, you will need to use different tests.

Measures of dispersion

As well as seeing where the centre of your data lies, you will be interested in how widely your data are spread around the centre. For example, if Natalia (**Student research in action 10.2(a) and 10.2(b)**) measured the number of children the women in her study had, she might find they all had the statutory 2.4 children (low dispersion), or the number of children could vary from none to many (high dispersion). This would be important to know if she wanted to understand how family size affected entrepreneurial behaviour.

Some common measures of dispersion include:

- maximum – the highest value in a data set (10 for our board members example)
- minimum – the lowest value in a data set (1 for our board members example)
- range – the distance between the maximum and the minimum (1–10 for our board members example)
- percentage rank – the percentage of responses lying below a specified value (the median value always has a percentage rank of 50%)
- percentile or quartile – the value which a given percentage (or quarter of the data) lie below (for example 20% of the data fall below 37)
- standard deviation – the variation around the mean, computed as the square root of the mean of the squared deviations of the observations from the mean
- variance – another measure of the variation around the mean, which is the square of the standard deviation (or the standard deviation is the square root of the variance).

As the measure of dispersion increases, the spread of your data around the mean increases; as it decreases, the data are closer to the mean. The **standard deviation** is one commonly reported measure of dispersion, because the central tendency and dispersion are the only two numbers you need to know to describe the data that are normally distributed. By knowing the mean and the standard deviation you have a complete picture of how those data are distributed as a normal distribution curve: how close or how far away data are from the mean.

A non-normal distribution might have more responses at the mean (centre) or close to the edges (or tails), so that they are bunched more closely in or spread more widely out than a true normal distribution. This is described as **kurtosis**. If your normal distribution curve looks 'tall' because more of your data lie close to the mean, and fewer in the tails, then your data have positive kurtosis, whilst if your normal distribution looks 'squashed', more data points lie in the extremes, then your data have negative kurtosis.

Thus, after you describe the frequency distribution of each variable, you can describe the central tendency and the dispersion for each variable (remembering that this is not appropriate for nominal and ordinal data), and start looking for patterns and trends in your data. You might want to prepare a summary table or set of tables that shows the frequency distribution and/or measures of central tendency and dispersion for each of your key variables, before you go on to the next step of your analysis. These can be useful in presenting your data to other people, for example an interim report on your research to your supervisor or your manager.

So where do you go next? The measures we have described above are useful in summarising your raw data and giving you some insights into your data. The frequency counts, tests of central tendency and tests of dispersion are **univariate tests**, because they only look at one variable at a time. This is useful information, and you need it before you do any more sophisticated statistical tests, but univariate tests do not usually answer research questions except in the most basic descriptive research. The only research question that this level of analysis really answers is 'how many?', not a very sophisticated research question. Here, we will introduce some simple **bivariate tests**, which test the relationships between pairs of variables.

 ## Bivariate statistics and simple hypothesis testing

To answer most research questions, we are interested in looking at more than one variable at a time. Most hypotheses are based on a relationship between at least two concepts – there is a relationship between variable A and variable B. (We will describe tests of the relationships between more than two variables – multivariate tests – in **Chapter 11**.)

You can use a number of simple statistical measures and tests to look at bivariate relationships, including measures of association, such as correlation coefficients or simple regression analysis, and measures of difference such as t-tests. Measures of association show the strength of the relationship between two variables, a common concern of business and management. 'Do men have more automobile accidents than women?' is an example of a question about the relationship between the variable of biological sex and driving performance. You may be interested in showing that there is a relationship, perhaps to justify lowering insurance rates for women, or there is not a relationship. This is a simple form of hypothesis testing.

Statistically analysing bivariate relationships might also be useful in showing that there are significant differences between two or more categories in your data, as shown in **Student research in action 10.2(c)**.

 Student research in action 10.2(c)

NATALIA'S HEAVENLY DELIGHTS (CONTINUED)

As Natalia's research project progressed, she became interested in seeing whether the barriers to the success of Asian women entrepreneurs mentioned in the popular press really existed, and if they existed, did they have an effect? For example, studies of women entrepreneurs often suggested that taking time out early in your career to have children was incompatible with becoming successful, yet most of the women she interviewed had had children at an early age and were also successful. Were there significant differences in the two groups, she wanted to know?

As you decide how you will test your data, you may want to ask yourself some of the questions suggested by O'Leary (2004: 192):

1. How does my sample compare to the larger population?
2. Are there differences between two or more groups of respondents?
3. Have my respondents changed over time?
4. Is there a relationship between two or more variables?

These questions often concern researchers. See, for example, **Student research in action 10.3**, where Costas was interested in two different groups of customers.

Student research in action 10.3

OH YES, WAIT A MINUTE MR POSTMAN

Costas, an MSc student, was interested in the effect of queuing on customer satisfaction. He designed a study to test the relationship between queuing times and customer satisfaction, using structured observation and a questionnaire rather than an experiment. He used the Greek post office as the setting for his field research, timing the length that customers waited in line, and using a questionnaire to collect information such as their satisfaction with the service.

Costas wanted to examine whether there was indeed a negative relationship between the length of time customers had to wait and their satisfaction with the service. He measured both the length of time and a Likert-type scale for customer satisfaction, and found that customer satisfaction was indeed lower when customers queued longer. The Pearson correlation of 0.77 also provided support for a relationship.

10.3.1 Correlation

You may want to investigate the strength of the relationship between pairs of variables in your data set, often reported in the descriptive statistics as the **correlation** between these variables. Researchers often compute correlations for survey data or secondary data. For example, suppose you had measured the size of each corporate board and the number of women sitting on the board. You could plot the two measures against each other, as shown in **Figure 10.7**. From the figure, you might expect that there is some relationship between the size of the board and the number of women who sit on it, and in fact the correlation is 0.462, indicating that there is a moderate relationship.

It might help if you can think of the values of one variable being plotted against the values of another variable as in **Figure 10.7**. How much one variable's values increase

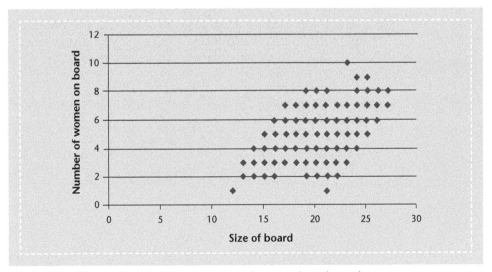

Figure 10.7 Data on board size and number of women board members

or decrease with a corresponding increase or decrease in the other variable's values indicates a stronger positive or negative relationship between the two. If for every one-unit rise in Variable A, there is a corresponding one-unit rise in Variable B, for example every time a respondent answers '3' for statement 1, he or she answers '4' for statement 2, and every time a respondent answers '4' for statement 1, the answer for 2 is '5', then there is a perfect positive correlation.

Interpreting correlations is fairly straightforward. The correlation between two variables will always fall between 1 and -1. The three possibilities are:

- Positively correlated – correlations that are close to +1 mean that there is a strong, positive linear correlation between two variables. In the example, the size of the board increases as the number of women increases, so they are positively correlated.
- Uncorrelated – correlations that are close to 0 indicate that there is no significant relationship between two variables. If there were no relationship between the size of the board and the number of women, you would expect a correlation of 0.
- Negatively correlated – correlations that are close to –1 indicate that there is a strong, negative linear correlation between two variables. If the number of women actually decreased with board size, the correlation would be negative.

The most common correlation measure is *Pearson's product moment correlation coefficient*, which describes the strength of the linear relationship between two variables, and is usually what is meant if you see the term correlation. Even a simple statistical procedure such as correlation requires some understanding of statistics: knowing the assumptions of the test is important. If your data are correlated, but not linear, you might be misled by a Pearson correlation of 0. The results of correlation are also affected by missing data – whether you choose pair-wise deletion (computing the correlation on the largest set of data) or list-wise deletion (computing the correlation on the most complete set of data) will significantly affect what you find.

Statistical significance

As well as reporting the strength of the correlation between any pair of variables, you should also report whether it is significant or not. In most research reports, and the outputs of most statistical software, you will see statistical significance reported. This shows the probability that the results you have found are due to chance, rather than a real underlying relationship or difference between variables.

Statistical significance ranges between 0 and 1. The closer it is to zero, the less chance there is that we have been misled into believing we have found support for our hypothesis when we have actually not. The accepted level of significance for business and management studies, as in most other disciplines, is .05 (or 1 chance in 20 that we are mistaken). Although you might sometimes see someone claim that a level above .05, say .10, is acceptable, it is not.

Because reporting statistical significance is integral to reporting statistical analysis results, instead of reporting the exact significance level, the following scheme is used to highlight different levels:

*   the significance level is less than .05 (1 chance in 20)
**   the significance level is less than .01 (1 chance in 100)
***   the significance level is less than .001 (1 chance in 1000)

Most spreadsheets will report only the correlation coefficient, but a statistical program such as SPSS will report both the correlation coefficient and the statistical significance. If you try to interpret statistical significance only by looking at the correlation coefficient, you may be misled, especially if you are working with a small data set.

If you calculate the correlation coefficient between all the pairs of variables in your data set simultaneously, you have a good chance of accepting a relationship as significant when it is due to chance. For example, if you calculate the correlations between 20 variables, you are calculating 20 correlations. If you accept an individual correlation as significant if $p < .05$, then you have a good chance of accepting a spurious (false) correlation. Most statistical programs will let you correct your significance tests if you want to compute multiple correlations.

10.3.2   Simple linear regression

If we know that two variables are related, we may want to use our knowledge of that relationship to predict a future behaviour. If two variables are significantly correlated, you should be able to use information about one variable and the relationship to predict the level of the other variable. You can use **simple linear regression** to see how variable B (customer satisfaction) increases or decreases with changes in variable A (queuing time). Linear regression attempts to find a linear (that is, straight-line) relationship between two variables by minimising the **sum of squares of the errors**, the squared distance of each data point from the line for all the values in the data set. (Although the mathematics of linear regression are somewhat complicated, you can ignore them and use Excel or a statistical program to compute the relevant coefficients.)

Simple linear regression represents the relationship between two variables in the form of a line that can be expressed with the y-intercept (b) and the slope (m) of the line ($y = mx + b$). You can then substitute any x into this equation to see what y would be at that level of x. For example, if you knew that customer satisfaction decreased with queuing time, you could predict the level of customer satisfaction for various queuing times, which could help you set service standards. You should note that even though you specify an independent variable (x) and a dependent variable (y) in linear regression, linear regression does not demonstrate that a cause-and-effect relationship exists, just that the two variables are related. For example, you could equally use the same method and data to predict the relationship between customer satisfaction and queuing time, even though it is not logical that customer satisfaction causes queuing time.

You can also compute measures of how well a line fits the relationship between the variables. These measures include the **goodness of fit** terms for the intercept, slope and the entire equation. This is important to know because the goodness of fit terms tell you how much confidence you should place in the results being real rather than chance. The **coefficient of determination** (R^2) measures the proportion of the variation in the dependent variable that is explained by the independent variable. R^2 is like the correlation coefficient, except that it varies between 0 (there is no relationship between the independent and dependent variable) and 1 (the independent variable perfectly explains the dependent variable). (In fact, R^2 is the square of the correlation between two variables.)

T-tests and ANOVAs

To answer many research questions, you will need to use statistical analysis to find out whether there are differences between one or more subgroups in your data, such as different categories of your respondents. The simplest statistical test that measures differences between two groups is the **t-test** (as discussed later, the ANOVA is a t-test for more than two groups).

Suppose Costas also wanted to test whether tourists would mind waiting in the post office queue less than residents. The data he would need to test this hypothesis include information about each respondent (whether a local resident or a visitor to the area) and the respondent's level of customer satisfaction with the post office transaction. By computing the means and standard deviations of the two groups, Costas found the following results, shown in **Table 10.9**.

The t-test looks for differences between the means of the two groups. Costas could use the statistical functions in Excel to find the probability that the two groups have the same mean.

The number that the t-test returns reflects the probability that a statistical difference between the two groups is due to chance rather than actual. For example, if the number (p) is .04, we would expect once out of 25 times that the difference is not statistically significant, or 24 times out of 25 it would be. Since the usual standard for business and management research is a $p < = .05$, then Costas should accept the t-test as showing a statistically significant difference between the two groups. If the difference had been .10, or 1 out of 10, he would have to reject this as showing a statistically significant difference in their level of customer satisfaction with the post office, even though there is a difference between the two means.

Although the t-test is a simple test, there is a little more you ought to know. An important assumption is that the data are normally distributed within each subgroup. It also requires a minimum sample size. If the two groups you are comparing come from different samples, you should use an **independent t-test**. For example, Costas cannot assume that locals and visitors are alike in other ways, so he should use an independent sample t-test. Costas does not need the same number of visitors and locals, because the t-test only uses the mean and standard deviation in its calculations. However, he does need to ensure that the standard deviation is not different for both groups.

If Costas knows that he has carefully matched the locals and the visitors, he can use a **paired t-test**. The **matched pair t-test** compares the scores of the two different groups (pair by pair) on the same measure. The difference between the matched pair and independent t-test is that there is more information available in the matched pair t-test, so the results are more likely to be significant if there actually is a difference. **Table 10.10** shows the results.

Table 10.9   Costas's results

	Number (N)	Mean	Standard deviation
Visitors	35	16.27	6.25
Locals	40	14.35	6.25

Table 10.10 Matched pair t-test

Pair	Satisfaction	
	Visitor	Local
1	19	23
2	15	22
3	11	7

The paired t-test compares the scores of the same respondent on two different measures. For example, Costas might have measured both the customer's satisfaction with the length of time he or she had to wait and their satisfaction with the service at the window. In this case, this extra information again gives a more precise test, as shown in **Table 10.11**.

A final variation on the t-test is the **one sample t-test**, which is used when the mean for your sample group varies from a constant value, for example zero. Costas might have been interested in whether the difference between the customer's estimate of the time they had to wait and the time they actually waited was consistently overestimated, underestimated or neutral. He could test the difference versus a constant value of zero to see whether this was true, as given in **Table 10.12**.

Table 10.11 Paired t-test

Respondent	Satisfaction	
	Queue	Window
1	19	23
2	16	21
3	14	9

Table 10.12 One sample t-test

Respondent	Satisfaction	
	Wait	Window
1	0.52	0
2	0	0
3	−0.37	0

You can use an **analysis of variance (ANOVA) test** when you want to test the difference in the means between more than two groups. Suppose Costas had studied customers at three different post offices (PO). He might then analyse his data set to see whether there were differences in queuing times and customer satisfaction between the three different samples. A one-way ANOVA is a better test here than three t-tests (PO1 versus PO2, PO1 versus PO3, and PO2 versus PO3), because it takes the data from the three sites into account simultaneously.

When an ANOVA is used as above, it is classified as a one-way test because only one way of splitting the sample is being used at a time. Although we won't discuss it here, the two-way ANOVA allows you to consider more than one way of splitting the sample at a time, for example testing the effects of post office location and time of day simultaneously.

10.3.4 Chi-squared test

The bivariate statistical tests we have described in this section are only appropriate for seeing whether two variables are significantly related if the variables are interval or ratio. But what if you want to test relationships between variables that do not meet this criterion? A useful test is the **chi-squared test**, which works with nominal, ordinal, interval and ratio data. You can compute the chi-square for any two variables that you can put into a 2 × 2 (or higher) table.

Most spreadsheets and statistical programs will perform a chi-squared test and return a number for the level of statistical significance, which you can interpret in the normal way. The chi-squared test is based on the expected distribution of the frequency counts if there is no relationship between the data and the actual distribution of the frequency counts.

Suppose you had been studying what people buy over the internet. You expect that there is a relationship between the sex of the consumer and the category that he or she has purchased items from, in other words, men and women have different internet purchasing habits. Suppose you have observed 100 internet purchases and come up with **Table 10.13** for your data. If there were no relationship between sex and what people bought, you would expect to see no differences in the purchases by category between men and women. The chi-squared test returns a probability of .0005, or a chance of 1 in 2000 that this is due to chance.

If you want to use a chi-squared test, like any other test you should read more about it in a quantitative methods book. One restriction on the chi-squared test is that every cell should have a minimum of five observations. Although it is possible to achieve this by combining cells with low frequencies, this is not always theoretically justified.

Table 10.13   Chi-squared example: internet purchases by sex

	Books	DVDs	Clothing	Sports	Total
Male	9	12	7	22	50
Female	21	8	15	6	50
Total	30	20	22	28	100

There are some other restrictions, such as degrees of freedom and the need to correct a 2 by 2 table, so you might want to ask an expert in statistical analysis or look in a good stats book if you want to use this test on a hypotheses.

10.4 Interpreting your quantitative results

The reader of a research report is usually at least as concerned with how you arrived at your findings (your process) as with what your findings are (your content). Academic readers are interested in how you have translated your research questions into a research design, and how your evidence answers those research questions. In other words, their focus is on the generalisability of your report, which requires validity. Practitioners, on the other hand, will be interested in how you propose that your answers might solve a practical problem. In other words, their focus is on the relevance of your recommendations, which requires rigour. As you will see in **Chapter 13**, this may lead you to write two separate reports, one for each audience, although you may be able to include common material in both. Before you start the writing-up process, however, you need to interpret what you have found out. It is not enough to present your raw (or summarised) data and hope that your reader can (or will) make sense of it for him- or herself.

Once you have collected and analysed your data, you have three key tasks:

1. **Interpret your data** – Understand what the data mean, with respect to your hypotheses
2. **Interpret your analysis** – Understand what the analysis means with respect to your conceptual framework
3. **Interpret your empirical research** – Understand what your findings mean for your theoretical and practical problem.

If you are doing your research from a quantitative perspective, once you have completed your statistical analysis you should ask yourself some tough questions about what you have found out (for example O'Leary 2004: 186–7). These questions include:

1. Do my data adequately capture the concepts and relationships I want to investigate?
2. Have I adequately measured these concepts and relationships with my statistical tests?
3. Do my data and statistical tests support or not support my hypotheses?
4. How does this analysis fit with my conceptual model?
5. Have I answered my research questions?
6. Do I need to go back to the literature to explain my findings from another perspective? Are there other ways I can interpret my findings? What did I not find out that I expected to find out? What did I find out that I didn't expect to find out?
7. Do I need to do further research to answer my research questions?
8. What have I learnt about my research setting, research methods, research questions or theory? What can this contribute to future research?

Along with your data and your analysis, the answers to these questions will provide the basis for your findings, discussion and conclusions when you present or write up your research.

10.4.1   Interpreting your data

Your first key task is to relate your data to the research questions you set out to investigate – making sure that the data you have collected are relevant to your research questions; as mentioned in the introduction, this is not always the case in research. **Chapter 10** presented simple statistical techniques and **Chapter 11** will present more sophisticated statistical techniques you can use to interrogate your data, ranging from simple descriptive statistics to advanced multivariate techniques. Applying these techniques rigorously, however, is no guarantee that your data have construct validity (they measure the concepts and/or relationships you set out to investigate) or face validity (they measure what you think they measure). This is a matter of judgement and hence research skill, rather than number-crunching.

You will also need to think about how you will identify the most important and relevant data to support your arguments. This can be a problem in both quantitative and qualitative research, because you will have usually gathered a lot more data than you can make sense of. If you have used a quantitative approach such as secondary analysis, survey or experiment, you are likely to begin your interpretation swamped by numbers – many numbers, raw data, tables, statistical formulae, statistical outputs. This may be too many numbers for you to be able to see the forest for the trees when you are writing up your research report or presenting your findings. Your reader will have no chance.

No matter how interesting you think each piece of data is, do not become a trainspotter. The data are nothing – your interpretation is everything. Try to focus first on those data that will help you to answer your research questions. A good way to get started on this is to reduce your data so you can identify the most *important* patterns, not every possible pattern. One of Kate's former colleagues called this 'holding down the data and torturing it until it surrenders'!

Since most of us find visual data easier to interpret than numbers, you might try converting your raw data into charts, graph, figures and tables. You can present many data more clearly in the form of charts or graphs, tables and figures. Most computer software, whether specialised statistical software, spreadsheet software or word-processing software, lets you create illustrations from your data. These should relate back to your conceptual framework and hence back to each of your research questions. You should generally present your data in the same order as your research questions (**Chapter 2**), which will determine the structure of your literature review, conceptual framework and so on.

The main dangers of this for students are that they waste too much time trying to get things to look 'just right', for example three-dimensional charts when two-dimensional would do, and they try to create a graph or chart for every possible aspect of the data, so inducing 'graph fatigue'. Try to create just the right amount of graphics to identify the story your data are telling. These are like the illustrations in a book – try to make 'your book' relatively grown-up rather than a children's picture book.

Tables

A *table* presents data in rows and columns of numbers and/or words. It is the most basic form of exhibit. 'Tables communicate precise numerical information to readers'

(Dunleavy 2003: 165). You should organise the layout of any table systematically, with the columns and rows in some logical order such as largest to smallest or most important to least important.

You can usually find many uses for tables in your project report. Tables seldom show raw data; they usually show data that have been processed in some way, for example to summarise or describe data or findings in compact form. Tables of raw data are rarely helpful in interpreting your data with respect to your research questions. If you look at academic research reported in high-quality academic journals such as the *Academy of Management Journal* or the *Administrative Science Quarterly*, you will see that the first table in most of these articles presents an overview of the key concepts and the relationships between them. This is a good idea for you when you are interpreting your data, before you start looking at the results of any statistical tests. The three things commonly reported in such a table are:

1. A measure of central tendency, such as the mean
2. A measure of dispersion, such as the standard deviation
3. A measure of bivariate relationships, such as Pearson's product moment correlation.

Such a table is invaluable to an experienced researcher, since he or she can often predict the significant findings and potential problems with the data based on this table alone, even before you present the results of any statistical tests. **Table 10.14**, from a project investigating the link between communication and group conflict, shows the means, standard deviations and correlations.

In fact, when you look at **Table 10.14**, the data suggest that face-to-face communication and telephone communication are associated with lower group conflict, but email communication is a bit more ambiguous. Perhaps this is because in the group studied, people who talk to each other face to face tend to talk to each other on the phone as well, but people who email do not communicate in other ways.

Table 10.14   A descriptive table for your variables

	Variable	Mean	SD	Pearson's product moment correlation					
				1	2	3	4	5	6
1	Face-to-face contact	13.4	3.1	1.00					
2	Telephone contact	10.2	5.1	.56	1.00				
3	Email contact	18.1	3.5	−.21	−.31	1.00			
4	Liking	4.5	1.01	.47	.20	−.36	1.00		
5	Preference	3.2	.87	.36	.33	.21	.39	1.00	
6	Attachment	3.5	.98	.09	.15	.22	.56	.37	1.00

Charts and graphs

Charts and graphs present numeric data effectively, especially if you want to look for patterns that tell a story. A chart is the term typically used for a figure that presents relationships among two or more independent variables. A *graph* is the term typically used for one that presents relationships among one or more sets of independent and dependent variables, especially where data follow a linear pattern. Microsoft Excel and other statistical programs make it easy to explore a range of charts. You should avoid 'dumbing down the data' too much (for example endless pie charts) and making it look like the front page of *USA Today*. Dunleavy (2003: 173) lists eight types of charts and graphs commonly used in research, which are shown in **Table 10.15**.

When you create your graphics, you should follow good practice (for example Dunleavey 2003: 163–4):

1. Label each exhibit with a heading or caption that clearly describes what is being shown.
2. Number each exhibit uniquely and systematically, preferably with a chapter number and unique figure number, for example **Figure 4.1**, **Table 17.2**.
3. Label the elements of the exhibit clearly, for example table columns, chart legends and the units of measurement. Make sure that each exhibit is self-explanatory.
4. Give brief details of where the data come from.

Table 10.15 Some common charts and graphs

Type	Use to present	Example
Scatterplot (X-Y) chart	The relationship between an independent and one or more dependent variables	Ice cream sales versus average monthly temperature
Line graph	The relationship between time and one or more dependent variables	Sales of Maylor's *Project Management* by month
Vertical bar chart	Discontinuous time-series data	Monthly sales of male deodorants
Horizontal bar chart	Non-time-series categorical data	Amount of time taken to complete activities
Grouped bar chart	Several discontinuous time-series data	Sales of the top three management books by month
Stacked bar chart	Relative shares of multiple categories	Share of grocery spending by different food categories by year for 10 years
Pie chart	Shares of a single overall category	Companies by number of employees in your sample
Layer chart	Several continuous time-series (or other continuous) data	Aggregate sales in three industrial sectors over the past 100 years

This systematic approach will make your life a lot easier when you present your graphics or incorporate them into your final project report. You must also make sure that you refer to each exhibit and explain it in words in your main text.

10.4.2 Interpreting your analysis

Your second task is to interpret the results of your statistical analysis. The goal of interpretation is not just to present your data and statistical test results, but to tell the story of how these data and tests relate to your research question. The structure of this story is determined by your research questions.

If you have analysed your data using statistical techniques, you need to interpret the results of your statistical analysis and turn this interpretation into your findings. This means not only reporting key data and key aspects of your statistical analysis, but also explaining them with respect to your hypothesis (or whatever statement is driving your research).

For each statistical test, you should always make sure that you describe:

1. **Your data** – What data you are analysing, where they come from and any data reduction or other transformation that you have applied to the data.
2. **Your tests** – What statistical test you have used to analyse your data, any important assumptions and what software package you have used in the analysis. If you are using a statistical test that is unlikely to be familiar to your reader, you may need to include details in an appendix.
3. **Your results** – In enough detail so that your reader can interpret them for him- or herself, but not so much detail that it is overwhelming. Include the key details, not every number reported in the analytical results. (If you don't know what those details are, you probably shouldn't be using that test.) You may need to include details of equations or outputs in an appendix if your reader might need to consult them in more or full detail.

As we mentioned above, this is where students often go to pieces. The purpose of gathering data is to answer your research questions, not to gather as much data as you can. Elegance is better than overkill. Similarly, the purpose of using statistical tests is not to test data in as many ways as possible, nor is it to apply as many different statistical tests as you can. We made the point in **Chapter 4** about the quantitative approach that ideally you would be able to specify the data and tests in advance of collecting data, to the point that you could mostly write up your project report before you ever started collecting data. Gathering a lot of data and testing it to death is an inductive strategy; data-mining has its place, but usually as the prelude to organised research rather than as part of it (it is sometimes referred to as 'data-gouging' for this reason).

What statistics should I be looking at?

A key part of interpreting your statistical tests will be to figure out what the most important and relevant statistical tests are, what they mean and how to present them. The statistics and statistical tests you are most interested in are those that help you to decide whether you have answered your research questions. If you have been following our advice for a systematic research process, you have translated your research questions into your research design by means of a conceptual diagram.

How you actually report your data and the story you tell will depend on your research project. If your research is mainly descriptive, you will present descriptive statistics, often in reduced form, and explain what they mean. If your research is more analytical, you need to present details of your analysis and relate it to your hypotheses. If your research is explanatory, you need to link it to the literature as well.

Figures

A good way to present your statistical tests (especially if you have more than one) is to integrate them with your conceptual model. Drawing your conceptual model and then showing which concepts and/or relationships you have tested and what the results are is a good way to do this. It is definitely a helpful way to begin visualising the story emerging from your research project.

Figure 10.8 illustrates a simple conceptual model with a single independent and a single dependent concept. Suppose you were investigating the link between communication and group conflict. You want to see whether the frequency with which people communicate with others in the same group, by face-to-face contact, telephone contact and email, affects intragroup conflict. Your participants have kept a diary recording the number of contacts with other group members per week. You want to see whether the type and frequency of communication affect how much people like each other, who they prefer to work with on projects and how attached they feel to the group. For this study, you might present the conceptual model in a figure and indicate the results of the hypothesised relationships and the direction of those relationships.

Figure 10.8 shows that your main hypothesis is that the more frequently members of a group communicate with each other, the lower the amount of group conflict. An experienced reader will also be able to tell from your figure what kind of data you have collected and what kind of statistical analysis you are likely to have used. Figures such as this are especially useful in showing relationships, which become essential when you have a complex conceptual model that your readers might find difficult to

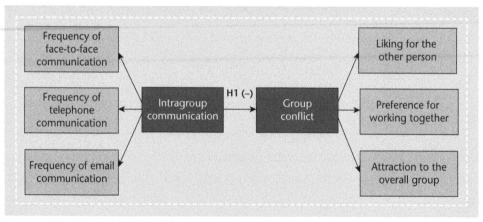

Figure 10.8 A conceptual model

follow if you present it only in words. You can think of a good figure as being a road map for your audience.

Statistical significance

A word to the wise. The ways in which students interpret statistical significance (p) is a source of endless hilarity to examiners and gnashing of teeth by quantitative methods teachers. Do make sure that you understand what a test of statistical significance means and how to interpret the level of statistical significance. The 'golden rule' in business and management research for determining whether a result is statistically significant is p < .05, or a 1 in 20 chance that we are falsely accepting a relationship when one does not exist. Any test where the result is p < .05 is significant; any test where the result is p > .05 is not significant. There is no such thing as almost or nearly significant.

You should also make sure that you are following the conventions for highlighting statistical significance in tables, which we show below:

```
*     p < = .05
**    p < = .01
***   p < = .001
```

10.4.3 Interpreting your empirical research

Once you have interpreted your data and your statistical tests, you have started to create the most important elements of your findings. Your findings are a central element of your research project and hence of any presentation or report. Your third task is to 'close the loop' between these findings and your research questions, to see how well you have done your job as a researcher. This will lead to a discussion of what your empirical research means in light of your research questions, and, usually, the theory that informs and supports those research questions. Remember that your data illustrate those questions and that theory in a particular research setting and sample.

One important aspect of interpreting your findings is to see how well you have done against the criteria on which the quality of your research will be assessed. It is not enough for research to be provocative or interesting; it needs to be done in an appropriate way. One criterion is whether you are able to express your results in the context of the existing knowledge in your area of interest. It also links with earlier parts of the study – the literature review in particular. You should also demonstrate how you have systematically addressed your research questions.

In order to close this loop, you need to see how the findings from your secondary analysis, survey or experiment fit with your literature. We described how to interpret the results of your statistical analysis above, to see whether your hypotheses are supported or not supported by your data. Since your hypotheses were deduced from your theory or conceptual framework, then you need to link this back to your research questions and the relevant theory (literature). This can help you to show that your data and analysis support your original framework, and whether you should consider any alternative frameworks to explore what you actually found out. You may need to conduct additional research – or at least identify the need to conduct additional research – as a result of this.

10.4.4 Quality in quantitative analysis

The final task in interpreting your evidence is to think about the quality of your research, primarily in terms of what you set out to do, but also with reference to the standards by which research is judged. The two lenses through which you might view your research are:

- **Scientific** – has it increased the reader's knowledge about/of the research problem and/or the method?
- **Advice** – what can the reader do/what is the reader empowered to do now that he/she has read the report?

Compared with qualitative researchers, quantitative researchers have a good deal of consensus on the scientific, or technical, criteria for judging quantitative research:

1. **Validity** – are your results accurate?
2. **Reliability** – are your results repeatable?
3. **Generalisability** – do your results have meaning beyond your data set?
4. **Credibility** – does the 'story' that your results tell appear plausible?

You should also highlight any actual or potential problems with the research you actually did, versus the research you planned to do (especially deviations from your research design). These deviations, which might include problems with missing data, sample size, violation of statistical assumptions or your instrument, might affect what you found out. You should also reveal anything that might influence your interpretation of your findings. Perhaps you should have used a different statistical test or added (or taken away) variables to (from) your model. These sorts of issues become important in drawing conclusions from your research.

Summary

This chapter has provided an overview of the basic techniques associated with analysing quantitative data. You should think of them as a way of starting to understand your quantitative data. This chapter will help you to understand the relationship between how you record the data and how you can analyse them. In **Chapter 11**, we will introduce some more sophisticated ways to analyse quantitative data than those presented here.

Answers to key questions

How can I record and manage quantitative data?

- You can record quantitative data by hand, in a spreadsheet or in a statistical program.
- You can proactively manage your data by taking care with the coding and cleaning of your data set so that you do not make assumptions based on faulty data.

How can I describe my quantitative data using statistics?

- You can describe your quantitative data using descriptive statistics such as frequency counts, measures of central tendency and measures of dispersion.
- You can present them using tables, charts and graphs.
- You should make sure that you understand the implications of types of measures – nominal, ordinal, interval and ratio – and the normal distribution for what you can do with your data.

What computer programs can I use to analyse quantitative data?

- You can use a spreadsheet or a specialised statistical program to analyse quantitative data.
  - A spreadsheet is adequate for descriptive statistics and basic inferential statistics.
  - A statistical program is useful for more sophisticated statistics and provides more guidance on the assumptions, limitations and other issues associated with a particular test.

How can I test relationships between variables or differences between groups using statistics?

- You can test the bivariate relationships between variables using measures of association such as correlation and simple linear regression, and measures of difference such as t-tests or ANOVAs and chi-squared tests.

How can I interpret my data?

- Reports need to be tailored to their audiences, for example academic and managerial readers may need different reports.
- Common ways of presenting data include tables, charts and graphs.
- Interpreting means making sense of the data with reference to your research question, not simply stating them.
- You should also report on how well you met the quantitative criteria such as validity, reliability, generalisability and credibility.

References

Denscombe, Martyn 2003. *The Good Research Guide for Small-Scale Social Research Projects,* 2nd edn. Maidenhead: Open University Press.

Dunleavy, Patrick 2003. *Authoring a PhD: How to Plan, Draft, Write and Finish a Doctoral Thesis or Dissertation.* Basingstoke: Palgrave Macmillan.

O'Leary, Zina 2004. *The Essential Guide to Doing Research.* Thousand Oaks, CA: Sage.

Additional resources

Bryman, A. and Cramer, D. 2001. *Quantitative Data Analysis with SPSS Release 10 for Windows.* London: Routledge.

Bryman, Alan and Bell, Emma 2003. *Business Research Methods.* Oxford: Oxford University Press.

Oakshott, L. 2001. *Essential Quantitative Methods for Business, Management, and Finance*, 2nd edn. Basingstoke: Palgrave Macmillan.

Swift, L. 2001. *Quantitative Methods for Business, Management and Finance*. Basingstoke: Palgrave Macmillan.

Key terms

analysis of variance (ANOVA) test, 312	median, 302
bivariate tests, 306	mode, 303
chi-squared test, 312	nominal, 296
coding, 295	nonparametric tests, 304
coefficient of determination, 309	normal distribution, 304
correlation, 307	one sample t-test, 311
data matrix, 293	ordinal, 297
frequency count, 300	paired t-test, 310
goodness of fit, 309	parametric tests, 304
histogram, 301	ratio, 298
independent t-test, 310	raw data, 292
interval, 297	simple linear regression, 309
kurtosis, 305	skew, 304
matched pair t-test, 310	standard deviation, 305
mean, 302	sum of squares of the errors, 309
measures of central tendency, 302	t-test, 310
measures of dispersion, 302	univariate tests, 306

Discussion questions

1 When should you start planning your data matrix and your data analysis in a quantitative research project?

2. Why are missing data a problem in quantitative research?

3. Many researchers treat ordinal responses as equally spaced. What would be the implications of this practice for a linear regression?

4. 'It is always better to use the most sophisticated software package and the most advanced statistical tests on your data if you want to get a good mark.' Discuss.

5. Is it true that managers don't need to know about statistical significance because you can tell the answer to most practical problems simply by 'eyeballing' the data?

6. If you have gathered data about a large number of variables from a large sample, why shouldn't you try to induce your hypotheses from a matrix of correlation coefficients?

7. Why should you always be sceptical about the statistical significance reported for a test? Doesn't it mean that a relationship must exist (or not exist)?

8. What might happen if you skip univariate analysis of your variables and go straight to bivariate analysis?

Workshop

Find a dataset that you can use for analysis or use the data in the workshop in **Chapter 5**.

- Set up a spreadsheet or data matrix by hand.
- What are the major decisions that you have in doing this?
- Enter the data.
- Have someone else check it.
- What kind of error rates have you found?
- What would this mean for the final analysis?
- Discuss with your project team or another student what kind of statistical tests you would use for testing these data.
- Use frequency counts, histograms or other statistics to show the distribution of at least two variables.
- Conduct at least one correlation analysis and one test of difference (such as t-test or ANOVA) between the two variables.
- Assess the results in terms of what you have learnt in this chapter.

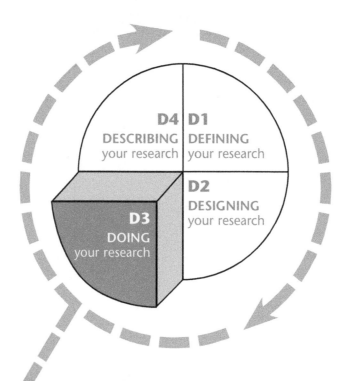

Relevant chapters
13 How do I write up my report?
14 What do I do now?

Key challenges
- Making sense of your findings
- Presenting your research to others
- Reflecting and learning from your research

4

Relevant chapters
1 What is research?
2 What should I study?
3 How do I find information?

Key challenges
- Understanding what academic research is
- Generating and clarifying ideas
- Using sources of information

1

D4
DESCRIBING your research

D1
DEFINING your research

D2
DESIGNING your research

D3
DOING your research

Relevant chapters
9 How do I do field research?
10 What do my quantitative data mean(1)?
11 **What do my quantitative data mean(2)?**
12 What do my qualitative data mean?

Key challenges
- Practical considerations in doing research
- Describing data using simple statistics
- **Carrying out statistical tests**
- Interpreting words and actions

3

Relevant chapters
4 What is my research approach?
5 How do I do quantitative research?
6 How do I do qualitative research?
7 How do I do case study research?
8 How do I make sure my research is ethical?

Key challenges
- Choosing a research approach
- Choosing a research design
- Collecting data using quantitative methods
- Collecting data using qualitative methods
- Integrating quantitative and qualitative methods

2

11

What do my quantitative data mean(2)?
Advanced statistical analysis

 Key questions

- What happens if I want to analyse relationships between more than two variables?
- How can a third variable influence the relationship between two variables?
- What statistical techniques can I use to analyse multivariate relationships?

 Learning outcomes

At the end of this chapter, you should be able to:

- Describe how multivariate analysis can help you to understand complex relationships
- Understand what kinds of questions multivariate statistics can help you to answer
- Identify the most common multivariate statistical techniques

Contents

Introduction

 Introduction

---

Research in action 11.1

BUT HE WAS SUCH A FUN GUY

Rugg and Petre (2004: 162) described an agricultural student who studied the growth of mushrooms for his doctorate. From the student's observations, he concluded that mushrooms grew in four-hour cycles. He found this exciting, because he would be the first person to observe such variation. The student made it all the way to his viva before his examiner pointed out that, instead of making a revolutionary finding about growth cycles, he had actually spent several years measuring the effect of the on/off cycle of central heating in the mushroom sheds. Not only had he failed to find anything, he overlooked one of the most obvious things he should have been studying. He also forgot one of the basic principles of experimental designs – eliminating extraneous variables (see **Chapter 5**).

Rugg and Petre's student above applied bivariate analysis to the relationship between time of day and mushroom growth; however, he ignored a second and equally important bivariate relationship between time of day and central heating cycles. Our experience as supervisors has been that many student research projects, whether they take a quantitative or qualitative approach, similarly over-rely on bivariate relationships and therefore ignore the true complexity of reality, which is multivariate. This is a threat to every single research design, quantitative or qualitative, and even to research done by experienced researchers.

In **Chapter 10**, we looked at how to analyse quantitative data using univariate and bivariate statistics, and this chapter we turn to multivariate analysis of the relationships between more than two variables. This chapter will briefly introduce the principles of multivariate analysis, illustrate some techniques for analysing data and help you to understand the statistical analysis you might have been reading about.

Given the vast and expanding universe of multivariate statistical techniques, we can only provide a brief overview here, so we will focus on explaining how you can apply multivariate logic to understanding your data and conceptual model. An understanding of the basic principles of multivariate analysis can illuminate both qualitative and quantitative data sets, as well as particular statistical methods. The relationships of interest in qualitative research are 'naturally' multivariate, even if qualitative researchers seldom use statistical techniques to analyse their data. Whilst you need not become an expert in multivariate analysis, you should know enough so that you can consult more advanced and specific references, or ask someone else for help in doing multivariate statistical analysis and interpret the results.

Section 11.1 explains why you should be interested in understanding the principles of multivariate research. Although you could use bivariate analysis to analyse the relationships among three variables one by one, such bivariate analysis does not always adequately test your hypotheses or give insights into a complex data set.

Section 11.2 explains the logic underlying the analysis of multivariate relationships. You must make sure that you have included the right variables in your research design in order to be able to do multivariate analysis. This means including every variable you want to investigate, and excluding those you do not want to investigate. You should draw the boundaries of your conceptual model based on theoretical considerations, rather than on data or practical considerations. However, as shown in the example at the beginning of the chapter, this is easier to say than to do.

Section 11.3 provides a brief overview of statistical techniques for analysing multivariate data. Whilst many undergraduate and master's level students do not consider using multivariate analysis because they are afraid it will be too complex, modern statistical software has greatly simplified the technical aspects of working with quantitative data, so these techniques have become more accessible.

After you finish this chapter, you should be able to look at your conceptual framework and data set – whether quantitative or qualitative – and decide whether to consider multiple bivariate or multivariate analysis. This analysis might be formal and statistical, or it might be informal and conceptual. This chapter's goal is for you to understand the logic of multivariate analysis, so that you can apply it to understanding possible relationships in your data. Once you understand this, you can get help in analysing these data from an expert, or take a 'cookbook' approach to perform multivariate analysis yourself using a user-friendly statistical program.

11.1 Understanding multivariate relationships

When you read a research report that reports that a significant relationship has been found between two variables (or, on the other hand that no significant relationship has been found where there ought to be one), the question you should immediately ask is: 'What other relationships might explain this significant relationship (or lack of one)?'

Plausible findings from good research often fail to hold up when they are re-examined by other studies because the original findings were based on too limited an analysis. This often occurs when the research study is based on examining the relationship between only two variables and failing to consider what other variables might have an effect, or examining the relationships between two or more variables but only considering the relationships pair-wise so that the simultaneous effect is ignored.

Deciding whether a bivariate relationship is both credible and sufficient is critically important if we want to make policy decisions or take other actions based on someone's research findings. For example, if research suggests that there is a link between playing video games and violent behaviour, we might decide to ban violent video games. If this decision is not based on reliable evidence, we might reduce people's freedom to play games without reducing the incidence of violence. If we decided that there is a credible link between listening to country music on the radio and suicide, we might propose that country music stations should be banned or run public service announcements advertising the Samaritans' telephone counselling services.

On the other hand, we do not want to take hasty action based on a **spurious** relationship, such as the one between the consumption of ice cream and deaths by shark attacks. The website http://tylervigen.com/spurious-correlations generates very plausible looking (and true) correlations between variables where there could be no logical link between them, e.g. annual series of 'number of people who drowned by falling into a pool' has a substantial correlation with 'number of films Nicholas Cage has appeared in'. This is because in any sufficiently large set of variables, we will be able to find multiple false correlations (if we do not correct for the set's size).

If we could use experiments to test critical research findings (as explained in **Chapter 5**), we could conduct more rigorous testing of cause-and-effect relationships and eliminate spurious associations. However, researchers might not be able to conduct an experiment for various time, practical or ethical reasons, or decision-makers might need to take urgent action. It would probably be both impractical and unethical to ask men to carry mobile phones in their pockets to see if their sperm counts are damaged by radiation, and it might be difficult to find a control group who could be convinced to completely avoid carrying phones. *The Guardian* in July 2004 reported that studies of whether aspirin was effective against a myriad of health problems could no longer be ethically continued because the proven benefits of aspirin against heart disease meant that giving someone a placebo instead of an aspirin might endanger his/her health (Jeffreys 2004). The studies were stopped and aspirin was recommended for all patients at risk.

Even if we could conduct experiments when we need to test cause-and-effect relationships, the need to investigate business and management research topics in their natural rather than a laboratory setting might make it impossible to do convincing experimental research. We simply might not be able to include enough factors, control the environment sufficiently or gather data from a large enough sample for statistically significant results. If we want to maximise the probability that we reject spurious relationships and accept valid ones, rule out alternate causes and strengthen the credibility of our findings, then the multivariate approach enables us to extend our analysis beyond bivariate relationships.

11.1.1 Multivariate analysis

Multivariate analysis is a method for analysing multiple variables simultaneously (Dillon and Goldstein 1984: 1). It is better than sequential bivariate analysis of multiple relationships for ruling out spurious relationships. Further, multivariate analysis lets us describe the structure of a data set in a more efficient way than multiple bivariate analyses do. If you look back to the discussion of correlation in **Chapter 10** it should be obvious why this is so.

Bryman and Bell (2003: 24) describe three situations in which multivariate analysis is useful to researchers:

1. Establishing whether the relationship between two variables is spurious or genuine;
2. Establishing whether there is a third variable that intervenes between the two variables you have studied;
3. Establishing whether there is a third variable that affects the relationship between the two variables that you have studied.

Spurious versus genuine relationships

If we have not accounted for the effect of one or more other variables which might affect the bivariate relationship between two variables, then the relationship loses its credibility. Many research projects fail to include all the relevant variables and end up drawing misleading conclusions. Leaving out one or more important variables could result from the theory guiding the research being incomplete, starting with an incomplete conceptual framework, or simply failing to include enough variables in the conceptual design or qualitative data-gathering.

Chapter 5 described Stack and Gundlach's (1992) study that argued that country music and suicide were linked: higher audiences for country music radio stations were linked to higher rates of suicide amongst audiences not composed of people of colour. Snipes and Maguire (1995) countered that the relationship between country music and suicide was spurious because the suicide rate in each metropolitan area could be explained equally well if you did not include the information about country radio listenership. Other researchers argued that differences in suicide between metropolitan areas could be explained by poverty, gun ownership, divorce and living in the south (which might also explain country music listening).

Unobserved variables

The original researchers on country music and suicide failed to consider whether some general underlying factor – perhaps southern rural culture – might create the same relationships between a number of variables (such as poverty or gun ownership) and suicide, as well as country music listenership. This is an **unobserved variable** in this study.

Researchers sometimes think that they have found a direct relationship between two variables when the relationship is actually caused by the relationship of each variable (A and B) to some unknown variable (C) that has not been observed – such as the heating cycle in the mushroom sheds mentioned earlier. C causes A, and C causes B, as shown in Figure 11.1, but A and B are only related through C, which hasn't been observed. The relationship between A and B is spurious because A and B are related to C and not to each other. For example, both ice cream sales and swimming in the ocean (where sharks hang out) increase with temperature, but consuming ice cream doesn't cause sharks to bite (or vice versa).

Intervening variables

Rather than causing variation in each variable (covariation), a third variable might also affect the relationship between two variables, or intervene in the relationship by coming between the two variables. We show an example of an **intervening variable**

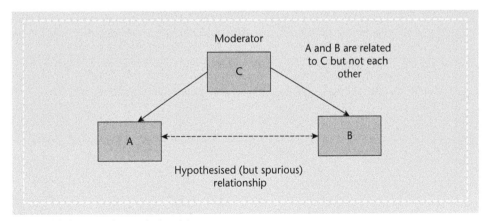

Figure 11.1 A spurious relationship

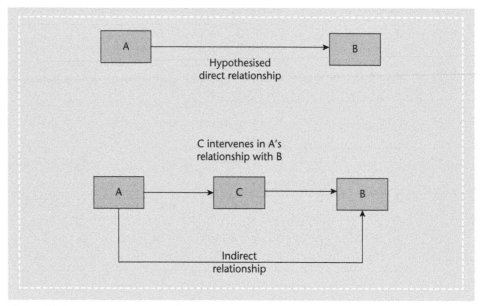

Figure 11.2 An intervening variable

in **Figure 11.2** where the intervening variable C directly affects B, whilst A has an indirect effect upon B.

Failing to include an intervening variable might make you conclude that no relationship exists when one actually does, or accept a spurious relationship. Many best-practice studies measure the adoption of specific techniques such as kaizen or six sigma and the firm's performance and then argue that adopting such best practices should improve the firm's performance. However, other variables might intervene between these practices and performance. It might not be enough to adopt best practice – the firm might not see any benefits without top management leadership or employee commitment.

ACTIVITY

In the UK the value of expanding higher education has been hotly debated over the past few years. An argument in favour of higher education is that graduates' lifetime earnings tend to be higher than nongraduates. However, some studies have failed to show a relationship between the two and you can find plenty of anecdotal evidence that some graduates earn less than some nongraduates (plumbers and other trades being a highly visible exception in these reports, where they are shown to earn considerably more on average than, for example, academics or social workers).

If you were designing a study of the relationship between level of education and earnings, what kinds of factors would you consider as intervening variables?

1.

2.

3.

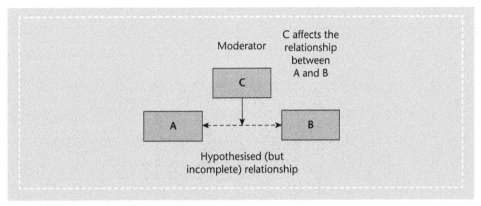

Figure 11.3 A moderating variable

Moderating variables

The third threat to the validity of a bivariate relationship that you might consider in your conceptual framework is whether there is a third, unidentified variable that might affect the strength of the relationship between your two variables – a **moderating variable**. Rather than intervening, this variable intensifies or weakens the relationship between the two variables, as shown in **Figure 11.3**.

This type of moderating variable is true for many research areas. In public health studies, social class (or income) moderates most of the relationships between behaviours and health, including obesity, smoking, fast-food consumption, fruit and vegetable consumption, exercise or dental care, and intervenes in many others. So if you fail to include social class in public health studies, you are likely to come up with an incomplete explanation. Similarly, in business and management studies, bivariate relationships are often affected by characteristics of the members of the sample, for example age or gender for people, and industry or size for organisations. Failure to take account of these demographic characteristics can lead to misleading results.

Mediating variable

The third possibility is that a third unidentified variable may act as a **mediating variable** in the relationship between two variables as shown in **Figure 11.4**. This is an extension of the intervening variable discussed previously where the indirect effect is changed to a direct effect.

An example of a mediated relationship occurs in the job market. The attractiveness of a university to job recruiters (C) may be directly related to the university's rankings in various guides (A). Higher ranked universities may also attract more intelligent students (B), who make the university more attractive to recruiters – an indirect influence of A on C.

Multivariate predictor or criterion variables

The final and perhaps most important reason we recommend a multivariate rather than a bivariate explanation in designing and doing your research is that bivariate relationships don't reflect the complexity of social reality very well. Two or more independent variables may contribute to one or more dependent variables, as shown

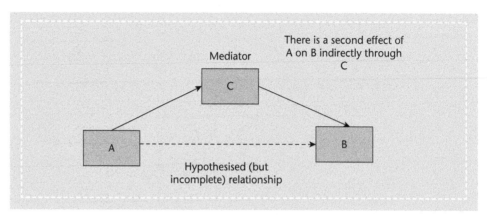

Figure 11.4 A mediating variable

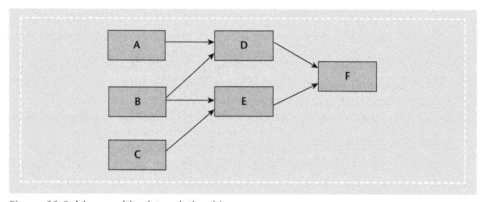

Figure 11.5 More multivariate relationships

in **Figure 11.5**. If you don't take account of these variables in designing your conceptual model, data collection and analysis, or when you are doing your statistical analysis, you are likely to come to misleading conclusions.

If you analyse each of these relationships separately using bivariate analysis, you are likely to end up making conclusions that leave out the simultaneous relationships between variables. For example, how would you know which variable is more strongly related to E, B or C? What is the true relationship between B and F?

We are not trying to *force* you to do multivariate statistical analysis on your data. In fact, students often use this as an excuse for fishing, or data-gouging. We believe, however, that all research projects can benefit from multivariate thinking in the design and interpretation stages. This is equally important when you decide what you will or won't investigate.

11.2 Analysing multivariate relationships

As noted above, few relationships in business or management – or life itself – are simple and bivariate. In most research projects, you need to consider whether multivariate relationships might exist and might be relevant when you are defining your research questions and designing your data collection.

If you don't recognise that you might have a multivariate relationship before you analyse your data, it is often too late to do anything about it. If you haven't measured an important variable, you cannot see if it affects your significant bivariate finding. You should try to identify a comprehensive (but not exhaustive) set of variables in the research design stage. On the other hand, each variable you collect has a cost in terms of time and effort. The worst-case scenario is that you present your research and someone points out that you have left out a key variable – perhaps one already identified in the literature. The example at the beginning of this chapter illustrates a situation where this had a huge impact.

ACTIVITY

If you wanted to open an ice cream stand, in predicting your daily sales what different variables would you consider? First, there is undoubtedly a relationship between ice cream sales and ambient temperature – people eat more ice cream in hot weather than cold weather. Is that enough?

11.2.1 Have I included all the right variables?

In your research design, you should collect information on any relevant variables. You can seldom go back and collect additional data to clarify those issues, especially in field studies. Cook and Campbell's (1979) threats to research validity identify some of the variables you might want to take into account, so any serious researcher might want to read what they have to say. Some threats are discussed below.

Time

As noted above, many researchers claim to have discovered a relationship between two variables, when both of them are related to a third, underlying variable that has not been investigated. This underlying variable is often time. Many factors vary predictably over time – hours, days, month or years. Others change predictably over the course of time. The science of forecasting explicitly recognises the importance of time to business and management activities.

Characteristics of your sample

One principle of experimental design is the use of random assignment and control groups. Where you cannot use this, and you cannot show that any two or more groups you are studying are absolutely equivalent, you need to use multivariate analysis to account for differences between groups to address this threat to validity. This occurs so often in journalists' reports on research that the authors are almost disappointed when it doesn't show up. For example, when we wrote the first edition of this book, we reported on a study where researchers concluded that the use of mobile phones was directly linked to lower sperm counts, but their study failed to show that other lifestyle factors associated with lower sperm counts were similar across groups of men. Early adopters of mobile phones might also be more likely to drink, smoke, have stressful jobs and wear tight underwear, all factors associated with lower sperm counts. (Now that mobile phone usage is nearly universal, this would be less of a threat to validity.)

Have I included too many variables?

Some students take the opposite view and try to collect as much data as they can, even if they don't know whether or why they might be important. This is sometimes known as 'going on a fishing expedition'. But data are not free; each variable you collect has a cost to your project in time and effort.

Many students are tempted, especially if they are using a program such as SPSS, to try to examine all possible relationships in their data simultaneously. These students set up a regression equation (for example) including all their independent variables at once to explain their dependent variable. So what's wrong with this?

Well, first, unless you have a large data set, you probably have too few observations per variable to get significant results. One author once had to explain to a management consultant that setting up a regression equation with 80 variables and 150 respondents (roughly two respondents per variable) was unlikely to result in significant results. In fact, he would have needed a minimum of 10–15 respondents per variable (or 800–1200 respondents) to test this model. This would have been several times larger than the complete population he wanted to sample!

Second, if you try such an approach, the relationships between the independent (predictor) variables (*collinearity*) may hide which variables are contributing significantly to the dependent (outcome) variable(s). This may be a bit more difficult to see, but if you have independent variables that are closely related it can happen. For example, suppose you wanted to see what factors affected a child's weight. Children's age is significantly and positively correlated with weight: children put on weight at a more or less continuous rate over their childhoods, and few children get lighter as they age. You might also expect children's weight to vary with their height, since taller children tend to be heavier. If you ran a regression equation with age and height as the independent variables, you would probably find that age, height and weight are all positively and significantly correlated. Logically speaking, however, age and height are the most likely independent variables (being taller or heavier is unlikely to make you older, and people do not get taller as they get heavier). Since age and weight are so highly correlated, it is difficult to separate each one's contribution for weight. A statistical analysis might show age as explaining all the variance and height none, height explaining all the variance and age none or a split between the two, making the relationship seem much weaker than it actually is. Performing a correlation test on all of the variables included in the regression will highlight any potential collinearity.

This illustrates the fact that each variable you include in your multivariate analysis has a statistical cost as well as the cost of data collection. Adding more variables will increase the explanatory power of your equation only up to a point, after that point it will decrease. If you have experience with multivariate regression, this explains why we look at adjusted R^2 statistics as well as plain R^2. Adjusted R^2 should be within .2 of R^2. If the difference is greater this indicates that the model is overfitted, i.e. it has variables in it that are not statistically significant. These variables should be removed.

11.2.3 Are my data appropriate for multivariate analysis?

To be analysed using most *multivariate analysis* techniques, your data need to meet fairly restrictive assumptions about data type and distribution, as noted in **Chapter 10**. If you remember our discussion of ordinal data, you may be surprised that researchers who use the familiar agree/disagree or other five-point items are among the biggest users of multivariate statistical techniques. What gives? In **Chapter 10**, we explained that ordinally scaled questions could not be analysed in the same way as interval or ratio-scaled questions, because we could not show that the distance between the numbers assigned to categories was proportional to the distance between categories. Some researchers combine several ordinally scaled questions to create a composite variable that is approximately normally distributed and can then be used in multi-variate analysis. (It is also possible to use the same logic to combine nominally scaled items into new variables using techniques such as Guttman scaling; however, this is beyond the scope of this book.)

First, though, a brief note on terminology. From this section on, we will refer frequently to the data you have collected using the terms questions, items, responses and scales. What we mean by this is:

- **Question** – a question or statement on a questionnaire or structured data collection instrument such as an interview schedule that asks respondents for data.
- **Item** – a single question or subpart of a multiple question on a questionnaire or interview schedule. A simple item might be Gender: M or F.
- **Response** – the range of possible answers to an item, including responses predefined by the researcher (closed-ended) and those not predefined (open-ended). Attitude questions commonly rely on responses of 1 = Strongly disagree to 5 = Strongly agree.
- **Scale** – a single item or group of items that relates to a single underlying variable.

Multiple items that measure different aspects of the same variable may be combined into a **scale**. (Some scales are composed of only one item, but this creates significant reliability problems.) A scale typically has three or more items. An example of where multiple items are better at capturing a variable than a single item might be happiness – you could measure different behaviours or aspects that each relate to some aspect of happiness rather than the single question 'How happy are you?' An example of a multi-item scale is shown below. This measures reliability in a service setting and is from SERVQUAL – the widely used instrument for measuring service quality (Zeithaml et al. 1990):

To what extent do you agree with the following statements?

When XYZ promises to do something by a certain time, it does so.

When you have problems, XYZ is sympathetic and reassuring.

XYZ is dependable.

XYZ provides its services at the time it promises to do so.

XYZ keeps its records accurately.

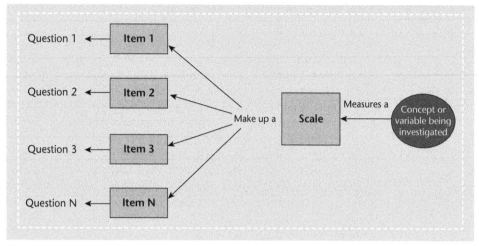

Figure 11.6 Relationship between items and scales

Figure 11.6 might help you understand how this might be useful. Many aspects of organisations are associated with organisation size, for example structure. One measure of organisation size is number of employees. However, you might expect some difference between a pizzeria with 15 employees, a high-tech start-up with 15 employees and a seasonal business with 15 employees. In this case, you might want to collect several measures each relating to organisation size. These measures can be combined to form a single, more accurate measurement of the underlying variable you are interested in.

So far we have talked about items as though descriptive statistics can be applied equally well to any measure. However, descriptive statistics other than frequency counts are more appropriate for interval and ratio measures than nominal or ordinal measures. Try to imagine interpreting the average response for sex, for example. The same is true for ordinal measurements: could someone be 50% in agreement and 50% neutral?

Unfortunately, many people don't think about the appropriateness of statistical measures before they calculate statistics using their spreadsheet or statistical analysis package. In particular, people often report means, standard deviations and other measures for ordinal measurements as though they were really interval and could be meaningfully analysed.

So when can you use statistics to analyse ordinal measures? Probably the best-known way is to use the method proposed by Rensis Likert as a new way to measure attitudes. Likert suggested the following process:

1. Develop multiple items measuring the same underlying attitude
2. Use the same set of responses (graded response) to measure all items in a set
3. Combine the responses from the multiple items to give a single indicator of the underlying item.

By combining the responses from multiple items, the score for a well-designed variable approaches the normal distribution. If you have five items and your responses are coded 1 to 5, the range of responses for the scale will be 5 to 25, with a midpoint of 15 if it is normally distributed.

You may sometimes see a *single* item referred to as a Likert-type scale, but a true Likert scale is composed of multiple items. The term is sometimes used loosely to describe graded responses. Researchers who specialise in attitude measurement have developed a number of techniques for determining what items do and don't belong in a particular scale, along with how to develop the graded responses to be used in the items. This will be discussed in the next section.

11.3 Where to go next: Understanding multivariate statistical techniques

O'Leary (2004: 187) suggests that the best way to learn about statistical methods is to 'get your hands dirty' using statistical programs. It is true that you can get good results from these programs without knowing much about the underlying details of different statistical techniques. As a result, most students don't have problems with the mechanics of data analysis, but with understanding the data and the logic of the relationships they are trying to test.

If you want to analyse your data using multivariate statistical techniques, but you haven't studied multivariate methods, you may want to get advice from your project supervisor or someone with experience before you decide on a particular test. In the remainder of this section we explain four of the most common statistical techniques that we frequently encounter when supervising students. This chapter's **Additional resources** lists several books you might find helpful.

11.3.1 Multivariate data analysis methods

The two main types of multivariate analysis are interdependence methods and dependence methods. In **interdependence methods**, there are no assumptions about independent and dependent variables – all the variables are equal. In **dependence methods**, the goal of multivariate analysis is to establish relationships between independent and dependent variables (that is, the kinds of cause-and-effect relationships examined in **Chapter 5** when we discussed experiments).

Interdependence methods include:

1. **Cluster analysis** – variables are assigned to groups based on similarity of features. Cluster analysis is used for classification, for example to see if there are any distinct groups of shoppers based on their spending patterns.
2. **Principal components analysis** and **exploratory factor analysis** – the goal is to reduce the number of variables into a smaller set by grouping them into factors or categories. These techniques are used to see if there are any obvious latent variables within the data. For example, as discussed previously, 'happiness' could be measured with a number of items.

Dependence methods include:

1. **Multiple regression** – examines the relationships between one dependent variable and multiple independent variables.

2. **Structural equation modelling (SEM)** – examines the relationship between multiple independent and multiple dependent variables. It can also be used to test intervening, moderating and mediating relationships between variables. SEM is used for *confirmatory factor analysis* and *path modelling*.

Cluster analysis

Cluster analysis is popular because it lets us reduce data and thus manage complexity. Cluster analysis identifies a smaller number of groups in data, where multiple respondents and multiple variables are being measured. You can cluster your data by cases (for example people or organisations), variables (your measurements) or both simultaneously. It is not a statistical technique, but an empirical one. People like cluster analysis because they often think using informal cluster analysis. For example, 'Men are from Mars, women are from Venus' clusters people by sex to predict a substantial amount of behaviour based on this one characteristic. Similarly, demographic classifications such as ABC cluster people on social class, occupation and other variables in order to make predictions.

Suppose you wanted to see what types of consumers eat in McDonald's restaurants. If you prefer quantitative research, you might start with a conceptual framework such as the one proposed by Gabriel and Lang (1995) in their catalogue of consumer types – consumer as chooser, communicator, explorer, identity-seeker, hedonist or artist, victim, rebel, activist and citizen. You would develop measures based on this catalogue and then classify the actual consumers you study into each of these types.

On the other hand, rather than imposing them, if you wanted to let the types emerge from the data, you could decide what data you want to collect, which variables to use to cluster the data and then use cluster analysis to identify clusters of consumers based on the data you have collected. Based on the aggregate characteristics of respondents in your clusters, you could assign each cluster a name or identity. (To complete the analysis, you could compare your clusters with those identified by Gabriel and Lang to see whether your findings are similar or different.)

The two main approaches in cluster analysis (there are many) are:

1. Start with all your data and split them into successively smaller clusters until each cluster has only one member
2. Start with one member in each cluster and create clusters until you have one big cluster that includes every data point.

Which method – and statistical technique – you use for clustering should be theoretically driven (based on your conceptual model) and not by trying all the methods and deciding which output you like the best. Also, we caution against including too many variables in the analysis. The results may be meaningless or difficult to interpret.

If you decide to use cluster analysis, remember that it is a descriptive technique. Although cluster analysis may reveal clusters that occur naturally in your data, it is more likely that you are imposing (somewhat) arbitrary clusters on messy data. If you identify clusters based on a set of variables, and then apply statistical tests to show that clusters differ on those variables, you are not actually testing anything worthwhile. You should also remember that the number of clusters is arbitrary.

Principal components and factor analysis

In a similar fashion to cluster analysis, principal components and factor analysis are used in dimension reduction. Factor analysis is often used if a researcher has decided to develop a multi-item scale for use in a survey. For example, if seven items are developed that are attempting to measure lean implementation these can be factor analysed in an exploratory factor analysis. All of the items should load on one factor – this is where the factor loading is greater than 0.5. If there is more than one factor present then the researcher needs to decide whether the scale should be purified (i.e. items removed), or whether two scales are more appropriate.

Multiple regression

Multiple regression is a popular method for multivariate analysis, because multiple regression is logically clear if you understand simple regression. There are numerous options within multiple regression. For example, logistic regression can be used to examine categorical variables. The most popular use is with scale variables. This is linear regression and is used to examine how multiple independent – or predictor – variables influence a dependent – or outcome – variable. When using regression to analyse your data, remember that there is one dependent variable and one or more independent variables. The independent variables need to be just that – independent. For example, the gross domestic product (GDP), private consumption and government expenditure are not independent as GDP is calculated using the other two variables. It is therefore worth ensuring that the variables are conceptually different. Before running the regression, it is worth running a simple correlation on the data. This will identify any problems with collinearity – an indicator that your independent variables may not be independent. Regression can be conducted on a large range of variables but as a researcher it is best for you to conceptualise potential relationships rather than throwing everything into the pot. You will have to discuss potential relationships if they are significant!

The output of linear regression is relatively easy to interpret. R^2 and R^2_{adj} statistics indicate how much of the variation in the model is explained by the variables. The difference between these needs to be no greater than 0.2. Typically researchers are not that interested in the R^2, they are more concerned with determining whether a variable has a statistically significant impact on the dependent variable. The regression model will also include a constant – this takes into account all of the other factors that generally are impossible to incorporate into the model. The independent variables will then have a beta variable that will be positive or negative and a statistical significance. It is the statistical significance that most researchers are interested in as this allows a hypothesis to be tested. If the statistical significance is high – typically 95% or $\alpha = \leq 0.05$ – then the hypothesis can be accepted.

Suppose you wanted to examine the relative contributions of the use of just-in-time, total quality management and supply chain management to manufacturing performance in terms of plant on-time delivery. Your conceptual model might look like the one in **Figure 11.7**.

If you didn't know about multivariate analysis, it would be easy to analyse the bivariate relationships in isolation and conclude that each of them contributed significantly to on-time manufacturing performance. (In fact, this kind of analysis is typical

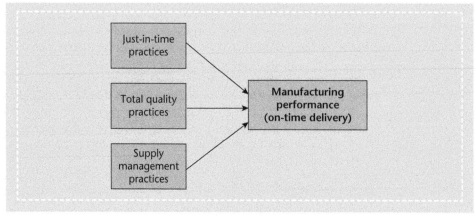

Figure 11.7 Model A of manufacturing performance

of journalism and consulting.) On the other hand, most researchers (and managers) would want to know, when we consider all three practices together, which contribute most and least to manufacturing performance.

If you used linear regression, you might find that when you include all three variables in a multiple regression equation, only supply management practices are statistically significant. This is very different from finding that all three are statistically significant. On the other hand, if you stop there, you might be making the same kind of conceptual error you made in using bivariate analysis. Suppose you couldn't implement supply chain management until you had implemented just-in-time, and you couldn't implement just-in-time without having total quality management in place? While you have treated the three practices as independent variables in this model, they are not necessarily independent of each other. In fact, the conceptual model might look like the one presented in **Figure 11.8**.

An experienced researcher could probably pick out a structure like this from analysing the relationships between the independent variables as well as the relationship between the independent variables and the dependent variable. To analyse more complex relationships between variables a different technique – structural equation modelling – can be used.

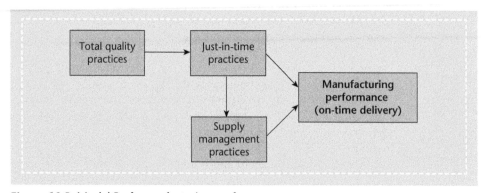

Figure 11.8 Model B of manufacturing performance

However, the real lesson is that our ability to perform multivariate statistical analysis usually outstrips our ability to relate it to conceptual models. Don't let the data or statistical methods drive your analysis; your conceptual model should drive it.

Structural equation modelling (SEM)

Structural equation modelling (SEM) is gaining in popularity amongst management researchers. It can be used to test how multiple variables – typically latent variables – affect other multiple variables, including mediating effects. Some of these models can incorporate a number of latents with a number of effects. It is for this reason that SEM has become popular. And whilst allowing far more sophisticated and complex analysis is a good thing, SEM needs larger sample sizes. These should typically be of the order of 10 responses per item. So for a 5 latent variable model – assuming 5 items per latent variable, a minimum of 250 responses are required. Building and testing an SEM model is not difficult but requires a number of steps. In our experience it takes far longer to understand the incredibly unfriendly user interfaces compared to the logic behind SEM! The logic of building and testing a structural equation model are explained below:

Conceptualise a theoretical model and collect the data. This could be along the lines of how do institutional pressures (one construct) influence technology uptake (a second construct)? Then, how does the technology uptake influence supply chain integration (a third construct)? How does integration affect operational performance (a fourth construct)? The link between technology uptake and operational performance can also tested. Not only does this stage guide the constructs (i.e. the latent variables), but the hypotheses that are to be tested later. There are numerous latent constructs available, and there are books that contain the most important scales used within disciplines.

Test the data for validity and reliability. This is a multi-stage process. In the first stage the Cronbach's alpha of each latent variable needs to be tested. This assesses whether the multiple items are measuring the same thing. Alpha needs to be above 0.7. Many of the existing scales are highly reliable so feel free to use those rather than re-inventing the wheel. The next stage is to construct a measurement model. The measurement model comprises all of the latent variables that are to be tested but instead of unidirectional paths between the constructs, bidirectional covariances are used. Once the model is built and run, convergent (the validity of a construct) and divergent validity (whether the constructs are measuring separate things) can be assessed. Convergent validity is tested using average variance extracted (AVE). This is the mean of the squared path coefficients for an individual construct. AVE needs to be above 0.5. Divergent validity is assessed by comparing the AVE of each pair of linked constructs with the squared correlation of the two constructs. The squared correlation needs to be lower than the lowest of the two AVE scores.

Run the model and evaluate the results. The model needs to incorporate paths that represent the hypotheses from your conceptual model. Of course, you can explore other paths that are not discussed in the literature but you are seeking to test hypotheses first and foremost and not search for the best fitting model. The model needs to be assessed for the statistical significance of each of the paths plus the overall model fit. The most popular SEM packages provide useful guidelines as to what these fit indices should be.

11.3.2 Software for multivariate analysis

Many software packages such as Minitab, SAS, SPSS and AMOS will let you analyse your data set using multivariate statistics. An advantage of using one of these packages is the number of help texts that have been written to go along with them, for example the excellent guides to SPSS by Bryman and colleagues that you can find listed by Amazon or in your bookstore.

Summary

This chapter has introduced the logic, analysis and techniques associated with multivariate analysis. Understanding the logic of multivariate analysis can help you to identify avenues in your data that you should explore, and potential threats to the credibility of your results. You can use the logic of multivariate analysis to identify unmeasured variables that might explain, intervene between or moderate the significant (or nonsignificant) bivariate relationship you found in your data.

If you suspect you might have multivariate relationships in your data, you should consider using multivariate analysis of your research problem and data so you can formulate some questions which you can answer statistically (or ask someone else to investigate statistically).

Finally, we have described some of the more common or important multivariate statistical techniques that you might want to learn to use or you might read about in your literature search.

Answers to key questions

What happens if I want to analyse relationships between more than two variables?

- You should use multivariate analysis.
- You should start with the conceptual framework and then use the techniques outlined here to determine if the hypothesised relationships exist.

How can a third variable influence the relationship between two variables?

- Underlie – where the variation in both observed variables is caused by a third, unobserved variable (mushroom study).
- Intervene – where there is a variable that comes between the two variables you are considering.
- Mediate – where there is a direct effect and an intervening variable.
- Moderate – there is another factor or factors that alter the effect of one variable on the other.

What statistical techniques can I use to analyse multivariate relationships?

- Dependence techniques – including multiple regression analysis and structural equation modelling.
- Interdependence techniques – including factor and cluster analysis.

References

Bryman, Alan and Bell, Emma 2003. *Business Research Methods*. Oxford: Oxford University Press.

Cook, T.D. and Campbell, D. 1979. *Quasi-Experimentation: Design and Analysis Issues for Field Settings*. London: Houghton Mifflin.

Dillon, William R. and Goldstein, Matthew 1984. *Multivariate Analysis: Methods and Application*. New York: John Wiley & Sons.

Gabriel, Yiannis and Lang, Tim 1995. *The Unmanageable Consumer*. London: Sage.

O'Leary, Z. 2004. *The Essential Guide to Doing Research*. London: Sage.

Jeffreys, D. 2004, 8 July. A victim of its own success, *The Guardian*. Available at: www.theguardian.com/education/2004/jul/08/research.highereducation (accessed 4 August 2016).

Rugg, Gordon and Petre, Marian 2004. *The Unwritten Rules of PhD Research*. Maidenhead: Open University Press.

Snipes, Jeffrey B. and Maguire, Edward R. 1995. Country music, suicide, and spuriousness, *Social Forces*, 74(1): 327–9.

Stack, S. and Gundlach, J. 1992. The effect of country music on suicide, *Social Forces*, 70(5): 211–18.

Zeithaml, Valarie A., Parasuraman, A. and Berry, Leonard L. 1990. *Delivering Quality Service: Balancing Customer Perceptions and Expectations*. New York: Simon and Schuster.

Additional resources

Bryman, A. and Cramer, D. 2000. *Quantitative Data Analysis with SPSS Release 10 for Windows*. London: Routledge.

Oakshott, Les 2001. *Essential Quantitative Methods for Business, Management, and Finance*, 2nd edn. Basingstoke: Palgrave Macmillan.

Swift, Louise 2001. *Quantitative Methods for Business, Management and Finance*. Basingstoke: Palgrave Macmillan.

Key terms

Discussion questions

1. What should you take into account when you are deciding whether to accept a causal relationship based on bivariate data?

2. How does an intervening variable differ from a moderating variable?

3. 'It's not necessary to understand how multivariate statistics work, so long as you have a user-friendly statistics software package.' Discuss.

4. What problems might you experience in trying to use nominal or ordinal data in multivariate analysis?

5. Where do you think most spurious relationships come from: faulty statistical analysis or faulty conceptual models?

6. What would happen if we included every possible variable in a conceptual model? What are the implications for research design?

7. Should you leave multivariate analysis to the experts?

Workshop

Find a quantitative study related to your research topic. Outline the theoretical framework based on the text. Compare this with the model in the figures (if provided).

1. What direct relationships are there among variables?

2. What indirect relationships are there?

3. Are any of these moderating/mediating?

4. Are the model/explanation/findings plausible?

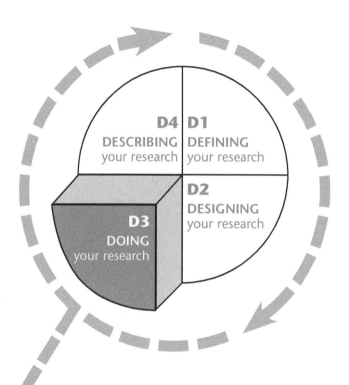

Relevant chapters
13 How do I write up my report?
14 What do I do now?

Key challenges
- Making sense of your findings
- Presenting your research to others
- Reflecting and learning from your research

4

Relevant chapters
1 What is research?
2 What should I study?
3 How do I find information?

Key challenges
- Understanding what academic research is
- Generating and clarifying ideas
- Using sources of information

1

D4
DESCRIBING
your research

D1
DEFINING
your research

D2
DESIGNING
your research

D3
DOING
your research

Relevant chapters
9 How do I do field research?
10 What do my quantitative data mean(1)?
11 What do my quantitative data mean(2)?
12 What do my qualitative data mean?

Key challenges
- Practical considerations in doing research
- Describing data using simple statistics
- Carrying out statistical tests
- **Interpreting words and actions**

3

Relevant chapters
4 What is my research approach?
5 How do I do quantitative research?
6 How do I do qualitative research?
7 How do I do case study research?
8 How do I make sure my research is ethical?

Key challenges
- Choosing a research approach
- Choosing a research design
- Collecting data using quantitative methods
- Collecting data using qualitative methods
- Integrating quantitative and qualitative methods

2

What do my qualitative data mean?

Interpreting interview and observational data

 Key questions

- How should I prepare my qualitative data for analysis?
- What are the main strategies for analysing qualitative data?
- What qualities should I aim for in my analysis?

 Learning outcomes

At the end of this chapter, you should be able to:

- Decide whether to analyse your qualitative data in a structured or unstructured way
- See if your data analysis is consistent with your research design
- Assess the quality of your data and analysis

Contents

Introduction

> Just as painters need both techniques and vision to bring their novel images to life on canvas, [qualitative] analysts need techniques to help them see beyond the ordinary and to arrive at new understandings of social life.
>
> **(Strauss and Corbin** 1996: 8).

If you have collected all your qualitative data and are sitting in front of a significant pile of transcripts, notes and other documents from your interviews or observations, you are probably wondering: 'What do I do with all of this? Where do I start?' At this point you realise you should have read **Chapter 6**, where it was made clear that you need to analyse your data as you go along, not wait until the end. However, all is not lost, and there are strategies that can be used to rescue the project.

Once you start collecting data using a qualitative research design, you will see the major difference between the deductive approach taken in quantitative research and the inductive approach taken in qualitative research. In a qualitative research design, you continually refine your data collection and analysis as you investigate your research problem, opening up new areas and closing off other ones. Your qualitative research design will evolve throughout the research process; a quantitative research design is 'frozen' once your data collection has started.

Because of this evolution and flexibility, you need to approach qualitative research as a creative process that requires your intuition and insight. This is one of the key skills associated with the ethnographer rather than the scientist as a role model. The scientist's creativity comes before and after the data analysis (for which there are strict rules), whilst the ethnographer's creativity is especially important in analysing and interpreting the evidence. This might be new to you, particularly if you come from a technical background where research follows the deductive logic. Although you may find this much less structured than statistical analysis, the procedures you can use for identifying themes in qualitative data are as rigorous, well developed and credible as statistical methods for analysing quantitative data.

This chapter presents two main approaches to analysing qualitative data, one structured and the other unstructured. Which one you choose will depend on your research design. The four qualitative research designs introduced in **Chapter 6** varied by how involved the researcher was in the research setting and with the research participants. There are a plethora of methods though that can be used and whilst we set out some that we have found appropriate for our students, you may wish to look further afield for your analysis strategy. As always in this book there is more detailed guidance contained in the **Additional resources** given at the end of this chapter.

In **Section 12.1**, we deal with some issues you must address before you even start analysing your qualitative data. You must organise your data, decide the general approach you will take – structured or unstructured – and whether you will analyse your data by hand or use specialised computer software.

In **Section 12.2**, we discuss key principles of qualitative analysis. We introduce methods for unstructured data analysis. We begin with Kolb's cycle, which is a general approach to analysing qualitative data. We then discuss principles of coding, concept extraction and framework-building.

Section 12.3 examines how to interpret the data and the themes associated with a qualitative analysis to see whether you have answered your research questions. We point out some useful strategies and common mistakes associated with this stage of doing your research. Since qualitative research does not necessarily start with a fixed and detailed conceptual framework, one may emerge from the analysis. This process will be more *iterative* than in quantitative research. However, you still need to relate what you have found out back to your research questions, so that you can see whether you have answered them. The experimenting that you do in this stage can help you see how to present your research in your project report. We conclude by describing the criteria by which you should assess the quality of your analysis.

After you have read this chapter, you should be able to plan how you will analyse your qualitative data. This makes it easier to collect data in a systematic way and analyse them. Since a major advantage of qualitative research design is that it enables you to look for unexpected or counterintuitive patterns in your data, you should make sure you capture as many of these insights as you can. Taking a systematic approach is especially important for an open-ended process such as qualitative analysis.

12.1 Managing your qualitative data

Before you start analysing your qualitative data, you will need to put them in a form that you can work with. This will be much easier if you have taken a systematic approach to collecting, handling and storing these data.

12.1.1 Managing qualitative data

As we saw in **Chapter 10**, you can record quantitative data in a data matrix by hand, in a spreadsheet or a statistical program, which helps you keep track of and analyse them relatively easily. Managing qualitative data presents more of a challenge because qualitative data:

- **Are not processed or transformed.** You must start your analysis with data in their raw form rather than in processed form. This is a major difference from quantitative research, where you might even analyse secondary data from a database where someone has already transformed the raw data into numbers.
- **Take many forms.** Qualitative data include interviews, personal statements, opinions, impressions and recollections, along with documents and other artefacts.
- **Are not standardised.** Each piece of qualitative data will be presented in its own way.
- **Are voluminous.** Because they haven't been transformed or processed, qualitative data cannot be expressed as concisely as quantitative data. It is not unusual for qualitative analysis, for example the results of a participant observation study, to start with hundreds or even thousands of pages of notes and transcripts.

In working with qualitative data, you must make sure that your data are:

- **Traceable.** You must be able to demonstrate where a particular piece of data came from. Who said (or wrote) it? Which organisation or field setting did it come from? When was it collected? Who collected it? See **Student research in action 12.1** for an example.
- **Reliable.** Your transcripts or other records must faithfully record your discussions or observations. Always write up your notes and impressions within 24 hours – we recommend immediately, if you can. This might even be before you leave the interview site – some researchers have even done this in the toilets for privacy.

- **Complete.** You should keep all your field notes, tapes and transcripts. **Student research in action 12.1** shows how a student did this for a project where she collected data in several different ways and from several different sources.

Student research in action 12.1

HANNAH AND HER CISTERNS

As part of a wine-marketing course, Hannah was investigating how market information gets up the supply chain from the sellers to the wine producers and finally the growers. She arranged to interview people at different stages in the supply process.

Following her interviews, Hannah logged her data sources as shown in **Table 12.1**. Hannah identified each different data element she collected using a simple system. She used a four-digit code to classify each interview or document according to its source and type. Each code contained information about the category of the organisation, the organisation, the individual who was interviewed and the type of data that were collected. She also kept careful track of the dates of the interviews.

These simple codes helped Hannah keep track of interviews and documents. By organising her data systematically, Hannah made sure that she could trace all her data back to their source. She could easily include the table in her research methods chapter in her project report, so that she could refer to them systematically. Also, since Hannah disguised the firms and individuals before she reported her findings, this table helped her keep track of the disguises she used for her firms. Finally, during her analysis and reporting, she used these codes to compare the views of participants located in different parts of the supply network.

Table 12.1   Hannah's list of contacts and documents

Place in supply chain	Company	Person interviewed	Date(s) of interview	Code(s)
Retail outlet	A	Store manager	7/12/2001	1–A–1 T (transcript)
		Beverage manager	7/12/2001	1-A-2 N (notes only – recording declined)
	B	Regional manager	14/12/2001	1-B-1 T 1-B-1-D (documents)
Distributor	C	Marketing manager	22/11/2001	2-C-1-T
	D	Category manager	18/12/2001	2-D-1-T
Producer	D	Marketing manager	19/12/2001	3-D-2-T
	E	Brand manager	7/11/2001	3-E-1-T 3-E-1-D
Grower	F	Vineyard owner	12/1/2002	4-F-1-T
		Vineyard manager	12/1/2002	4-F-2-T
	G	Planning manager	25/11/2001	4-G-1-T

12.1.2 Software for qualitative analysis

Even though qualitative research designs usually collect data from a small sample compared with quantitative research designs such as surveys, they result in as much or even more data. As we noted above, you may record or transcribe thousands of words, especially in a long or group project: a doctoral student who takes this approach may often transcribe more than a thousand pages of interviews or observations.

We recommend that, unless you are collecting a lot of data, working in a team or doing a complex analysis you collect and analyse your qualitative data using a simple word-processing program such as Microsoft Word. You should decide early on whether you will analyse your qualitative data by hand, using a word-processing program, or using a specialised computer program. This will affect not only your analysis, but also how you collect and record your data. If you make this decision early in the research process, you will avoid having to convert your data to a new format before you can analyse it or, more disastrously, having to type it all in at the last minute.

Just as you can use statistical software to manage the complexity of statistical analysis, you can use ethnographic software to manage the complexity of qualitative analysis. You may hear this software generically referred to as **computer-assisted qualitative data analysis software** (CAQDAS). Specialised software such as Ethnograph (www.qualisresearch.com), NVivo (see www.qsrinternational.com for the software and Bazeley and Jackson, 2013 on how to use it), and winMAX (see www.scolari.com) are all used by researchers. Although experienced qualitative researchers have differing opinions about CAQDAS software, you may find it useful if you have the time to spend learning to use it (Bryman and Bell, 2011). Professional researchers use this software for the routine mechanical work of coding data and finding all the instances of a particular code so they can concentrate on interpreting the data. As O'Leary (2013: 203) points out, the researcher still needs to 'strategically, creatively, and intuitively analyse the data'.

Table 12.2 summarises the arguments for and against using CAQDAS software.

In addition to these tools, we see an increasing array of specialist tools used by researchers. One of these is Leximancer which analyses patterns of word usage in data and has been used following the collection of data from social media platforms. The following example demonstrates how this works.

Table 12.2   The advantages and disadvantages of using qualitative analysis software

Pros	Cons
Ease of document management – particularly for very large amounts of data	Doesn't do anything that cannot be done by other means
Traceability of concepts ensured	Can result in loss of contextual information
Does allow you to demonstrate your methods and obtain high-quality output	Significant learning curve – takes time to get to be proficient with the software
	Doesn't do the analysis for you
	May deter you from using more effective graphical means
	Requires all data to be entered in the same format – can be highly time consuming where you have nonstandard data
	A fool with a tool is still a fool…

Research in action 12.1

LEXIMANCER

Using Leximancer: by Professor Saleem Gul, Institute of Management Sciences, Peshawar.

1. Leximancer Description

Leximancer is a thesaurus-based searching algorithm that automatically builds, through a recursive process, a thesaurus from the data being analysed. The generated thesaurus is based on the concept of 'co-occurrence' of words within the corpus under analysis. Through the use of Leximancer it is possible to obtain data relating to centrality, incidence, and networking of concepts. Leximancer has been shown to improve the management of text data and increase the validity of interpretations.

2. Leximancer's Algorithms and Example of *Cinderella*: Or, *the Little Glass Slipper* by Dalziel (1817)

Leximancer uses a three-phase algorithm to analyse text data. A brief description of each algorithm along with sample output from the Leximancer software is provided below.

Phase 1 Conceptual Analysis: This phase involves identification of the main word concepts in the texts being analysed; this is based purely on a word count performed on the text. See the sample output in Figure 12.1.

Name-Like	Count	Relevance	
CINDERELLA	12	100%	
Prince	5	42%	
King's	2	17%	
Court	2	17%	

Word-Like	Count	Relevance	
ball	8	67%	
godmother	8	67%	
sisters	6	50%	
lady	6	50%	
beautiful	5	42%	
wand	5	42%	
changed	5	42%	
glass	4	33%	
slipper	4	33%	
coach	4	33%	
moment	3	25%	
old	3	25%	
gave	3	25%	
home	3	25%	
clock	3	25%	
rats	2	17%	
coachman	2	17%	
son	2	17%	
postilion	2	17%	
arrived	2	17%	
splendid	2	17%	

Figure 12.1 Sample output – Phase 1 Conceptual Analysis

Theme	Connectivity	Relevance
godmother	100%	
ball	95%	
King's	45%	
coach	43%	
glass	26%	
changed	25%	
home	06%	
splendid	06%	
clock	04%	

Figure 12.2 Sample output – Phase 2 Semantic Analysis

Phase 2 Semantic Analysis: In this phase the software established relationships between the concepts; this is performed based on a word count analysis of the text, where the count is focused on the co-occurrence of two words. The more times any two words co-occur, the greater is the semantic relationship between the two. See the sample output in Figure 12.2.

Phase 3 Concept Mapping: This phase results in the production of concept maps that present a visual representation of the analysed text showing: the main concepts, their relative frequency, frequency of co-occurrence of concepts, centrality of each concept, and thematic contexts in which they co-occur. Concepts appear on the map as clusters as shown in Figure 12.3.

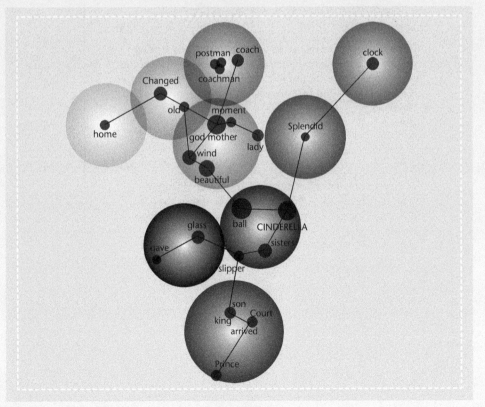

Figure 12.3 Sample output – Phase 3 Concept Mapping

Users may at any time view each theme in more detail, as shown in the example of Figure 12.4:

THEME: ball

(ball, CINDERELLA, sisters, slipper)

---

ball   *(Hits:* 8)

your tears you shall go to the grand ball Go into you must do just as I bid you. **Cinderella** brought the garden and bring me a pumpkin."
more...

CINDERELLA   *(Hits:* 12)

say in praise of the lady, that **Cinderella** expressed a desire to go to the next ball to see the **Princess;** but
this only served to bring out their dislike of
still
more...

sisters   *(Hits:* 6)

The next evening the two sisters went to the ball, and also, who was still more splendidly dressed than before. Her enjoyment was even greater than at the first ball, and she was so occupied with the **Prince's** tender sayings that she was not so quick in marking the **Cinderella**
more...

slipper   *(Hits:* 4)

When her sisters arrived after the ball, they spoke in terms of rapture of the unknown **Princess**, and told **Cinderella** about the little glass slipper she had dropped, and how the **Prince** picked it up. It was evident to all the
Court that the **Prince** was determined if possible, to find out the owner of the slipper; and a few days afterwards a royal herald proclaimed that the **King's** son would
more...

Figure 12.4 The 'ball' theme in more detail

Additionally, custom queries can be posed to explore specific words and their occurrence within the text. For example, the following query shown in Figure 12.5 is based on the word 'Slipper'.

/cinderella.pdf/cinderella~1.html 1 68   Add to Log | Full Text

This proclamation caused a great sensation. *Ladies* of ranks were permitted to make a trial of the slipper "Let me but it was of no use.

/cinderella.pdf/cinderella~1.html 1 67   Add to Log | Full Text

the glass slipper should be found

/cinderella.pdf/cinderella~1.html 1 64   Add to Log | Full Text

When her sisters arrived after the ball, they spoke in terms of rapture of the unknown *Princess*, and told *Cinderella* about the little glass slipper she had dropped, and how the *Prince* picked it up. It was evident to all the
Court that the **Prince** was determined if possible, to find out the owner of the slipper; and a few days afterwards a royal herald proclaimed that the **King's** son would

/cinderella.pdf/cinderella~1.html 1 74   Add to Log | Full Text

astonishment when *Cinderella* took the fellow slipper out of her pocket At that moment the godmother appeared, and touched *Cinderella's* clothes with her wand. Her sisters then saw that she was the beautiful lady they had met at the ball,

Figure 12.5 Query on the word 'slipper'

Examples of the use of Leximancer in professional research include Kordestani et al. (2015) and Bal et al. (2010).

12.2 Analysing your qualitative data

In **Chapter 4**, we characterised the logic underlying quantitative research as deductive and qualitative research as inductive. As we have noted, quantitative research (at least in the abstract) is a more or less linear process. Qualitative research, however, is usually much messier. Research design, data collection and data analysis may overlap; you may even cycle back and forth between them repeatedly. As a result, you may not be able to tell how you will analyse your data until you have collected them. You may not even know what data you will end up collecting.

This has a significant impact on this stage of the research process, because you do not know how much time and energy you will spend analysing your data. Compared with quantitative data analysis, where only your interpretation cannot be predicted in your research design, the analysis of qualitative data can be complex and open-ended, so new researchers sometimes find this frustrating. This stage may be very time consuming, but skimping on it will mean that you don't find out anything worthwhile. Worse, if you rush your analysis, even if you do find out something interesting, you may not be able to support your findings.

12.2.1 Using Kolb's learning cycle for qualitative data analysis

A fundamental strength of qualitative data analysis is its ability to evolve during the study. A good model which many researchers use to analyse qualitative data is based on **Kolb's learning cycle** (Kolb 1985), and is shown in **Figure 12.6**. We will describe a simple technique – based on Kolb's learning cycle – and a more complicated technique – concept extraction – for this.

Kolb's cycle starts with what he terms **concrete experience**. Your concrete experience may be very personal, such as a series of feelings or memories, or research-based, such as transcripts of interviews. Your analysis is based on this concrete experience.

The second stage of **reflective observation** involves three separate activities. The first activity is **familiarisation**, becoming intimately familiar with your data. This is particularly important for group projects or where you are analysing your data after a time lapse. Many researchers believe (re)familiarisation to be key to high-quality qualitative analysis.

The second activity is **spending time with the issues and the data**. You are not specifically looking for anything, but unhurriedly reflecting on what is happening. The final activity is **reordering**, or summarising the data to reflect the patterns you see in the data.

Once you have reordered your data, you should spend some time in **abstract conceptualisation**. This sounds horrendous, but it is actually very simple. You extract concepts (or the key themes) from your data. A **concept** is 'a descriptor for an issue, movement, thought or pattern of words that would be recognisable particularly to the researcher' (Kolb 1985). A simple example of the identification of what became a very important concept in a piece of research is described in **Student research in action 12.2**.

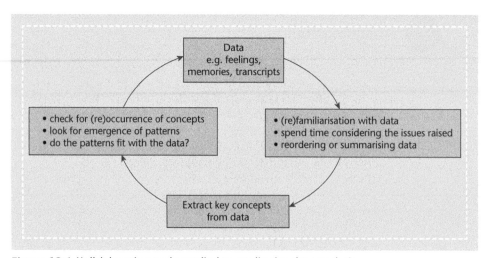

Figure 12.6 Kolb's learning cycle applied to qualitative data analysis

Student research in action 12.2

FLUFFY THE VAMPIRE SLAYER

A student group was interviewing people in a firm about benchmarking. They noticed that the people they interviewed would start talking about benchmarking but become very vague once they had got beyond a simple statement of the word. The students identified this vagueness as 'going fluffy'.

Once they had identified 'going fluffy' as a concept, the students marked the occasions in their transcripts where they thought respondents had 'gone fluffy'. By identifying episodes of 'going fluffy' in the transcripts, the students saw that vagueness was associated with low levels of application, and even lower levels of benefits being achieved. They were then able to relate where this occurred to people's experiences with the benchmarking initiative, and later to its relative success. They concluded that there were significant pockets within the organisation where knowledge levels were low ('being fluffy') and that if the firm wanted to gain greater success from its initiative, these knowledge deficiencies would have to be addressed.

The final stage of Kolb's learning cycle is **active experimentation** with your data to see where a concept or group of concepts occurs. In this stage, you can see whether any patterns are emerging from your data, or whether your data are starting to fit with theories, models or concepts suggested in the literature. A concept can include actions, so you can analyse actions using Kolb's learning cycle, as illustrated in **Student research in action 12.3**. You will then need to see if these patterns fit with the reality of your data – do they really fit your concrete experience? We will discuss how you can do this in **Section 12.2**.

Student research in action 12.3

PLEASE DON'T SQUEEZE THE KIWIS

A team of students were investigating whether people would purchase fresh vegetables over the internet and what kinds of customers were likely to use internet shopping. They decided to investigate buyer behaviour and spent a considerable amount of time lurking round the vegetable counters of a major supermarket observing and recording the behaviour of different customers. As this was a nonparticipant observation study, they had to unobtrusively record their observations of the movements and actions of shoppers to avoid alerting customers to the fact that they were being watched.

The students started their data collection by observing how people selected fresh produce. These differences included how the person looked for items (browsers versus list shoppers) and how they then selected the actual produce to buy. They noted the process of produce selection by using a series of symbols for structured observation. They modified a standard set of symbols to include special activities that emerged from their analysis – specifically 'squeeze', 'sniff' or 'tap and listen'.

For each observation they carefully noted the shopper's characteristics. This included whether the shopper was a man or a woman, whether they had a basket or trolley (small or large shopping expedition), their apparent age and their appearance. This provided background information for later analysis.

Once they had observed a sufficient number of shoppers, they examined the sequence of actions by each customer and compared these sequences across the range of shoppers. As part of the abstract conceptualisation stage, they classified shoppers into the following three behaviours:

- Pickers – Pick the first thing that they see
- Lookers – Have a perfunctory look to check that it is OK before confirming their selection
- Squeezers – Do a thorough analysis, including one or more of the special activities listed above.

▶

They then tried to see whether each behaviour could be associated with a particular category of customer. Some of the propositions they identified were:

- Older people are more likely to be squeezers
- Younger people are more likely to be pickers.

They tested these propositions by going back to their original data set. They then hypothesised that the main group of prospective purchasers via the internet would be pickers, shoppers who were less discriminating about their vegetables. These would most likely be younger shoppers (under 40). Older people, who checked out their vegetables more thoroughly, were less likely to spend their 'grey pound' via the internet, at least on vegetables, since they would not be able to do a thorough analysis.

By examining how people select fresh produce, the students could understand some general principles of shopping behaviours after observing a small sample of buyers in one store. Since the students hadn't started with any particular hypotheses to test, such as 'Older shoppers are less likely to buy vegetables via the internet', they were free to let the findings emerge from the data they collected rather than imposing an interpretation on it (and making it less likely that they would recognise any unexpected or counterintuitive evidence). They might have missed these different behaviours if they had administered a survey and statistically analysed the data. However, they could argue that their findings were as generalisable as survey data, since there was nothing special about the store, its location or the customers). As part of their 'areas for further investigation', they suggested that the findings could be further tested through a survey of a wider population.

12.2.2 Unstructured versus structured analysis

As described above, Kolb's cycle is a relatively unstructured approach to finding out the meaning of your qualitative data. In an **unstructured analysis**, you let meanings and themes emerge from your data, rather than imposing them on the data. You can then look for conceptual frameworks that help you to understand and explain these themes.

Unstructured approach to qualitative analysis

Although an unstructured approach is excellent for maximising the creativity you can bring to interpreting your data and the chances that you may develop some new and unique insights from your evidence, it can create real challenges for student researchers. An unstructured approach takes no account of deadlines – it is done when it is done and not any sooner. This means that it is open-ended, and that you may take weeks, or even months, to do a thorough job of your data analysis and interpretation.

Structured analysis of qualitative data

If you are collecting qualitative data, but you have to meet a project deadline, you might want to consider taking a more structured approach to analysing your qualitative data. Instead of trying to induce everything, up to and including your conceptual framework, from your data, you can use concepts and/or conceptual frameworks from the literature to structure your data analysis and interpretation.

In a **structured analysis** of qualitative data, you compare your findings to a conceptual framework you have developed or found in the literature. This will help to guide your analysis and interpretation, but still allow you to identify those aspects of your evidence that differ from what other researchers have previously found.

Some researchers use pre-existing concepts and frameworks to apply even more structure than the comparative method we have just described. That is, they analyse their qualitative data through the lens of a conceptual framework they have already selected. This process is similar to the 'classical' scientific approach, but it substitutes thematic analysis for statistical analysis.

Since the structured approach is so similar to the analysis of quantitative data, we will not focus on it in this chapter. Instead, the following considers how quantitative techniques can be applied to qualitative data.

Statistical analysis of qualitative data

There is nothing to prevent you from statistically analysing data you have gathered using a qualitative research method such as participant observation or unstructured interviews. Indeed, quantitative research is often based on quantitative data that started out as qualitative data. We often reduce the complexity of qualitative data, such as attitudes, opinions or behaviours, to numbers by quantification so that we can analyse them more conveniently using the statistical methods described in **Chapters 10** and **11**. You are likely to be familiar with these shortcuts. For example, many questionnaires ask you to quantify an opinion on a scale of 'completely disagree' to 'completely agree', or a behaviour on a scale of 'rarely or never' to 'frequently or always' by circling a number.

You can analyse any qualitative data set – for example the thousand-page interview transcript or notes based on participant observation – in a quantitative way. If you want to analyse your qualitative data statistically, you will need to make sure that you meet the other requirements for quantitative analysis. Qualitative research designs often involve in-depth investigation of a small number of cases. You will have to make sure that you have a large enough sample to analyse statistically. Small sample sizes and other factors may make it difficult for you to use the inferential statistics described in **Chapters 10** and **11**. Since many qualitative research designs do not meet minimum sample sizes, continuous measurements or normal distributions, you may need to use special techniques, known as nonparametric methods.

However, the main objection to analysing qualitative data statistically is not small sample size. The complexity of the conceptual frameworks (theories and models) that people investigate in qualitative research designs means that multivariate thinking (if not statistical techniques) may be useful in developing and evaluating your findings. If you reduce qualitative data to categorical data, you risk losing much of the data's richness and any unique insights. For example, if you classified people as only 'satisfied' or 'dissatisfied', you might miss out on insights from your data that reveal why they were dissatisfied or whether all dissatisfied customers are alike – are there different kinds of dissatisfaction?

Which approach should you take?

Figure 12.7 shows how the unstructured and structured approaches to analysing qualitative data fit with the different research designs discussed in **Chapter 6**, where we classified qualitative research designs by how close the researcher was to the subject

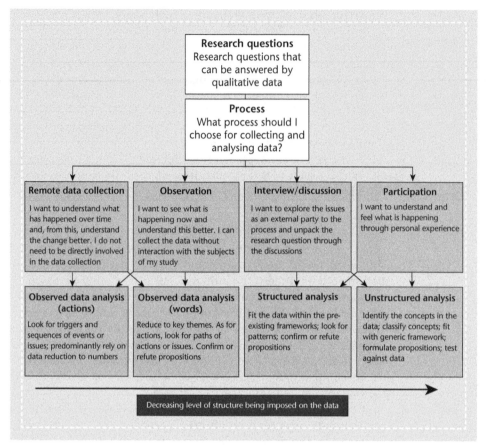

Figure 12.7 Methods for collecting and analysing qualitative data

of the research. Your approach should match the data you have collected. Where you position your data analysis depends on your research problem and questions, and on the data you have collected. Research questions that ask 'why?' and look for underlying meaning in situations suggest unstructured techniques, whilst research questions such as 'what?' suggest more structured techniques.

In an unstructured approach to analysing your qualitative data, you will not have a predetermined structure, as in structured qualitative or quantitative analysis. As you analyse your data and collect more data, you will change the methods and perhaps even the questions you are asking. You still need to take a systematic approach to managing the analytic process, no matter what technique you decide to use.

12.2.3 Extracting concepts from your data

A more complex technique for identifying concepts and developing or testing conceptual frameworks is **concept extraction**. Concept extraction is often used in analysing structured and unstructured interviews and participant observation. In concept extraction, your concepts emerge from your data, rather than from your literature review. This can be used in either the structured or unstructured approaches described above. With either approach, the first step in the process is immersion in the data – spending time making sure you have a high level of familiarity with the data, with both its content, its context and any inferences in the way that something was said.

Concept identification

The next step in concept extraction is to identify the key issues, ideas or other meaning units in your data. Many people find this easiest to do manually, by going through a transcript line by line and marking each occurrence of a potential concept. (You can also do this on the computer or using specialised software.) You should try to summarise each concept in a word or a short phrase. You may want to play around with different ways of expressing a concept.

If you have found the concept expressed in different words by different interviewees or sources of data, you may want to call the concepts by slightly different names. This might be easier to see in an example where two interviewees were discussing change in their organisations. They frequently mentioned the measures being applied to the individuals and teams during the interviews, but they focused on different aspects such as those measures that had an impact on pay systems. The researchers identified measures as a concept, but showed the different measures as 'Measures1' and 'Measures2'. You should also note the context in which these issues are being discussed, and any other issues (discussed before or after) associated with them.

Open coding

A systematic process for identifying concepts is **open coding**. Open coding starts with codes that emerge when the researcher highlights the key ideas.

Table 12.3 presents a detailed example of how you can change your raw data – words – into concepts, based on a transcript of an actual interview. The study addressed the research question: 'Where do new ideas for changes to new product development processes come from, and how are they implemented?' After some structured questions, the interviewer asked the respondents more open-ended questions about how new ideas came into the department to find out how innovation was being applied to new product development (NPD). The table shows how the researcher has highlighted those concepts in the transcript associated with where new product ideas come from.

The researcher has identified the exact words used by the manager with **codes** in the right-hand column that represent concepts. The term 'coding' is used differently in qualitative analysis, where it involves identifying the key idea present in the text, whereas in quantitative analysis coding is purely data recording. 'Coding' the data in the way shown here makes it easier to compare data from interviews from different managers, and starts to create the raw material for the next stage of classification.

It is worth noting that as you look at this example you may disagree with the allocation of codes or feel that they may not seem intuitive to you. This is to be expected as the researcher involved (Harvey) had spent a long time with the managers and the data.

Coding starts to translate your respondent's language (here the manager's words) into your own language of concepts. As you can see, people don't speak in concepts, particularly if they are formulating ideas as they speak. In this case, the manager describes what goes on inside his organisation; the researcher translates his words into more abstract codes for concepts that describe the flow of ideas. For example,

Table 12.3   Transcribed interview

Interviewer's question	Manager's answer	Code/concept
I was just wondering how you find out about other things that are going on in the company?	We used to find out about these things through colleagues, and curiously enough it often comes from one particular area of the firm – that of silicon chip design. These chips are at the heart of all our products and are highly complex. The guys working down there tend to generate very quick processes for what they do, and they are then taken up by other parts of the design process, so **they tend to lead** the way.	Internal sources Perceived excellence
So they've got something different going on there? Do they have different pressures on the process that means they have to innovate more quickly?	I think that what is different there is that we do our bit first. They are then under pretty **severe schedule pressure**. It is also a fairly deterministic part of the product in that if you get it right, it stays right.	Time-driven
Is that because it's too expensive to change it?	No, it's because of the nature of the design – it's digital design. Once you've come up with the digital design, you can make a million of them. From the point of view of the rest of the product, there's a lot more to do after you've come up with the design. For some reason, it does generate an immense amount of schedule pressure on those guys up front and as a result of that there is a strong recognition that it is necessary to get the chips right first time, and that's **fundamental to the health of the overall development programme.**	Pressure Critical
	So they tend to **invest more in novel techniques** to make it happen right and quickly. They do all sorts of things like they'll think nothing of buying some sort of simulator package that we use that costs say a quarter of a million pounds, to save three weeks on a project. They'll probably only use it for a few weeks, but the **payback is in time, so it's worth it.** To kind of complete that, what happens is that **those guys tend to find out new techniques,** then it kind of seeps out if you like. **They start talking about it, you go along, you review it. You think this looks good – I can apply it some way; then you do it yourself.** What does not happen and perhaps ought to happen is we don't get ideas coming from the corporate HQ. They have teams of people studying the product development processes. They then come round and say, '**we've got a great new technique for you,**' and **you don't go to the seminar** because we've discovered in the past that what they've really got is something that invariably you were doing a lot of years ago, because they're actually going round polling all of us and getting the best practices from us; **it doesn't help.**	Investment Time-driven Pull of ideas – chance External push – rejection Evaluation – ineffective

Is there any other help from the corporation?	No – they are just playing at it really. We just have to do it as well as we possibly can.	
Are there any other sources that you use to find new ideas?	Often from **best practice within the corporation** rather than corporate HQ telling you. This is a good way of doing it. Often at the beginning of a programme, you might find yourself, you get this **breathing space when you are planning**, you use this time to go and visit other parts of the corporation that you know are being successful. So you've got the Laser Printer people who have gone and seen what the disk people are doing, what techniques they are using and seeing if there is anything here we can use?	Pull of ideas – Opportunity available
That would be an informal process then?	Yes, it would be up to the **initiative** of the people involved in the new programme. They'd want to go and find out that stuff. For instance, we wouldn't use universities or educational establishments. I can't remember any times when we do.	Individual initiative
Just as a matter of interest, is there any particular reason for that?	**We don't tend to look outside these walls.** Specifically, why we don't go to academia I couldn't tell you, other than whenever something like that happens, often they're not well engaged; you get the impression they've read every book there is but they haven't actually done any of this stuff. There's an element of having to **win your spurs** here.	Internal sources Credibility

one code refers to the pull of ideas. Pull is where you go looking for that something; push is where someone from outside your area is telling you to do something. You can identify two examples of the pull of ideas in the transcript in **Table 12.3**.

You will also find that your own questioning may have made perfect sense at the time, but when you read it on the page, it may not be what you intended, or certainly nowhere near as clear – this is a skill that comes with time and reflection on the transcripts. The transcript therefore is a substantially different data source than a report, for instance. You may have some challenges decoding what respondents were talking about before you can do the analysis. Beware here that you don't impose an interpretation – if there is ambiguity, either go back to them to seek clarification or treat this with care.

Bryman and Bell (2011) suggest that you:

● Code as soon as possible, preferably as you are going along, to make sense of your data and avoid being swamped at the end
● Read through all your materials before you start coding or interpreting them
● Read through once and generate your basic codes
● Review your codes to see whether you can group codes into common categories

- Start to look for more general theoretical ideas
- Don't worry about generating too many codes, finding a single interpretation of your data or analysing your data.

Classification

Once you have coded your data, you can start to group together the concepts you have identified. Numbering or otherwise identifying your concepts (as in **Table 12.3**) will let you track where your data came from. You may want to write down each code or concept on an index card or Post-it note and group them physically, or list them on the computer and start rearranging them. You may see hierarchical patterns in the concepts (concept, subconcept, sub-subconcept and so on).

Table 12.4 shows one possible arrangement of the concepts from **Table 12.3**. As you can see, each significant group of concepts, such as source of ideas, drivers for ideas, search process and so on, defines a **category** representing a real-world **phenomenon** (Bryman and Bell 2011). A category has **properties**, which are aspects or attributes. Each property has one or more **dimensions**, representing the range of values it can take on, which are derived from your original concepts. For instance, in the transcript, ideas were noted to come from either inside the firm (internal) or outside (external). So, internal and external become the two dimensions of the property 'location'.

Conceptual framework

Once you have developed categories, you can start to develop a conceptual framework and propositions about the relationships between concepts, or compare your findings with a pre-existing framework, for example a conceptual framework you have identified in the literature. This provides the input into the next stage of qualitative analysis. **Student research in action 12.4** illustrates how such a framework can emerge as you explore the relationships between concepts.

Table 12.4   Organising concepts by themes

Category	Property	Dimension
Source of ideas	Location Mechanism Perception of source	Internal/external Push/pull Excellence/ineffective Credible/not credible
Drivers for ideas	Criticality of process	Time-driven High/low
Idea-searching process	Involvement in searching Type of searching process Instigation	Active/passive Planned/chance Individual/corporate initiative
Implementation	Opportunity	Available/not available

Student research in action 12.4
BUDDY, MY BUDDY

Suzie was considering the role of networks between individuals in knowledge transfer within and between organisations. She focused on the social aspects of knowledge management – she proposed that the more socially active a member of staff was, the more likely he or she was to share knowledge with others. Suzie developed a conceptual framework to show the concepts and relations that she wanted to develop, as shown in **Figure 12.8**.

At the start of her study, Suzie did not know how she would identify socially active employees or measure their behaviour. As she collected and analysed data, she started to see patterns emerge. A concept that consistently emerged during the interviews and observations was the number and duration of non-work-related discussions that took place, either directly or by phone or email. These were often wrapped around discussions of work-related issues. Suzie's analysis suggested that there was a link between non-work discussions and work-related discussions that was worth investigating further.

Axial coding

Strauss and Corbin (1999) present a method for putting the codes back together in a new way once you have completed your open coding. They explain how you can experiment with your codes and categories, so you can test out different scenarios to explain what you think is happening. This approach is helpful if your goal is to build a conceptual model based on your qualitative data.

This process of building up a conceptual model from your open codes and categories is called **axial coding**. Axial coding lets you elaborate each of your data categories in terms of the relationships that may exist between properties and their dimensions. You can use axial coding to figure out what is going on in each of these conceptual

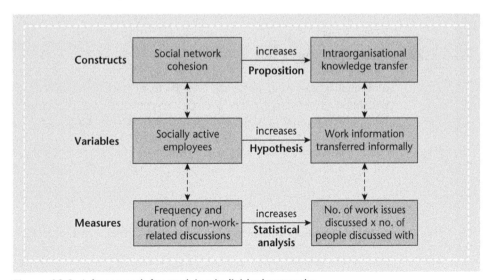

Figure 12.8 A framework for studying individual networks

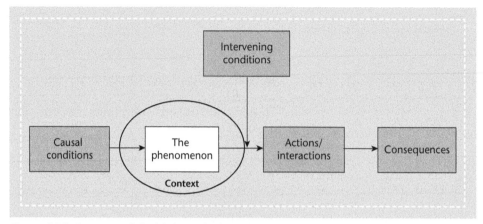

Figure 12.9 Strauss and Corbin's model for axial coding

categories: what it is, when it happens, when it doesn't happen, what are its consequences. Strauss and Corbin suggest that you link your categories to the causal conditions, contexts, intervening conditions, actions/interactions and consequences of the phenomenon you are investigating, as shown in **Figure 12.9**.

For example, you might be interested in whether there is any relationship between playing video games frequently and failure in exams. You could use the process of axial coding to examine the conceptual category of video game-playing. The phenomenon is the behaviour you are actually studying, whether it is solitary game-playing or group game-playing. You might want to distinguish between high and low levels of game-playing. Is four hours a day a high, moderate or low amount? Does this vary depending on whether it is a school day or a holiday? Finally, you would want to see what consequences game-playing has for study, social activities and so on.

12.2.4 Mapping concepts

Some qualitative researchers find it easier to explore qualitative data using graphical techniques rather than verbal ones such as the axial coding process described above. You could experiment with mind maps, influence diagrams and logic diagrams as ways of identifying patterns in your qualitative data. Mind maps have already been shown in **Chapter 3** and you might find them useful for graphically displaying and linking the concepts that have emerged from your study.

Influence diagrams

An **influence diagram** not only shows the concepts and whether there are relationships between them, it also shows the proposed cause-and-effect relationships. You can use an influence diagram to show where different forces may be acting in a particular situation (see Coyle 2001). An example influence diagram is shown in **Figure 12.10**.

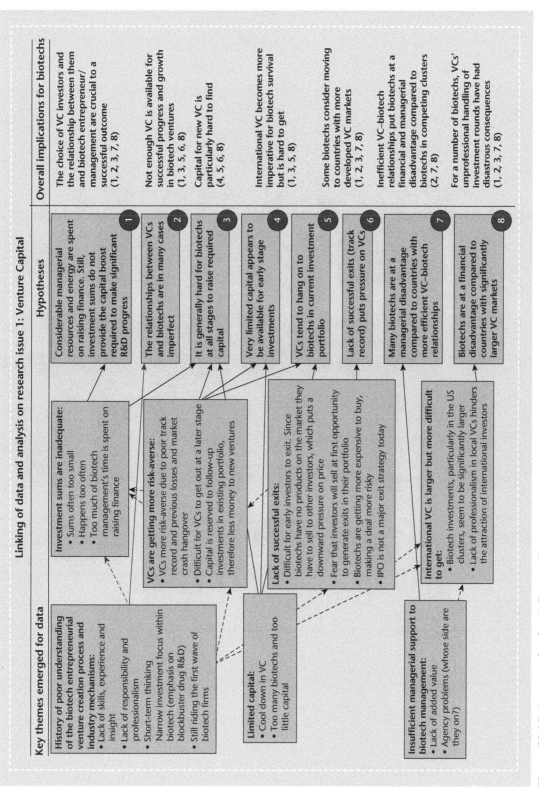

Figure 12.10 An example of an influence diagram

Source: Courtesy of Jes Batting

Logic diagrams

Logic diagrams show the logic or preconditions for an event or set of circumstances to occur. Logic diagrams provide the ability either to structure the logic of the current situation, or to indicate the necessary conditions for that situation to arise (see also Schragenheim 1998). The example shown in **Figure 12.11** enabled the researcher to

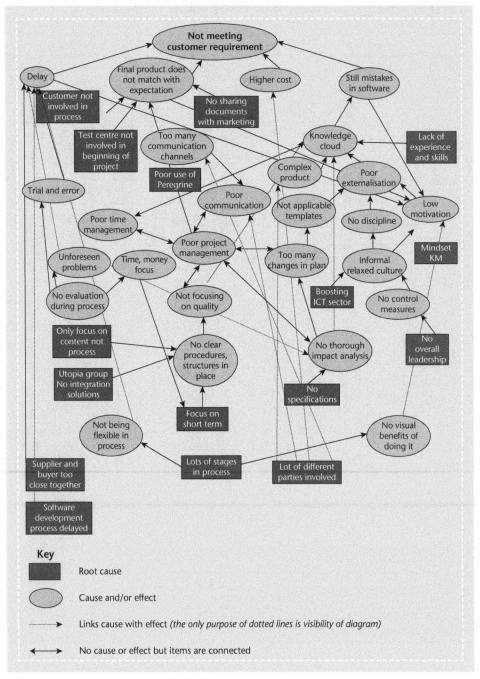

Figure 12.11 An example of a logic diagram

determine the root causes of particular phenomena. The basis for the figure is the logic that *if* the first condition arises, *then* it will logically lead to those that are indicated by the arrows.

Finishing your analysis

Students frequently ask how they will know when their qualitative data collection is complete. Unlike quantitative research designs, where you can determine the sample size required for your statistical data analysis before you start collecting data, in qualitative research designs it may be difficult to tell when you can stop collecting data, and then when your analysis is complete. In qualitative research, the term that is often used is **theoretical saturation**. You have reached theoretical saturation when additional data no longer add extra information to your concepts, when you are no longer getting any new insights from coding your data or reviewing your concepts or categories.

You have done enough when you have achieved your goal, which might include:

- **Description.** A better description of a particular phenomenon, the elements that constitute it and its dynamics, for instance how a situation changes over time.
- **Categorisation.** A classification of elements of an issue of interest, for example how people behave or perform particular tasks.
- **Inter-relation.** Establishing relationships between concepts, for instance as illustrated in **Table 12.4**.
- **Explanation.** Explaining a particular action or behaviour by describing what caused it or the circumstances in which it occurred.
- **Prediction.** A better prediction of the circumstances under which some action may work, for example the produce buying case in **Student research in action 12.3**.

12.2.5 Where to look for more information

In this section, we have only looked at structured and unstructured techniques for analysing qualitative data. However, you will find many different approaches to qualitative data analysis discussed in the research methods literature, including those highlighted by O'Leary (2013) and by Bryman and Bell (2011):

- **Analytic induction**, a rigorous approach to testing hypotheses from qualitative data
- **Content analysis**, which can be used to identify themes in texts or other materials. Researchers use both qualitative content analysis, where the emphasis is on searching out underlying themes, and quantitative content analysis, where the emphasis is on counting instances of these themes for quantitative analysis
- **Discourse analysis**, which can be used to interpret language in its social and historical context
- **Narrative analysis**, which can be used to interpret the stories told by individuals and focuses on the patterns people find in their lives over time
- **Conversation analysis**, which can be used to understand the structure of conversations
- **Semiotics**, which can be used to interpret the meaning behind signs and symbols, to show how messages are communicated as systems of cultural meaning

- **Hermeneutics**, which can be used to interpret texts, originally sacred texts such as the Bible, but today applied to both documents and social actions
- **Grounded theory**, which can be used to generate theory directly from data (which we briefly discussed in **Chapter 7** in the context of grounded case studies).

You may want to look at the **Additional resources** at the end of this chapter if any sound interesting. You can find many articles and even entire books written on these approaches.

12.3 Interpreting your qualitative results

In **Section 12.2**, we described a process for thematically analysing qualitative research. In qualitative analysis, you are inevitably interpreting your findings as you are analysing your data, because you need to build codes and categories from the raw data. This means that the interpretation aspect of this stage of your research process differs from this stage of a quantitative research project where you can separate analysing and interpreting. As with quantitative research, the main issue you need to address is linking what you have done with your research questions.

12.3.1 Interpreting patterns

In interpreting qualitative research, you will need to link your data with a theory you have identified because of doing your research. This means that you will find it difficult, if not impossible, to adopt the same structured approach to interpreting your research as you did for quantitative research. In qualitative research, your main goal is to weave together a convincing narrative from what you have done. A major task in interpreting is to identify the data that support this story, so that it is grounded in your empirical data as well as in your thematic analysis (for example your use of Kolb's cycle or concept extraction, as described in **Section 12.1**).

As the qualitative research process is usually iterative, cycling back and forth between processes of conceptualisation, data collection and data analysis, you will need to combine these in your interpretation of what you have found out. In qualitative research, you end up creating a conceptual framework, rather than starting with one. Your conceptual framework will emerge from your data, rather than being 'borrowed' from the literature. This means that interpreting your qualitative research report can be difficult because you can identify many different ways to make sense of it. Two different ways for organising emerging ideas and themes are:

- **Categorical** – reporting your categories and progressively focusing in or out. These categories can be predetermined or emerge from your data analysis
- **Thematic** – presenting your overall conceptual framework, then reporting each theme.

Many students find it useful to refer to examples of qualitative research to see how other researchers have induced themes and conceptual frameworks from their rich, qualitative data. It is even more important to understand the 'story' emerging from your research, even if it is not the only story that could emerge. You are depending mainly on the story you tell, or the narrative you create, to communicate the essence of the research you have done, and tables and figures are not as much a part of that story.

Students have found Miles, Huberman and Saldana's (2013) *Qualitative Data Analysis* useful for reading about the details of particular strategies for data analysis that go beyond the methods presented here. You may be able to find a good model for your own research among the many examples they present. You might also go back to an article or book you have consulted in your research project, and map how it structured its discussion.

Instead of basing your interpretation on data summarised in the form of tables and charts, as in quantitative research, you will usually need to work with the critical incidents, concepts or themes that emerge from your data. Many students have found it useful to use physical methods of working with keywords or phrases. For example, market researchers have developed sophisticated ways of sorting ideas written on index cards, using either R-sort or Q-sort procedures. (The main differences in sorting approaches tend to be whether you start with every idea in the same structure and split them progressively into smaller and smaller groups, or whether you start with individual ideas and combine them progressively into larger groups.) Other qualitative researchers have found it useful to use whiteboards or Post-it notes at this stage.

Kate Fox's *Watching the English: The Hidden Rules of English Behaviour*, an ethnographic study of the 'everyday' behaviour of English people, provides a good full-length example of organising around themes (Fox 2014). Fox identifies two main themes from her investigation, which she describes as 'conversation codes' and 'behaviour codes'. These are then used to organise all subsequent subthemes, for example conversation codes start with 'the weather' and end with 'pub talk', while behaviour codes start with rules that apply at home and take in sex, food and work along the way. Conversation codes and behaviour codes represent 'meta-themes'.

Either way, it may be useful to refer back and forth to 'verbatim quoting' from your transcripts and observation notes, comparing them with your argument, and interpreting and commenting on that evidence as you go along. (You need to have carefully catalogued your data, as recommended in **Section 12.1**, to be able to trace your quotes back to the interview or observation they came from.)

12.3.2 Linking your results to the literature

Because you are not basing your research plan on a deep exploration of the literature, in interpreting your qualitative research it is especially important to link what you have found to the literature. One criticism of qualitative research as currently practised is that too little of this linking is done, so there is very little accumulation of knowledge and much repetition. On the other hand, since you are inducing or developing further a conceptual model from your data whilst doing your research, as a qualitative researcher you should be in an excellent position to do a wide sweep for relevant literature, since you will have 'already found out what you are going to find out'.

Your interpretation may point towards particular themes or strands in the literature that might explain your findings or your findings might help to explain. You are moving in the opposite direction of the relationship between theory and data found in quantitative research. Again, it may be helpful to look at some examples of qualitative research on your topic for guidance in this area. There is no reason that a qualitative research project cannot be theoretically rich and use this richness to make sure that it is robust.

12.3.3 Presenting your qualitative results

Qualitative research is also challenging for students who are using this approach for the first time, especially if this is their first major research project. The outcome of interpreting the qualitative research you have done is another story! If the role model for the quantitative researcher is objective, independent scientist, then the role model for the qualitative research as ethnographer has clear implications for how you interpret qualitative research. Your major task is to develop this story, or narrative, and figure out the best way to tell it.

Reading an account of qualitative research is much closer to reading a work of fiction, such as a novel, than reading a scientific report. You would probably be surprised to read the following in a quantitative report:

> As a single, 30 year old woman, I could uninhibitedly ask other women to go to lunch; however, asking the men, most of whom were also older than me, was not as comfortable and seemed to require more of a justification.
>
> (**Schultze** 2000)

Although all qualitative reports have more in common with each other than they do with quantitative reports, there are three important models of how to interpret and present your qualitative evidence:

- As a narrative
- As thick description
- As a personal journey.

Narrative

The narrative form is probably the closest that qualitative research comes to the quantitative approach, and may be a good choice if your research is more structured than unstructured. If you have used a relatively non-involved qualitative design for your research such as indirect observation or secondary source data, your story may be a chronological story, which relates events – both in what you have studied and your research process – as they happened over time. If you develop your interpretation as a narrative, you may focus mostly on the factual details of what you observed and what it meant.

Thick description

If you have been more involved in your research setting, for example as a participant observer, you may want to include more of your own experience in interpreting your research. The style that is often associated with the more participative types of qualitative research is *thick description*, which incorporates how it felt for you to be doing research as well as what you observed. According to Geertz (1973), thick description comes from the tradition of ethnographic research in anthropology, where researchers such as Malinowski and Mead were describing people and contexts such as Pacific Islanders, with whom their readers were unfamiliar. The goal of thick description is to make your reader feel as though he or she is actually present in the research setting, and perhaps even as if he or she is doing the research. You may describe the physical situation in detail, for example how it looked, felt, smelt and so on.

Business and management researchers who are influenced by this tradition use thick description to describe less exotic situations, such as Bruno Latour and Steve Woolgar's (1986) observations in scientific laboratories or Barbara Ehrenreich's (2002) participant observation in retirement homes. Even though they are observing cultures much closer to home, for example, as in Po Branson's (1999) *Nudist on the Late Shift*, they interpret the setting and events for their readers in much the same way. John van Maanen's (1988) *Tales of the Field* gives a number of vivid examples from his own experience as an ethnographer.

When you read thick description, you can place yourself in the scene it describes: this style of writing could just as easily come from a novel or short story, and is completely different from the factual description found in a quantitative research report. For example, Diane Forsythe (2001: 170) conducted participant observation in a computer lab where several incidents had occurred that made the atmosphere a bit tense for the women in the lab. Forsythe describes how she herself, as well as the other women in the lab, reacted to the screensavers, eventually bringing the matter up with the head of the lab. She discusses the feelings and reactions not only of the people she was observing, but also her own reactions, and what these might mean in a wider context. Forsythe's work is vividly descriptive, and she puts herself into the story as a major character and takes part in the action. This is a major break with quantitative research, where the researcher writes as an omniscient, neutral 'we', if at all. Especially in direct observation and participant observation, the researcher becomes an active character in the story being told in the research and, to some extent, your reader does too.

Personal journey

As noted above, some forms of qualitative research reports include the researcher as a major actor, rather than as an observer who mainly observes and reacts. In some forms of qualitative research, for example participative action research or cooperative inquiry, the researcher becomes as much an object of the study as the people in the organisation or context being studied. In this case, your interpretation of what you have done may focus on reflections on how you felt or changed during the research, as well as what you learnt/observed from the field study.

Ulricke Schultze (2000), mentioned above, incorporated her experiences as a researcher into her vivid description of what she saw. To give her reader a feel for reflexive research as a process rather than an outcome, she presents excerpts from her research diary in her report so that the reader gets a sense of the progress (or lack of progress) she was making at various points in the project. She presents her reflections on what is going on (how can I interpret this, how does it make me feel) and her reflections on this reflection – a kind of hyper-reflexivity that she describes as 'ex-pressing'. Again, this is very different from the mostly retrospective sense-making imposed on research done from a scientific perspective. This is not to say that scientists never write in an ethnographic style. James Watson, for example, describes the discovery of the structure of DNA in very much this way. But scientists do this outside reporting research, usually in biographies written for popular audiences.

You may want to talk to your project supervisor, and look at some previous project reports, before you decide how much of your own experience and reflections you need to incorporate when you are interpreting what you have done. Some academic supervisors will expect and/or encourage it, but some may find it inappropriate.

If you are using this as the basis for a report to your business sponsor, you should tread carefully! Your business sponsor may be completely uninterested in this aspect of your placement or sponsored project (although it is not completely unknown), and it can be politically risky for both yourself and the people in the organisation to reveal detailed information. The major exception would be, obviously, situations in which you were explicitly engaged to do action research or other similar research.

12.3.4 Assessing the quality of your findings

Figure 12.12 shows the key elements of this assessment and the questions you should ask of your work before, during and after you have analysed your qualitative data. Each element is now discussed in turn.

Is your research reliable?

Whilst the detailed specification of the conceptual framework and methods of quantitative studies are assumed to lead to higher levels of reliability, qualitative studies – particularly those that are unstructured – would be difficult to repeat exactly. If you

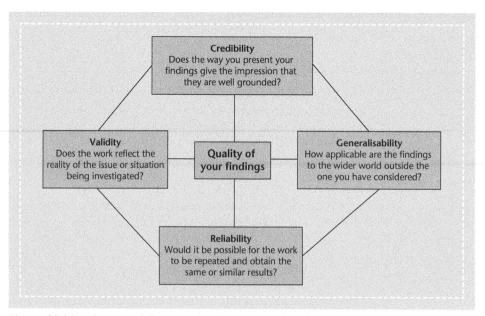

Figure 12.12 A framework for assessing the quality of qualitative research

were to do a short period of participant observation, it would be unlikely that someone else could go and join the same group and achieve exactly the same findings. Situations, people and dynamics change over time, resulting in this being more of a theoretical question – 'If I went back and did this study again, would I get the same results, and if it had been done by someone else, would they have got the same results?' In a qualitative study, it is unlikely that the results would be the same in either case, but the main points and conclusions should be fairly robust rather than fragile. Both of these questions force reflection on your own interaction and influence with the system you are researching.

Is your research valid?

Validity refers to the extent to which you have captured the underlying truth of the situation and not been misled by particular influences. Student projects can be biased by the views of key individuals – maybe someone who has been closely associated with the project and who may have his/her own agenda to press. Furthermore, there is always the issue of whether you have been *rigorous* in your analysis, or succumbed to a shallow *impressionistic* analysis of your data. Whilst there is ample space in the scope of methods used here to allow you to form impressions from your data, you should be able to demonstrate how you got from there to your findings. Documenting and explaining how you got from your data to your conclusions, using strategies such as those described in this chapter (which are explored in more depth in **Chapter 13**), is one way to show this.

Is your research generalisable?

Generalisability in the context of qualitative research is very challenging as a concept. Many researchers overstate their findings (this is what we found in this organisation/place and therefore it is true for all organisations/places/the entire world) or understate them (these findings are only true in the situation we investigated and have no relevance anywhere else). You might think that a single case study means that you have a sample size of only one, which makes it difficult to generalise from the sample to the population. Exactly. You should be thinking about where your theoretical proposition generalises and not your sample. It is possible to learn from a sample of one by thinking about areas where the findings of a similar piece of work may be similar, and where its particular circumstances would make it different (for example different competitive/legislative/geographical environments or schools/business organisations).

Is your research credible?

Shipman (1982) included **credibility** – how you present your findings and your research – as a vital factor in assessing the quality of qualitative research. It is important that you present evidence to support any contentions made, including key quotations and evidence from numerous sources (see the discussion of triangulation in **Chapter 7**). In analysing your qualitative data, you should identify suitable key pieces of data that can be presented in your report.

The last task in interpreting qualitative data is to assess your research against the standards you have set for your research project and the standards for qualitative research. There is much debate over whether qualitative research should be judged by the standards for qualitative research or those for quantitative research.

One aspect of the scientific approach is that there is very little room for innovation or improvisation in the way you interpret and present your research. How you present your data and statistical analysis needs in some ways to stand by itself. On the other hand, the actual style of the writing – the aesthetic effect – matters little as long as you get the job done. Whilst there are wide variations in writing ability among quantitative researchers, this has little effect on the credibility of what they say (although it may affect the willingness of other people to read it in the first place). The scientific style intentionally effaces the researcher – rather than highlights his or her role in the research – the findings are what counts.

In qualitative research, especially in thick description or research as personal journey, the aesthetics of the writing style and presentation play an important role in how the quality of your research is assessed. If you are writing a report using qualitative research, you usually mean your reader to take it seriously as a narrative and as a text. You are also being assessed on the additional criterion – how well is this project report written? This includes the quality of your writing, as well as its effect on your reader. Some of the criteria applied to assessing qualitative research, as well as validity and reliability, may be:

- **Aesthetic** – what reactions does it arouse in the reader?
- **Moral** – does the research raise or clarify any moral issues relating to the research problem and/or the reader him/herself?
- **Activist** – what can the reader do/what is the reader empowered to do now that he/she has read the report?

Summary

This chapter introduced methods for analysing qualitative data. These methods range from highly structured, which are close to quantitative analysis, to highly unstructured, which are not. Which method you should choose depends on how involved you are with the data source, whether you have started with a conceptual framework or expect one to emerge from your analysis, and your research questions.

Many studies start with a conceptual framework, but it is also possible to let the structure emerge. You can use various graphical techniques to experiment with your concepts as suggested by Kolb, including mind maps, influence diagrams and logic diagrams, which help you to formulate propositions that can be compared with the data you have collected.

The data analysis process will pass the findings to the discussion and reporting stage of the project in a range of forms. The quality of this outcome is evaluated in terms of reliability, validity, generalisability and credibility. The use of IT support in your process may provide benefits but, for short projects where the volume of data is limited, may take more time to learn how to use than will provide benefit to the project.

Answers to key questions

How should I prepare my qualitative data for analysis?
- Verbal data should be transcribed and put in order, with a reference for each piece of data.

What are the main strategies for analysing qualitative data?
- Use structured analysis to fit your data into a predetermined framework.
- Use unstructured analysis to let your framework emerge.

What qualities should I aim for in my analysis?
- Reliability.
- Validity.
- Generalisability.
- Credibility.

References

Bal, A.S., Campbell, C.L., Payne, N.J. and Pitt, L. 2010. Political ad portraits: A visual analysis of viewer reaction to online political spoof advertisements, *Journal of Public Affairs*, 10(4): 313–28.

Bazeley, Patricia and Jackson, Kristi (eds) 2013. *Qualitative Data Analysis with Nvivo*. London: Sage Publications.

Branson, Po 1999. *Nudist on the Late Shift: And Other True Tales of Silicon Valley*. New York: Random House.

Bryman, Alan and Bell, Emma 2011. *Business Research Methods*, 3rd edn. Oxford: Oxford University Press.

Coyle, R.G. 2001. *Systems Dynamics Modelling: A Practical Approach*. London: Chapman & Hall/CRC.

Ehrenreich, Barbara 2002. *Nickel and Dimed: On (Not) Getting By in America*. New York: Metropolitan Books.

Forsythe, Diane E. 2001. *Studying Those Who Study Us: An Anthropologist in the World of Artificial Intelligence*. Stanford, CA: Stanford University Press.

Fox, Kate 2014. *Watching the English*, 2nd edn. New York: Nicholas Brealey Press.

Geertz, Clifford 1973. *The Interpretation of Cultures: Selected Essays*. New York: Basic Book.

Kolb, David A. 1985. *Experiential Learning*. Englewood Cliffs, NJ: Pearson

Kordestani, Arash, Peighambari, Kaveh and Foster, Tim 2015. Emerging trends in sustainability research: A look back as we begin to look forward, *International Journal of Environment and Sustainable Development* 14(2), 154–69.

Latour, Bruno and Woolgar, Steve 1986. *Laboratory Life: The Construction of Scientific Facts*. Princeton, NJ: Princeton University Press.

Miles, Matthew B., Huberman, A. Michael and Saldana, Jonny 2013. *Qualitative Data Analysis*, 3rd edn. Beverly Hills, CA: Sage.

O'Leary, Zina 2013. *The Essential Guide to Doing Research*, 2nd edn. London: Sage.

Schragenheim, E. 1998. *Management Dilemmas*. Boca Raton, FL: St Lucie Press.

Schultze, Ulricke 2000. A confessional account of an ethnography about knowledge work, *MIS Quarterly*, 24(1), 1–39.

Shipman, M. 1982. *The Limitations of Social Research*. London: Longman.

Strauss, Anselm L. and Corbin, Juliet 1999. *Basics of Qualitative Research: Grounded Theory Procedures & Techniques*, 2nd edn. Thousand Oaks, CA: Sage.

Van Maanen, John 1988. *Tales of the Field: On Writing Ethnography*. Chicago: University of Chicago Press.

Additional resources

Bryman, Alan and Burgess, R.G. (eds). 1994. *Analysing Qualitative Data*. London: Routledge.

Buzan, A. 2000. *The Mind Map Book*. London: BBC Books.

Cameron, S. 2001. *The MBA Handbook*. Harlow: Financial Times/Prentice Hall.

Denzin, Norman 1970. *The Research Act: A Theoretical Introduction to Sociological Methods*. Chicago: Aldine.

Denzin, Norman and Lincoln, Y. 1994. *Handbook of Qualitative Research*. Thousand Oaks, CA: Sage.

Dubin, Robert 1978. *Theory Building: A Practical Guide to the Construction and Testing of Theoretical Models*, 2nd edn. New York: Free Press.

Gibbs, Graham R. 2002. *Qualitative Data Analysis: Explorations with NVivo*. Maidenhead: Open University Press.

Glaser, Barney G. and Strauss, Anselm L. 1967. *The Discovery of Grounded Theory: Strategies of Qualitative Research*. London: Wiedenfeld & Nicholson.

Guba, E. 1985. The context of emergent paradigm research. In Y. Lincoln (ed.), *Organizational Theory and Inquiry: The Paradigm Revolution*. Thousand Oaks, CA: Sage. pp. 287–306.

Gummesson, Evert 2000. *Qualitative Methods in Management Research*, 2nd edn. Thousand Oaks, CA: Sage.

Kolb, D.A., Rubin, I.M. and MacIntyre, J.M. 1984. *Organisational Psychology*. Harlow: Prentice Hall.

Reason, Peter and Bradbury, Hilary (eds) 2000. *Handbook of Action Research*. London: Sage.

Symon, Gillian and Cassell, Catherine (eds) 1998. *Qualitative Methods and Analysis in Organisational Research*. London: Sage.

Key terms

Discussion questions

1. How is qualitative analysis different from quantitative analysis?

2. What techniques for analysis are usually associated with which research methods?

3. Why should you try to capture data as close to the source as possible, for instance by recording all notes within a short time of an interview?

4. What is the role of a learning cycle approach in analysing data?

5. What is coding?

6. What research philosophy might be associated with structured data analysis?

7. Do codes exist in the data or should you impose them?

8. What is the difference between a construct, a variable and a measure?

9. What is the end point of qualitative analysis?

10. How would you assess the quality of the research you have carried out and that reported (for example in journals) by others?

Workshop

Background

In previous workshops you have conducted interviews on the subject of the changes that people go through when they move into higher education.

Task

1. If you did not record the interviews in **Chapter 6**'s workshop, in pairs conduct an interview on the subject of the changes that each other has experienced in their move into higher education. Each interview should last no more than 10 minutes. Use this time to explore any particular issues that the interviewees found challenging and what it was that made the issue challenging or important to them. Record the interviews, if at all possible (computers, some mobile phones, i-Pods and other devices can be used for recording purposes, if you do not have a tape recorder handy).

2. Relisten to the interview and transcribe the most important two minutes (this is not a general practice, but is used here for pragmatic purposes).

3. Use the coding procedures shown in **Table 12.3** to identify the key concepts that emerged from the interviews.

4. How would further data (interviews) help here?

5. If you had many more interviews (say 100), how would you handle the data?

6. Describe a process for storing, retrieving and analysing such a large volume of data.

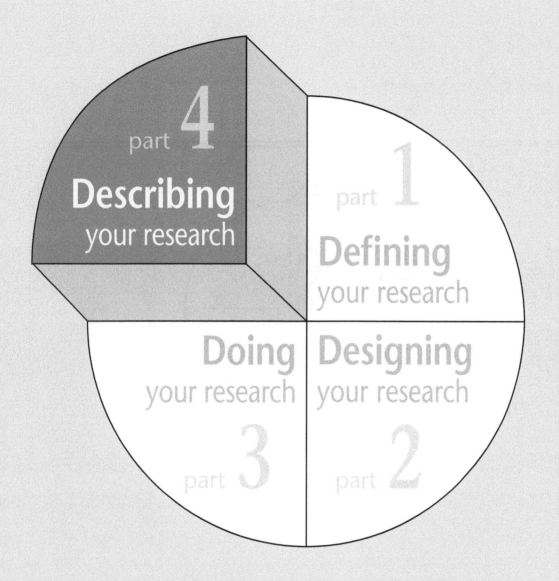

part 4

Describing
your research

part 1

Defining
your research

Doing
your research

Designing
your research

part 3

part 2

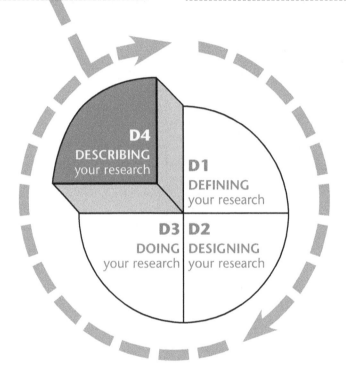

Relevant chapters
13 How do I write up my report?
14 What do I do now?

Key challenges
- Making sense of your findings
- Presenting your research to others
- Reflecting and learning from your research

4

Relevant chapters
1 What is research?
2 What should I study?
3 How do I find information?

Key challenges
- Understanding what academic research is
- Generating and clarifying ideas
- Using sources of information

1

D4
DESCRIBING
your research

D1
DEFINING
your research

D3
DOING
your research

D2
DESIGNING
your research

Relevant chapters
9 How do I do field research?
10 What do my quantitative data mean(1)?
11 What do my quantitative data mean(2)?
12 What do my qualitative data mean?

Key challenges
- Practical considerations in doing research
- Describing data using simple statistics
- Carrying out statistical tests
- Interpreting words and actions

3

Relevant chapters
4 What is my research approach?
5 How do I do quantitative research?
6 How do I do qualitative research?
7 How do I do case study research?
8 How do I make sure my research is ethical?

Key challenges
- Choosing a research approach
- Choosing a research design
- Collecting data using quantitative methods
- Collecting data using qualitative methods
- Integrating quantitative and qualitative methods

2

13 How do I write up my report?
Describing what you have done and found

chapter

 Key questions

- How should I report my research?
- What are the differences between reports on quantitative and on qualitative research?
- What are the differences between an academic and a business presentation?
- How can I manage the writing process effectively?
- How do I write and edit the project report?
- How do I prepare for an oral presentation or viva?

 Learning outcomes

By the time that you have completed this chapter, you should be able to:

- Manage the report writing process
- Vary the generic report structure and style to suit different research approaches and different audiences
- Plan and deliver your written report or oral presentation, or prepare for a viva voce examination
- Avoid common writing errors that detract from the quality of your project report

Contents

Introduction

Once you know the answers to your research questions (**Chapters 9** *through Chapter 11*), your project may seem practically complete. Although the finish line is in sight, don't let up on the accelerator just yet! *'Research is judged not by what you did, but by your ability to report on what you did'* (O'Leary, 2013). If you have been writing all along, well done! You will have a good head start in preparing your project report, and you should be able to write, edit and polish it up into a brilliant piece of work, without staying up all night, drinking vast amounts of coffee or Red Bull, or panicking. If not, you will find some practical tips and strategies here for getting your project report on track, and for avoiding wasting time and effort that you can't spare in this final stage.

A well-done project report is critical to satisfying your stakeholders and to getting a good mark. Because other people can only experience your research and judge its quality based on your project report, it is no less important than actually doing your research. Your project report tells your audience what you did in your research, including why you did it, how you did it, what you found out and why it matters. An excellent report may not totally make up for a project gone wrong, but it may tip the scales between passing and failing. A poorly done report on even the most brilliant research, on the other hand, will underwhelm your readers.

Section 13.1 presents a generic structure for project reports and identifies the elements that every project report must include. You can combine these elements in different ways depending on your research approach, your audience and your project requirements and assessment criteria, including how long and how formal your report needs to be. If you are writing for both academic and business audiences, you may need to write different reports. Academic readers will be interested in how well you executed your research and what you have contributed to academic knowledge, while business readers will be interested in how well you have solved the specific problem that they face.

Section 13.2 suggests how you can manage the writing process more effectively, especially if you are writing with other people, or working to a tight deadline. If you are a Type 2 student (discussed in **Chapter 1**), you may have been able to scrape along quite well in writing essays, coursework, or short project reports by keeping everything in your head and writing it down as a stream of consciousness, and then rearranging it into some sort of organised structure. For long or complex project reports, though, Type 2 habits lead to what Harvey calls the *'beginning, muddle, end'*. A structured writing process will help you identify the most appropriate content, structure and style for your audience, set out a writing plan and develop a detailed outline of your project report or presentation. This makes it easier to track how well your writing is coming along and to turn the project report that you have visualised into reality. Furthermore, if you are writing with other people, it is easier to work to a clearly articulated vision and plan.

Section 13.3 focuses on technical writing skills. If you are balancing study and full-time work, if you have returned to study after a gap, if you don't write much on your degree, or even if you have extensive experience of other types of writing, you will need different skills to write a high-quality project report. We highlight some common student errors of grammar and style that cost marks. We also identify some style and writing manuals that you can consult.

13.1 How do I structure my project report?

Spend some time visualising your project report – if you haven't already. You will find it much easier to get started on writing your project report if you know what it should contain and how it should be structured. Thinking about the process and output will make it easier to write your project report, to manage your writing process and to produce a high-quality project report for the audience for whom you did your research including your project supervisor, examiners and business sponsor. As you read through this chapter, you should consider:

- **Rationale**: Why are you writing your report? Who will read it? What will they want to know? How will you present it?
- **Content**: What are the major themes of your report? How should you structure your report? What is the main evidence you need to include in your report? What other evidence do you need to support this? What should go in and what should you leave out?
- **Process**: How can you put together a rough draft? How can you turn this rough draft into a first draft? How can you edit this into a finished draft? How long will it take and who needs to review it along the way?

We begin this section by presenting a generic project report structure and reviewing the elements that every project report must include. Even though a short, informal report and a long, formal report may differ substantially in details, their structure and content will be similar, because every project report must tell your **reader** what you did, why you did it, how you did it, and what you found out. However, you cannot just take a 'fill-in-the-blank' approach to reporting what you studied, so this section will also show you how to customise this generic structure to reflect your research project and your audience. We will also briefly discuss how to approach oral presentations and examinations.

13.1.1 The elements of your project report

Figure 13.1 presents a generic project structure consisting of five main elements – front matter, introduction, core, conclusions and back matter. Although no two project reports will be exactly the same, the first two and last two elements are similar for all reports, and most of the variation occurs in the main body, which describes your particular research project. Based on the elements, which we will describe below, you can develop a preliminary outline for your project report.

Once you know what elements you need to include in your project report, you can begin to visualise your project report and your audience. Outlining your project report will help you answer these questions:

- What do I need to include in my project report?
- How should I structure my report?
- What are the major themes of my report?
- What is the main evidence that I will present in my report?

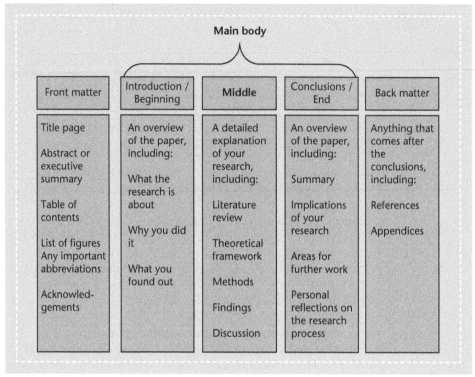

Figure 13.1 A generic project report structure

Even if you need to revise it later, outlining will help you clarify your thinking and visualise the finished project report. As you prepare your outline, think not only about what you want to say, but about what evidence you want to include in the form of charts, tables and figures, and how you will include this in your project report. This is also a good time to think about material you need to include in the body of your report, and what should be put in appendices, especially if you have a word or page limit.

13.1.2 What do I include in the main body of my report?

The **main body** of your project report leads your reader through the introduction, telling them what you are going to tell them (in summary form) in the rest of the report. It then moves onto the middle to look at five aspects of your research: research context, theoretical background, research methods, findings and discussion. The ending or conclusions tells your reader what you have told them – again in summary form.

Introduction

Your **introduction** is the starting point for your project report. Its main purpose is to provide an overview of your research that places the research project in context and tells your reader:

- What you investigated;
- Why your research is important to you and should be interesting to the rest of the world;

- What your main findings were;
- What your reader will find in the rest of the report, chapter by chapter.

Some students are concerned that if you tell your readers what you found out in your introduction, they will not want to read any farther. A research report is not a detective novel. You need to report your findings early on, rather than leaving them to a *big reveal* on the final page.

Even though it comes first in the main text, you will usually (re)write your introduction after you've written your paper because your readers will pay more attention to it than to any other part of your project. A well-written introduction helps 'sell' your report's recommendations or contribution to knowledge to your readers, so it is worth spending time on. In support, the editors of the *Academy of Management Journal* found that on average the authors who won 'Best Paper' awards in that journal rewrote their introduction at least 10 times (Grant and Pollock, 2011).

Research context – where does my research fit in?

Early on in your project report, you need to position your research project in its larger context and establish why your research is interesting and important. (See **Chapter 1** if you need a refresher.) Your *research topic* explains what your research is generally about. You develop the general research topic into a more detailed description of the specific *research problem* that you set out to solve and the *research questions* that you investigated. You may also put the topic in its context and set out, if you need to, which part of business and management you are drawing on.

Theoretical background – what am I looking for?

The next element of the main body is a **literature review** that links your research topic and questions to previous research that is relevant to your research problem and questions. **Chapter 3** discussed doing a literature search and writing a literature review in depth, and mentioned Chris Hart's two excellent books, *Doing a Literature Review* and *Doing a Literature Search*. If your readers are unfamiliar with your research topic, after they have read your literature review they should know (O'Leary 2013):

- What are the developments in the field?
- Is this researcher credible?
- Is this topic worth studying?

Researching and writing your literature review may take as much time and effort as data analysis, so don't wait to start your literature review until you are writing up. You may find it difficult to do a good job on both at once. It is much easier if you have been constantly revisiting the literature as you gather data, analyse it, and interpret your findings. Things to watch out for when writing your literature review include:

- Being uncritical or hypercritical
- Lacking focus or having too many focuses
- Not linking the literature review to the research questions
- Not leaving enough time to search and review the literature
- Using the wrong sources (e.g. over-reliance on web articles and blogs rather than peer reviewed articles).

If you are taking a quantitative approach, your literature review typically starts with a broad overview of the topic and progressively narrows it down using a deductive logic or **focus-down strategy** (Dunleavy 2003), which is very much in line with the hierarchy of concepts model that we introduced in **Chapter 2**. After reading your literature review, your readers should be able to anticipate your findings. On the other hand, if you are taking a qualitative approach, your literature review typically compares and contrasts themes in the literature you are reviewing, and may be intertwined with your findings, as we describe below.

We find that even if you are not starting your research with a fully worked out theoretical model, it can be helpful to summarise what you are doing in the form of a conceptual framework at the end of the literature review (as mentioned in **Chapter 3**) to bring the relevant elements of your work together. For the quantitative approach, this may show your variables and your hypothesised relationships between them, while for the qualitative approach this may simply be a 'mind map' of your key high-level constructs.

Research methods – how did I carry out my research?

Next, the main body of your project report should describe how you answered your research questions and provided a solution to your research problem (the topic of **Chapters 5 to 7**). This section explains:

- **Research design** and methods – How did I/we investigate the research problem?
- **Research quality** – How well did we do this research and was this the best way to investigate it?

You must provide enough detail in this section to show your reader that you are a competent researcher, and why you used the particular methods and techniques that you did. Your project supervisor can advise you how much you need to 'show' your readers, for example whether you need to discuss your research approach in detail, include a copy of a survey instrument or an interview *pro forma*. Make sure to cite the authorities that you consulted on methods, for example Stake (1995) or Yin (2003) on case study, or Stringer (1996) or Reason and Bradbury-Huang (2013) on action research, or particular examples that you followed. Starting by citing this book is a particularly fine idea – Maylor, Blackmon and Huemann 2017 – especially if one of us is marking your project.

You should also address how you analysed or interpreted your evidence and its quality:

- Why you collected the data you did;
- What data you collected, where you collected it, when it was collected and how it was collected;
- How you analysed the data;
- Why you chose these methods;
- Strengths and weaknesses of your choices, perhaps with reference to alternative approaches that you might have taken, but didn't.

If you have chosen a well-established set of techniques and procedures for investigating your particular research topic, you would probably not include a section on your *research approach*, which underlies your research design (see **Chapter 4**). This may be needed if there is controversy over the best method, or you have used a non-traditional method. Otherwise, unless you have expertise in philosophy, it's a good idea to leave it out as it is difficult to get right.

Your project report will also describe the *research context*; that is, your research setting and either your sample or the social objects of interest that you selected. The *research setting* describes the people, organisation, industry, country, or other collectivity that you studied. You should also give details of how you identified and selected your sample or cases, and any relevant details and related issues such as response rates and non-respondent bias.

Findings – what am I looking for?

The fourth part of the main body is your **findings**, which will introduce your reader to your data (Denscombe 2014), tell your reader what you found out in your research, and explain what it means. According to Dunleavy (2003), this answers *'what does the reader need to know?'*. You should look at **Chapters 9, 10 and 11** again if you get stuck here.

If your project is data-driven, which is characteristic of the quantitative approach, you may summarise your analysis in the main text, in the form of charts and tables, and provide the full analysis and data in an appendix. Focus on reducing the data and communicating them clearly, rather than overwhelming your reader with undigested numbers and graphs, considering:

- What is the main evidence you need to include in your report?
- What other evidence do you need to support this?
- What are the major themes of your report?

For a qualitative approach, this section would be more focused around the 'story' that you are telling based on ethnographic observation or other qualitative methods. You would not usually reduce the data to tables or figures, although you might use them to highlight relevant quotations or critical incidents, for example, that support the storyline.

Discussion – did I answer my research questions?

Next comes your **discussion**, which relates your findings to the more general research problem and questions that you set out to investigate, and to the literature, and is separate from your findings. The discussion describes whether your research answered your research questions, interprets your findings in light of your research questions (Denscombe 2014), and explains how your research addressed the research problem. You will also need to discuss what your findings mean within the broader context of the research project, including the theoretical literature and/or frameworks that were presented in the literature review. Because your discussion establishes the strength of your contribution to academic and managerial knowledge, it should highlight key aspects of your research including how your findings relate to the literature.

Conclusions – what did I find out?

Use the last part of your project report's main body to draw some general **conclusions** for your readers, which highlight the contribution and implications of your research, and suggest a way forward to them. This provides an opportunity to reflect on your research project in its larger context and with respect to your goals. You might highlight:

- What are your main/most important findings? What are the main lessons learnt from the study?
- What should be done as a result of your research? What are their implications for stakeholders – academics, managers or policy makers?
- What are any weaknesses/limitations of your findings? What problems did you face? How did you overcome them?
- What future research should be conducted? What would you do differently if you were starting the work now?

Summary

Your conclusions should also include a summary, which provides a précis of what you did and what you found out. Like your introduction, your readers will pay close attention to this part, so you should make sure that you have written really good conclusions. It's no secret that examiners often read selectively – they skim the middle of your project report and start reading closely again when they reach the conclusions and recommendations. Grab their interest again, and *help them make sense of your research.*

13.1.3 What else do I include in my report?

What else you need to include in your report depends on many factors, including (1) how formal the report is; (2) how long the report is; (3) what your project guidelines or marking criteria tell you to include, (4) your supervisor or advisor's particular preferences. The most common additional elements are front matter, i.e. anything that comes before the main body, and back matter, i.e. anything that comes after the main body.

Front matter

Front matter helps your reader navigate through your project report and make sense of the report, especially if it is long, technical or complicated. This front matter comes before the introduction and main body, and may include a title page, abstract, acknowledgements, a table of contents, and other 'maps' of the content and structure of your project report.

Your **title page** may include the name of your project, the name of the author(s) (unless you are being marked anonymously) or their examinations, the date and the unit or the degree for which you are submitting this report. Your main research questions may be the best source of your *title*. Make sure that your title expresses your research topic clearly and concisely. Avoid obscure or 'clever' titles – you are supposed to communicate your research to your reader, not show off.

All but very short project reports may include either an abstract or an executive summary that provides a brief précis of your report. An **abstract** is typically 75 to

500 words long, follows the title page and summarises your research topic, the main themes of your research, and your main findings. The abstract may be published or circulated independently of the rest of the project report, for example in library holdings. *Note that (unless otherwise specified) your abstract is NOT the first few paragraphs of your introduction – it is freestanding from the rest of your paper.* Anything you say in your abstract or executive summary needs to be repeated in the introduction.

In a business report, an **executive summary** may appear instead of an abstract. This presents a short (about one page or 250 words) summary of the practical problem, your analysis of the practical problem, the alternative solutions, your recommendations and any implementation issues. An executive summary lets a busy manager who reads only that part of your report understand and accept your recommendation without having to trawl through the report. The emphasis is on decision making. Like the abstract, an executive summary is a separate part of your business report and not the first part of the introduction.

Short **acknowledgements** may sometimes be appropriate for thanking people who have significantly helped you with your research, such as your supervisor, sponsor and research participants. In general, only significant *research* help warrants an acknowledgement. Try not to be too smarmy or suck-up if you thank your academic supervisor or project sponsor, especially if he or she will be marking your work. Because he or she is getting paid to supervise you, unless they've gone beyond the call of duty, provide very simple thanks only. Leave out your current girlfriend/boyfriend/best mate/cat unless they have provided you with project resources or data (endless cups of tea may be borderline).

In a *long* project report, a **table of contents** helps your reader navigate its contents or flip to a specific place quickly. (Someone who needs a table of contents for a short report needs more help than this book can give.) Many word-processing programmes can generate a table of contents automatically from headings.

Other front matter that may be found in long/complex/technical project reports includes:

- **a list of tables**;
- **a list of illustrations**;
- a **glossary** of unfamiliar terms;
- **a list of abbreviations**.

Back matter

Any back matter you include depends on your project requirements and the complexity of your report. **Back matter** includes a bibliography or list of references, and appendices of additional material that help your reader understand what you have presented and to amplify their understanding, although even brief reports may include back matter. Back matter typically includes the following:

1. Your **list of sources** lists either all of the resources that you consulted for the research project ('Works consulted'), or only those sources that you have actually cited in the main text ('References'). Consult your project guidelines and/or project supervisor to see which one is appropriate.

   Make sure that your references are complete, that you have included every source you have cited in your main text, and that you have not included irrelevant sources just to pad out your list. This will be much easier if you have been keeping good records of your sources during your project; if not, we will take this opportunity to say '*I told you so*'. Some examiners will turn first to your references, as we noted in **Chapter 3**, and interpret the quality of your citations and references as an overall guide to the quality of your research. If your project requirements do not specify a format, you should use the Harvard author–date system.

2. An **appendix** or several *appendices* contain anything that might be useful to understanding the report but not important enough to go in the main text, such as:
   - Copies of your research instruments, such as a blank questionnaire or an interview schedule;
   - Full details of your research setting and sample, which you have summarised in the main text;
   - Additional analyses, such as tables;
   - Full details of your analysis, which you have summarised in the main body.

Balance not wasting space in your main body with material that doesn't belong there with not hiding any of your key points in your appendices – many examiners do not bother to read them. One example of a questionnaire or transcript will usually do. Don't include all completed questionnaires or all completed interview transcripts unless you have been instructed to do so by your supervisor or project requirements.

13.1.4 Varying your report structure to reflect your research approach

We now come to an important fork in the road. If you are writing up a report that takes the scientific approach, then you will most likely follow the 'generic structure' for writing up scientific research: introduction, literature review, methods, findings, discussion, conclusions. You do not have much choice over the elements. All you have left to do now is to park your bottom in a chair to write and edit it.

On the other hand, if you are writing up a report using the qualitative approach, you need to think much more carefully about how you will structure your report. (The front and back matter will normally be exactly the same for both kinds of reports – the main variation will be in the core chapters of the report.) You have multiple choices in how you weave the theory and data together to make these elements part of your story or narrative.

If you have used both quantitative and qualitative methods (multiple method research), you will need to decide whether you should structure your project report around the quantitative or the qualitative aspect or keep them separate.

How to structure a project report based on the quantitative approach

A 'generic' report structure suits the deductive approach of quantitative research well because it is based on the scientific reporting style central to quantitative research. As shown in **Figure 13.2**, there is a symmetry across your project report elements, especially in the main body.

A more subtle hint for writing this kind of project report is to structure your report around your research hypotheses. Once you know what these are, you can structure your theoretical background, findings and discussion chapters around them, as shown in **Figure 13.3**. If you have more than one hypothesis, keeping the discussion

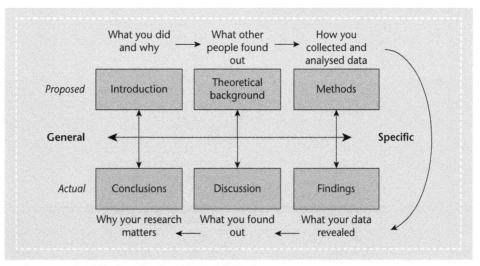

Figure 13.2 Quantitative project report symmetry

always in the same order (Hypothesis 1, Hypothesis 2, etc.) across your project report will greatly improve readability and reduce confusion.

How to structure a project report based on qualitative or mixed research

Although you could also use the generic elements and structure above for qualitative or multiple method research, we suggest that you do not, since your report should reflect your research approach. Qualitative research is usually written in a more fluid and less structured way that reflects its emergent nature, uses a more flexible structure than quantitative research and reflects the different ethos of qualitative research. A report on an ethnography, for example, would reflect its emergent and provisional nature and the unique characteristics of each piece of ethnography.

A good way of structuring the core of your project report is around the themes that emerged during your analysis (e.g. Miles et al. 2013), as described in **Chapter 12**. We suggest that you use these themes to guide your micro-structure in the same way as in the hypotheses and conceptual framework in quantitative research reports, even though they emerge from your data collection and analysis rather than preceding it. Instead of a section or chapter presenting all of the hypotheses, as in a quantitative report, you would have a section or chapter on Theme 1, another on Theme 2, etc., as shown below in **Figure 13.4**. In writing up qualitative research, researchers often integrate the literature review, data analysis and interpretation around each theme in turn, and then present the conceptual framework that binds them all together after they have discussed them all. Alternatively, Wolcott (2008) suggests that your structure might coalesce around the personal journey that you took as a researcher.

If you have done a research study with an initial quantitative phase followed by a qualitative phase, it might make sense to report the quantitative phase in a set of core chapters structured as we suggest for quantitative research, followed by a set of core chapters structured as we suggest for qualitative research. (Or vice versa, if you have done qualitative followed by quantitative research.)

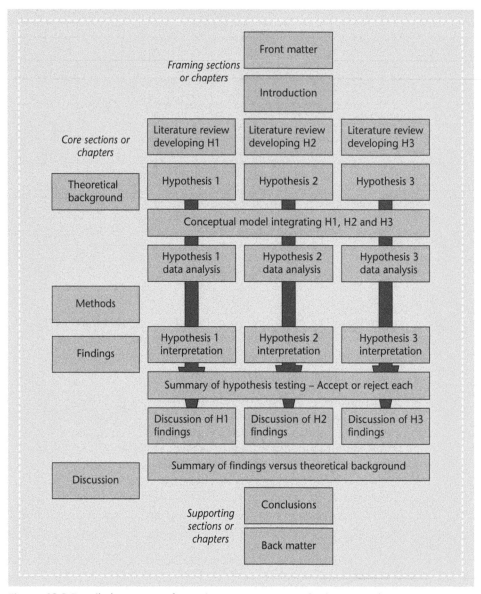

Figure 13.3 Detailed structure of a project report on quantitative research

13.1.5 Writing your project report for different readers and audiences

Below, we suggest how you might customise your project report to reflect other sources of variation in project reports which answer questions including:

- Who will read your project report?
- How will you present your research to them?
- What should your readers know after reading your project report?

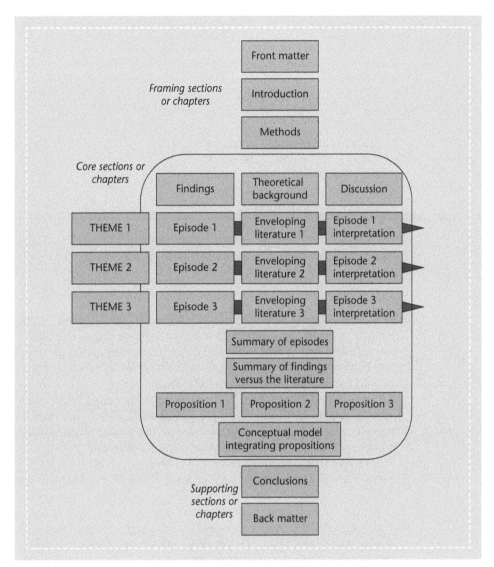

Figure 13.4 Core structure of a project report on qualitative research

Who will read your project report?

Visualise your project report as starting a conversation with an audience (O'Leary 2013). You need to target not only the contents and structure of your report to this reader, but also its style, so identify this *audience* – or audiences – before you start writing or preparing your project report. Who is your ideal or actual *reader*? What knowledge, assumptions or expectations will they bring to reading your report? Your main reader will be your examiner(s) and/or your business sponsor, as discussed in **Chapter 2** and **Chapter 14**, but don't forget about your project supervisor or other academic advisors, your business sponsors, the people who have supported or participated in your research, and the wider community of business and management researchers and managers.

How will you present your research to your readers?

How will you present your research to this reader or readers? The project report format will affect not only how you will physically present your research, but also how much depth you can go into and what you need to include. Your project requirements should tell you how you will present your research and how it will be assessed, usually one or more of:

- Short project report – 20 pages
- Long project report – 100 pages
- Brief oral presentation – 15 minutes
- Long oral presentation – 1 hour
- Viva voce examination

You should also have agreed with your business sponsor, if you have one, what they expect as far as any additional reports or presentations in your project brief.

What should your readers know after reading your project report?

An *academic audience* is traditionally more interested in the conceptual side of your research problem than the practical, so your project report should focus on showing how you have translated your research topic into research questions, and designed your research to answer those questions. However, this is where it is worth knowing the particular preferences of your examiners.

A *business audience* is more likely to be more interested in the practical side of your research and its implications for practice than academic theory or models. Your project report for managers should focus especially on the practical problem: your analysis, your potential solutions and your recommendation.

It is likely that the more senior the manager, the less time he or she will actually spend reading your project report, and a very senior manager will probably only read your report's executive summary or sit through a brief presentation. A business reader is primarily interested in your recommendations about how to address the particular practical problem or decision that they face, and only interested in everything else such as what you did and how you did it insofar as it supports your recommendations.

Given these differences, you may wonder if you can get by with writing just one single report if you are presenting your research to both academic and business audiences. It is often difficult to make the same project report suit both academic and business readers. Although Easterby-Smith, Thorpe and Lowe (2012) argue that the distance between academic and business audiences is decreasing as more managers study business and management, we suggest that you should consider managers and academics as two different audiences. These two types of readers will want to know different things and the constraints on their time and attention differ vastly, so definitely do not read a project report or listen to a project presentation in the same way.

Although you may be able to identify common themes and elements across both audiences, it is probably best to think at this stage of your target being two different reports. We recommend a structure as shown in **Figure 13.5**, which focuses on the practical problem faced by the organisation or people, and is supported by the academic problem. You should identify the potential solutions to the problem, the feasibility, costs and benefits of each, and your recommendation of the potential solution.

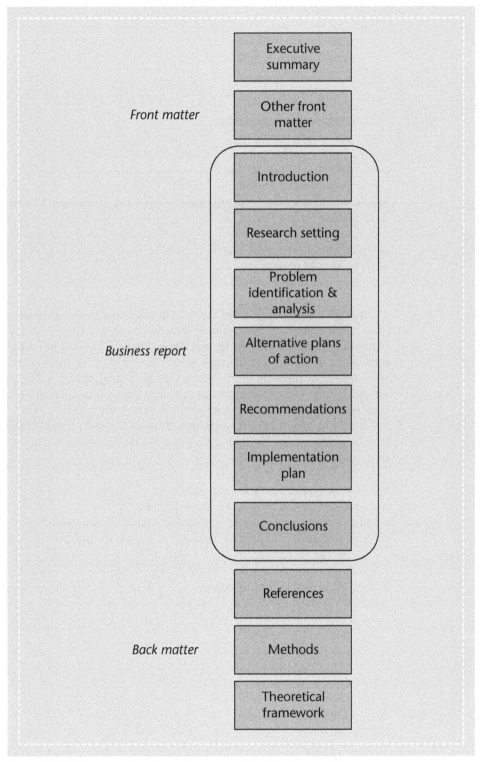

Figure 13.5 Core structure of a project report for a business audience

No business plan is complete without an implementation plan which discusses how to put your recommendation into action, along with the time and cost requirements. You should provide the academic framework for your research in an appendix or appendices so that your business sponsor or other reader can consult them if they want further details.

13.1.6 Oral presentations and vivas

Many research projects involve a formal or informal presentation, such as an **oral presentation** to fellow students or business sponsors, or a **viva voce examination**, a formal presentation. You should prepare for an oral presentation or a viva as carefully as you would a written report. Issues you should think about during the planning stage include:

- What should the presentation include?
- Who should present it?
- How sophisticated does it need to be?

Although many students feel nervous or self-conscious about oral presentations, an oral examination may be relatively informal, such as a question-and-answer session. Presenting your research to an audience can help you build career skills and self-confidence. It can also enhance your written project report by building enthusiasm and support for the project, allow you to explore project angles that you missed in the written report, and expand the discussion of interesting areas of the project, perhaps even some that you couldn't include in your written report.

You should review your project requirements to see if any criteria apply specifically to your presentation or if they differ from the written project criteria. The main thing that examiners look for are:

- How confidently do you present your report?
- How well do you bring your material to life?
- How well have you prepared your materials and visual aids?
- How well can you answer questions, and depart from the 'script' if necessary?

You might want to consider whether all group members will take turns presenting, or only the strongest and most confident. If you are presenting to examiners, you should probably make every effort to include every team member in the presentation, unless there is a genuine reason why someone cannot actively participate. It is usually better for everyone to play at least some role, even if only to introduce the people who will do the substantive speaking. If you are presenting to a business audience, you may want to let the more confident members dominate, but everyone should still participate.

While you can look up past projects to see what they are like, you cannot observe a viva to see what one is like, which makes some students nervous. On the brighter side, rarely will you get one or more intelligent examiners to listen so intently to you talking about your research project. You might talk to students who have already undergone the same examination to see what it is like – but beware of believing that horror stories are the norm. Everyone likes to tell stories about awful examinations, just like they do about driving tests.

In her book *How to Survive Your Viva*, Rowena Murray (2015) suggests that in a viva, or a formal examination by one or more examiners, the main concerns will be:

- Did you do the work yourself?
- Do you understand the business and management research?
- Do you have a good knowledge of the research project?
- Are you a competent researcher?
- Did you learn anything?

Tips for preparing for an oral presentation or a viva

If your audience has thoroughly read your written report in advance, avoid simply repeating the main points in your report, and instead add value through your presentation by bringing something new to the material that you are presenting or presenting some aspects of your research that perhaps you could not include in the written report. On the other hand, if the people attending your presentation haven't read your report in advance, you should focus on summarising the key points and conveying the research story.

If you are using presentation software such as PowerPoint or Prezi, a typical structure will be:

- Title slide – project title, researcher name(s), sponsor (if any)
- Aims and objectives
- Background and context of the research
- How you did the research
- Your key findings
- Your analysis and discussion
- Your conclusions and recommendations

A good rule of thumb is to prepare one slide for every five minutes if your presentation is over an hour; one slide for every three minutes if under an hour. Try to avoid slides that are too busy or too dense. Try not to overload slides with text – on the other hand, don't put up an overhead with just a few words. One danger of using presentation software is that students get too wrapped up in selecting colours, music, special effects, etc., and the content is often not as carefully thought out as the presentation.

You should rehearse your presentation enough times so that you deliver your presentation smoothly and in the right amount of time. Rehearsing with technical aids is essential. If you haven't used an overhead projector, slide projector, whiteboard, flip chart, video/DVD, visualiser, or other aid before, you should practise with it until you are comfortable. You should also work carefully on timing – presentations that are much longer or shorter come across as ill-prepared. If your report runs over, you may find yourself cut off without having covered all of your material.

Presentation nerves

Even experienced speakers expect to have some 'butterflies' before they start speaking. Many believe that if you aren't at least a little nervous, your delivery will be flat. We know from experience that you will feel less nervous *and* sound much better if you take a deep breath before you speak your first word.

If you are not normally a confident speaker, you should make sure to practise alone or with friends until you are comfortable speaking. Practise in front of a mirror to see whether you are using your body language and your gestures effectively. Get a friend to give you feedback if possible. If you are really nervous, then you might try some sort of humour as an icebreaker – Dilbert cartoons are currently popular – but remember that humour can fall flat. You should also think about any questions that are likely to come up, and how you might answer them. Once you get started, your audience will focus on what you are presenting, unless you distract them. As long as you don't fall down, giggle uncontrollably, pass out or run off stage – all of which we have seen in student presentations – the audience will stick with you.

13.2 How can I manage the writing process?

Once you have identified what kind of report you're writing, for whom, and its structure and contents, actually writing it should be straightforward. In principle, that is certainly the case. However, *no plan survives first contact with the enemy*. We have found that writing is simpler if you set yourself a schedule and stick to it, if you create a rhythm of work and get support from others. Even though main milestones of writing up your project report or preparing your project presentation will simply be a rough draft, a first draft, and a finished report that describe what you did and what it means, the report-writing phase of your research will be cyclical and messy, and not linear and orderly. Some parts of your report may be in their finished form before you start collecting your data; others may come together only at the last minute.

As well as writing your report and preparing any presentations, you will also have to manage the writing process, including yourself (and your project group if you have one). Think about where and how you write most effectively. Consider your working habit and working environment, and your group dynamics, in order to make the most of this phase.

How straightforward the rest of the writing process will be depends in part on your research approach, which will be reflected in your project report's content and structure (as noted above). If you are working within the quantitative approach, especially if you are working on a large and formal project, you may have been able to complete much of your writing early on in the research process before you began your field research. You will have identified your research problem, research questions and any propositions or hypotheses that you are putting forward in your research proposal, and you will have defined your methodology, including methods for gathering and analysing data early on as well. You can even write up early versions of your findings, discussion and conclusions before or while you are collecting and analysing your data.

On the other hand, if you are working within the qualitative approach, you will typically be collecting and analysing data and reviewing the literature at the same time, so you won't be able to do as much writing early in the project. However, you should be taking field and reflective notes all during the process, and therefore you should have a good deal of the text to hand by the time you finish your fieldwork.

The challenge is then to work out the structure for presenting your research, as described in **Section 13.1**, and to whip it into shape for the finished project report.

The skills that have got you this far in your studies writing essays or short projects of 20 pages or so may no longer be adequate. As we have noted before, your project report may often be the biggest written project that you have done to date, because the project is so much longer, and more complex. Furthermore, if you have been working in a group, this may be the first time that you have written anything substantial with other people. You will face another substantial challenge in managing the group process. You will need to manage yourself and/or your group so that you not only finish on time but you also leave yourself plenty of time to get your project report right in the process. This is so important that we come back to it below in **Section 13.3**.

13.2.1 Drafting and editing your project report

As we noted above, writing your project report will be considerably easier if you have been writing as you go along, for example by producing early drafts of results chapters. The three main phases of any project report are rough draft, first draft and final report. You can add more stages if you like, but most people don't usually have time.

Your rough draft – capturing what you did

Your **rough draft** will be the first time you will write down your complete argument in a more or less coherent form, and try to cover all of the points and get your main argument right. At this stage, you shouldn't worry about getting the detailed writing exactly right. However, it is important to write a rough draft because it is the foundation of your project report.

In preparing a rough draft, focus mainly on your core chapters – the literature review, methods, findings and discussion – and hold off on your front and back end chapters – introduction and conclusions – and any front and back matter until later, because you will waste time writing and rewriting these chapters to reflect a constantly changing report. Your rough draft should be no more than 60%–80% of your total word length, since you have quite a bit to add to this.

Once you have written this rough draft, you can:

- Add to it – new material, ideas or thinking,
- Subtract from it,
- Change the structure around,
- Make it communicate better to your readers.

How you get to a rough draft may vary. Some writers 'sculpt in marble', writing an initial draft of the report or a chapter following the order and sequence of the outline, then editing and revising it until it fits the requirements. Others 'sculpt in clay', writing bits in any order and then filling in each of the points in greater detail until they have a complete draft. We suggest that if you are writing your first long report or if several people are working together that you will find it more effective to write in a more orderly way, and to complete a chapter at a time. Keep going back to your outline if you need to.

Your first draft – joining up the pieces

Your rough draft provides a starting point that you can revise and edit into your **first draft**, the first complete version of your project report. A first draft is *not* simply a spell-checked and grammar-corrected rough draft. The quality of your final report is almost entirely determined by the quality of your first draft, so make sure that you give enough time and attention to writing your first draft.

At this point, don't worry too much about polishing your written text word-by-word so that you have chosen the absolute best word and best sentence structure. You may end up editing out or rewriting large sections of what you have written in your rough draft, so it doesn't really matter how well-written those sections were. Instead, you should try to see how well the overall structure of your report is working, especially if you have taken a qualitative approach and there is more than one way to present your research.

Many project reports are marked down because they are essentially edited rough drafts, rather than polished first drafts. Turning a rough draft into a first draft requires you to join up all of the disparate bits into a complete and coherent account of your research. Do you have the right chapters in the right order? This is much more of a problem for people writing up qualitative or mixed-method research than those writing up quantitative research. Second, do you have the sections in each chapter in the best order possible? Booth et al. (2008) suggest that 'Since readers read each sentence in light of how they see it contributing to the whole, it makes sense to diagnose first the largest elements, then focus on the clarity of your sentences, and only last on matters of correctness, spelling and punctuation.'

You should read through your text and see if you have achieved the following:

- Is the information presented in a logical sequence?
- Does each section have a central message?
- Does each item lead to the next?
- Is there any unnecessary material that could go into an appendix?

The main difference between a rough draft and a first draft is in the audience for whom the draft is being written. Whereas it is OK to write your rough draft from your own perspective, you must write your first draft from your reader's perspective. Much of your work in editing your first draft will therefore be thinking from the perspective of your readers, who were not there doing the research with you. This shifts the draft from what you want to say about your research to what your reader wants and needs to know.

In particular, a first draft includes quite a lot of writing that highlights the important or interesting things that you have done and to help your reader navigate through the report. Murray (2015) suggests that these four tactics will help your reader understand what you want to say:

- **Repetition** – repeating concepts, arguments and other key points for linking and emphasis;
- **Forecasting** – letting readers know in advance what you will and will not be doing in your project report;
- **Signalling** – highlighting links and other key aspects of the text;
- **Signposting** – constantly reminding your readers where they are in the thesis, using headings, topic sentences and other devices.

Although you know very well what you mean to say, what you have written is seldom so obvious and straightforward that your reader doesn't need any extra help. Even though it may seem crystal clear to you – at least when you read it, your reader doesn't have the advantage of the hours and weeks that you have put into your research project, and they may be spending only minutes reading through your report. Don't shoot yourself in the foot here!

Only after you are satisfied with the structure and flow of your first draft – and only then – should you write your introduction and conclusions and add any additional elements such as front and back matter (title page, table of contents, table of figures, acknowledgements, abstract, executive summary, glossary, reference list or bibliography, index and/or appendices). You should now check that your page numbering, headers, footers, etc., are correct and in the correct format. If you start including these too early in the writing process, you will waste a lot of time playing with them.

The length of your first draft once you have included these remaining elements is a good guide to whether your report is within the word and/or page limits specified in your project requirements. Most, if not all, word-processing programmes will count words for you either automatically or with a menu command. If you haven't put your report in its final format, a good estimate is 250 words per page (in double-spaced, standard-margin, 12-point Times New Roman font). You should try to be within plus or minus about 20% of your word limit when you put together your first draft.

Your final report – editing and refining

Once you are satisfied with your first draft (or more realistically you run out of time and your deadline is approaching), you can edit it into your **final draft**. Editing is critical to making this your best possible report, so make sure that you have allowed enough time for this stage. Good editing may be able to turn *'a pig's ear in to a silk purse'*, by revising how you have organised your paper to make sure that your argument and everything else in your paper is clear to your readers.

Use charts, figures and tables wherever they are clearer than written descriptions. A picture can often replace 1000 words! Make sure that you link these back to the text, and interpret them – or highlight their implications – in the text rather than just sticking them in anywhere and expecting your reader to figure out what they mean for him- or herself.

At this point, you can do detailed editing for sense and length. Remove unneeded words. Although some people write very concisely and economically even in their rough draft, most of us can slash 25% to 50% of what we write in the first draft without changing any content or losing any meaning. Most of us include wordy 'throat-clearing' phrases that don't actually mean anything: 'In this project report we will …' – well, where else would you be doing it? Replace 'in the way that' with 'how' or 'in order to' with 'to'. Also look for places where you need to add extra words to clarify your meaning.

Figure 13.6 presents some hints for editing by ear from the social scientist Howard S. Becker.

We also list some specialised sources on writing in the **Additional resources**. Basic references include dictionaries, usage manuals and thesauruses, which increasingly can be accessed online. Good reference books on the technical aspects of formal and academic writing include professional style and usage guides such as the *Chicago Manual of Style* and the *Oxford Style Manual*. These will answer technical questions

1. **Avoid throat-clearing phrases.** If it's important to do it, don't talk about it, do it.
2. **Order is important.** Use order to reinforce meaning.
3. **Seek out and simplify wordy phrases.** Eliminate needless words.
4. **Make the abstract concrete.** Use description to bring your subject matter alive.
5. **Keep writing until you get it right.** Each change leads to more changes.

Figure 13.6 Becker on editing by ear
Source: Becker 1986: 74ff.

such as how to prepare a table of contents, number pages, do a reference list, etc., and so are especially useful when you are preparing your final draft.

If you are working on a long, complicated, or multi-authored project report (such as the second edition of this very book), you may want to invest in a specialist guide to your word-processing programme. Programmes such as Microsoft Word duplicate many of the same features as professional page-setting programmes. Being able to number tables and figures and update references to them, and update them automatically rather than by hand, can save you considerable time and frustration. You can keep your text broken up into smaller units such as chapters, especially if different people are writing different bits of the text, and then to use your word-processing software to edit and print them as a single virtual text.

13.2.2 Managing collaborative writing

Writing is generally a solitary activity (like smoking behind the bike sheds), so writing with other people can be especially challenging. If you have taken a quantitative approach, you may find that it is easy to split up the project report chapters or even sections so that individual team members can write independently. For example, one person could take responsibility for the research methods chapter, one for the literature review, and so on. This may be difficult if you have taken a qualitative approach, since it is much more difficult to split up the different elements.

Consider the extent to which you will be writing individually versus writing collaboratively. If you are writing with other people, you should make time to discuss explicitly as a group how you will organise the writing process and specify each person's responsibilities and deadlines. As a project team, you may want to stick with the same strategy that you have used in defining, designing and doing your research project, or you may want to try a new pattern. Some groups prefer to assign roles, with a single person – or a pair – responsible for editing, and others writing the text. Other groups divide up responsibility equally for writing and editing.

Consistency poses more of a challenge than you would think when deadlines loom for a group. If you split up the writing between several people you will need to put a lot more effort into editing your report. Some people are better writers than others, so your overall project report will be only as good as your weakest writer. Even if everyone writes well, since people will have different writing styles it may be difficult to keep a consistent voice and style across the chapters. Although you may find that splitting up the writing task reduces interpersonal conflicts, 'cutting and pasting' the resulting text together is not always the best solution. Individual writers may go 'off

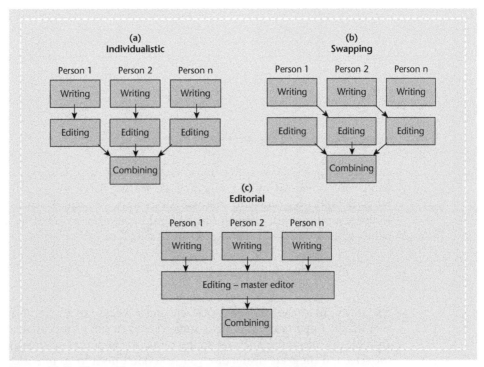

Figure 13.7 **Alternative strategies for writing and editing**

message', so that your report contradicts itself, confusing your readers. We have read some student project reports that don't even agree what topic they researched – each section started with a different interpretation! Needless to say, the examiner would have preferred a group consensus on whether the topic was corporate social responsibility, corporate ethics or corporate governance.

If you share writing and editing responsibilities, because different people are responsible for writing and editing the differences can be homogenised across the different individuals or teams, as shown in **Figure 13.7(a)**. If you are writing up quantitative research, shared responsibility for writing and editing may work very well, since there are generally accepted conventions for structure and style that most people understand and can imitate well. In addition, if different people are writing and editing then you have more chances to catch any mistakes or misstatements that may creep as in **Fig 13.7(b)**.

In qualitative writing, however, it may be difficult to split up the writing between different people, since you are weaving together your data, conceptual framework and findings as you present them, rather than having them in separate sections. It may work better to appoint a **master editor** as shown in **Figure 13.7(c)**, to edit all of the chapters and attain a 'seamless' style across different writers, especially if different people are writing different sections. This is a good way of using a group member who is particularly talented at editing, but you may burn that person out if the editing task is too big and there is too little time left to do it in.

File sharing (Dropbox or Google Docs) definitely makes the process easier, particularly when it comes to managing *version control* – making sure that only the latest version of the document is being worked on – and in ensuring that the process does not become reliant on a single memory stick.

Writing collaboratively involves significant interpersonal challenges as well as technical challenges. People with similar writing habits, such as Harvey and Kate, can share similar dysfunctions (mostly involving procrastination)! Different writing habits may also cause stress and conflict. It might be useful for your team to discuss work habits and expectation before you start writing. Ignorance is definitely not bliss here!

13.2.3 Managing yourself during the writing process

Whilst having a good working environment is important, you need to actually write while you're there. Most of us already have writing habits and working practices that we have built over time and that will affect how we write. For many of us, writing is also bound up with elaborate rituals and habits that many of us need to execute before getting down to a major piece of writing.

Creating a good writing environment

Good lighting, comfortable seating, enough space to work, neither too hot nor not too cold, the right level of ambient noise, etc. make it easier to work without distraction. It is especially important not to work somewhere you can't concentrate on your writing. Turn off the 'incoming' message sound on your computer and smartphone and blank the screen, if these are distracting you. You don't need to go into monastic solitude – many people write better with some background noise such as the radio, television or music, but choose your background noise carefully, so that it isn't distracting. Classical music (and more generally instrumental music) has been shown to be better for intellectual pursuits than music with lyrics. Put a 'do not disturb' sign on your door if necessary.

This doesn't always mean working in the same place. Sometimes Kate works best at home, sometimes in her office (mostly original research and rough drafts); other times, she writes best in a particular chair in the lounge with her netbook in her lap (revising a rough draft into a first draft); or even in the local Starbucks or the Museum of Natural History. Martina does her best writing in her kitchen at home and sometimes in her sleep. Harvey allegedly writes by dictating into a voice recorded whilst hanging by his feet like a bat. (One of the above statements may not be correct)

Comfort habits

Comfort habits are anxiety-reducing routines or rituals associated with stressful activities such as writing. Kate and a class of doctoral students once shared their writing rituals. Nearly everyone had to use a particular kind of writing instrument, for example, only a No. 2 pencil or a particular type of gel pen, or write on a particular kind of paper, for example, yellow legal pads or quadrille paper. One student could not start writing until he had made a cup of tea, and allowed it to cool down completely. While the students assumed these were unique and embarrassing, and that they were the only ones to have such rituals, they were embarrassed to admit to them, but everyone has them. Comfort habits are only a problem if they prevent you from writing when you need to. You should reinforce good habits, especially those that enable you to start writing or keep going, and minimise bad ones, that keep you from getting started or encourage you to stop.

Avoid procrastinating

Procrastination has been described as the art of putting off tomorrow what we really should be doing today (Blaxter et al. 2010). Although approaching deadlines to help motivate us, waiting until the last possible minute does not result in significantly better project reports, but it does increase the possibility that something will go wrong. Blaxter and her colleagues (2010) give four tips for overcoming procrastination:

- Make notes on your reading, the results of your research, or your discussion with your supervisor or manager.
- Write one of the easier sections of your report, such as the table of contents, references or bibliography.
- Prepare the outline of one of the sections or chapters, and start adding quotations, points, etc..
- Set yourself a target for writing a set amount of time or number of words, don't do anything else until you have done it, and give yourself a treat once you have finished it.

We are all experts at avoiding things that we don't really want to do and fooling ourselves. Procrastination stimulates students (and academics) to new heights of creativity in **displacement**, substituting an activity that is indeed worthwhile, but not essential for writing, for example cleaning the cooker, tidying your room/desk or switching your summer and winter wardrobes. These activities are really just excuses for not sitting down to writing or marking.

If you are working alone, finding someone to be a moral support or 'buddy' can be an effective way to overcome procrastination. For example, you can talk about your writing with someone else or ask someone else to be your 'conscience'.

Know thyself

If you are lazy, slack, neurotic, avoidant, obsessive-compulsive or have other dysfunctional tendencies, you may have to accept this as a given in the short term, and consciously manage the writing process around this instead of letting it manage you.

Some Type 1 students finish early and then keep working because they don't know when to stop. For most of us, this is unlikely because we have procrastinated and generally fooled around and wasted time. Most students stop writing when they absolutely have to stop writing to turn their project report in on time. However, if you have finished early, and you have met your objectives for the report, hand it in.

This is more likely to be a problem with postgraduate research students, who may not have a fixed deadline for handing in their work (although the research councils in the United Kingdom do impose these, as may universities), whilst most undergraduates and postgraduate taught students are usually working towards fixed – and in some cases immoveable – deadlines.

Break your writing into smaller tasks with deadlines

You can avoid procrastinating or wasting time by building rewards for good behaviour into your writing routine. For example, when marking stacks of hundreds of exam papers – even more painful than writing – Kate used to line up the contents

Week 3	Mon	Tue	Wed	Thu	Fri	Sat
Writing						
Work on Chapter 6 rough draft						
--Section 6.1	X	X				
--Section 6.2			X	X		
Send draft to Esther					X	Day off if finished!
Check references in library				X		
Etc.						

Figure 13.8 Kerry's star chart

of a bag of Skittles in rainbow order and reward herself with a Skittle each time she completed marking five examination scripts. One bag of Skittles later, the entire stack of marking was done. Healthy rewards include a stretch, a short walk, a run or a session in the gym after doing a set task, writing time, or number of words.

The 'star charts' that are used to motivate small children can also be a surprisingly effective too. An example is shown in **Figure 13.8**.

13.3 How can I avoid common writing errors?

Thus far in the research project, you have had to learn and use various sets of skills. Writing the project report is no different. Every project report will be unique, but the process of writing any project report will call on the same set of generic technical skills. These are:

- Writing correctly
- Writing stylishly
- Writing persuasively

Your project report, at a minimum, should:

- Achieve good standards of spelling and grammar
- Develop logical links from one section to another
- Use headings and sub-headings to divide the text into clear sections
- Be consistent in the use of the referencing style
- Use care with the page layout
- Present tables and figures properly

13.3.1 Technical writing skills

Some believe that ideas about writing correctly are old-fashioned, but to write persuasively and convincingly, you need to master spelling, grammar and punctuation. Many people have problems writing correctly and idiomatically in English, however. You may have dyslexia or another learning impairment; you may not have been taught how to write correctly; English might not be your first language. Whatever the cause, your readers will consciously or unconsciously judge your research as being of poorer quality if you make errors of spelling, grammar and punctuation in your project report, presentation hand-outs and overheads, presentations, your cover letters, and any other documents that you produce. If you make more than a few errors your reader will mentally downgrade their opinion of the quality of your research report, and, by extension, your research. You run the risk of being marked by someone who does care passionately about these aspects of writing. At the very least, errors distract your reader's attention from your content, and they may notice problems with your logic or other core aspects of your research that might otherwise have gone unnoticed.

Take advantage of any opportunities that your university provides for improving your written and spoken English. Many universities offer assistance to international students, including pre-sessional English courses, continuing English training, and even personal coaching. You may want to ask your supervisor or project co-ordinator whether you are allowed to use a proofreader (it is not ethical to hire someone to actually write the report for you).

13.3.2 Check your spelling

Most readers will assume that if you misspell more than a few words in your project report that you were in too much of a rush do a good job, that you don't know what a good job is, or even that you don't care about the quality of your work. Don't forget to check the correct spelling of any people or organisations that you mention in your report. Misspelling the name of a major researcher in your literature review – and this happens more frequently than you would think – makes your command of the literature look shaky. Kate recently received a project report for remarking (i.e. it failed the first time) that misspelled the name of the instructor, who was also the director of studies for the degree, and she has seen her own name similarly misspelt by students! If you get the name of a major organisation wrong (McDonald's is correct, not MacDonald's or McDonalds), your reader may assume you can't get other basic data and analyses right.

You will catch more misspellings if you:

- Use a dictionary when you write, to answer tricky questions such as: 'it's or its'?
- Leave time between your final editing and printing out your report, so that you can read through with a fresh eye;
- Get someone else to read through your report;
- Read through your report backwards – from back to front, bottom to top and left to right.

Don't rely just on the spellchecker in your word-processing programme. Although most will highlight words that are obviously misspelled or that don't exist in any dictionary, if you substitute a correctly spelled word for the word you meant to write, for example 'from' for 'form', even the most sophisticated computer spellchecker won't always catch your mistake. Some even query correctly spelled words that are commonly misused – 'it's' for 'its'.

You should also use your dictionary to check for correct word usage, especially on tricky words or words you haven't used before. People often misuse fancy-sounding words when they want to impress others or appear more sophisticated than they actually are. This is not usually a good idea, unless you want your readers to snort coffee out of their nose and onto your carefully designed and expensively printed report. These errors are called malapropisms, after Mrs Malaprop, a character in Sheridan's play The Rivals, who constantly misused words to try to impress her listeners. '[P]romise to forget this fellow – to *illiterate* him, I say, quite from your memory.' (Richard Sheridan, *The Rivals*, Act I, Scene II, Line 178) emphasis ours.

A good dictionary will also help you identify clichés and other hackneyed expressions in your writing and avoid them. O'Connor (1996) lists some of the *'usual suspects'*: acid test, bite the bullet, bottom line, can of worms, foregone conclusion, foreseeable future, tip of the iceberg, viable alternative. Be especially aware of managerialisms (or manager-speak) gone mad. 'Only recently I came across someone trying to tell me that a company was experiencing a "negative fiscal productivity scenario", which I took to mean "making a loss".' (Nick Smith, on the IET Forum, www.theiet.org/Forums/).

Check your punctuation

Punctuation clarifies the structure of a sentence and prevents you from misreading it (Cook 1985: 108), and is a key aspect of your writing style. *'Prose writers are interested mostly in life and commas'*, argues Ursula Le Guin (1998: 35). Vampire Weekend even wrote a song about the serial, or Oxford, comma. You can use punctuation to decorate your writing (Cook 1985). The public interest in punctuation was revealed by Lynne Truss's book on punctuation, *Eats, Shoots and Leaves,* which was a bestseller on both sides of the Atlantic in 2003.

It would be nice to think that students only have problems with sophisticated punctuation marks such as the colon, but even the poor 'full stop' gets abused in student reports. If you have any doubts about punctuation, then consult the wide range of reference manuals in your library, bookshop, or online. If you're not confident with your punctuation, stick to simple, short sentences: even if your report sounds a bit choppy, you may come across as the next Ernest Hemingway if you're lucky. We (and our students) can enthusiastically recommend the following books (full details in **Additional resources**):

- Patricia T. O'Connor's *Woe is I: The Grammarphobe's Guide to Better English in Plain English*, described by the author as a 'survival guide for intelligent people', which provides 'commonsense tips on how to avoid stumbling into … the worst pitfalls of everyday language' (x);
- Karen Elizabeth Gordon's *The New Well-Tempered Sentence: A Punctuation Handbook for the Innocent, the Eager, and the Doomed*, in which 'the punctuation marks themselves [are] stirring up trouble and inviting raffish comrades in for drinks', not to mention 'taking off their clothes, throwing masked balls, [and] sending insinuating letters to cellists, divas, and Eurobankers' (vii).

Check your grammar

A report that is filled with grammatical mistakes also gives your reader a poor impression. **Grammar** describes the technical rules governing the parts of speech (nouns, verbs, verbals, adjectives and adverbs, pronouns), and how we employ them (agreement, phrases and clauses). *'Grammar is a sine qua non of language, placing its demons in the light of sense, sentencing them to the plight of prose'* (Gordon 1993a: xv).

If you aren't sure about any aspects of grammar, consult a good usage guide and/ or a friend or professional with a good ear for language and a good understanding of the rules – also see **Additional resources**. Cook (1985: viii) reviews the most common grammatical faults that cause readers the greatest problems in reading and understanding:

- **Imprecise relations between subjects and verbs** ... A fancy way of saying that the subject and verbs in the sentence should agree. This sounds easy; however, this can be tricky when you have a compound subject (Bob and John ... are ... is?), when your subject and verb are separated by other elements of your sentence (The experiment that was carried out by the students under controlled conditions in a laboratory setting ... are ... is?), or when you have a tricky subject such as 'per cent' or 'none'.
- **... and between pronouns and antecedents.** The same goes for pronoun agreement. Most native speakers wouldn't say 'John ... she ... her' but things can get tricky (The company ... its or their?), especially when you are trying to avoid non-sexist and gender-neutral language (The examiner awarded his ... her ... their? mark).
- **Words in the wrong order.** Words end in the wrong order generally for one of two reasons. First, word processing makes it easy to shift sentence elements around, and to leave words dangling at the beginning of a sentence or marooned in random parts of the sentence. A more subtle problem occurs when words are not in the wrong logical order, but are not in the order that a native English speaker would put them, that is in idiomatic English. This takes a more practised editorial ear to find, because it is usually difficult to articulate why 'the red big house', for example, sounds awkward whereas the 'big red house' doesn't.
- **Equivalent but unbalanced sentence elements.** You can write your entire report in simple sentences. This would start to sound monotonous after a while. When we use conjunctions, punctuation and other strategies to join up simple sentences into more complex ones, we run the danger that there are inconsistencies between the joined-up phrases or sentences. You should check to make sure that they are parallel, that is, written the same way. *'Harvey designed the survey chapters, the data were analysed by Kate, and writing the report was the job of Martina'* joins up three different kinds of sentences. It would be better to write *'Harvey designed the survey, Kate analysed the data and Martina wrote the report'*.

13.3.3 Writing with style

As well as the aspects of writing correctly that we outlined above, you should pay some attention to your writing style, especially if your goal is first-class marks rather than just passing. Style distinguishes a good report from a great report with the same content. Style includes the sound of the language that you use, punctuation, syntax, sentences and paragraphs. Style is presentation. Anyone who has watched the *Masterchef* cooking competition on television has heard John Torode and Gregg Wallace tell a contestant that *"this tastes great, but it looks like a mess on the plate"*. A professional chef not only knows how to prepare a good meal, but also knows how to arrange it on the plate for maximum impact and eye appeal.

Although style is not one of the main criteria by which we judge a project report, unlike poetry or fiction, how you write does affect our ability to make sense of what you have written and how we interpret your meaning. The style of your project report or presentation plays an important role in creating a persuasive, as well as accurate, account of your research, especially through your ability to construct sentences and paragraphs, and to generate and order ideas (Williams 1990: xiv).

Your readers will also bring their experience of the research approach you have used, and their expectation about how you will write about it. O'Leary (2013) suggests that approaching writing as a craft includes setting the style and finding a voice. In qualitative research, your style helps 'paint the picture' of the real-life context where you have observed people and organisations. If I am reading a project report written in the qualitative research tradition, I will expect you to write in the much more conversational and storytelling style associated with ethnography, and to use the first person, present tense, and many active sentences. You might express your observations of a Fortune 500 corporation's boardroom in more formal language than your observations of a web design firm's open-plan office where everyone sits together. If I am reading a project report written in the quantitative tradition, I will expect you to write in a scientific style, and to use the third person, past tense and many passive sentences (Denscombe 2014). In quantitative research, an impersonal, authoritative, omniscient voice helps you establish and maintain the credibility of what you have done, through creating an authoritative picture.

Many books deal with the finer points of style. Strunk and White's short (less than 100 pages) book *The Elements of Style* has withstood the test of time for generations of American students. Joseph M. Williams's *Style: Toward Clarity and Grace*, and Jacques Barzun's *Simple and Direct* are two invaluable handbooks for more advanced writers who want to *really* understand the mechanics of writing well at a high level.

These books point out that some things that writers work on in communicating complicated ideas in a simple manner include attention to:

- **Narrative** – Remember that a research report is a type of story, and try to put yourself in the shoes of the person who is hearing the story for the first time and trying to make sense of it;
- **Agency** – Name the subjects of your sentences. This is why you are told to 'avoid passive sentences' – passive sentences 'pass the buck' about responsibility. 'The staff were laid off' versus 'The division managers laid off the staff'. These subjects can be people, organisations, collectivities, or figurative ('studies').
- **Action** – Use active verbs wherever possible. Avoid weak linking verbs – is, are, were – where you can replace them with stronger verbs that describe physical movements, mental processes, feelings or relationships. If you combine active verbs with agency, you can't help improving your writing.
- **Cohesion** – Linking your sentences so that one sentence follows on from the next.

Writing clearly and concisely

On the other hand, voice and style does not mean imitating 'academic writing', which usually creates a turgid, impenetrable mess. Joseph Williams suggests that good writing is difficult because:

- We don't actually intend to write well: we try to impress other people with pretentious writing or academic writing when we think our ideas won't be good enough, like trying to cover up a bad steak with a fancy sauce.
- We never learned how to write well: we think that writing that is technically correct (no spelling or grammatical errors) is enough, without writing clearly as well.
- We can't write this particular report well: we don't have enough experience in doing this kind of writing or we don't really know for whom we're writing.

An important part of your job is to write clearly: 'Whatever else a well-educated person can do, that person should be able to write clearly and to understand what it means to do that.' (Williams 1990: 2). A logical and clear report may get much higher marks than a report that is muddled and hard to follow, even if both reports are written on the same research and with the same content.

Williams (1990) suggests that writing clearly begins with writing clear sentences. These sentences then need to be joined up into coherent paragraphs, which maintain the flow of meaning between sentences. Paragraphs are joined up into sections. Sections are combined in a chapter. Each chapter needs to flow into the next.

Choosing your voice

Voice refers to the tone that is taken in the relationship between reader and writer, and describes how you express yourself (Blaxter et al. 2010) to your real or imagined audience, and your distinctive *point of view*. If you are part of a group project, is the paper being written by the group, or by a collective 'we' persona? Are you (the person writing the report) omniscient, as in quantitative research, or is your viewpoint limited to what you observed, as in much qualitative research? In quantitative research, you are addressing an academic audience, usually your academic supervisor and/or examiner(s). In qualitative research, though, is the audience (assessor/sponsor) the same as for a quantitative report, or is it different? Miles, Huberman and Saldana (2013) suggest that you should consider your reader as a co-analyst, who is looking at and interpreting the evidence in your qualitative report.

ACTIVITY

Take a representative page from somewhere in your first draft and do one or more of the following activities:

- Circle the subjects of your sentences and underline the verbs. How many sentences have explicit subjects? How many have active verbs? Passive, indirect sentences are like a long stretch of the motorway – they can lull you to sleep.

▶

- Count the number of words in the sentences on the page. Most people average about 20 words per sentence. To vary the pace of your writing, make some sentences shorter, and some longer.
- Circle the last sentence of each paragraph and first sentence of the next paragraph on the page and see how they relate to each other. If you are having continuity problems, this is a good way to see why this happens.

13.3.4 A final word

We would never argue that *how* you present your research should be more important than *what* you present, but what is written on the page or shown and said in the presentation can significantly distract your reader from paying attention to the research that you have done. We have seen many students do their research projects a great disservice by presenting them carelessly. If you get voice, style and grammar right, your reader should be oblivious to how you write, and your research will speak for itself. If you get any of these wrong, your reader will be distracted from the content by it, and be more inclined to find fault with the research.

Summary

Section 13.1 described the process for planning your project report, writing your rough draft, revising your rough draft into a first draft and editing your project report into a finished draft. **Section 13.2** suggested some tips for writing alone or as part of a project group. **Section 13.3** concluded with some of the technical aspects of project report writing: developing an argument, writing correctly and writing with style.

Answers to key questions

How should I report my research?
- This depends on the requirements of your project – it may be a report and/or a presentation.
- The formats for each of these are well-defined.
- You should follow one of the recommended formats.

What are the differences between reports on quantitative and on qualitative research?
- The formats for quantitative reports are based on a generic format with little variation.
- The formats for qualitative research may vary depending on the narrative or story being told.

What are the differences between an academic and a business presentation?

- Length, audience, purpose and format are all different between these two forms.

How can I manage the writing process effectively?

- Plan before you start.
- Start early and write often.
- Get regular feedback on the process.
- Manage your group and yourself.

How do I write and edit the project report?

- You should pay attention to style, voice and the technical content of your work.

How do I prepare for an oral presentation or viva?

- Prepare your formal presentation.
- Check the audience – their interest and purpose for attending.
- Practise what you will say.
- Anticipate questions.

 References

Barzun, Jacques 1985. *Simple and Direct: A Rhetoric for Writers*, revised edn. Chicago: University of Chicago Press.

Becker, Howard S. 1986. *Writing for Social Scientists*. Chicago: University of Chicago Press.

Blaxter, Lorraine, Hughes, Christine, and Tight, Malcolm 2010. *How to Research*, 4th edn. Maidenhead: Open University.

Booth, Wayne C., Colomb, Gregory G. and Williams, Joseph M. 2008. *The Craft of Research*, 3rd edn. Chicago, IL: University of Chicago Press.

Cook, Claire Kehrwald 1985. *Line by Line: How to Edit Your Own Writing*. Boston: Houghton Mifflin.

Denscombe, Martyn 2014. *The Good Research Guide for Small-Scale Social Research Projects*, 5th edn. Maidenhead: Open University Press.

Dunleavy, Patrick 2003. *Authoring a PhD: How to Plan, Draft, Write and Finish a Doctoral Thesis or Dissertation*. Basingstoke: Palgrave Macmillan.

Easterby-Smith, Mark, Thorpe, Richard and Lowe, Andy 2012. *Management Research: An Introduction*, 4th edn. London: Sage.

Gordon, Karen E. 1993. *The Deluxe Transitive Vampire: The Ultimate Handbook for the Innocent, the Eager, and the Doomed*. New York: Pantheon Books.

Grant, Adam M. and Pollock, Timothy G. 2011. From the editors publishing in *AMJ* – Part 3: Setting the hook, *Academy of Management Journal*, 54 (5): 873–9.

Le Guin, Ursula K. 1998. *Steering the Craft: Exercises and Discussions on Story Writing for the Lone Navigator or the Mutinous Crew*. Portland, OR: Eighth Mountain Press.

Miles, Matthew B., Huberman, A. Michael and Saldana, Jonny 2013. *Qualitative Data Analysis*, 3rd edn. Beverly Hills, CA: Sage.

Murray, Rowena 2015. *How to Survive Your Viva: Defending a Thesis in an Oral Examination*, 3rd edn. Maidenhead: Open University Press.

O'Connor, Patricia T. 1996. *Woe Is I: The Grammarphobe's Guide to Better English in Plain English*. New York: Riverhead Books.

O'Leary, Zina 2013. *The Essential Guide to Doing Research*, 2nd edn. London: Sage.

Reason, Peter, and Bradbury-Huang, Hilary (eds) 2013. *The Sage Handbook of Action Research: Participative Inquiry and Practice*, 2nd edn. Thousand Oaks, CA: Sage.

Stake, Robert E. 1995. *The Art of Case Study Research*. Thousand Oaks, CA: Sage.

Stringer, Ernest T. 1996. *Action Research: A Handbook for Practitioners*. London: Sage.

Strunk, William I. and White, E.B. 1999. *The Elements of Style*. Boston: Allyn and Bacon.

Truss, Lynne 2003. *Eats, Shoots and Leaves: The Zero Tolerance Approach to Punctuation*. London: Profile Books.

Williams, Joseph M. 1990. *Style: Toward Clarity and Grace*. Chicago: University of Chicago Press.

Wolcott, Harry F. 2008. *Writing up Qualitative Research*, 3rd edn. Thousand Oaks, CA: Sage Publications.

Yin, Robert K. 2003. *Case Study Research: Design and Methods*, 3rd edn. Thousand Oaks, CA: Sage.

Additional resources

Bell, Judith and Opie, Clive 2002. *Learning from Research: Getting More from Your Data*. Maidenhead: Open University Press.

Gordon, Karen E. 1993b. *The New Well-Tempered Sentence: A Punctuation Handbook for the Innocent, the Eager, and the Doomed*. Boston: Houghton Mifflin.

Locke, Lawrence F., Silverman, Stephen J. and Spirduso, Waneen W. 2009. *Reading and Understanding Research*, 2nd edn. Thousand Oaks, CA: Sage.

Ritter, Robert M. 2002. *The Oxford Style Manual*. Oxford: Oxford University Press.

University of Chicago 2003. *The Chicago Manual of Style: For Authors, Editors and Copywriters*, 15th edn. Chicago: University of Chicago Press.

Key terms

Frequently asked questions

How long will it take?

Experience suggests that any piece of written work will take 10% longer than the absolute maximum of time that you have available to do it in. However, you can include how much time to leave for preparing, writing, and editing early on in your project plan.

If you know the length of your project, either total number of words or pages, you can estimate about how long it will take you based on how quickly you normally work. An average page formatted with double-spacing, 12-point Times New Roman font will be about 250 words. The most you can reasonably expect to write in a single day is 6000 words, working at an inspired pace. A more reasonable target is 2000 words working at a steady pace, or 1000 words if you are a slow writer.

This would require you to work the following amounts of time, just on writing (not researching or reading):

1–5 days for a coursework project of 1500–5000 words (6–20 pages);

5–20 days for a dissertation of 20,000 words

You will also need to factor in time for collecting your materials and planning your report structure, and for editing your first draft. Thus, you should allow about three times as long for the entire writing process as for the writing itself. Obviously, if you write as you go along, you will be able to streamline this stage of the research process; if you leave it all to the last minute, forget about it and just go into panic mode, work all night and drink lots of caffeinated beverages.

What should it look like?

If you have been given specifications for the format of the written report, you should follow these – exactly. In this case, you can use this section to help understand what to do and how to get there. You will probably find it useful to consult student reports from previous years, if you have access to them, so that you can see how other students have presented their research.

If you are not working to a specified format, **Section 13.1** will help you visualise your format and decide how to get there.

Who will read this report?

Unlike most things that you have read during your course and research, research reports are typically written for a very small audience. Your main 'customers' for your report will be your supervisor, your examiners (if different), your sponsor (if you have one) and perhaps the participants in your study. Sometimes research reports from student projects will reach a wider audience, but this isn't one of their characteristics.

Discussion questions

1. Why is it important to approach your project report as a special kind of writing rather than just 'business as usual'?
2. Is there a special format that all project reports must follow?
3. Why is it important to understand who will be reading your report before you start writing?
4. Should you write your report in the same order as the chapters?
5. Where can you go to get help with writing if English is not your primary language?
6. What challenges occur when you are writing as part of a group that are not relevant when you are writing alone?
7. Why is procrastination an enemy of good reports rather than just a different way of working?
8. What are the habits that you can identify around how you write and/or get started writing?
9. How can good writing help your reader understand your research project? How can it help you?
10. Why might quantitative and qualitative research reports differ? Academic and business reports? Individual and group reports?

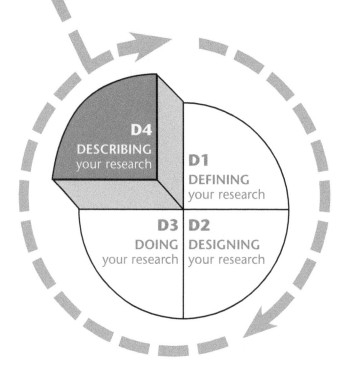

Relevant chapters
13 How do I write up my report?
14 **What do I do now?**

Key challenges
- Making sense of your findings
- Presenting your research to others
- **Reflecting and learning from your research**

4

Relevant chapters
1   What is research?
2   What should I study?
3   How do I find information?

Key challenges
- Understanding what academic research is
- Generating and clarifying ideas
- Using sources of information

1

D4
DESCRIBING
your research

D1
DEFINING
your research

D3
DOING
your research

D2
DESIGNING
your research

Relevant chapters
9   How do I do field research?
10 What do my quantitative data mean(1)?
11 What do my quantitative data mean(2)?
12 What do my qualitative data mean?

Key challenges
- Practical considerations in doing research
- Describing data using simple statistics
- Carrying out statistical tests
- Interpreting words and actions

3

Relevant chapters
4   What is my research approach?
5   How do I do quantitative research?
6   How do I do qualitative research?
7   How do I do case study research?
8   How do I make sure my research is ethical?

Key challenges
- Choosing a research approach
- Choosing a research design
- Collecting data using quantitative methods
- Collecting data using qualitative methods
- Integrating quantitative and qualitative methods

2

14 chapter

What do I do now?
Learning from your research

 Key questions

- What makes my research project more likely to achieve a distinction?
- What makes my research project less likely to fail?
- What should I do when I finish the project?
- What can I learn from this project that will help me in the future?

 Learning outcomes

At the end of this chapter, you should be able to:
- Identify how your research project will be marked;
- Explain the difference between a fail, pass and distinction;
- Relate your project to your personal objectives and career.

Contents

⊕ Introduction

'If only one could have two lives, the first in which to make one's mistakes...the second in which to profit by them.'

D.H. Lawrence

In **Chapter 1** we suggested that you should begin any research project with the end in mind. As a brief history lesson, remind yourself of your original personal and research objectives, and your project goals. One of your original goals was almost certainly to pass, or even to achieve a distinction. Understanding both what standards your project will be marked against and the process by which your examiners will mark your project will help you to put those finishing touches to your work, if you have left that buffer that we described in **Chapter 9**. In **Section 14.1**, we describe how projects are marked and what examiners look for when they mark a project. This should help you target that final draft of your project report and/or oral presentation so that you get the fullest credit for the hard work that you have done, by writing that draft intentionally *for* the criteria your examiners will be seeking.

In **Section 14.2**, we describe the factors that will keep your project from passing and almost certainly doom you to failure; for instance, if you don't turn it in on time, violate other essential project guidelines, or get caught plagiarising or violating other ethical guidelines. Most students want to achieve more than just a bare pass. We also describe what makes a really good project good.

We conclude this chapter and the book with some reflections about research and the research process in **Section 14.3**. We suggest that once you are near completing or have completed your project or course, you need not stop just yet. Towards the end of your research project, you may be cheering yourself up with the thought that you are nearly finished, and, if your project is the last thing standing between you and your degree, then you do not ever have to do another research project again. This feeling is perfectly natural; however, we strongly suggest that you take time between completing your research and submitting your project report to reflect on what you have learnt about your topic and about your research, and, if you can, incorporate these insights into your report.

You can reflect and learn from your project more broadly. What have you learned in your project about business and management, about the research process and about yourself? A good way of '*closing the loop*' is debrief yourself (and your project team) at the end of the project to capture your reflections before you forget them. At the end of a project, most of us, even experienced researchers, imagine that if we could go through our research project again we would do it much better the second time around. We would not only be able to avoid dead ends and wasted effort, we would know more about our research topic, and be more experienced researchers.

Your reflections on what you have learnt will be useful not only to future research projects, but also to your studies, your career and your personal development. You might build on your project experience to get a 'leg-up' in the job market. The business and management world values research skills, information search, knowledge synthesis, critical thinking and the discipline of writing that you have acquired. Just as important is your ability to be reflective about what you have done. These are tough skills to learn, but can become habits of thought – if you practise them. You might even use your project experience to launch an exciting career as a researcher!

14.1 Maximise your project marks

Before you hand in your project report, you should make sure that you have explicitly addressed each criterion given in the project guidelines. (We reviewed marking and project guidelines in **Chapter 2**.) The guidelines examiners are given will be the exactly the same as the ones you were given at the beginning of your project. For instance, if you are asked to relate your project findings to business and management research, make sure that you do it. Likewise, if you are asked to reflect on what you have learned from the project, explicitly discuss this somewhere. If one of these criteria is not addressed in the report, then it is likely to be marked down or even failed. You may even want to explicitly highlight each criterion by mentioning it in the relevant chapter or section title, and in the introduction to the chapter or section.

Student research in action 14.1
JUST DO IT!

Kate includes a rubric, a detailed list of points that each student must address, in the assignment for the Research Methods module on the MSc in Major Programme Management. The rubric directs the student to discuss briefly '*What do you expect to find out as a result of your research?*' Savvy students include a section titled '*Expected research findings*' to highlight that they have addressed this point.

Informal marking criteria of correct spelling, grammar and overall presentation of your research are so widely known and accepted that they may not be spelt out for you. Given that marking is a *subjective* process – don't give them a chance to nit-pick. Many examiners expect to see a minimum of typos, since many of these can be detected by spell- and grammar checkers. Such lack of attention to detail is especially dangerous, since your examiners may assume that students who get 'basics' wrong have made more fundamental errors or mistakes in their research. Whilst your project will not pass or fail on presentation alone, a neat and attractive presentation will contribute substantially to a positive impression as stated in **Chapter 13**.

Once you've finished and received your mark, a look back at the marking criteria may 'close the loop' for your next project by helping you to understand why you got the project mark you did.

The characteristics of a distinction

Most students are concerned not only with not failing or just barely passing their research project; they want to do well on it. To be awarded a distinction, it is not enough just to do everything to the letter – you must also produce a project that is distinguished, in concept, in execution and in its reporting. Good research is like Ronseal: it does what it says on the tin. Probably the best guideline to whether a project is a distinction or not is whether the examiner comes away with the feeling that '*I'd like to have done that project*'.

In this section, we look at what makes an excellent project. **Table 14.1** lists seven factors that often weigh on whether a report receives a pass or a distinction. You should of course consider these factors in conjunction with any that are produced by the organisation or individuals that will be assessing your work.

Table 14.1 Characteristics of a distinction

Issue	Characteristic
The fundamentals	Like the foundations of a great building, the work is nothing unless it has a good basis. The report presented must at least be acceptable on all the criteria outlined in **Section 14.1**. This is a *qualifier*, without which you will not get a distinction, no matter how well any of the other criteria are rated.
Interest	The work has answered the 'so what?' question, not only in the context of the particular research setting, but also says something to a wider audience.
Critique	The report has assimilated a wide literature and had something interesting to say about the wider issues in the literature, including identification of inconsistencies, contradictions and gaps.
The story	It is a defining characteristic of distinction-level projects that the quality starts at the first page. Here the story is outlined and the rest of the document picks it up and guides the reader through the work and, like a good story, it leaves you wanting more, for example explicitly stating identified areas for further research.
Sense-making	The scenario may be complex and the literature certainly will be. An excellent piece of work will take all of this in, and find ways to turn the complexity into something accessible, without oversimplifying it.
Initiative	As a marker, a piece of work distinguishes itself when it has done something that sets it aside from the rest of the pile of your marking – possibly in the level of effort that has gone into the method, or the unusual twist that someone has added to an established research method or the 'extra mile' that has been travelled in preparing the literature review (for example inclusion of hard-to-find journal articles).
Learning is evident	One of the great disappointments in reading a project report is when you check it against the question – 'could the person have produced this work without taking the course of study?' If the answer is yes, one is left wondering what value the course has added. On the other hand, a distinction-level project leaves the reader in no doubt that the writer has come through a tremendous personal journey and this report is the culmination of the thinking processes and perspectives gleaned, not necessarily from the whole course, but at least from substantial chunks of it.

14.1.1 What do I want my reader to believe after reading my report?

A good report has a clear and simple story, and underlying argument or thesis, that links the whole report together and helps the reader make sense of it. Excellent reports identify the themes of the research at the very beginning and then carry them through each of the major sections.

Your themes are introduced upfront in the *Introduction*. These themes are then explicitly developed as research questions in the *Theoretical Background* or *Literature Review*, making sure to note the implications of the literature for those themes. The *Research Methods* chapter shows how the themes are specifically addressed through an appropriate methodology, specific research methods for collecting and analysing

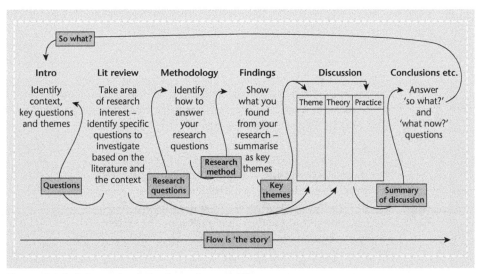

Figure 14.1 Schematic of the flow of an excellent report

data. The *Findings* show how you carried this out, and what you found out (*Results*), structured around your key themes. Your *Discussion* then takes the themes and links them back to the *Literature Review* through a comparison with the relevant theory (and hence expectations) that were there. These provide the basis for the points of similarity and difference in those themes as the basis for the discussion. Your *Summary and Conclusions* include the outcomes and recommendations, relative to the themes. These linkages and carry-overs are shown in **Figure 14.1**. Finally, look at the balance across all of the different aspects of your research report. You must also make sure that no section is over- or under-emphasised relative to its importance. Remember that your report is no stronger than its weakest section (or weakest link between sections). This is illustrated in **Figure 14.1**.

14.1.2 What have we done that matters?

Chapter 13 suggested you should direct the attention of the readers to parts of your report that are good or innovative. In the project described in **Student research in action 12.3**, the students failed to signal that the covert observation of supermarket shoppers was an innovative research method, or to highlight their interesting research findings, such as the rituals that people go through in choosing fresh products. Thus, their research project came across as pedestrian to the markers, even though it was original and definitely different.

One of the best places to do this signalling is in your chapter (or section) introduction and summary. Providing such explicit **cues** will highlight the best aspects of your report (and take attention away from the weaker aspects).

Make sure to highlight your report's contributions, in a realistic way. State what you did in concise terms, yes, but don't forget to draw attention to what you did differently that adds real value or points of interest to your work. This shows that you put yourself out to do the work.

To understand why you need to 'market' your research findings, imagine yourself in your examiner's shoes, facing a towering stack of project reports. Show your reader where you have used imagination and creatively tackled the problem.

Most student research projects simply require you to design a research project and carry it out competently, but your project guidelines may also require that you make an *original contribution* (see **Chapter 1**) to business and management in your research, or this may be a specific criterion for a first-class or distinction. An original contribution may be any of the following:

- To review and synthesise existing knowledge
- To investigate some existing situation or problem
- To provide solutions to a problem
- To explore and analyse more general issues
- To construct or create a new procedure or system
- To explain a new phenomenon
- To generate new knowledge

You do not need to make a major breakthrough in a project for an undergraduate or taught master's degree, but you do need to show some contribution in one or more of the areas listed above.

14.1.3 Was this research worth doing in the first place?

If you have done all of this, you only need to be able to answer one further question – *'so what?'* Many studies focus on an interesting research problem and questions, apply an interesting research method to an existing research problem, or investigate an innovative research setting, but fall down because they don't connect the research back to reality. In other words, they forget to say something useful based on the work carried out, or forget to do research that does this in the first place. This process of connecting back to reality and making something useful from your work is called *impact*.

Make sure that you can answer the 'so what' question about your research. If you could have answered your research questions without having done your project, you are in big trouble. If you are in any doubt, imagine you have met one of your colleagues from your course in the street who doesn't know what you have been doing in your project. In 15 seconds (no more, otherwise they will get bored) you need to give them the 'punch lines' – what you have done and found.

Student research in action 14.2
I'M FREE!

A student group found many different algorithms in the scheduling literature. To find out whether the use of any of these would improve business performance and whether any were actually used in small businesses, they gathered data from three small businesses about how the owner-managers scheduled their work and decided which orders to work on first. The students then put their data in the algorithms, but this was where their research project ended, with the outcomes from the algorithms showing how the owner-managers *could* have scheduled their systems.

When the examiners looked at the research, the 'so what' question revealed that this research project had made no practical contribution at all to any of the firms that the students had studied (about how using scheduling algorithms would improve their cash flow, for example). Neither did it increase academic knowledge about the algorithms and their applicability. For instance, algorithms may only work well where there is considerable accurate historic data about how long a job will take, and they don't handle the uncertainty inherent in a small business. All in all, the students made no link between the theory and their empirical research to show why it was important and useful.

The student group in the example might have answered the 'so what' question by reporting: 'We worked with three SMEs to look at how they scheduled work. They were not optimally scheduling their resources and by the use of a simple algorithm could have improved their turnover by 23% in one year.'

14.2 Fatal errors to avoid

As we discussed in **Chapter 2**, your examiners may not have met you personally – and may not even recognise your name (or increasingly, number). They have your only report to go on in assessing the quality of your work. Therefore, there is no substitute for a well-written project report, an oral presentation, a viva voce examination or a combination of these, as shown in **Figure 14.2**.

Because failures make everyone associated with them look and feel bad, mercifully most projects don't fail. Even though few students begin their research project intending to fail, inevitably some do. In hindsight, the seeds of failure are usually obvious from the first day of the project – and sometimes even before.

This section reviews some ways that we have seen students snatch failure from the jaws of success. Some projects fail on one single criterion; others fail resoundingly on every aspect. Some students simply refuse to follow the project guidelines or they commit plagiarism or other ethical violations; others ignore advice or warnings from their supervisors that could stop them from failing.

14.2.1 What happens if I turn the project report in late?

Ignoring one or more project guidelines is a sure-fire way to ensure that your project fails. One of the least flexible of these guidelines is the project deadline. If you fail to hand in your project on time, or you hand in an incomplete project, you are unlikely

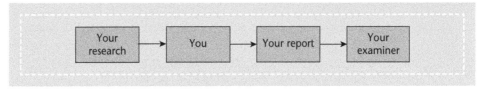

Figure 14.2 Your examiner only sees your research project indirectly

to get a second chance and your examiners may be required to fail you, no matter how good your excuse. Your project deadline will have been set well in advance and is unlikely to be flexible unless you have a genuine medical or personal emergency *and* you have received an extension from your course director (or whoever is named in your course handbook) well in advance of your project deadline.

⊕ *Student research in action 14.3*
ACHY BREAKY HEART

There was a time when a word with a tutor would ensure that an extension to a deadline could be obtained. In many places today, this is no longer the case and does mean that getting any sort of extension requires forms to be filled in and approval sought. The criteria for granting extensions are usually clear and often staff do not have any flexibility, so do not assume that an extension will be forthcoming. One of Kate's students came to her in considerable emotional distress two weeks before a major assignment was due because of major family problems. Kate suggested that rather than take a fail he ask for an extension on his assignment; but the student was told that 'a broken heart' did not justify extending the deadline. The student had to take non-submission as a failure, and the maximum mark for his re-submission was capped at 50.

14.2.2 What happens if I exceed the word limit?

You should always obey the project word limit if you have been given one, including the minimum and maximum word limit in the project guidelines. Ignoring your word limit can definitely cause you to lose a specified number of marks per word, be demoted a degree class, or even failed. Always check to make sure you understand exactly what is included in the word limit – is it every single word? A maximum page length? Are references included? What about figures and tables? If your assignment guidelines aren't clear, ask your supervisor, the course coordinator or the examinations officer to clarify this for you.

Before they start writing, students most often worry about being unable to meet the minimum word limit, especially for long pieces of work such as theses and dissertations, but few have trouble writing at least the minimum number of words. In fact, most complete first drafts will run substantially over the word limit.

If your report is too long, this isn't too bad, you should be able to edit it down to the required length by taking out excess words, repetition and plain old 'throat-clearing'. Your examiner will thank you, and your business sponsor will probably only read the first three pages, and skim the rest, anyway. The rainforest will also thank you.

Even though some students inevitably try, it is difficult if not impossible to fool an examiner using 'creative' tricks such as adjusting font sizes or page margins to try to squeeze in more words or disguise too few. An experienced examiner knows word lengths without even counting words and can easily estimate how many pages 15,000 words is or what a 1-inch margin looks like. If you are caught outside the word limit, or even worse, lying about the word limit, your examiner may have the option to fail you outright without even reading your paper.

Student research in action 14.4

IN SYMPATHY

Kate recently set an assignment with a 3000-word limit, including figures and tables, but not references. She went over this guideline in class, and put this chapter on the students' reading list. When she received the assignments, one looked suspiciously bulky. It was three times the page length of any of the other assignments, but there wasn't any more white space than the other papers; in fact, it looked much denser. Was it really only 2997 words long as it claimed? A simple reconversion of the file from pdf to Word showed that it more like 12,000 words! For such a breach, staff are required *not* to mark it, and as a result it failed. The assignment showed considerable effort had been expended, but the rules were clear. It sometimes does take a lot longer to write a short assignment than a long one.

In cutting your report to the right length you will have learnt more about your project than when you started editing. Writing concisely gives a better impression of your research and your command of the topic much more than an excessively wordy report.

If you are required to give an oral presentation of your research, your time limits are just as important as word limits are for your written report. If you have 15 minutes to present, going over looks bad and suggests that you haven't bothered to plan your presentation properly. At the very least, your audience will stop listening to your presentation and start thinking about marking exams, what's for dinner or summer holidays. If you go on much longer than the project guidelines allow, your examiners may 'pull the plug' on the presentation and you may not get to the summary and conclusions that pull your research project together. Even your examiners have better things to do with their time than to listen to you drivel on, and your business sponsors definitely do. Time is money. Don't waste their time or yours.

Students often think the deadline for word length, report formatting and other guidelines about report presentation are optional rather than mandatory. Deliberately flouting the guidelines (or common sense/customs and practice) simply annoys everyone and wastes time. Pay attention to unwritten guidelines (or norms), as shown in **Student research in action 14.5**.

Student research in action 14.5

THERE'S NO RULE AGAINST IT, BUT ...

A doctoral student handed in his thesis printed entirely on bright turquoise paper. Even though the thesis regulations did not specifically prohibit printing on coloured paper, they did require that the thesis be legible, which unfortunately this was not. He had to have his thesis reprinted and rebound, which cost both time and money. His supervisor and examiners were unimpressed, too.

Finally, don't try to be clever and outwit the project guidelines. Anything in the project regulations is generally there because it was found to be essential over generations of research projects. If you have a problem interpreting the guidelines, or if you think that they are wrong, take the matter up with your supervisor or the project co-ordinator.

What happens if I get caught plagiarising or cheating?

OK, so you've handed in your project on time, and within the word limits. How else can you ensure that your project gets a big, fat ZERO? One of the most serious unethical behaviours in academia, and generally an automatic '*red card*', is **plagiarism**, failing to properly credit the originator of any words or ideas that you have used. We discussed plagiarism in **Chapter 8**, but many students manage to forget about this under pressure to get their project turned in on time.

The kinds of plagiarism we have seen in handed-in project reports ranges from wholesale 'cut-and-paste' from online sources to narrow paraphrasing without giving credit for the original words. No matter how under pressure you feel, plagiarising only makes things worse. Penalties may range from losing marks or failing your research project to being expelled from your degree course. Your examiners will not take into account the effect that this might have on your glittering career prospects. Your university will have a written policy on plagiarism (for example, in the Student Handbook which you were given on the first day of your first year). You have had a reasonable chance to read it, and you are expected to obey it whether you remember it or not. Many universities nowadays have online plagiarism training that students need to complete.

Your university may use formal plagiarism detection software such as Turnitin, but experienced examiners may detect plagiarism through familiarity with the original material or even through changes in style and voice in your report. There is no substitute for good old-fashioned knowledge, however, as **Student research in action 14.6** below illustrates.

⊕ *Student research in action 14.6*
THERE'S NO ESCAPING THE LONG ARM OF THE LAW

Students on a course recently must have thought that they had 'got away with it' when they submitted a group assignment. The work was given good marks by two **internal examiners**. It was then sent to the external examiner at another university. The **external examiner** quickly realised that much of the work from the group had been copied word-for-word from his own book. As in the urban legend, he was very tempted to comment that 'I like what you wrote, but it only got a 2ii when I originally wrote it'. The students were failed for plagiarism and required to leave the programme without completing their degrees.

It is obviously wrong to buy a research paper from an 'essay mill' on the internet, and to submit it whole or with substantial changes. Deliberately plagiarising also includes using material that you have downloaded from the web without attribution. (See **Chapter 8** and **Chapter 13** for a reminder of good practice in citations and referencing.) As we noted in **Chapter 8**, it is increasingly simple for students to plagiarise, as search engines and the mechanics of internet sources ('cut and paste') make plagiarism even more tempting than when students had to type out all of the material to be plagiarised by hand, which took about as long as writing it in the first place. Even simply downloading a paper from one of these custom essay writing sites is now a violation in many universities – so may be selling one of your own papers, writing a paper on commission, or even uploading one of your own papers in return for being able to download someone else's.

On the other hand, the same computer technologies also make it increasingly easy for examiners to search for the same sources through search engines and/or to demonstrate plagiarism using specialised software programmes for detecting unauthorised copying. Even without recourse to the internet or Turnitin, your examiner can usually detect material that you have not written yourself, as it will stand out stylistically from the material that you have written, particularly when you are not a fluent writer or a native English speaker.

Student research in action 14.7

FOOTPRINTS IN THE BUTTER

Another student went to the library of a neighbouring institution, copied a dissertation report and submitted it with his name on it. This was easily picked up by the examiner, as the literature review was at least 10 years out of date and contained references to many sources to which the student did not have access. It didn't take long for the assessor to track down the original.

You can be penalised even if your plagiarism is inadvertent – accidentally leaving out the source – rather than intentional. When you write the final draft of your project report, always double-check that you have credited the source of any ideas or words that you have taken directly or indirectly from someone else, and that you have listed all of the relevant sources in your reference list or bibliography. Preventing the problem in the first place is better than having to deal with it once it has occurred.

You may also be failed for *self-plagiarism*, which covers recycling work that you have previously turned in for credit. (Since it is difficult to steal from yourself, the term plagiarism is not quite correct, but the penalties are often the same.) Most universities have or are in the process of adopting formal policies prohibiting **recycling**.

How seriously examiners and universities take plagiarism is illustrated in **Student research in action 14.8**. If you get away with plagiarism in your written report, it might still be detected during an oral presentation or viva voce examination. Your examiners can ask you detailed questions about any source that you cite, any facts or opinions that you have not cited a source for, or any material that they suspect that you have cut and pasted.

Student research in action 14.8

GO DIRECTLY TO JAIL, DO NOT PASS GO

A student plagiarised on a coursework resit. His tutors spotted the (poorly executed) cut-and-paste job and easily found the original references that he had copied from. He was expelled from the master's programme, one week before graduation, and his offer of a postgraduate research place was immediately cancelled. He was also barred from campus, so that he couldn't even see his friends (or girlfriend) graduate. For the lack of an hour's extra work, he jeopardised his whole future.

Another master's student recycled an entire chapter from a course textbook in his final project. It was not that hard for the examiner (from another academic area) to spot, including the change in font and font size for the chapter, the mention of a date 15 years before as 'recent', and the transcription of grammatical and other errors from the original source. It took 10 minutes in the library to find the source in one of the books listed on the reading list, even though the material was so old it was not on the internet. The student was referred to the university authorities, and failed the entire master's degree as a result.

It may seem as though we are overstating the problem of plagiarism, but in fact it seems to be increasing in frequency rather than decreasing. Here are a few links that you may find helpful if you are still having trouble understanding what plagiarism is or how to avoid committing it:

- The Writing Tutorial Services at the University of Indiana (www.indiana.edu/~wts/pamphlets.shtml).
- The student judiciary at the University of California at Davis (http://sja.ucdavis.edu/academic-integrity-page2.html).
- The Faculty of Arts at the University of British Columbia (http://help.library.ubc.ca/planning-your-research/academic-integrity-plagiarism/).

Make sure to be equally scrupulous in preparing your report to your business sponsor or placement manager in checking for plagiarism. They may not care that much about academic integrity – but they will expect full value for the money that they have paid you and the access that they have given you to their organisation. Plagiarising in your business is just as bad as misrepresenting your data or not honestly interpreting your findings.

Other forms of unethical behaviour include deception of participants, etc.. You must absolutely avoid any form of unethical behaviour if you want to have any credibility as a researcher, as we mentioned in **Chapter 8**. The penalty for unethical behaviour can be quite severe.

14.3 ## What should I do when I've submitted my research project?

In his book *Project Management*, Harvey suggests that the final phase of any project is to develop the process so that you can do it better next time. Why? At the end of most projects, people are so focused on moving on to the next thing (always pressing, generally more 'sexy' than what has just been finished) that they miss many opportunities for learning. Research projects are special not least because they are so personal and all-involving. In future projects you may repeat the same mistakes, or run into the same problems, if you abandon your **learning process** when you submit your project report. Also, you may overlook key findings and learning points about what did work, or simply do not give them the attention they deserve.

The end of the project is also a good opportunity to capture what you have learned about yourself. Doing a research project is a good way to learn about your own strengths and weaknesses, in academic, personal and interpersonal skills. Make a list of what you have learned about yourself from doing your research, both good and bad. For example, you might have learned that you are good at planning but not so good at execution. Some people find out that they are bad at writing, but good at editing. You might find out that you are good at teamwork, or that you never want to work on a team project again (at least with certain people or types of people).

Unexpected benefits include friends you have made or any contacts you have added to your personal network. One student found that the other students in the project group pulled together and covered the work she missed when a family member died. Another student, unfortunately, found out that her best friend was not very reliable, going clubbing on days that she had claimed to be too ill or too busy to attend group project meetings! As we discuss below, many students use the contacts they make during their placements or projects to find a job after graduation.

Assuming you have submitted your report and presented the recommendations to your assessors, what next? Among the suggestions made by Rugg and Petre (2004) are to relax by reading a good book or taking a long bath, or to get organised by tidying and filing your research materials, sorting out your wardrobe or otherwise getting rid of junk. These are all constructive activities. But before you completely abandon researcher mode, this book's authors suggest that you **PARTY**:

- **P – persist** until the project is truly finished, not 95, or 99, but 100% complete, printed, bound and 'pushed over the edge';
- **A – arrange** a holiday, a trip or discussion on a new project;
- **R – reflect** on your learning;
- **T – take time out** to allow the real lessons from the project to come to you (this can need some time);
- **Y – yield manage** – make sure that you maximise any benefits to yourself and others from the project.

14.3.1 Persist – closing down the project

Good practice suggests that once your project is 100% complete, you might also:

- **Send a thank you letter** to everyone who provided support to the project. Enclose a copy of your findings to anyone who participated in the project. If you did an in-company project, this might be better as a 1–2 page summary of the project and its findings, rather than the entire report. Make sure that you don't violate any confidentiality agreements.
- **Thank your project supervisor** and **business sponsor** and give him or her any feedback about the project process that might help them next time. Your supervisor might like a copy of the report, if he or she doesn't already receive one.
- **Return any books or other materials** you have borrowed to the library or to their owners. You can lose your sponsor or supervisor's goodwill if you don't! This may cost you dearly when it comes to getting recommendation letters.

14.3.2 Arrange – don't just sit there, do something!

We recommend arranging something fun or special for a few days after the deadline for a project. You may well have earned a holiday if you have just completed a major project, such as a dissertation that marks the end of a course of study. Taking a break has a number of benefits, not least:

- Avoiding the last mood phase of the project (deflation).
- Ensuring that you have really finished everything – there's nothing like a holiday deadline to make sure that you have cleared your desk and completed your work.
- People who have a holiday booked have never, in our experience of student projects, missed their submission deadline.
- Going on a break forces you to take time out and perhaps to use the time to reflect.

14.3.3 Reflect – project review

Probably the last thing you want to do when you have just handed in a project is to talk about your project again. However, according to Harvey you should carry out an immediate **project review** at the end of a project. If you have been working on a group project, then a brief meeting, perhaps over coffee or in the pub, would be a good way to do this. If you have been working on a project solo, then you could do this in front of *The Great British Bake Off* (Kate's favourite TV show), or while waiting for the bus, anywhere you have a few minutes to think. If you don't capture this information with a week or so of when you complete your project, then you will forget about it until the next project (no matter how many times you say 'never again...').

In your project review (or project *post-mortem* as some like to call them), you should cover the following elements: review how the project went; identify any long-term or short-term changes you should make to improve your performance on the next project; any challenges or obstacles that you faced and how you overcame them. If you have done well on your project, then your review should focus on what you think you did well, so you can repeat it, and what you could have done better next time. If you did more poorly than you wanted to, you should think about what you could do better next time, but also about anything that went right with your project so you can build on it. Some supervisors ask that this step is included explicitly in the final chapter of your project report.

14.3.4 Take time out

Other insights from the work that you have done are only revealed as time elapses. Your subconscious works on issues over time. This can give you a 'eureka' moment – often when you least expect it, even if your examiner cannot give you credit for it! These insights *will* be useful when you are working on projects or having to manage yourself or others in the future. For instance, one student studied enterprise and the behaviour of entrepreneurs in his project. The student found the project interesting at the time, but the long-term benefit was understanding the processes that a small company, one of his suppliers, was going through during the development of a new product.

Taking *time out*, though, is not just for intellectual purpose. Most people find creating a report and submitting it emotionally draining, and you need time for both your mind and body (and sometimes your soul) to recuperate.

14.3.5 Yield manage – using your research experience on the jobs market

If you are finishing up a degree course and looking for a job, you can draw on your project experience as a key selling point in job interviews. Potential employers may not be interested in the particular content of your research project, but they do want to know about your strengths and weaknesses, and you can mine your project experience for examples. You can also use a successful group project as evidence that you can work well in groups, a skill highly sought after by employers.

Use your research skills in a job search. After all, it is also a research process, which develops skills that include:

- Searching for information,
- Recording and keeping track of information,
- Managing the process using project management,
- Writing skills (applications and thank you letters),
- Time management,
- Interviewing (think about what it's like to be on the other side of the desk),
- Working or visiting organisational settings (what to wear, how to act),
- Observation (useful when you are starting a new job).

If you get on well with your supervisor, you might want to talk to them about opportunities to do further research. Although being good at research isn't a guarantee that you will complete an MPhil or a PhD, it's much easier than if you are bad at it.

If you don't want to commit to a **research career**, you might still be interested in an internship as a research officer. If you are interested in a research career, you should keep an eye on the following sources:

- The *Times Higher Education Supplement* – www.timeshighereducation.com,
- www.jobs.ac.uk, www.academia.edu and www.researchgate.net,
- *The Guardian* weekly education supplement and website,
- *The Chronicle of Higher Education*, for opportunities in North America.

14.4 Some final thoughts

14.4.1 Parting words of wisdom

And finally, despite all that has been written already about business and management, there is still so much of the subject left that we know very little about. A research project is a wonderful opportunity for researchers to contribute not just to their own knowledge base, but in some way, however small, to make new findings that will improve what we know overall. The experience that we have had as supervisors of student projects over the past 25 years reinforces this – so many projects have questioned, critiqued, confirmed or denied what has been accepted as 'knowledge', all in so doing contributing to the knowledge base.

As we always suggest at the end of a piece of work, there should be two questions addressed. The first is *'so what?'*. The *'so what?'* is that you should now have a good knowledge of the content and process of research – if you have read this book, studied the questions and identified relevant areas of further reading you have all that you need for now. The second question is *'what now?'*. Your *'what now?'* depends on whether you have been using this book as part of a course on research methods or to support you in doing your research project (or both). Whichever, we wish you every success and that you profit from the challenges, grow through the frustrations and in the end enjoy the great satisfaction that researching business and management can bring. Now, where is that party...

Summary

In this chapter, we suggested that you should take a little time between completing your work and submitting it, to make sure that it has the best chance of achieving your objectives. Also, that instead of abandoning your project when you have finally delivered your report(s), you should spend some time reflecting on your project and seeing what you can learn from it.

In **Section 14.1**, we opened the lid on the art and process of assessment. We start by discussing some issues that cause projects to fail in **Section 14.2** – avoid them at all costs. Some mistakes will only cost you marks, but you should try to avoid them as well. We discussed some of the characteristics of excellent work which we hope will provide you with something to aim for – gaining a distinction is not a science, but we hope we have enlightened the art just a little.

Later on, as well as the general reflection and learning discussed in the first section, we suggested that you reflect on and learn from your project mark. This section was intended to help make sense of that. We concluded in **Section 14.3** by suggesting that you take some time to review your project, as well as relaxing and celebrating. You can use a project review to capture any insights into your research and personal objectives, and identify any feedback that you need to provide to others. You can also note what went well and badly, and what you should work on for next time. We also suggested that you reflect on how you can use what you have learnt in the process in planning for the next stage of your career. Research skills will be helpful in searching for a job, and perhaps even provide the first step on the career ladder.

Answers to key questions

What makes my project more likely to achieve a distinction?

- It will meet all of the requirements for a research project at your institution AND has shown both effort and imagination in tackling an interesting research question.
- It will provide a synthesis of what is already known and use this as a platform to generate new and valuable insights with a good warrant from a systematic research process.

What makes my project less likely to fail?

- It will meet all of the requirements for a research project at your institution, including the ethical requirements.
- It will demonstrate a sound knowledge of the topic / problem, the context in which it is placed, the perspective from which it is approached, the methods used to investigate it and reports these in a coherent manner.

What should I do when I finish the project?

- Relax and celebrate.
- Conduct an immediate project review.

What can I learn from this project that will help me in the future?

- You can use your research skills and your research findings in researching and applying for a job.
- You can use your research skills as the basis for postgraduate work or study.

References

Rugg, Gordon and Petre, Marian 2004. *The Unwritten Rules of PhD Research*. Maidenhead: Open University Press.

Additional resources

Bell, Judith and Opie, Clive 2002. *Learning from Research: Getting More from Your Data*. Maidenhead: Open University Press.

Bryman, Alan and Bell, Emma 2011. *Business Research Methods*, 3rd edn. Oxford: Oxford University Press.

Campbell, John P., Daft, Richard L. and Hulin, Charles L. 1982. *What to Study: Generating and Developing Research Questions*. Beverly Hills, CA: Sage Publications.

Collis, Jill and Hussey, Roger 2013. *Business Research*, 4th edn. Basingstoke: Palgrave Macmillan.

Drucker, Peter F. 1955. *The Practice of Management*. Portsmouth, NH: Heinemann.

Easterby-Smith, Mark, Thorpe, Richard and Lowe, Andy 2012. *Management Research: An Introduction*, 4th edn. London: Sage.

Maylor, Harvey 2017. *Project Management*, 5th edn. London: Prentice Hall.

Sagan, Carl 1997. *The Demon-Haunted World: Science as a Candle in the Dark*. New York: Ballantine Books.

Saunders, Mark, Lewis, Phillip and Thornhill, Adrian 2012. *Research Methods for Business Students*, 6th edn. Harlow: Financial Times/Prentice Hall.

Stringer, Ernest T. 1996. *Action Research: A Handbook for Practitioners*. London: Sage Publications.

Wilkinson, Barry 1998. *Project Guidance Notes 1998/99*, Executive MBA Programme. School of Management, University of Bath, November.

Yin, Robert K. 2014. *Case Study Research: Design and Methods*, 5th edn. Thousand Oaks, CA: Sage.

Zikmund, William G. 2000. *Business Research Methods*, 6th edn. Orlando, FL: Dryden Press/Harcourt College Publishers.

Key terms

Workshop

Carry out a personal learning review of previous projects that you have been involved with. You should consider:

1. What was the outcome of each of the projects – were you pleased with the outcome? If not, specify why not.

2. Your structuring of the technical (or subject-specific) issues around the project – how did you handle the complexity of the subject in particular?

3. How did you manage the process – did you set up a plan, use it to control your process, did you finish on time, was there adequate buffer for when problems arose?

4. Based on the above, what will you try to do differently next time?

Index